VILNA

FACSIMILE EDITION

with an introduction by
ESTHER HAUTZIG

THE JEWISH PUBLICATION SOCIETY
Philadelphia   Jerusalem
5752/1992

VILNA

By

ISRAEL COHEN

PHILADELPHIA
THE JEWISH PUBLICATION SOCIETY OF AMERICA
5704–1943

Originally published as
Jewish Communities Series: Vilna
Copyright 1943 by
The Jewish Publication Society of America

Introduction copyright © 1992 by
The Jewish Publication Society
All rights reserved
Manufactured in the United States of America

Cataloging-in-Publication Data
Cohen, Israel, 1879–1961.
Vilna/by Israel Cohen. —Facsim. ed./
with an introduction by Esther Hautzig.
p.   cm. —(Jewish communities series)
Includes bibliographical references and index.
ISBN 0–8276–0415–7. —ISBN 0–8276–0416–5 (pbk.)
1. Jews—Lithuania—Vilnius—History.
2. Vilnius (Lithuania)—Ethnic relations.
I. Title. II. Series.
DS135.R93V5 1992
947'.5—dc20   92–6162
CIP

*Monument at Ponar, donated by Yeshayahu Epstein
in memory of the 70,000 Jews from Vilna and vicinity,
murdered by the Nazis and their helpers
in the years 1941 to 1944.*

This facsimile edition is made possible

by a grant in memory of

SAMUEL AND RAYA ZUNSER RUDOMIN

CONTENTS

CHAPTER I

The founding of Vilna — Conflicting views about date of
origin of Jewish community — Early settlement under
Sigismund I — Settlements in other towns before end of
14th century — Political union of Poland and Lithuania
— Grand Duke Witold's Charter — Charter of Boleslav
and Casimir — Charter of the Jews of Grodno — Casimir
Jagiello's Charter of 1453 — Grand Duke Alexander's
decree of expulsion and its revocation — Attitude of
Sigismund I and Sigismund II — Anti-Jewish articles of
Constitution of Pietrokow.

CHAPTER II

Effect of union with Poland upon Jewish position —
Attitude of nobles and burghers — The Magdeburg
Law — How the legal settlement of the Jews in Vilna
was facilitated — The first synagogue — The first anti-
Jewish attack — Sigismund III's Charter of 1593 —
Charter of 1629 — Royal instructions to municipality —
Charter of 1633 — Establishment of ghetto — Fourfold
ordinance of Wladislav IV — The burghers' hostility —
"Relazioni" Court's decision of 1644 — Evading domi-
ciliary restrictions.

CHAPTER III

Jewish gold embroiderers forbidden — The Chmielnicki
atrocities — Flight from Vilna and return — Burghers'
raid upon Jewish quarter — Complaints of Christian
butchers and glaziers — King Michael's friendly pro-

CHAPTER XIII

CHAPTER XIV

CHAPTER XVII

CHAPTER XVIII

CHAPTER XXI

SUPPLEMENTARY NOTES

LIST OF ILLUSTRATIONS

INTRODUCTION TO *VILNA*
BY ISRAEL COHEN

Esther Hautzig

IN the preface to his remarkable book, *Vilna*, the distinguished British scholar, Israel Cohen, wrote nearly half a century ago, "The desire to write it suggested itself to me when I first visited the city some fifteen years ago, for it exercised so fascinating a spell that I immediately began to interest myself in its Jewish aspect...."

The "spell" Vilna cast over Israel Cohen also binds me, reflecting my own feelings for the city where I was born and where I spent an idyllic childhood in the 1930s. Its spell over me has never diminished; perhaps it is so strong because of my mother's wise advice never to return to Vilna after the Holocaust. "My child," she often said, "don't make a ruin of your beautiful memories."

When The Jewish Publication Society asked me to write a new introduction to their facsimile edition of Israel Cohen's splendid volume, I was honored and excited. However, composing it has proven very daunting. Israel Cohen's text is woven in a luminous blend of textures and colors. His words are also blessed with perfect pitch—an attribute one seldom encounters in historical works. It

Introduction

rings pure and true not only because I love Vilna but because the tenor of Cohen's prose is not academic in the modern sense of the word, but passionate and engaged.

In my remarks I have striven to achieve a tone and texture harmonious with Israel Cohen's work. The various yarns I have woven into the introduction—calling attention to the riches inside *Vilna* the book and Vilna the city; connecting both as briefly as possible with events that have taken place since its publication in 1943; and putting down my own recollections and memories of Vilna—have not always formed a smooth, even fabric. As I was writing, there were times that I wished for a loom instead of a typewriter to intertwine Cohen's *Vilna* with my own memories and thoughts. Yet I take comfort in knowing that irregularities in the weave of a fabric do not impair its use and durability but rather make it unique.

Israel Cohen's book opens with the legend about the origin of Vilna in 1322:

The city of Vilna, which has played so notable a part in the history of the Lithuanians, the Poles and the Jews, owes its origin to a dream, according to a local tradition. Gedymin, who ruled over the Grand Duchy of Lithuania in the earlier half of the fourteenth century, at first lived in the fortified town of Troki. One day he and his retinue set out on a hunting expedition in Troki's outskirts and shot an arrow in the direction of one of the hills overlooking the River Vilia. The arrow felled an ox on a spot near a house of idolatrous worship, for the people of the land were then still pagans, and Gedymin spent the night there. In his sleep he dreamed that he saw a big wolf wearing an iron shield and howling as loudly as a hundred wolves together. Awaking in fear, he asked the chief of his priests, Lezdeika, to interpret his dream. Lezdeika replied that the big wolf represented a strong fortress and a great city which would arise on that place, and that the roar indicated the fame of the fortress and the city, which would travel to distant parts of the earth. Gedymin was pleased with this interpretation and immediately began to build a city with a fortress, which, owing to the River Vilia flowing through it, was called Vilna.

I first heard this tale when I was four or five years old as I played with my cousins near the ruins of the fortress built by Prince Gedymin. This fortress dominated the city's skyline as it dominated my childhood imagination. Learning in school that Jews had lived in Vilna almost from its beginnings reinforced my own feelings of belonging, of being at one with the place of my birth.

My own deep involvement with Cohen's *Vilna* came about six years ago when a friend suggested that I write a book about the city of my youth. I took his words to heart, filled my loose-leaf notebook with fresh paper, and set to work.

I began my research at the YIVO Institute Library in New York. YIVO, the acronym for Yiddisher Visenshaftliker Institute, was founded by a group of Jewish scholars at a meeting in Berlin in 1925, but it was based in Vilna until the outbreak of World War II. YIVO's aim in the beginning, and to a large degree even now, was to teach and to preserve Yiddish material mirroring Jewish life in Eastern Europe, to collect Jewish folklore, and to study Jewish problems in a scientific manner. As a child in Vilna, I would sometimes accompany my mother on visits to YIVO. Only later did I learn of the important work being done there, work that continues to this day.

In those first days and weeks of research, the more I read about Vilna and wrote down in my loose-leaf binder, the more I retreated into my own thoughts and feelings about *home,* which is what Vilna has always been in my soul. No other place on earth holds the same meaning for me. Though sometimes chagrined at the narrowness of my own parameter, I've been reassured by William Faulkner's words, "I discovered that my own little postage stamp of native soil was worth writing about and that I would never live long enough to exhaust it."

One day, as I sat at a table at the YIVO library, the chief librarian, Dina Abramowicz, now my beloved friend and at one time librarian in Vilna's Kinderbibliotek of the Centrale Bildungs Komitet (CBK), who had introduced me to the first library I ever knew, passed by me, looked down at the mass of papers surrounding me, and murmured, "Why don't you read *Vilna* by Israel Cohen? It's the best one-volume history of Vilna in English."

My first glance at Cohen's table of contents revealed the immense scope of this man's work. I opened *Vilna* at random and read of Moses ben David, an ancestor of the famous Gaon of Vilna, Rabbi Elijah. Israel Cohen's vivid portrait of this seventeenth-century sage enthralled me:

The seventh in the line of Vilna's rabbis was a notable character, Moses ben David, a native of Cracow, and the ancestor of the Gaon Elijah. He was surnamed Kraemer, which means "shopkeeper," because, on accepting the appointment of rabbi, he declined to take a salary, being content to live on the earnings of a little provision-store kept by his wife. As he was very popular, all the members of the community made their purchases at this store. When Rabbi Moses noticed that his wife was conducting the household on a rather liberal scale, he questioned her, for he suspected that she was secretly receiving the salary he refused. But when she explained that this prosperity was due to the extensive customers she enjoyed, he drew up a careful calculation of their weekly expenditures and told her that there was no need for them to earn more. He accordingly insisted that, as soon as she found that she had enough money for the rest of the week, she should at once close the shop, even if it was only Sunday afternoon, so that the other shopkeepers might also be able to earn enough to cover their needs.

Another story, that of Count Valentin Potocki, the Ger Zedek (Righteous Proselyte), touched a personal memory. Israel Cohen notes that "the somewhat monotonous course of the Jews' economic struggle in Vilna was suddenly relieved in the middle of the eighteenth century by a remarkable event which lay quite outside all mundane affairs. It was the trial and condemnation to death of a Polish nobleman, Count Valentin Potocki, who had committed the heinous sin of abandoning the Christian for the Jewish faith." I remember my father telling me of going to the grave of the Ger Zedek on the Count's yahrzeit (the anniversary of his death) and saying kaddish with a large group of Vilna's Jews who came yearly to honor his memory.

These tales and countless others like them, framed within a wealth of historical information, quickly spun a web around me; I was captivated. Here was a book based on scholarship of the first magnitude, yet it was full, too, of wonderful, unforgettable *stories*.

Unable to take the book home from YIVO or to find it

elsewhere, I spent many hours reading it in the library. Here was a book I never could have written—nor did I really want to. How could I ever duplicate Cohen's words? Instead, it encouraged me to write *Remember Who You Are: Stories About Being Jewish,* which recounts life in Vilna when I was young and tells of friends and family whose lives touched mine before the war and throughout my life.

Israel Cohen's book is indeed quite different from any personal memoir. It is a "yerusha," a legacy, not only for people from Vilna, but also an erudite yet totally readable volume for all who care about the lost world of Jewish life in Europe.

Cohen's book reveals a history filled with people who are famous throughout the world. Each chapter is studded with the names of those who have risen to great fame as writers of religious works and secular literature, who became giants in the fields of art, music, and medicine. And in our own century Vilna has continued to give birth or spiritual sustenance to prominent artists, musicians, scholars, and writers as diverse as Chaim Soutine and Jascha Heifetz, Abraham Joshua Heschel and Chaim Grade, Abraham Sutskever and the devoutly Catholic Nobel Laureate Czeslaw Milosz, who learned Hebrew in order to translate Jewish liturgical works into Polish.

In his autobiographical work, *Native Realm,* Milosz comments warmly and movingly on his youth and education in Vilna, or Wilno as he, a Pole, calls it. Elsewhere he writes that "Vilnius, or as it also has been called, Wilno, is the city of my adolescence and youth. After many decades, it is still the center of my internal geography. And I know by experience how many obstacles confront a writer who wants to talk about its architectural beauty, tragic history and national imbroglios" (*The New Republic*, May 18, 1990).

Yet despite such obstacles, many important books have been written in this century about or by writers from Vilna: Chaim Grade's monumental *Rabbis and Wives, The Well,* and *My Mother's Sabbath Days,* first published in Yiddish and now widely read in English as well; Joseph Buloff's *From the Old Market Place;* Tadeusz Konwicki's novels written in Polish and translated into English; Lucy Davidowicz's *From That Place and Time,* a memoir of the period she spent at the YIVO in 1939 and after the Holocaust; and Leyzer Ran's vast compilation of photographs and documents in a multi-volume work called *The Jerusalem of Lithuania.*

One of the introductory essays in Ran's book was written by Rabbi Abraham Joshua Heschel, who attended the Reál Gymnasium in Vilna, led and nurtured by my great-uncle Dr. Leib Turbowicz, the first fully accredited gymnasium teaching all its subjects in Yiddish and preparing students for entry into state universities. Heschel writes:

Other Jewish communities were also rich in creative person-alities—rabbis, rosh yeshivas, scholars, writers, artists, cantors, and preachers— and in philanthropic, political and cultural insti-tutions, yeshivas, and modern schools. But all of those com-bined—such color, such diversity of colors, such scope—in this respect Vilna ranks above all other communities. The writer of these lines, who lived in Vilna for a while and was a co-founder of "Young Vilna" [a group of writers], was privileged to absorb the spirit of the city, where even the poorest were the bearers of refinement and spiritual exaltation. The readiness of self-sacrifice for justice and the dignity of man, inherited from many holy generations, was also glowing in the modern Jew. So many secular Jews lived the lives of saints and did not know it!

In another essay in Ran's collection, the scholar Ben-Zion Dinur writes, "One could not help feeling that the city had a soul, and that the soul was in harmony with the body." Dinur recalls visiting the grave of the Gaon of Vilna, where supplicants would bring written requests for his intercession on their behalf. "Unable to restrain my curiosity, I picked up a few of them and read. One said, 'I pray and beg mercy that I succeed in choosing the right books for reading. Shloimo, the son of Gittel.'"

Perhaps a religious custom influenced Shloimo's signature. But, I like to think, he chose to identify himself as the son of his mother, because mothers and fathers had equal status in Vilna. At least that is how I remember families there—particularly the far-flung and numerous branches of my own clan. Two of my great-grandmothers were undisputed heads of their businesses and families, and women were educated quite as diligently as men.

We all remember what we wish to remember. Secular Yiddishists recall Vilna from a different vantage point from that of yeshiva graduates; Zionists have a different frame of reference from that of Bundists. Nevertheless, Vilna's Jewish community tried to accommodate them all: members of Po'ale Zion, the Zionist Socialists, and the Bundists. In Israel Cohen's words, the community attempted "to form a synthesis of the different principles that [these various organizations] embodied."

Now, years later, when people from Vilna meet in New

York at lectures sponsored by "Nusach Vilne," a group of people who gather to remember Vilna, to say kaddish for its victims, to celebrate past and present accomplishments of its native sons and daughters, and to fund and administer a literary prize, we often disagree about "the way it really was." My cousin Danka Turow, herself a survivor of the Vilna ghetto, once perceptively remarked: "Maybe only a brilliant historian can capture [Vilna] properly...."

Israel Cohen, a historian of immense skill and humanity, has done just that, capturing Vilna with the wide lens of today's camera, not through the narrow scope of an early Kodak Brownie. If the period between the two world wars receives a less detailed account in Cohen's work than the years up to 1914, perhaps it is because Cohen was writing *Vilna* in the late 1930's as war was looming. At the time, he might not have had sufficient access to primary sources or documents of that period nor perhaps the ease of spirit to write as fully as he did of previous centuries and decades.

In 1943, when Israel Cohen wrote the epilogue, he could not fully realize, nor could the rest of the world community, what was then befalling the Jews of Vilna and the rest of Europe. In it he reports the murder of 60,000 men, women, and children in Ponar, where they were brought by the Nazis and machine-gunned. His report was based on a June 16, 1942, story in the *London Evening Standard*. It is significant that his footnote to this account cautions, "It is naturally impossible to check the accuracy of these figures." Indeed.

Unfortunately, we now *can* check the accuracy of such

figures. In the years since Cohen's work was published, many important historical works have appeared, documenting in chilling detail what happened to his beloved Vilna. One of the most significant books is *Ghetto in Flames: The Struggle and Destruction of the Jews of Vilna in the Holocaust* by Dr. Itzhak Arad, present director of Yad Vashem and a retired brigadier general of the Israeli army. He was 13-year-old Isaac Rudnicki when he escaped from Warsaw to a small town near Vilna two years ahead of the Nazi occupation. As a member of a partisan group, the author participated in derailing German military trains. *Ghetto in Flames* is part of the Holocaust Library that was created and is managed by survivors in New York. Its mission is "to offer to the reading public authentic material, not readily available, and to preserve the memory of our martyrs and heroes, untainted by arbitrary and inadvertent distortions."

Herman Kruk's Diary From the Vilna Ghetto, translated by Barbara and Benjamin Harshav; *Diary of the Vilna Ghetto* by Yitzhok Rudashevski, translated by Percy Matenko; and many other first-hand and historical accounts, as well as the recent film *The Partisans of Vilna,* directed by Joshua Waletzky and produced by Aviva Kempner, and Joshua Sobol's controversial plays, the trilogy *Ghetto,* are modern echoes of the lamentation with which Cohen opens his book's epilogue: "How doth the city sit solitary, that was full of people!"

Despite the tragic ending that eventually befell the Vilna ghetto, its last years represent a moving testament to its Jewish inhabitants' courage and love of learning and life. Remarkably, as long as there were still people alive in the ghetto, an almost unimaginable cultural life went on in the midst of doom. Not everyone approved and participated at first. When a symphony orchestra was organized and gave public performances, leaflets protesting the event were handed out, paraphrasing Herman Kruk's anguished "Theatrical performances should not be held in cemeteries." But according to Itzhak Arad, "The political groups which at first were against concerts eventually reconciled themselves to these events and even came to accept them. Concerts became a popular social event and a spur to the growth of cultural and social life in the pent-up community. Kruk, who himself had sharply criticized the first concert in the ghetto, was to write on March 8, 1942: 'And yet life is stronger than anything else.'"

In addition to the orchestra, there were two choirs, one Hebrew and one Yiddish, scientific seminars, an association of writers and another of musicians, a marionette theater, and a sports club. Recitations and performances of the work of writers, poets, and musicians were arranged. Alexander Tamir, a leading pianist and teacher now living in Israel, won a musical competition in the Vilna ghetto at the age of twelve. His song, "Shtiler, shtiler lomir shveigen, kvorim vaksn do"—"Quiet, quiet, let's be silent, graves are growing here"—with words by Szmerke Kaczerginski, is sung at nearly every ghetto commemoration around the world.

Most moving of all was the establishment in Vilna of the only ghetto library to operate during the Holocaust. Dina Abramowicz, that steadfast link between books and people, was asked by Herman Kruk to work in the library he set up with the permission of the Jewish ghetto government. In an interview in *The New York Jewish Week* (November 1, 1990), a reporter challenged Ms. Abramowicz: "But how could a library exist in the ghetto, where human beings were reduced to living like animals?" She explained:

> It was a kind of spiritual resistance and protest. On the territory of the ghetto remained a former Jewish library of Vilna, abandoned and devastated but not completely destroyed. Kruk wanted to prevent it from destruction. Of course, nobody knew what ghetto life would be like.... Books found in empty apartments there bore mute testimony. People found [books] scattered everywhere in abandoned houses.... Books were found in and outside the ghetto, so the library was fed books all the time. Some of the readers never came back.

In the midst of the destruction, Abramowicz worked from eleven in the morning to seven in the evening, signing out books and talking to readers. She recounts: "In the afternoon schoolchildren came in droves to the library. They had no other entertainment, there were no playgrounds, so books were an outlet for the ghetto child to satisfy his interest in the world, in adventures and travels—what young people like to read about...."

The library operated for two years. The little mud-encrusted diary of fourteen-year-old Yitzhok Rudashevski, found in the ruins of the Vilna ghetto after the war, has as one of its last entries, "The book unites us with the future, the book unites us with the world."

Only a few months ago, I met two representatives of the present-day Jewish community of Vilnius. They were in the United States to explore arrangements for the publication of books with Jewish content in Lithuania. They told me that one of the first books they want to make available to all readers in their part of the world is Israel Cohen's *Vilna*. It is their aim to integrate, to underscore, the rich Jewish history which, to them, is part of Vilnius, Lithuania, in the 1990s, just as it was for centuries before our time.

I liked both people immensely. One of them spoke a beautiful, pure Yiddish, the other hardly a word. One urged me to come to Vilnius; the other understood my reluctance. Upon parting, they gave me a book in Luthuanian about Vilnius and other cities in their newly independent country. They gave me as well a key ring with a picture of the castle where I played as a child. Alas, I have no keys for any doors in Vilnius.

They also gave me a leaflet describing the aims and plans of their newly established publishing company, the "Zalman Rejzen Foundation for Jewish Culture." It felt surreal to me when I read this name on their brochure, for Zalman Rejzen was one of the founders of YIVO, an editor of the famous Vilna Yiddish newspaper *Der Tog*, and the author of many books on Yiddish grammar, including his seminal four-volume *Lexicon of Jewish Literature, Press and Philology*, and *Pinkos*, which Cohen used as a reference source. The leaflet from Vilnius announced that one of the chief goals of this new enterprise was to "redeem the historical memory, religious and spiritual values of Lithuanian

Jewry." Among their projected activities were a camp for
Jewish teenagers, a Jewish folk theater, a Purim-shpil, a
Passover seder, and a Jerusalem Day holiday.

How is one to reconcile the aims of this fledgling organization with the news that came out of Lithuania in
1991? Recent articles do not bode well for the resurgence
of Jewish life there. The same Lithuanian government,
which voices support for the plans of the Rejzen
Foundation, has granted pardons to some Lithuanians
who have been accused of crimes against Jews during the
Holocaust and has issued a stream of contradictory statements about these actions. Since Lithuania's independence from the Soviet Union, reports from Vilnius
mention restitution proceedings for owners whose properties were confiscated by Nazis and later by Soviet
authorities. At this time, "the law permits claims only
from current Lithuanian citizens, not from Jewish emi-
grants to Israel or elsewhere..." (*Los Angeles Times*,
September 16, 1991).

Similarly, optimism for reunification of recently found
YIVO documents in Vilnius with those in the New York
archives, where they rightly belong, waxes and wanes,
despite the government's promise that the material will be
transferred. Is there a future for these precious remnants
of Vilna's Jewish past in Vilnius?

According to an article in *The Village Voice* (March 20,
1991), "Ninety-six per cent of Lithuania's 300,000 Jews
were murdered by Hitler, and the culture their survivors
tried to resuscitate after the war was quashed by Stalin.
Nowadays, Lithuanian Jews are fleeing the country for

Israel at the rate of 1500 per year. By the end of the decade, community leaders estimate there will be only a thousand Jews left, most of them elderly. When they die, who will say kaddish for them?"

Is there an answer?

Aaron Lansky, founder and director of the National Yiddish Book Center in America, recently brought Yiddish books to the remaining Jews of Lithuania. Some were intended for the Lithuanian Book Palace in Vilnius, where Esfir Bramson Alperniene, a native of Vilna and survivor of the Holocaust, helps with the identification and classification of Jewish documents. Upon his return to the United States, Lansky wrote in the *Yiddish Book Peddler* (Winter 1990–91) that Fira [diminutive for Esfir] agreed to accompany him to Ponar:

As we walked along the winding path between the craters in the silence of the forest, we came upon another group of visitors: an old man and two elderly women. Speaking in Yiddish, they explained that they were preparing to leave Vilna for Israel and had come to Ponar one last time. "There is nothing left for us in Lithuania.... Here, at Ponar, are the only people to whom we must say goodbye."

Until recently, there was no marker or even a mound to mark the Jewish graves at Ponar. A large monument, a pavilion and paved paths through the woods commemorated the site simply as an "Official Memorial of the Great Patriotic War." In the summer of 1991, the Lithuanian government finally agreed to have a new monument erected in Ponar, initiated and funded by Yeshayahu

Epstein, a Vilna survivor of the Holocaust who now lives in Israel. Though it provides only small solace to victims and survivors, it now declares in Hebrew and Yiddish:

> In eternal memory of the 70,000 Jews from Vilna and vicinity whom the Nazi criminals and their helpers murdered and burned, here in Ponar, in the years 1941–1944.

Even in the midst of such horror, Aaron Lansky found reason for hope when he noted upon his return from Lithuania, "Who could believe that we, the children and grandchildren of those who left or died, would be returning with copies of the very books they destroyed? No one thought there would be Jews here again, only ashes. That's the final triumph of our trip. Our arrival is an act of defiance. They didn't succeed. Our culture survives" (*Smithsonian Magazine*, January 1991).

One prays, though with a heavy heart, that Israel Cohen would agree with Lansky. In the final pages of his epilogue, Cohen wonders whether "the glorious traditions of the 'Jerusalem of Lithuania' will ever be renewed. Will the Jews ever rise again from the desolation and devastation around them, rebuild their ruined lives, and restore their shattered community? It would be hazardous and perhaps idle, though natural, to indulge in the consolation of pleasant prophecy, and yet the accumulated experiences of a long and eventful past counsel hope."

Perhaps the people who came to New York from Vilnius to discuss the publication of *Vilna* in Lithuania really do have reason to take Cohen's words to heart. It *is* true that our culture lives on, that miracles can happen despite apocalyptic changes in the world. Yet our greatest triumph and strength as a people, the one certainty we have had from the beginning of time, is that the written word sustains us and makes immortal the richness of our traditions and faith.

Israel Cohen's *Vilna* preserves and celebrates the glory of a special place and remarkable people and brings their world to life in the pages of this book as well as in the minds and hearts of all those who immerse themselves in it.

New York
January, 1992

PREFACE

THIS is, so far as I am aware, the first comprehensive history, in any language, of the Jewish community of Vilna from its earliest times to the present day. The desire to write it suggested itself to me when I first visited the city some fifteen years ago, for it exercised so fascinating a spell that I immediately began to interest myself in its Jewish aspect, although this naturally appealed to me for quite different reasons. The opportunity of realizing that desire also came to me, by a happy coincidence, in Vilna, for it was while staying there, on another occasion many years later, that the invitation to write this book reached me. I therefore prolonged my visit in order to equip myself for the task by delving into the early annals of the community, studying its checkered evolution and inspiring traditions, familiarizing myself with the Jewish quarter and all its manifold institutions and personalities, steeping myself in its atmosphere and legends, and collecting all the books and brochures about Vilna Jewry that were then obtainable in the city itself. In these preparatory steps I enjoyed the advantage of the very friendly and instructive help of Haikel Lunski, the scholarly librarian of the Strashun Library, who has himself written extensively on the community, and whom I found a veritable walking encyclopedia.

Chief among the literary booty that I brought home were the two Hebrew classics, Finn's *Kiryah Ne'emanah* ("Faithful City") and Noah Maggid Steinschneider's *'Ir Vilna* ("City of Vilna"). These pioneer products of painstaking research provide the basic and indispensable material for any history of the Jews in Vilna. They complement and partly duplicate one another in their voluminous contents. The first presents a brief chronicle up to the reign of Tsar Alexander II and includes classified biographies of most of the men of importance associated with the community from its birth; the second is mainly a biographical dictionary, covering every significant phase of intellectual and communal activity, based partly, like its predecessor, upon a careful scrutiny of the tombstone inscriptions in the Jewish cemeteries, but containing many more lives, much greater detail, and a more lavish supply of footnotes.

Essential as these two works are as source-books, they concentrate far too much upon the personal element; and Finn's miscellany, with all its merits (especially in the revised and annotated edition by Matthias Strashun), fails to provide an adequate account even of the period that it covers. The lack in this respect was made good to some extent, only a few years ago, by Israel Klausner in his *Toledot ha-Kehillah ha-'Ivrit b'Vilna* ("History of the Jewish Community in Vilna"), of which so far only the first part has appeared. It contains a scholarly presentation of the social, political, and economic evolution of Vilna Jewry until the end of the eight-

eenth century, at least one-third being devoted to
a detailed investigation of the tangled and unedifying
story of the Kahal's finances. It is the fruit of much
laborious research among the State, municipal, and
other archives, and the records of all communal
institutions, as attested by a formidable array of
references, and I gratefully acknowledge the help
that I have derived from it.

There are two other books to which I am equally
indebted, both in Yiddish and of rather mammoth
proportions. One is the *Pinkos* compiled by Zalman
Reisen, a large folio volume of nearly 950 pages of
double columns of small type, containing circumstantial and graphic descriptions by a number of
writers of the community's tribulations in the years
1914–1922. The other is the bulky *Zammelbuch*
("Miscellany") of 1,000 pages, edited by Ephim H.
Jeshurin, and published, in celebration of its silver
jubilee, by the Wilner Branch 367 — Workmen's
Circle, New York. This imposing collection of
contributions, in prose and verse, by a numerous
band of writers, with an abundance of illustrations,
provides a comprehensive and life-like picture of
most of the manifold facets of the community's
record. While, by virtue of its origin, it naturally
gives pride of place to the Jewish labor movement
and the struggle for political liberty, it also reflects
and reveals more faithfully than any other work the
soul and genius of Vilna Jewry, the humanity that
pervaded its ghetto, and the humor that occasionally enlivened it. As for the many other sources
that I have consulted, they are given either in the

notes or the bibliography, although the latter does
not claim to be a complete list of all works relating
to the subject, as there are some, such as the *Yovel
Buch* ("Jubilee Book") 1906–1936, issued by the
Jewish printers of Vilna, to which I have been unable
to obtain access.

Among those from whom I have obtained additional information not available in any publication,
I should like to record my gratitude to Professor
Isaac D. Markon, Mr. E. C. Sosnowicz (a graduate
of the Vilna University), and Dr. G. Haus (also
formerly of Vilna), while my thanks are likewise
tendered to Dr. Cecil Roth and Dr. D. Mowshowitch
for the loan of valuable material.

A word about the spelling of the name of the
city. Before the World War of 1914–1918, the
Russian spelling, "Wilna," was fairly universal.
After the city came into the possession of the Poles,
the name became "Wilno," though with "Wilna"
as its genitive. During the brief Lithuanian regime,
the name was changed to "Vilnius," and since the
German occupation the spelling "Wilna" again came
into vogue. But as the pronunciation in English-
speaking countries has always been "Vilna," and
that, too, is the pronunciation current in Jewish
circles, there seems to be no reason for not adopting
the corresponding spelling. Moreover, in the translit-
eration of Yiddish words, I have, where phonetic fidelity required it, deviated from the German equivalent.

This book was first planned in the halcyon days of
peace, but the writing of it, owing to other more

pressing tasks, was not begun until after the outbreak of war. This delay unfortunately prevented
me from paying another visit to Vilna, which I had
fondly contemplated, but it has had a compensating
advantage, for it has afforded me the melancholy
satisfaction of bringing this history down to the end
of a definite epoch. Moreover, in consequence of the
tragic march of events, some phases of life and
institutions described in the present tense most
probably now belong to memories of the past.
Although, in comparison with many other Jewish
communities in Europe, that of Vilna appeared upon
the scene rather late, it has exercised a potent and
determining influence upon the religious and cultural
development of the Jews throughout Eastern
Europe — an influence that has even been borne
to numberless centers throughout the world by
its numerous offspring who have sought their
fortunes in other climes. It has, in truth, been
a bastion of Judaism and Jewish life, which, like so
many other strongholds of Jewish culture, has fallen
victim to the ravages of the present war. But
although it has suffered such a terrible and devastating martyrdom, greatly overshadowing even the
most tragic calamities that had ever befallen it, and
inevitably evoking the exclamation: *"Ichabod—
the glory is departed!"*, one cannot but wonder
whether its glory will not some day be revived in a
happier future.

ISRAEL COHEN

London, July 14, 1943.

VILNA

CHAPTER I

THE EARLY HISTORY OF
LITHUANIAN JEWRY

THE city of Vilna, which has played so notable a part in the history of the Lithuanians, the Poles and the Jews, owes its origin, according to a local tradition, to a dream. Gedymin, who ruled over the Grand Duchy of Lithuania in the earlier half of the fourteenth century, at first lived in the fortified town of Troki. One day he and his retinue set out on a hunting expedition in Troki's outskirts and shot an arrow in the direction of one of the hills overlooking the River Vilia. The arrow felled an ox on a spot near a house of idolatrous worship, for the people of the land were then still pagans, and Gedymin spent the night there. In his sleep he dreamed that he saw a big wolf wearing an iron shield and howling as loudly as a hundred wolves together. Awaking in fear, he asked the chief of his priests, Lezdeika, to interpret his dream. Lezdeika replied that the big wolf represented a strong fortress and a great city which would arise on that place, and that the roar indicated the fame of the fortress and the city, which would travel to distant parts of the earth. Gedymin was pleased with this interpretation and immediately began to build a city with a fortress, which, owing to the River Vilia flowing through it, was called Vilna.

Whatever truth there may be in this story, historians are at least agreed that in 1322 Gedymin made Vilna, then a small town, capital of the Grand Duchy of Lithuania, although its foundation dated from the tenth century and was attributed to the Normans. He displayed much energy and enterprise in its development, and made it known far and wide that he wished people to come and settle there. Tillers of the soil were invited to take possession of fields that awaited cultivation, and were promised exemption from any payment to the State for ten years; merchants and craftsmen were likewise attracted by a similar promise to transfer their activities to the new city. The settlers included not only Lithuanians from other parts of the country, but also many Russians and Germans. It would be plausible to suppose that Jews, who were already domiciled in other towns in Lithuania, likewise responded to Gedymin's invitation, but there is no definite evidence of their having done so. Narbutt, historian of Vilna, states that there was a large Jewish community in the city in the days of Gedymin and that the space occupied by the streets inhabited by Jews was about a fifth of the area of the whole city. Another historian, Bialinsky, maintains that there was a considerable community in the reign of Gedymin's successor, Olgierd (1345–1377), a view which is supported by some other writers, including Shereshevsky, author of a work on the Jewish records of the city. But the Russian historian Sergei Berschadski, who, at a later date, wrote a historical sketch of the Jewish community of Vilna (in *Vos-*

khod, 1881), declared that he had made a very thorough investigation of its archives and could find no trace of evidence that a recognized Jewish congregation had existed before the middle of the sixteenth century.[1]

There is a local tradition that an old Jewish cemetery on the further side of the River Vilia was laid out in 1487, but there are no documentary or other proofs that can be advanced in its support. Jews were, indeed, already settled in the neighboring town of Troki in 1388, and individual Jews may have begun to dribble into Vilna in the course of the fifteenth century, but it was not until the last decade of that century that we have any evidence of Jews having lived there. In 1490 the plenipotentiary of the Grand Duke of Moscow complained, in a letter to King Casimir Jagiello, of the excessive tax imposed upon merchants travelling to and from Moscow through Vilna by Michael Danilow, the Jewish lessee of taxes. In 1495 the Grand Duke of Lithuania presented to the city of Vilna some property which had formerly been owned by a Jew named Janishewsky.

In the reign of King Sigismund I (1506–1548), who was distinguished for his liberal outlook, Jews probably began to settle in Vilna in appreciable numbers. In the year after he ascended the Polish throne King Sigismund wrote that he had bought various goods from the Jewish merchant, Michael Rebinkowitz. There are also statements of accounts by Jewish

[1] See Supplementary Note 1.

tax-farmers in Vilna and Brisk (Brest-Litovsk) dating from the following year. By 1527 the number
of Jews in Vilna must have become too large for
the peace of mind of the burghers, although that
does not necessarily mean that it was considerable,
as in that year the King granted a charter to the
burghers which contained a prohibition against Jews
living or trading in the city.[1] It was owing to the
determined opposition of the local inhabitants, based
solely on the fear of economic competition, that a
Jewish community was so slow in developing.
Despite the terms of his charter, however, King
Sigismund appointed a Jew, Joshua Paskowitz, as
chief collector of taxes on wax in the market of
Vilna.

A sidelight upon the social conditions of the Jews
in the city in the middle of the sixteenth century
is afforded by the fact that in 1550 a certain Jewess,
Fanna Kasparova, refused to surrender to the Jewish
court in Vilna the Jew, Chatzka Issakowitz, and
defied the Jewish court-messenger sent to take him,
although she had previously given a bond for his
appearance. Nor is that the only evidence relating
to the presence of Jews in Vilna at that time, for in
1551 special permission was given to two Jews from
Cracow, Simon Doktorowicz and Israel ben Joseph,
to rent dwellings and shops in the city and to trade
and open a money exchange. Four years later King
Sigismund II, Augustus (1548–1572), leased to a
certain Jew in Vilna the privilege of minting coins

---

[1] This chapter was entitled, *De non tolerandis judaeis.*

for three years. Those who secured this concession in Vilna in 1560 are also known to have been Jews, named Felix and Borodavka. By 1568 there must have been a properly organized Jewish community, for in that year the King issued an order commanding it to pay the taxes due to his treasury. But it was not till 1573 that the first synagogue was built, proof that the number of Jews had now attained fair proportions and that they enjoyed a good measure of economic stability, although, as in the case of all other communities, there must have been a preliminary period during which the Jews met for religious worship in some temporary structure or in private houses.

Long before the Vilna community assumed definite form, however, there were Jewish settlements in all the more important towns in Lithuania. Some of them were already in existence before the end of the fourteenth century, particularly those of Brisk or Brest (better known as Brest-Litovsk), Grodno, Troki, Luzk, and Vladimir. The first Jews who settled in Lithuania are believed to have come in two different currents of immigration — an earlier one through southern Russia from the east, and a later one from the west, mainly Germany. They enjoyed a considerable degree of tolerance and even goodwill on the part of the rulers, largely owing to the comparatively late date at which Christianity was introduced into the country, and also to the time that it took for the fanaticism of the Catholic clergy in the adjoining territory of Poland to penetrate across its borders. In 1386 the Grand

Duke of Lithuania, Wladislav II, Jagiello, a grandson
of Gedymin, married Jadwiga, Queen of Poland,
and signalized the event by adopting her faith; and,
although he left his capital to become King of
Poland and to found a dynasty which lasted two
hundred years, the people of Lithuania followed his
example in abandoning paganism. They were, indeed, the last nation in Europe to accept Christianity, an event which was signalized by an impressive
scene in Vilna. On February 17, 1387, a stately
procession of nobles and prelates, headed by King
Wladislav and his brother, Skirgiello, the new Grand
Duke, marched forth to the ancient grove of oaks,
where countless generations had practiced their
heathen cult. There the royal convert hewed down
the trees that had been worshipped by his ancestors,
destroyed the idols, extinguished the sacred fire, and
elevated the Cross over the heathen altars. The
introduction of Christianity gradually brought about
an approximation in the position of the Jews in
Lithuania to that of their brethren in other lands,
for, although the Grand Dukes were just and even
friendly to their Jewish subjects, they were unable
to resist the aggressiveness of the priests and monks,
who soon exercised their baleful influence.

Another factor that affected the Jewish position in
Lithuania adversely was the union of that country
with Poland, which resulted from the marriage of
Wladislav Jagiello. Lithuania continued, indeed,
to be ruled as a separate State for over a century
and a half, but from 1386 her fortunes were very
intimately bound up with those of Poland. In 1401

the two countries agreed upon a political alliance, which was confirmed in 1432; from 1447 they both had the same rulers, apart from a brief interval of ten years (1492–1501); and in 1569 their formal and permanent union was enacted at a historic meeting of the *Seym* (Diet) at Lublin, which gave them a common legislature and a common government. The result of this culminating act was that Lithuania gradually sank into a state of dependence upon Poland and ultimately shared in her downfall at the end of the eighteenth century.

The development of Vilna received a powerful stimulus from the Grand Duke Witold, a cousin of Wladislav Jagiello, who combined martial vigor with a sense of justice to all his subjects. After contenting himself at first with the principality of Grodno, Witold secured the removal of his cousin, Skirgiello, from Vilna in 1392, when he made a compact with Wladislav at Ostrowo, and added to his territory by victorious battles with his neighbors. He fought against the Tatars and brought many of them captive from the Crimea to Lithuania: among these were a number of Karaites — according to their own tradition — who were taken to Troki, where they founded their first settlement in Lithuania. Witold was the first who authorized the existence of the Jewish communities in the Grand Duchy, and he displayed towards them a benevolence which was not only remarkable at the time but could well serve as an example to many governments in Central and Eastern Europe of the present day. In 1388 he granted a charter to the Jews of

Brest and other towns, and in the following year he gave a special charter to those of Grodno. The charter of 1388 was based upon that given to the Jews in Poland by the Grand Duke Boleslav the Pious in 1264 and confirmed by King Casimir the Great in 1334 and 1357.

The charter of Boleslav and Casimir, which constituted the foundation of the legal position of the Jews in Poland, was twofold in character. It consisted of positive rights, ensuring the Jews the opportunity for economic progress, and of preventive provisions for safeguarding their personal and religious security. Their rights comprised freedom of transit, of trade, and of financial operations — the paragraphs relating to the lending of money occupying a rather prominent place in the document. The charter conferred upon the Jews the right of receiving all kinds of pledges as well as mortgages upon the estates of the nobility; it prescribed that the Christians who were a month in arrear in the payment of interest due to a Jew must pay double, and that a Jew could not be forced to return his pledges on Sabbaths and festivals. The Jews were exempted from the jurisdiction of the ecclesiastical and the municipal law-courts, both of which were hostile to them, and were placed under the protection of the king. Their jurisdiction was entrusted to the *Voivode* (Governor) and the *Starosta* (County Lieutenant), two dignitaries of high rank, who were the king's representatives in the various provinces and towns. They were to be judged by a special officer appointed by the *Voivode*, who, although a

Christian, was, on account of his functions, designated the "Jewish Judge." In order to guard against any miscarriage of justice, the testimony of a Christian against a Jew had to be corroborated by a Jewish witness. If a Christian injured a Jew, he had to compensate him for his illness and pay for his cure, besides paying a fine to the State treasury; and if he killed a Jew, he was to be punished by the law, and all his goods and chattels became forfeit to the State. There was a special paragraph expressly based on the instructions issued by the Pope, forbidding any accusation to be made against a Jew of killing a Christian child to drink his blood, and ordering that if it were found after investigation that the Christian witnesses had testified falsely against him, then "as they had thought to do unto him, so shall be done unto them." Whoever kidnapped a Jewish child was to be punished, and whoever threw a stone at a synagogue or did damage to a Jewish cemetery was liable to be fined. The Jews were granted permission to dwell in the neighborhood of their synagogues and wherever they deemed proper. They were given the right to buy and sell everything, including corn and bread, and if any Christian molested them the culprits should be punished with a fine. There were also a number of paragraphs containing the germ of the system of autonomy which the Jewish communities, first in Poland and then in Lithuania, enjoyed for a period of two hundred years, until the middle of the eighteenth century.

The charter for the Jews of Grodno, given in

1389, shows that they were in possession of houses and plots in particular streets, as well as of a synagogue and cemetery. In return for a special tax payable to the Grand Duke, they had the right to sell spirituous liquor in their houses and — like all other citizens — to offer goods for sale in the streets as well as in their shops. The document also mentions that the Jews were occupied as artisans and that, upon payment of a land-tax, they could own lands, fields and meadows.

After the death of Witold, which occurred in 1430, there was a period of recurring war and unrest, but his example of tolerance was followed by Casimir Jagiello, a liberal-minded monarch and a friend of Italian humanism. Casimir became Grand Duke in 1440, when only a boy of thirteen, ascended the Polish throne in 1447, and then reigned over both Poland and Lithuania until 1492. He maintained the Jews' charter granted by Witold, bestowed a limited form of autonomy upon the Karaites at Troki, and employed Jews as financiers and tax-farmers in order to increase his income. In Poland he stoutly resisted the reactionary party of Bishop Olesnicki, who had presided over the regency council during his minority. At the request of the Jewish community, in 1453, he issued a charter confirming all its rights and privileges, in which he wrote: "It is our wish that the Jews, whom we take under our special protection in our own interest as well as that of the State, shall feel well and safe during our fortunate reign." This charter, which guaranteed the Jews not only the right of settlement, freedom of trade, inviolability of life and property, and protection from slanderous accusations and attacks, but also communal autonomy and autonomous law courts, aroused the bitter hostility of Bishop Olesnicki. The bigoted prelate, who was raised to the dignity of cardinal, secured the cooperation of the Papal Legate, Capistrano, in his efforts to get the charter abolished. He even alleged that the document containing the terms of the historic charter of Casimir the Great, which the Jews had submitted to the king for confirmation, was forged: the fact being that, as the original of that charter had been burned in a fire at Posen, only a copy could be produced. Finally, when the Polish army was defeated in 1454 by the Teutonic Order of Knights, the cardinal told the king that this disaster was due to his flouting the principles and interests of the Church, and compelled him to sign the Statute of Nieszawa, which contained an article annulling all the privileges formerly granted to the Jews which were "in conflict with the Divine law and the statute of the land."

The king ignored this statute, however, as he took advantage of the increasing Jewish immigration from Germany into Poland and Lithuania in order to utilize the commercial abilities of the newcomers. He leased to the Jews in Lithuania cultivated and uncultivated lands, and gave them the right to trade freely in agricultural products, dairy produce and whiskey. Jews were also granted the concession for collecting customs dues on the Polish-Lithuanian frontier as well as on the internal boundaries, and proved a source of considerable gain to the royal treasury. The larger customs contractors enjoyed a privileged position: they were exempt from the payment of taxes and were placed under the immediate protection of the king. This liberal treatment of the Jews resulted in inciting against them the hostility of the main sections of the population: clergy, townsfolk and farmers.

Upon the death of Casimir Jagiello, he was succeeded by his son, John Albert, as King of Poland (1492–1501) and by another son, Alexander Jagiello, as Grand Duke of Lithuania (1492–1506). Both had been pupils of the Polish historian, Jan Dlugosz, and had been infected by something of his Jew-hatred. King John confirmed the Statute of Nieszawa, which subordinated the legal rights of the Jews to the control of the Church. Grand Duke Alexander was at first kindly disposed towards the Jews. He renewed the charter granted by his father to the Karaites at Troki and even supplemented it; he leased to Jews his various Grand Ducal perquisites, especially customs dues; he fulfilled the obligations of his father to Jewish financiers, and himself borrowed money from them. All the more astonishing, therefore, was the decree of expulsion which he issued in 1495 against all the the Jews in Lithuania. It is not clear whether this cruel edict was due to clerical influence or to the wish of Alexander and the Lithuanian magnates to get rid of their Jewish creditors; it has even been suggested that it might have been prompted by the example set by Spain three years earlier. After the Jews had left the country the Grand Duke confiscated the whole of their immovable property and presented part of it to their former neighbors. The majority of the exiles were allowed to settle in near-by Polish towns, while a number who had originated from Volhynia and Kiev went to the Crimea, with whose commercial center, Kaffa, they had previously carried on trade. Their banishment, however, was of comparatively short duration, for when Alexander succeeded to the Polish crown, on his brother's death in 1501, and consequently had to take over his own former Jewish subjects who had found asylum in Poland, he allowed them to return to their old homes in Lithuania. He agreed with his advisers that there was no sense in keeping them in overcrowded towns in Poland while sparsely populated districts in Lithuania suffered from their absence. Accordingly, they received official permission in 1503 to return to Lithuania, where they were reinstated in the possession of their former dwellings and had all their property — houses, farms, synagogues, cemeteries — restored to them.

Alexander realized that the budget of the Grand Duchy could not well be covered without the financial services of Jewish tax-farmers, and therefore again made use of them. The richest Jew in his employment was Josko (Joseph), who held the lease of all the tolls on the frontier as well as of the road tolls in nearly half of Poland. Alexander showed his appreciation by exempting Josko and his officials from the jurisdiction of the local authority and placing them under the direct jurisdiction of the

Royal Court. Moreover, he had Boleslav's charter
to the Jews incorporated in the codex of Polish
fundamental laws, although he maintained that this
did not imply a confirmation of the charter but was
intended solely to defend the population from the
Jews.

A more benevolent attitude towards the Jews was
adopted by Alexander's brother and successor,
Sigismund I (1506–1548), the youngest son of
Casimir Jagiello, although his friendliness may have
been inspired to some extent by his own material interests. In Lithuania, in 1514, he appointed
as Court Banker and Royal Treasurer Michael
Josefowicz of Brest who acted as general lessee of
taxes and tolls throughout the country and had to
pay his officials' salaries out of the money collected,
besides satisfying his princely creditors. This Jewish
financier (whose brother, Abraham, had previously
held the post of Treasurer of the Grand Duchy under
Alexander and subsequently adopted Christianity)
enjoyed a position of unique importance and authority. He was created "the Senior and Judge of all
the communities in Lithuania;" he was the sole
representative of Jewish affairs before the King and
Grand Duke; he had the right to exercise judicial
powers, to impose money fines, and to pronounce
sentences of imprisonment. He even had the right,
in case of need, to appoint a rabbi to utter the ban
of excommunication (*Ḥerem*), since he could not
exercise any rabbinical prerogatives himself. This
multiplication of authority in the person of his
financial agent was due to the monarch's wish to

bring him into the closest contact with the autonomous administration of the Jewish communities:
similarly he appointed Abraham Bohemus (i. e. from
Bohemia) "Senior" of the Jewish communities of
Poland. This attempt to interfere in the internal
communal life of the Jews met with no success,
although the system of tax-farming, whereby Jewish
notables secured a certain influence in the affairs
both of the State and of Jewry, continued in force
until the Polish *Szlachta* (nobility) pressed their
claim to have control of public offices. In Lithuania,
however, the position of the Jews in general was
much better than in Poland: there were friendlier
relations with their Christian neighbors, who were
less infected with Jew-hatred than the populace in
Poland, and the king was subjected to less interference with his authority on the part of the nobles.

Sigismund was apparently constrained to forbid
the settlement of Jews in Vilna by the charter
granted to the burghers of that city in 1527, for a
much more generous spirit breathed in the decree
which he issued from Vilna in 1533 to all Lithuanian
Voivodes, *Starostas*, and town councils, strictly en-
joining them to maintain the rights and liberties
guaranteed to the Jews and to lighten their heavy
burdens of taxation. "For," said the decree, "the
Jews would surely collapse completely beneath the
burden imposed upon them if justice were not shown
to them in their affairs." The discrimination that
Sigismund exercised in favor of the Jews in Lithuania was further evidenced in connection with the
adoption by the Diet at Pietrokow, in 1538, of a

constitution which contained a number of restrictions against the Jews. It prescribed that in future they must be excluded from the positions of lessees or collectors of tolls, which must be strictly reserved for the nobility and professing Christians; that Jews should not have the general right to trade but must obtain the special permission of the king or the consent of the local municipality; that they were altogether forbidden to trade in villages; and that they must resume wearing a distinctive hat of yellow material. These various legal changes were applied only to the Jews in Poland and not to those in Lithuania.

The king's friendly interest in the Jews was again displayed in the following year, when a story was spread in many parts of Poland, especially in the district of Cracow, that a number of Christians had adopted Judaism, undergone circumcision, and fled to Lithuania. Incited by informers and troubled by religious scruples, the king ordered the heads of the Jewish communities in Cracow and Posen to be arrested, and sent special commissioners to Lithuania to seize the alleged converts. The arrival of the commissioners, who searched many houses and made numerous arrests, though all in vain, threw the Jews into a panic. A deputation from the Jewish communities of Brest, Grodno, and other cities complained to the king of the wrong that had been done to them, and gave him their assurance that they were loyal and had no fugitive proselytes in their houses. Investigation having shown that the story was entirely unfounded,

Sigismund ordered that the Jews of Lithuania should not be molested any more. He signed a rescript in Vilna, in 1540, in which he acquitted the Jews of all suspicion and expressed the wish that no regard should be paid to any calumnies that might be levelled against them in future.

Sigismund I was succeeded by his son, Sigismund II, generally called Sigismund Augustus (1548–1572), who continued his father's policy of benevolence. At the request of the Jews of Great Poland, Sigismund Augustus immediately after his ascension confirmed their charter of 1453, granted by Casimir Jagiello, and in the same year gave the Jews of Cracow a special charter in which he confirmed their rights and privileges. He appointed Jewish physicians to his Court and employed Jewish financiers in Lithuania to act as receivers of tolls. But he also decided to utilize the Jews as a permanent source of income as well as agents for collecting revenue. He issued a decree, in 1549, imposing a special tax of one zloty per head upon all Jews, irrespective of age and sex, in return for freeing all male Jews from military service, and he left it to the elders of the community to collect the tax. This was only one of the many functions with which the Kahal, or community, was entrusted, for in 1551 Sigismund Augustus enlarged the scope of its autonomy. He gave the rabbis and the elders of the Kahal wide authority in the sphere of administration and the dispensation of Jewish law, and even in disputes between Jews and Christians, heard in the Court of the *Voivode*, Jewish elders acted as assessors or assistant judges. The privilege of being placed under the jurisdiction of the royal governors was limited, however, to the Jews living on the estates of the Crown, as the governors had no right to concern themselves with those Jews who lived on the estates of the nobles and were consequently under the latter's protection.

The king showed his personal concern for his Jewish subjects in a letter that he wrote, in 1550, to Tsar Ivan the Terrible. In the peace treaties between Poland and Russia, the free entry of Polish and Lithuanian merchants to Moscow was solemnly guaranteed, and Jews had not to put up with anything worse than their Christian fellow-merchants. But Ivan the Terrible was an enemy of the Jews, and several Jewish merchants from Lithuania who went to Moscow were arrested and robbed of their goods. Thereupon Sigismund Augustus wrote a letter to the tsar, protesting against such treatment and asking for the safe admission of the Jews to his dominions. But Ivan returned a churlish reply, denouncing the Jews as evil-doers and declaring that he would not tolerate them.

Sigismund Augustus was zealous in upholding the rights of the Jews, since he regarded them as a valuable element in the urban population. He was particularly solicitous in defending them against charges of ritual murder, which were unfortunately increasing in frequency. He issued decrees in 1564 and 1566 forbidding the local authorities to accuse Jews of this alleged crime, as all such accusations had been proved to be devoid of any foundation, and in any case no charge could be made unless based on the testimony of three Christians and three Jews, as provided in previous charters. But despite his stand on behalf of the Jews, the anti-Jewish parties in the *Seym* (Diet) succeeded in securing the confirmation, in 1562 and 1565, of the constitution of Pietrokow passed in 1538. The consequence was that the anti-Jewish articles of this constitution were embodied in the Lithuanian statute which was proclaimed in 1566. The statute forbade the Jews to dress like Christians, to wear showy clothes, to own Christian slaves, or to employ Christian servants. But these were only minor restrictions in comparison with the general results of the political union of Poland and Lithuania, which was enacted at the famous Lublin Diet of 1569, for that event brought the Jews of Lithuania under the common government and the common legislature of the two countries and exercised a detrimental influence upon their subsequent development.

CHAPTER II

THE CHARTERS OF SIGISMUND III
AND WLADISLAV IV

The history of the Jews in Vilna as a community began at a critical turning point in the destinies of Lithuania, which was caused by two events of fundamental and far-reaching significance: the union with Poland and the ending of the hereditary monarchy. Owing to the amalgamation of the two countries, the Jews in Vilna, as in Lithuania generally, became subject to the reactionary and hostile influences exercised by both the Church and the *Seym*; and owing to the termination of the hereditary system of sovereignty, the power of the king, whose interest it had always been to protect the Jews, was considerably weakened. The Jagiello dynasty, which had ruled over the two countries from 1386 for nearly two hundred years, expired with the death of Sigismund Augustus in 1572. It was followed, after a brief interregnum of two years, by the introduction of a republican regime combined with an elective monarchy. Henceforth the king was always appointed by the *Seym*, which consisted solely of the *Szlachta* or nobles, with the result that, as he owed his crown to the latter and depended upon their goodwill, he was no longer able to command the same authority as before. He had no power over the principal affairs of State — military or political,

administrative or financial — which were all concentrated in the *Seym*. Indeed, he was often
reminded of his humiliating position and was even
browbeaten and insulted by the nobles. One of the
consequences of this lowered status of the monarch
was that the Jews could no longer receive the same
effective protection from him as before.

Fortunately the nobles needed the Jews just as
much as did the king, for while the latter used them
as sources of income and collectors of revenue, the
former employed them in various business and
administrative capacities. The nobles regarded it as
utterly derogatory to their dignity to engage in any
form of work or trade; they spent their lives in the
capital, at the Court, in the Diet, and on adventures
and amusement. Their lands were cultivated by
peasants, who were treated by them as mere serfs;
but they also needed stewards or bailiffs of their
estates, who should see that these were properly
worked and would hand over to the lordly landowners the proceeds from their agricultural and
dairy farms, as well as from their mills, distilleries
and inns, which dotted their rural domains. It was
in such positions — as estate managers, superin-
tendents of mills and distilleries, and innkeepers —
that Jews were largely employed by the nobles.
Consequently the latter were interested in protecting
the Jews from the hostility of the clergy and especially from attacks by the burghers. The Jews
incurred no little odium among the population as
dispensers of liquor, but this was a vocation into
which they were practically driven by the *Szlachta*.

It was the burghers who formed the principal and
most persistent antagonists of the Jews in Lithuania
as in Poland. They constituted the middle class,
were mainly engaged in trade and handicrafts, and
therefore looked upon the Jews as competitors and
adversaries. Many of them had come from Germany,
whence they had been tempted to migrate by the
offer of local self-government. The king had granted
them the so-called "Magdeburg Law," which assured
them complete autonomy in the cities in which they
settled and protected them from the encroachments
of the nobility; and since all authority in the municipalities was in their hands they exercised it jealously
and vigorously to the detriment of the Jews. For
centuries there was an almost incessant struggle in
the various cities between the burghers and the Jews,
the latter seeking systematically to establish themselves in different economic positions and the
burghers opposing their efforts with equal determination, combined with occasional violence. In this
bitter conflict the Jews repeatedly had to invoke the
assistance of the king and the nobles, and it was
readily given. Their disputes with the burghers often
engaged the attention of the law courts; and, since
there were courts of different jurisdiction, cases
dragged on for months and even for years and
decades. In Vilna there were three separate courts:
the Court of the Municipality, commonly called the
Magistracy, to which alone the burghers were subject; the Court of the Bishop, or Ecclesiastical Court;
and the Court of the Fortress, which was presided
over by the *Voivode* or governor, the king's repre-

sentative. There were also the king's own court, known as the Royal Court, and the Lithuanian Supreme Tribunal, which held its sessions in different cities. All these various courts were occupied at some time or other with the disputes between the burghers of Vilna, sometimes with the very same dispute.

The burghers of Vilna were granted the privilege of "Magdeburg Law" by the Grand Duke in 1387, which carried with it the right to engage in trade and industry within the city. In 1432 and in later years their privileges were enlarged by the Grand Duke, who forbade the *Voivode* and his officers to interfere in the affairs of the city. The municipality was given the monopoly of the revenue from wine, beer, and mead, as well as the monopoly of the weighing-machine on which all merchants were obliged to weigh all goods bought or sold in large quantities.

It was thanks to the instrumentality of the nobles that it first became possible for the Jews to settle in Vilna legally. In 1551 the Lithuanian Diet decided that any houses bought by members of the Council of the Grand Duke for their own purposes should not be subject to the jurisdiction of the Municipal Court and should be exempt from the payment of taxes to the municipality. This decision ingeniously facilitated the entry of the Jews, for as soon as the members of the Council began to buy houses that were not subject to the municipality's jurisdiction, Jews were able to occupy them under the protection of their owners. In 1552 Stanislav Kishko bought a house in the Niemiecka (German) Street, and the

king not only exempted him and his heirs from the
jurisdiction of the municipality, but also enacted
that this privilege was transferable to future owners
of the tenement.

Although the Jews were thus able to secure domicile in the city, they were still forbidden to engage
in trade or to establish a synagogue, and they therefore naturally directed their efforts towards attain-
ing those objectives. In their economic struggle they
were also aided by the nobles, whose position became
much stronger after the Union in 1569. The first
Jews to settle in the city were presumably persons of
substance, such as moneylenders, tax-farmers, and
lessees and directors of mints, probably accompanied
by Jewish employees and servants, and followed soon
afterwards by small merchants and artisans. They
doubtless met for public worship in some temporary
structure or in private houses before they proceeded
to the building of their first synagogue on a site
belonging to one of the nobles. The date of its construction is generally accepted as 1573, the year in
which the Warsaw Confederation proclaimed freedom of religion. Anybody who has visited that
venerable sanctuary, which, when last seen, was
still in an excellent state of preservation, must have
been impressed by its large and lofty proportions and
must have come to the conclusion that the community erecting a shrine of such massive grandeur
could not but have been numerous and economically
well established. A street close by, called Zydowska
(Jews' Street), already bore that name in 1592.

The burghers strongly resented the settlement of

the Jews in their midst in violation of the prohibition
of 1527. They nursed their wrath for some decades
and at last gave vent to it in an outbreak of violence.
On May 7, 1592, a mob made an attack upon the
synagogue and upon some shops and dwellings of
the Jews in the Zydowska. The assailants were
headed by a salt-merchant, who lived opposite the
synagogue courtyard, and included two members
of the Municipal Council. The Jews summoned the
burghers before the Lithuanian Supreme Court,
which happened then to meet in Vilna for the first
time, but the culprits declined to appear before this
body on the ground that they were not subject to
its jurisdiction. The Supreme Court decided that
the defendants must pay damages to the Jews
amounting to 13,350 Lithuanian *shock* and also
serve six weeks in prison. The burghers ignored
this judgment, and there was no power to enforce
it. A year later, however, on May 30, 1593, a settlement was arrived at between the Jews and the
burghers.

In order to safeguard themselves against any
similar attack in the future, the Jews appealed to
the king, Sigismund III (1587–1632), to legalize
their residence in Vilna. The response was satisfactory, for on June 3, 1593, they received the following charter:

> At the request of the Jews of Vilna, and
> upon the intervention of certain nobles of
> our Council on their behalf, we have granted
> permission to the Jews to rent and to buy
> from the nobles houses in the capital of the

Grand Duchy of Lithuania, in Vilna, for this reason in particular, that when we ascended the throne of the Kingdom of Poland and Lithuania we already found the Jews living in Vilna. Therefore we grant the Jews of Vilna permission from now to dwell without restriction in our city of Vilna in the houses of nobles, to pray according to the customs of their religion, and to engage in trade like our other subjects who dwell in the cities of the Grand Duchy of Lithuania.

King Sigismund exempted the Jews from the payment of any tax for the benefit of the municipality on the houses they rented or bought from the nobles, and declared that they were answerable only to the Court of the *Voivode*. He also gave them a further charter (or *Privilegium*), permitting them to establish the communal institutions that they needed, such as cemetery, slaughter-house, and baths; authorizing them to settle their private disputes in their own court of law (*Bet Din*); and confirming their ownership of the synagogue and of the houses they had bought.

Despite the benevolence shown by the king, however, the burghers continued from time to time to commit acts of violence against the Jews. In 1606, after an attack upon their houses and synagogue, the Jews submitted a complaint to the Lithuanian Tribunal against the burghers, but that body would not deal with the matter as it considered that it lay outside its competence. Not content with their position, the leader of the community resolved to secure an enlargement and consolidation of their rights, and they were effectively assisted in their efforts by two rich and influential Jews, Samuel ben Moses and Eliezer ben Moses, brothers, who originated from Frankfort-on-the-Main and afterwards lived in Bohemia, from where they, with other Jews, migrated to Vilna. On March 26, 1629, they were granted a charter for all the Jews of Lithuania, which was naturally more valuable than one issued to an individual city. This general charter prescribed that Jewish artisans were allowed to do any kind of work without belonging to the Christian workers' guilds, and thus at last provided the legal basis required by the Jews for economic activity in Vilna. It also stipulated that Jews were obliged to pay to the municipality all the usual taxes on houses contributed by the rest of the population, but exempted them from extraordinary taxes since they paid a poll-tax. It stated, furthermore, that in those cities where special agreements were made between the Jews and the burghers, the Jews should pay according to the amounts fixed in those documents. Should it be found necessary to sue a Jew, the only court to which he could be summoned was the Fortress Court, and, if that failed, recourse could be had to the Royal Court. In criminal cases Jews could be tried only by the Fortress Court, and not by the Municipal Court.

A further charter was given to the Jews in Vilna soon afterwards by King Sigismund, granting them the right to trade as well as to work. The effect of this was to incite the burghers to renewed hostility,

whereupon the Jews again appealed for royal protection. The king, thereupon, addressed an injunction to the municipality, on May 24, 1632, forbidding
it to do any violence against the Jews or to interfere
with their trade. This document gave the Jews the
right to buy from citizens and from travelling merchants, to use the ordinary weights and measures,
to engage in work, and to sell spirits. It recalled
that the right to rent houses had been granted to
the Jews of Vilna by previous charters, although
King Sigismund was in fact the first to accord this
right, which he formally confirmed; and it advised
the burghers not to waste money on litigation, but
to seek an agreement with the Jews and allow them
to deal in any kind of goods. The king showed partiality towards the Jews, for while they were allowed
to carry on retail trade and could engage in any
handicraft, travelling merchants were restricted to
dealing wholesale with local merchants, and no
artisan could practice a handicraft unless he belonged
to a guild. Moreover, the municipality had to pay
the royal treasury for permission to distill and sell
spirits, whereas the Jews enjoyed this right gratuitously. The effect of this document upon the
burghers was to inflame their anger and resentment.

King Sigismund's benevolent attitude towards
the Jews was emulated by his eldest son, Wladislav
IV (1632-1648), who greatly improved upon the pa-
ternal example. Delegations of all the Jewish communities in Lithuania attended the Coronation Diet
in order to have their respective privileges ratified by

the new sovereign. The leaders of the delegations were the two influential Jews from Vilna, Samuel ben Moses and Eliezer ben Moses, who received a confirmation of the charter for all the Jews of Lithuania on February 15, 1633. They also obtained a separate instrument for Vilna, which constitutes a considerable advance upon previous ones and may be designated the fundamental charter of the Vilna community. While confirming for its benefit all rights already bestowed upon the Jews of Lithuania by previous Grand Dukes, from Witold, it also included some additional ones. It contained a number of detailed provisions relating to trade and work. Jews were permitted to keep open shops dealing in woolen and cotton goods, carpets, wares from Turkey, spices, linen, glass, iron, and all kinds of other goods kept by small shopkeepers. They could sell retail or wholesale, like other Vilna tradespeople; they could buy and sell silver, gold, and ornaments; they could trade wherever and with whomsoever they wished, in the market-place or in shops, with local tradesmen or travelling merchants. They were allowed to engage in work, especially in branches that had no guild; but Jewish tailors could make clothes only for Jews, and not for Christians. They could buy prepared skins in any quantity for cutting and sewing, and buy and sell them in houses or on the street; they could make and sell all kinds of drinks; use the municipal weighing-machine at the usual fees; buy different kinds of cattle in the city or the market, but only for their own needs and not for sale or export beyond the city; and sell unredeemed pledges after a year and six weeks, without notice, at a price officially assessed.

This charter of 1633 exempted the Jews from taxes on their cemetery and slaughter-house, and restricted the use of their bathhouse to Jews. It also contained an innovation as compared with previous charters, for it delimited for the first time the area within which the Jews were allowed to dwell. Whatever may have been the reasons for the establishment of a ghetto in other cities, it was intended in Vilna to subserve the interests of the Jews by ensuring their living in a quarter which was not subject to the jurisdiction of the municipality and which would afford them protection from attack. The boundaries of the Jewish quarter, fixed by an official of the Grand Duchy, a priest named Marzian Trizna, comprised only the following streets: (a) Zydowska, both sides, (b) Jatkowa ("Slaughterers' Street"), only the side adjoining Zydowska, and (c) St. Michael Street, both sides. In the Niemiecka Street the Jews were allowed to buy plots not abutting on the street and to build houses thereon; but an exception was made in favor of the large house of the Dukes of Slutzki, which was free from municipal jurisdiction and which the Jews could own, sell, or transfer to others. The charter required that the Jews should, within fifteen years, purchase and occupy the houses within the area assigned to them, and stipulated that after that period they would not be allowed to live outside that area. If a Christian refused to sell a house to a Jew, or any

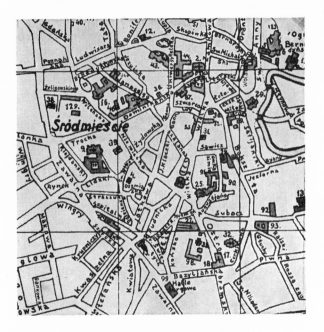

The Jewish District and its Environs

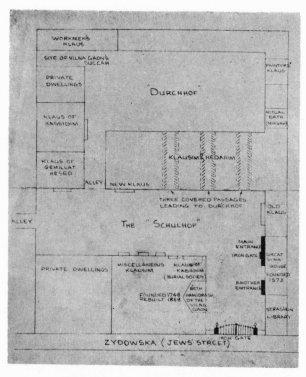

Plan of the Vilna Synagogue Courtyard

other difficulty arose in connection with its transfer, then the Municipal Council or the king's Commissioner must fix the price. The water cisterns in the houses in the Jewish quarter should remain, and the municipality must look after them, see that they were supplied with water, and demand payment from the Jewish tenants as from other inhabitants. If the house of a burgher outside the ghetto should pass into the hands of a Jew for a debt, the latter could own it, but the burgher could redeem it upon discharging the debt. The charter concluded with an admonition to the burghers that any regulations in their own "privileges" that might conflict with the provisions in the Jews' charter could not be upheld. The king followed up this document by giving the Jews permission to erect a synagogue of stone, stipulating that it should not be higher than other buildings in the vicinity and should not look like a church or monastery.

The two brothers, Samuel ben Moses and Eliezer ben Moses, who had taken such a leading part in securing the royal charter, also induced the *Seym* to pass a resolution, in 1633, ostensibly in the interest of free trade. This resolution stated that, in view of the rise of prices in Lithuania, which was detrimental to the burghers, all the members of the *Seym* requested that the Jews be allowed, especially in Vilna, to engage in all kinds of business both in shops and houses. The burghers stoutly protested against this decision as being opposed to their own privileges, and submitted their charters to the Royal Court, to which the Jews submitted their own for reaffirmation, but this court would not decide between the opposing claims. King Wladislav, who was in Vilna at this time, thereupon appointed an inquiry commission and, after it had completed its labor, he confirmed an Ordinance which set forth anew the conditions regulating the economic activity of the Jews.

This Ordinance consisted of four main parts, dealing with trade, work, domicile, and taxation. It gave the Jews permission, ostensibly in the interests of the nobles, to keep, for the next ten years, twelve shops opening on the Zydowska, in which they could deal in all sorts of articles — skins, furs, clothes, linen, woven stuffs, silver, gold, ornaments and spices. It laid down various restrictions, however, in regard to other commodities. Jews could buy rye only for their own requirements; they could buy salt and herrings only in large quantities from the burghers for sale; and they could sell hemp in the city only to burghers. They could trade in flax, fat and mead in any place, use the municipality's weighing machine, and keep seals in their own shops. They could buy cattle for slaughter, though not for sale to others; but they could sell the meat both to Jews and Christians in the slaughter-house near the synagogue. They could sell spirits, beer and mead to Jews in any quantity, but to Christians only wholesale. They were forbidden to do any kind of work for Christians for which there was an artisans' guild, but they could perform work for which there was no guild, such as glaziery, jewelry, and furriery, and they could do any kind of work for Jews. They were allowed to live on both sides of the Jatkowa Street, buy houses in any part of the Niemiecka, but they could not have gates leading into the latter, although they could have windows looking on it. They were forbidden to rent or buy houses outside the area assigned to them, although they could remain in such houses if they had owned them at the time when the Ordinance was published. The houses that had belonged to the Dukes of Slutzki and Kishko were to remain permanently in Jewish hands, with all the rights pertaining to them. The question of houses belonging to hospitals and situated within the Jewish quarter was referred to the bishop. As regards matters connected with real estate, the Jews had to appear before the court under whose jurisdiction the property stood; but in civil and criminal cases they were answerable to the Fortress Court. They were exempt from giving lodging to visitors when the Supreme Tribunal was holding a session, even when the king was on a visit to Vilna. The Jews were exempted from all municipal taxes, but they were required to pay to the municipality 300 gulden a year in peace and 500 gulden in wartime, and this money was to be devoted to strengthening and improving the city. The Ordinance concluded, like previous documents, with an exhortation to Jews and burghers to observe it carefully, and with a request to the municipality to protect the Jews from attacks in future.

King Wladislav had not left the city long, before

the Jews had cause to complain again that the
burghers would not let them carry on their trade
and threatened them with violence. The king
promptly sent a warning to the municipality not
to do any harm to the Jews on pain of a substantial
fine and loss of its rights, but his words had only a
short-lived effect. On March 3, 1634, a large mob
of shopkeepers, workmen and others made an attack
upon the Jewish cemetery, which resulted in injury
to twenty-four Jews. Twelve months later the
burghers organized an assault upon the large synagogue, removed three doors and tore and defiled
scrolls of the Torah, while they also broke into and
looted the houses of some Jews. Not until early in
1636 did the king appoint a commission to investigate these attacks, consisting of the Bishop of Vilna,
the *Voivode* and other high dignitaries. The commission wished to prevent a recurrence of such outrages
and also to secure compensation for the Jews without fining the burghers. They therefore adopted the
following resolutions: that the Jews should have the
right to construct gates at the corners of Zydowska
and Jatkowa Streets; that the municipality, the fortress authorities, and the bishop must investigate the
latest disorder and punish the culprits, and that if
another attack were made upon the Jews and the
municipality took no counter-measures, it should
be punished as the king would decide; that, as compensation for the loss they had incurred, the Jews
be given permission to sell spirits in twenty houses
in their possession up to any quantity, but only in

small quantities to Christians on condition that they did not drink on the premises; and that the Jews, in return, must pay the municipality 600 gulden every year, which should be spent on repairing the walls of the city. In all these matters the commission reaffirmed the provisions of the Ordinance of 1633.

The benevolence of King Wladislav towards the Jews was illustrated by a significant incident in connection with the trade relations between his country and Russia. He had occasion, in 1638, to send a letter to Tsar Michael, asking that permission be given to his representative, Aron Markowicz of Vilna, to visit Russia. But the tsar intolerantly replied that he would gladly let any Polish merchant come in, but never the Jews, "of whom there had never been any in Russia and with whom the Christians may not have any intercourse at all."

Although, according to the Ordinance, the Jews received the right to carry on business in open shops only for ten years, they secured the assent of the king to prolong this for another ten years. The burghers thereupon complained that they were becoming impoverished by the competition of the Jews, that the latter were living beyond the boundaries assigned to them, that they were selling spirits in more than twenty houses, that the traffic in drink at night resulted in disturbances, and that it was impossible to safeguard the protection of the Jews as their streets had not been provided with gates.

The Court of Appeal,[1] which considered these complaints, decided, on December 16, 1644, that the prolongation of the Ordinance in respect of open shops should be reduced to five years, after which period the Jews would be able to trade only in closed shops in all articles except herrings, salt, flax and hemp. It further resolved that the Jews could live in as many houses outside the ghetto as there were houses within it still unredeemed by them, that the houses within the ghetto must all be redeemed within twenty-five years, that the Jews must fix gates at the entrances of the Zydowska and Jatkowa Streets within three years, and that the sale of spirits in Jewish taverns be allowed only until nine o'clock in the evening. Finally, the Court emphasized that it was the duty of the municipality, with the help of the authorities of the fortress and the bishop, to prevent any further attacks upon the Jews.

The plan to induce or force the Jews to confine themselves to the ghetto was doomed to frustration. An inquiry conducted by the municipality in 1645 showed that of thirty-two houses in that area, only twenty-one belonged to Jews, while the latter owned seventeen outside. The restrictions regarding the occupation of houses by Jews beyond the ghetto led to the practice of transferring houses within it to Christian moneylenders on pledges. Thereupon the

---

[1] The *Relazioni* Court, presided over by the king himself, with his ministers as associate judges. Cf. E. N. Frenk, *Ha-'Ironim ve-ha-Yehudim be-Polin*, p. 69.

king issued an order forbidding Christians to transfer houses in the ghetto to themselves for occupation. The Christian owners were obliged to let or sell the houses to Jews, and if no Jewish purchaser could be found, then the Jewish community had to redeem the house according to official assessment. But all these various rules and regulations proved in vain. The Jews secured repeated postponements of their enforceability until the question of the ghetto, with the lapse of time, simply faded away.

CHAPTER III

FROM KING JOHN CASIMIR TO KING
JOHN SOBIESKI

AFTER the almost incessant struggle conducted by
the Jews in Vilna for over fifty years to secure the
rights of dwelling, working and trading in the city,
they enjoyed a brief respite. King John Casimir
(1648–1688), who had been a cardinal and succeeded his brother Wladislav IV, was not quite so
favorably disposed towards them at first. Although
he confirmed all the charters granted to the Jews
in the preceding reign, yet, when he was confronted
in 1650 with a dispute in which they were involved,
he decided against them. The Christian guild of
gold embroiderers summoned to court the Jews
engaged in this handicraft on the ground that, as
they were not members of the guild, they were
forbidden to practice it. But the Jews replied that
they were entitled to do so by virtue of the charters
of the two preceding kings, which they had received
before the embroiderers' guild came into existence.
John Casimir, however, ruled, on the basis of the
guild's charter, that the Jews had no right to
practice gold embroidery even for their own requirements. Apart from this case, the Jews were undisturbed by any economic conflict for some time,
but they were overtaken by a far more serious
calamity which made all questions of guild rights

pale into utter insignificance. It was the Cossack massacres, which raged through the greater part of Poland and Lithuania for a whole decade, from 1648, and which swept the Jews out of Vilna altogether for a period of six years.

The catastrophe was brought about by the harsh treatment of the people in the Ukraine at the hands of the Polish magnates, who had begun to colonize that territory at the end of the sixteenth century. While remaining at a safe distance themselves, they sent their agents and stewards to exploit the Ukrainians and to extract whatever wealth they could from the country and from the toil of its inhabitants. Among these stewards were many Jews, employed as collectors of tolls and customs, and as lessees who farmed the products of the mills, dairies, distilleries and fishing and game preserves belonging to the Polish nobles. The Ukrainians were treated like serfs, and in addition to being oppressed physically were also tormented spiritually, for they were lured or forced to abandon their Greek Orthodox faith for the Roman Catholic. Their sufferings goaded them at last to revolt under the leadership of Bogdan Chmielnicki, who secured the cooperation of their brethren beyond the Dnieper, the Cossacks, as well as of their former enemies, the Tatars, eager to join in a war that promised plenty of booty. The united hordes of Ukrainians, Cossacks, and Tatars easily overthrew a Polish army sent against them, and then began an orgy of carnage which has few parallels in history. Their fury was directed not only against the Polish magnates and the Catholic

priests, but also against the Jews, whom they
regarded as the immediate instruments of their
oppression. Beginning with Podolia and Volhynia,
they penetrated, by way of Galicia and the region
of Lublin, as far as the borders of Lithuania and
White Russia, wreaking death and devastation
wherever they went. In their onslaughts upon the
Jews they perpetrated the most unspeakable bar-
barities, sparing neither men nor women, neither
old nor young. Whole communities were wiped out
in a single day, the first victims being the six thousand Jews in Nemirov (Podolia) who were massacred
on Sivan 20, 5408 (1648).

All Jews who could fled from the marauding
bandits as from an earthquake. They poured in
floods into Germany and other parts of Central
Europe, into Holland and Italy, and even into
Turkey and Egypt. Thousands swarmed into Lithuania, where they received a friendly welcome. The
Va'ad (Council) of the Union of Jewish Communities
in Lithuania imposed upon all local communities
the duty of giving the utmost support to these
victims of Cossack savagery, and many Jews borrowed money for the purpose from Christian priests
on the security of their houses. They declared that
the 20th of Sivan, which hitherto had been observed
as a fast-day for the Crusades, must in future be
observed as a fast-day by all the communities in
the country to commemorate the blood-bath of
Nemirov; and as a mark of grief for the martyrs
they forbade the wearing of any clothes made of
silk, velvet, or brocade for three years. But the

Jews of Lithuania were themselves soon overwhelmed by the avalanche of butchery, for in 1653
their country was overrun not only by the Ukrainians and Cossacks but also by the Russians and
Swedes.

The city of Vilna was occupied, on August 8,
1655, by Muscovite and Cossack troops. The
greater part of the Jewish population fled in terror,
and all who stayed behind were slaughtered piti-
lessly, together with many of the rest of the population. The invaders set the city on fire, and the
flames raged for seventeen days, consuming the
Jewish quarter as well as other sections. A brief
yet moving account of those tragic events has come
down to us in the following passage of the introduction to a Hebrew commentary on the *Shulhan Aruk*
entitled *Be'er ha-Golah* ("Well of Exile"), composed
by Rabbi Moses Rivkes, a famous scholar who
succeeded in reaching Amsterdam:

> Throughout the whole of Lithuania there
> then roamed bands of Russians and Cos-
> sacks, who devastated the cities and occupied,
> among others, Polock, Vitebsk and Minsk.
> Wherever the Cossacks appeared they, in
> their lust for spoil, seized all the belongings
> of the Jews, whom they slaughtered in masses.
> When the army, spreading alarm and terror,
> approached the gates of Vilna, the *Voivode*
> Radziwill, together with his troops, quickly
> fled, and many of the inhabitants of the city
> followed his example. On Wednesday, the
> 24th of Tammuz, 5415, almost the whole

Jewish community ran for their lives like one man: those who had horses and carts went forth with their wives, sons and daughters and some of their belongings, and others went on foot, carrying their children on their shoulders.

I went forth with my stick in my right hand, after seizing my bag of phylacteries, and with my left hand I grasped a book on the calendar, murmuring unto myself, "Who knows where I shall find rest in my exile?" I left my house full of good things and abandoned my inheritance, a treasury of all that was desirable, a house full of books, both those which I had inherited from my father, of blessed memory and those which the Lord enabled me to buy. Among them were a few books and tractates which I had worked on and annotated, especially the tractates Zebaḥim and Menaḥot. Long and wearisomely had I labored and much time had I spent until I had annotated the two tractates properly; they were all left there. And we went whithersoever we could go, and the earth was rent with the cries and wailing of the fugitives, and from my eyes too poured tears in torrents. We came to the border of the land of Samogitia close to the frontier of Prussia, but there too we found no rest from the sword of war. The hosts of the kingdom of Sweden stripped us to the skin, and after this oppression I and some of the children of my house and also other people entered a ship in the heart of the sea and set our faces towards Amsterdam. And when we arrived there the Sephardic scholars and rich men had pity upon us and dealt kindly and charitably with us, and they spent much money in giving every one of us lodging, and food, and clothing for the naked. And as for the other ships which came after that, since the city was unable to cope with so many, because of the dearness of the dwellings and the food, they sent many ships at their expense to the congregation of Frankfort and they gave them provender (and the community of Frankfort and other communities in Germany showed many kindnesses to the exiles). But I remained there, for the chief rabbi and scholar, Saul Halevi Morteira, and the chief rabbi, the saintly Isaac Aboab, befriended me most generously and with the aid of the princely philanthropists they made me a comfortable home.

It was while he was in Amsterdam that Rabbi Moses Rivkes was asked to supervise the publication of an edition of the *Shulhan Aruk*, and to this edition, which appeared in 1661, he contributed his commentary under its appropriate title. He then returned to Vilna, where he died about 1671.[1]

---

[1] Further reference to the flight of the Jews from Vilna is made in the "Beth Hillel" on *Yoreh De'ah* (section 21). Among the exiles were the following rabbis: Aaron Samuel b. Israel Koidanower (who afterwards became Rabbi of Cracow, and who used to supplement his signature with the words, "the exile from the city of Vilna"); Shabbetai b. Meir ha-Kohen (author of *Megillat Ayefah*, in which the catastrophe of 1655 is described); and Ephraim b. Aaron (author of *Sha'ar Efrayim*).

The municipality of Vilna took advantage of the Russian occupation to address a petition to Tsar Alexei Michailowitsch asking that Jews be forbidden to live within the city, but kept on the outskirts — a request which was promptly granted. But when the Polish army at last recovered possession of the city in March, 1661, the Jews returned and were allowed to rebuild their ruined habitations. King John Casimir also permitted them to rent houses in all parts of the city and to sell spirits there, pending the restoration of their former dwellings and shops. In their efforts to re-establish themselves, the Jews received unexpected aid from the Jesuit priests, who derived a large income by letting houses to them and allowing them to build some on their land. The king tried to be helpful by twice requesting the municipality to exempt Jews from the payment of their annual tax, but without avail. Nor did he meet with any greater success in his attempts to resist the bigoted demand that Jews be forbidden to employ Christian servants. He had been obliged by the *Seym*, in 1653, to confirm the canon law to this effect, and when the Bishop of Vilna complained to him, in 1663, that the Jews, in defiance of the *Seym's* decision and his own royal decree, still employed Christian servants, he issued an order that the law must be scrupulously observed, otherwise the State entrusted to his care would again suffer "Divine punishments."

The endeavors of the Jews to recover their former economic positions were seriously hampered by the burghers, who resumed the stubborn struggle. In

1665 the guild of salt-vendors, who also dealt in herring, hemp and flax, organized an attack on the Zydowska Street, in which the Jews had resettled. A band of about eighty men and ten soldiers with firearms rushed into the street with the cry: "Beat the Jews with whatever you can; their time is now come!" They raided the houses of the Jews, assaulted men, women and children, smashed windows, looted shops, loaded goods upon carts, and, as they left, uttered a warning that that was only a beginning. But this attack did not prevent the Jews from continuing the sale of the articles that had provoked it.

The next trade to be challenged was that of the butchers. The Christian butchers noticed that the sale of cattle and meat by Jewish butchers was increasing, and this they wanted to prevent. They therefore submitted a series of complaints to the *Voivode's* Court: that the Jews bought cattle outside the city and brought the beasts inside for sale, that the number of Jewish butchers exceeded the previously agreed upon quota of six, that they took away the Christian apprentices who left owing money to their Christian employers, that they slaughtered diseased cattle and sold the meat to Christians, that they had slaughter-places near Christian churches, that on every Friday and on the day of the great fast (Ash Wednesday) they exposed meat for sale in their slaughter-house near the synagogue, which was passed by Christians, including priests and monks on their way to the Franciscan church, that the Christian butchers

contributed towards the upkeep of the altar in the
church of Saint Casimir while the Jews did not,
and that, finally, if the Jews were allowed to trade
in meat without restriction the Christian trade
would decline. The Jews contended that they could
not limit their number of butchers to six, that if
they did and bought less cattle it would injure the
interests of the *Szlachta*, that they were permitted
by the Ordinance of 1633 to buy cattle within the
city though forbidden to export any, that the
Christian butchers also slaughtered in the city,
that they did not take away Christian assistants,
and that they were willing to give an annual undertaking — like the Christians — that they would not
sell diseased meat. The *Voivode's* Court referred
the matter to the Royal Court, which gave its
judgment in 1667. The court decided that the
charters of both Jewish and Christian butchers
should remain in force, that the Jews be forbidden
to buy beasts outside the city and bring them in for
sale, that they should be limited to six slaughterers
and to six slaughter-houses near the synagogue and
that they take an oath every year not to sell diseased meat, that they each pay half a stone of fat
for the benefit of the church of Saint Casimir, that
they must not take away Christian assistants, and
that they must not sell meat on Fridays and on the
great Christian fast, though they could do so pri-
vately behind the synagogue. The Jews accordingly
paid an annual contribution to the church in the
form of a tax on the site near the Troki gate, which
belonged to the church and was assigned for a Jewish

slaughter-house; but the priests subsequently demanded that each Jewish butcher should give them a whole stone of fat.

The Jewish glaziers were also involved about the same time. In 1663 the Christians formed a glaziers' guild, which included in its constitution clauses stipulating that Jewish glaziers were forbidden to work for Christians, as they were not registered in the guild; that they must not send their lads with crates of glass to houses, otherwise the crates would be destroyed; that they must not accept Christian apprentices, and any whom they were already training must immediately go over to Christian glaziers belonging to the guild. The Christian glaziers took steps to enforce their own rules. On one occasion, in 1669, they attacked a Jewish glazier, Samuel ben David, who was plodding along a street in search of work. They robbed him of all his materials, injured him, and warned him that if any Jewish glazier dared to work for Christians they would kill him.

In 1664 the fishermen's guild excluded Jews from the fishing trade, and the king, yielding to the request of the burghers, prohibited them from engaging in the crafts of silversmiths and goldsmiths. Two years later they were excluded from the grain business, in 1667 from tanning, and in 1669 from the manufacture of bristles. But all these exclusions were only transitory in effect.

The impoverishment which the Jews had sustained through their enforced flight from the city and the destruction of their homes and businesses, com-

bined with their hard struggle to secure the elementary right to earn a living, aroused the sympathy
not only of King John Casimir but also of his
successor, Michael Korybut Wisniowiecki (1669–
1673), and indeed of several later sovereigns. King
Michael Korybut,[1] who was only a poor nobleman
when he was elevated to the throne, is said to have
wept when that unexpected and unwelcome honor
was thrust upon him. He was invariably kind to
the Jews. He extended for another twenty years the
period within which they could redeem houses in
the Jewish quarter, without limiting the number
of houses they could also occupy outside it; he
renewed their permit to sell spirits for another
twelve years; he secured the consent of the municipality to reduce their tax for fifteen years; and
he granted them a moratorium for the payment of
debts. He also ruled in their favor in regard to the
employment of Christian servants, concerning which
there were complaints from the municipality. He
accepted the pleading of Levka Josefowicz, an elder
of the Brest community, that it was impossible
to enforce the canon law, as Jews engaged as lessees
of farms, managers of distilleries and innkeepers
needed Christian employees, and the curtailment of
Jewish activity in these positions would affect the
income of both the king and the *Szlachta*. He
accordingly issued an edict, in 1670, that the canon
law applied only to permanently engaged servants,

[1] A son of Jeremi Wisniowiecki, chastiser of the Cossacks and
a friend of the Jews.

but that the employment of Christians as hired laborers in distilleries and inns, and also as drivers and stable servants, was both allowable and desirable, as the needy members of the Christian populace thus had the opportunity of earning a livelihood.

King Michael Korybut had to intervene also in the struggle with the guilds. The Christian furriers had formed a guild with a regulation that Jewish furriers were forbidden to employ Christian workers. They then complained that, as the Jews violated this rule, there were no workers available for themselves. They alleged that the Jews sold furs not only in shops but also in the market and on the streets, and maintained that they were entitled to destroy the goods of Jewish furriers who traded in the open air. They promptly proceeded to action, in which they had the support of the municipality, organizing an attack upon the Jewish furriers and looting some of their wares. The Jews thereupon addressed a complaint to the king that the municipality was guilty of infringing the charter of 1633 in allowing the formation of new guilds with anti-Jewish regulations, as well as in damaging goods which Jews brought to be weighed by the municipal weighing-machine, and in requisitioning the houses of Jews to lodge visiting judges of the Lithuanian Tribunal. The king, in reply, warned the municipality not to do any harm to any Jewish tradesman or worker, and confirmed the charter of 1633, by virtue of which the Jews were allowed to engage in any branch of work for which there was no guild, such as furriery, glaziery and jewelry.

Trouble was also caused by the Christian tanners, who demanded that Jewish merchants, Tatars, and even Christian travellers should not take hides out of the city. Their demand was acceded to, but the Jews, who claimed that the Ordinance of 1633 allowed them to trade in hides with travellers, continued to buy and sell. The tanners thereupon attacked the Jewish dealers, stole a lot of skins from them, and pretended that their action was approved by the heads of the municipality. They contended that the Ordinance of 1633 had been given for only ten years and was no longer valid. The Jews showed that this time limit applied only to open shops and that the rest of the Ordinance was in force. The Jews must have continued dealing in hides and sending them out of the city, as an order was issued in 1744, by King Augustus III, forbidding Jews and Tatars to buy skins and take them out of the city, even if they came from a Jewish slaughter-house.

The latter half of the seventeenth century was marked by increasing hostility on the part of the Christians against the Jews in Lithuania as in Poland. It was hostility engendered by the general demoralization brought about by the wars, with their aftermath of poverty, and was favored by the division of authority and the conflict of interest between the central government and the municipalities. The anti-Jewish feeling was fomented by clerical fanatics, who disseminated the ritual-murder libel and tried to persuade the *Seym* to pass special laws against the Jews. The Jesuits were particularly active in implanting Jew-hatred among the pupils of their colleges, with the result that these students regularly organized attacks upon the Jews. In order to ward off these assaults the Kahal, the executive board of the community, found itself obliged to give money to the college authorities for partial distribution among the bellicose students, and this blackmail developed into the annual payment of tribute. Such was the state of affairs not only in Vilna, but also in other cities in Lithuania and Poland, such as Brest, Cracow, and Posen, when the throne was ascended by King John Sobieski (1674–1696), who covered himself with glory by his heroic delivery of Vienna from the Turkish occupation. This martial monarch displayed his spirit of tolerance, which coincided with his own interest, in appointing a Jewish financial agent, Bezalel, as customs-farmer in Ruthenia, and another Jew, Emanuel de Jona, as physician at his Court at Zolkiew. At his instigation, in the early years of his reign, the *Seym* decided to suppress the anti-Jewish riots and ordered the local authorities to mete out severe punishment to the hooligans, and especially the students who were guilty of excesses. The need for drastic action was proved by a particularly flagrant outrage which occurred in Vilna.

In 1681 the Municipal Council of Vilna ordered all male Jews to assemble outside the city in order to be registered, together with the members of the Christian guilds, for the purpose of local defense. The Jews were afraid to go out to the field where the Christians and tradesmen were mustered with firearms, for they scented danger; they begged the

Council to allow their registration to be carried out separately in the palace of the *Voivode*, and offered to pay a large sum for this concession. The Council declined and assured them that nothing would happen to them. But no sooner had the Jews reached the field than they were attacked by the artisans and tradesmen, who brutally belabored them with their weapons, robbed them of everything they carried, and tore their clothes from off their backs. They would have suffered even more severely but for the sudden intervention of the Jesuit students, who hurried to their rescue, an act which was not as altruistic as it seemed, since it was prompted by the fact that the Jews owed them money for protection. The members of the Municipal Council, according to a contemporary chronicle, had remained passive during the attack and looked on "with pleasure." As soon as King John Sobieski heard of the outrage he sent a sharp warning to the municipality, demanded that the culprits be punished, and ordered that the Jews be exempted from such registration in the future.

On a later occasion, however, the Jesuit students took a leading part in an organized assault upon the Jews. They used to be employed, together even with members of the *Szlachta*, in collecting debts from impoverished Jews who had borrowed from Christian moneylenders, and they did not refrain from using force in the process. Early on the morning of March 26, 1687, the Zydowska Street was invaded by a mob of workmen and shopkeepers, headed by students, who broke the iron grilles protecting the windows, forced their way into houses and shops, and robbed and brutally assaulted every Jew upon whom they could lay their hands. Some Jews were killed; some pregnant women died of fright and others gave birth prematurely. The amount of damage inflicted, which included the loss of gold, silver and other articles, and of pledges deposited by some nobles with Jewish moneylenders, was 120,000 gulden. The Jews rushed to the municipality for help, but found that the Council had connived at the outrage. They would have been in a sorry plight if the Jesuit priests, spurred by a stricken conscience, had not hurried to their rescue and prevented the destruction of the synagogue upon which the rioters had already begun. It was not until the evening that the Municipal Council sent some armed artisans for the "protection" of the Jews, after the trouble was over.

When King John Sobieski heard of this pogrom he threatened to send troops to the city, to be stationed there at its expense, in order to maintain peace and order. He placed the responsibility for the safety of the Jews and their property upon the burghers, and prohibited the practice of employing students and nobles for the collecting of debts. He ordered that a register be kept of all students in the city, so that others should be unable to masquerade in their guise. He also reminded the burghers that they were forbidden to interfere with Jewish glaziers and hat-makers who plied their trade in the streets, and that members of the Supreme Tribunal could not be billeted in the houses of Jews, as the latter paid

their annual tax to the municipality. Owing to the
poverty of the Jewish community, the King renewed
the moratorium, which had been granted by his
predecessor, for another ten years.

The religious fanaticism of the populace, which
broke out so frequently in slander and violence
against the Jews in mediaeval Poland and Lithuania, claimed several victims in the reign of John
Sobieski. In 1680 the daughter of a Jewish land-
factor, who had become a Catholic, disappeared
from the house of a Polish official in Brest. The
suspicion arose that the apostate girl had been
abducted by her relatives, with the assent of the
elders of the community, and murdered by them.
Thereupon not only her family but also five heads
of the community were condemned to death by the
Vilna tribunal. Ten years later the charge of
"ritual-murder" was brought against some Jews
in Vilna. A Christian nurse carelessly let a child
fall into the river, where it was drowned, and, as
she was afraid of the anger of its parents, she hid
the body in a cornfield. When it was found, she
said that the child had been abducted and murdered
by Jews. Three of them were then arrested and
tortured to death. The sufferings of the martyrs
and the consternation and grief of the Vilna community are vividly described in a Yiddish rhymed
Volkslied, which was printed in Amsterdam about
1692 and has been preserved in the Bodleian Library
at Oxford.[1] In the same year, 1690, there was also
an alleged "ritual-murder" in Bialystok of a Russian-

[1] See Supplementary Note 2.

דאס ביזבליאו מיך די דריא

קדושים
בק"ק ווילנא

וויהרן גיאמאלט ניך דיעם ח"ב לוויה אות אן דער
מ ביז יון דר ת חיגעם ווהדין גיטראחכט · חיך
דיער ודריא נע יין מא נחן רטן הנדרן ח"ב חין
רי פרסיה חיתהות ווהרק חריין גיבראלט · זיער
נפאין מיו גיואגין ר' יחוקאל מוג' ר' אסה חונ' ר'
חברק ה"ר · מוג' ורהם חיו פס לוויה אחולגאך
ח"ב ווהרן גיסכפלט · דן חין ח"ב וגיין לוויים וגו'
לוונאין חותיות פר מפלט · חוג' לוויית אות לוויים
מוג' לו ניג · מיו פיר חוג' פירלין · מיו א"ר מא
א"ר אלבט רק" · וויסטרו רי תרה ווהט קומס
מרים מוס רען ח"ב וחול מין אוין יוסר זין פר
דער ליבה סליגה ליין וועגין דאם רייגה רק
וועם פון ריקרוסיק מיו וחרן פר נתסן · מוג'
מו רי עלוות וחלין ווהרין פון ישראל פר סלוהסן
מאן :

נדפס באמשטרדם

Title-Page of the Ballad on the Martyrs of the
Vilna Blood Libel

The Oldest Jewish Cemetery in Vilna

Orthodox boy, Gabriel Zabludowsky, whose preserved body was kept as a "holy relic" in a church
in the village of Zabludowa and afterwards transferred to Sluzk, where it became an object of pilgrimage for superstitious Russians until recent times.

The leaders of the community were often in danger
in cases of alleged "ritual-murder," as the ignorant
mob generally pointed to the synagogue as the place
of the crime and the elders of the Kahal were accused
of being privy to it. In order to be able to take the
requisite measures in such emergencies, the *Va'ad*
of Lithuania, and likewise that of Poland, always
had a reserve fund for rebutting false accusations
(*'Alilot Sheker*). It was used to defray the expenses
of a *Shtadlan* (advocate) who was sent to Warsaw,
or to pay legal defenders to secure the reversal of
unjust sentences. Thanks to the energy thus displayed by the elders of the Kahal, many Jewish
lives were saved and many a pogrom averted.

John Sobieski was too enlightened a man to place
any credence in these monstrous charges, but not
powerful enough as a king to effect their suppression.
His last act in the interests of the Jews was to forbid
the kidnapping of Jewish children and their forcible
conversion to Christianity, an outrage often committed in Lithuania in the latter years of his reign.
For the purpose of blunting the complaints of
clerical zealots he issued an order that a Jew should
be free to choose whatever religion he preferred, and
that if he wished to change his faith he should be
examined by a commission of Jews and Christians
specially appointed by the Court.

CHAPTER IV

FROM KING AUGUSTUS II TO KING AUGUSTUS III

THE closing years of the seventeenth century and the earlier part of the eighteenth were marked by a succession of unfortunate events which followed upon one another with the inexorable force of a cumulative tragedy. It was a period of civil strife, war, famine, plague and fires, each of which brought increased suffering upon the inhabitants in general and the Jews in particular. First came the bitter conflict, bred of rivalry in authority, between Bishop Brzostovski and the *Voivode* Sapieha, which was fought out violently by their respective followers and retainers, often by the method of bloody street affrays, and which disturbed the peace of the city from 1694 to 1700. This was but a mild prelude, however, to the distress and terror caused by the Great Northern War which laid waste so much of Northern and Central Europe from 1700 to 1720 and in which Swedes, Saxons and Russians not only lived on the dual state of Poland and Lithuania but plundered it systematically. The successor of John Sobieski, King Augustus II, had sought, in alliance with Tsar Peter the Great, to wrest Livonia from Sweden. He succeeded only in bringing the Swedish army, under its inspiring commander,

Charles XII, into his dominion; so that, after a brief
reign (1698–1706), he was compelled to cede his
crown to his rival, Stanislav Leszczynski (1706–
1709). The Swedes occupied Vilna from 1702 to
1708, imposed heavy taxation upon the city and
exacted large sums from the Jews; the Russians,
under Peter the Great, lorded it over the city in
1705 and indulged in the same depredations as the
Swedes, whom they had expelled; and in the following year the Swedes returned and continued the
process of confiscation and plunder. Not until the
defeat of the Swedes by Peter at the battle of
Poltava, in 1709, was a semblance of peace restored
under Augustus II, who then continued in undisturbed possession of his throne until his death in
1733.

Owing to the ravages of the countryside committed during six years of war; famine raged from
1708 to 1710, and was followed by an outbreak of
plague. The number of those who died of this
calamity in Vilna is stated (by the Polish historians,
Kraszewski and Bialinsky) to have been about 30,000
Christians and 4,000 Jews. These figures are probably an exaggeration, as the Jewish community at
that time could hardly have been so large, but that
the Jewish victims were very numerous can be
concluded from the order issued by the Lithuanian
commander, Ludovik Foze, forbidding interference
with the burial by the Jews of their dead in plots
near their cemetery.

The Jewish community, owing to the succession
of disasters, had become so poor and its debts had

become so great, that it was unable to pay even the interest upon them. Augustus II had granted them a moratorium soon after his accession in 1698, and again in 1713, for a period of ten years on each occasion. The community had the utmost difficulty in scraping money together for the poll-tax, which the army collected by force for its own needs, and the Lithuanian commander, Wisniowiecki, therefore, out of consideration for their distress, remitted the tax in 1706. In the same year there broke out the first of a series of fires which afflicted the city at intervals during the next forty-three years, and in which the Jews were among the principal sufferers. Many of their houses were burned in this first fire, and the military commander therefore exempted the Jews who had been affected from the payment of the window-tax, from which all other citizens had already been released. Fires broke out again in 1724 and 1734, damaging many houses of Jews, and when the latter sought the help of Christian work-men to repair or rebuild their ruined homes, the municipality forbade this. In 1737 the disaster was serious enough to be called the Great Fire; it sur-rounded the whole Jewish quarter, and the Great Synagogue as well as the old *Bet ha-Midrash* were almost entirely burned down. So extensive was the damage that the Vilna community appealed to the Jews of Amsterdam for help, with the result that the Ashkenazi congregation sent 400 guilders "to restore the crown, to uplift the house of our God by rebuilding the glorious synagogue, and the *Bate Midrashim*, which were consumed by the flames in a moment," and the Sephardi congregation sent 150 guilders.

After an interval of eleven years, in 1748, another big fire broke out, which destroyed almost the entire Jewish quarter. It started in three separate places, spread rapidly through the Niemiecka, Jatkowa, and Zydowska Streets, and destroyed 469 houses, 15 mansions and 12 churches. The *Schulhof* (the synagogue courtyard) was also in flames and serious damage was done to the Great Synagogue, the *Bet ha-Midrash*, the communal office, the synagogue of the *Hebra Kaddisha*, the baths and various other buildings. Many Jews were burned or suffocated by the smoke, and many of their shops were ruined. The Jews were accused of being responsible for all these fires, and a certain writer, Jachimowitz, who was commissioned by the municipality to compile a register of the buildings destroyed, also put the blame upon them. He must have realized that the fire that started in the house of a Jew, named Reuben, beyond the River Vilia, could have had no connection with the fires which broke out at the same time in the middle of the city, but that did not prevent him from indulging in a general indictment in some abusive verses. Scarcely had the damage caused by this fire been made good than another conflagration broke out in 1749, which engulfed the Jewish quarter and destroyed the synagogue courtyard and all Jewish shops, but this time no blame was imputed to the Jews.

The peace of the community was also shattered only too often by repeated "ritual-murder" accusations in different parts of the country, in one of which Jan Serafinowicz, a baptized Jew who was married to the daughter of a rabbi of Vilna, was personally concerned. Serafinowicz (born in 1685) had held the posts of rabbi at Sluzk and Brest before his mind became unhinged in consequence of excessive mental strain. After he had been taken to the *Ba'al-Shem* of Zolkiew to be "treated" for his madness, he became a Christian under the name of Michael Neophyt. He submitted a delirious statement to the Ecclesiastical Court at Sandomierz, that Jews used blood for their "magic arts" and that he himself had tortured two Christian children. But when he was invited to meet some rabbis in Warsaw for the purpose of a disputation on the subject, he failed to respond. One of the results of the slanderous agitation was that, at the request of the priest Zuchowski, Augustus II, on April 28, 1712, signed a decree quite contrary to the views of all his predecessors on the Polish throne, that "the perfidious, unbelieving Jews shed the blood of Christian children in an outrageous manner in secret, which cried for Divine vengeance."

In addition to this sequence of events which disturbed the peace and undermined the welfare of the Jews in Vilna, they were constantly hampered and harassed in their daily lives by the battle for elementary economic rights. Hitherto they had enjoyed the good will and active support of the Crown in the struggle with the burghers, but Augustus II, the first Polish king of German origin and breeding, was not so helpful, although he gave the Jews documents guaranteeing them protection in return for substantial payment. The difficulties under which the Jews had to labor may be gathered from some of the points in the municipal regulations which were drawn up in 1712 by the Crown officials in conjunction with members of the Municipal Council of Vilna. These regulations prescribed that neither Christians nor Jews might open their inns on Christian festivals before the conclusion of the church service; that they were both forbidden to keep their shops open on those days under the threat of confiscation of their goods; that Jewish tailors and furriers were forbidden to work for Christians, while Jewish goldsmiths were not allowed to carry on their work at all; that Jews must not make purchases from farmers supplying markets until nine o'clock in the morning, when the Christian townsfolk would have satisfied their own requirements; and that the Jews who wanted to buy provisions were not permitted to go out to meet the peasants in the suburbs or on the country road. The regulations also reaffirmed that the Jews must not live outside the streets assigned to them in Vilna, and that they were forbidden, as were likewise the Tatars, to employ any Christian workers except brewers and drivers. In the case of any violation of the latter restriction the employer had to pay a heavy fine and the employee was threatened with a flogging or imprisonment.

The Jews of Vilna were tired of the constant wrangling with the burghers and therefore, in 1713, attempted to reach a reconciliation. Their delegates to the *Seym*, Dr. Aaron Gordon and Judah ben Isaac, the beadle (a far more important post then than nowadays), met the delegates of the city of Vilna in Warsaw, and agreed that a commission should examine their respective charters and draw up terms of a settlement whereby they could live in peace. But the Christian delegates did not agree with the composition of the commission (which included two bishops and the *Voivode* of Vilna), and so no settlement was possible. But in the same year Augustus II, who had previously confirmed the Jewish charters in 1698, confirmed them anew. Out of regard for all the sufferings of the Jews since the beginning of the century, he gave them permission to dwell and buy houses in all parts of the city, and also to sell liquor. He further allowed them for another twenty years to sell all kinds of goods in shops opening on the street; freed the Jewish artisans from payments for the benefit of Christian artisans' guilds; and exempted Jewish houses from giving lodging to visiting members of the *Szlachta*.

The burghers resumed the fight in 1720, when the municipality and the merchants' guild summoned the Jews to the Royal Court to answer the charge that they were trespassing beyond their prescribed rights; but the Jews declined to appear, as they were afraid of an unfavorable decision. In April, 1724, the heads of the community announced that their charters and other important documents, which had lain in chests in the communal office, had been nibbled by mice, and they brought the chests to the office of the Fortress Court so that the documents could be examined. The Royal Court then heard the plaint of the municipality in the absence of the Jews, sentenced the latter to pay a heavy fine to the municipality, and ordered that the synagogue and Jewish shops should be closed until the money was paid. It was not, however, until August 3, 1726, that the Deputy-*Voivode*, accompanied by Court officials, attempted to close the synagogue and take possession of some Jewish houses, but they were prevented by the Jews with the help of some noblemen and priests who owned houses in the same streets. Not only these priests but also higher Church dignitaries at the time were, on the whole, rather friendly. Bishop Brzostovski issued regulations to facilitate Jewish funerals and burials; Bishop Panczesinski allowed Jews, in 1725, to open their shops on Sunday without interference; and Bishop Sinkiewicz, whose medical attendant was Dr. Aaron Gordon, allowed them to place a fence around the cemetery.

The municipality resumed its crusade against the Jews in 1713, when it complained that the Jewish community ignored the Ordinance and the decision of the Royal Court and failed to pay the annual tax of 600 gulden. In the following year the municipality and the merchants' guild again summoned the community to the Royal Court, though without effect. The Municipal Council gave particular vent to their hostility when the Russian army was once more in Vilna in 1734. They ordered the Jews to provide food for the soldiers for a fortnight and a further big supply when they left the city; they told the Russian General that the Jews removed the bodies of Cossacks from near the Jewish cemetery, where they were buried, and threw them into the Vilia; and they also spread the story that Jewish merchants and others gave secret information to the Polish troops. The result was that the Jews had to pay substantial sums to the Russians in order to save themselves from punishment.

After a brief respite the municipality returned to the attack in the reign of King Augustus III (1734–1763). This king confirmed all the charters of the Jewish community on May 29, 1738, and prolonged the right of the Jews to have open shops and to sell liquor for twenty years. The municipality thereupon instructed its deputies in the *Seym* to request the chancellor to prevent the Jews from obtaining any new rights or a confirmation of their charters, but without avail. The Municipal Council protested that the king had been misled by the Jews in granting them a confirmatory charter, contended that this was in conflict with the Ordinance of 1633, and summoned the Jews to the Royal Court to answer its charges. The court pronounced judgment on December 18, 1740, in favor of the municipality and even resurrected the old charter of 1527, which forbade the Jews to live in the city. The Jews thereupon appealed to the king for a letter of protection against the burghers, but in vain. The burghers next took steps to interfere with Jewish merchants and artisans, drove them from the market with the aid of the hangman, and even threatened to expel all Jews from the city. The latter, in their

distress, appealed to the *Voivode*, Prince Wisniowiecki, commander of the Lithuanian army, who
ordered his adjutant-general, Stanislav Lopota, to
defend the Jews from oppression both on the ground
of justice and in the interest of the revenue of the
country. The *Voivode* also asked his kinsman, the
Lithuanian chancellor, Jan Sapieha, to try to get
the Court's decision rescinded, but the latter, in his
reply, wrote that he could not hope to induce the
king, who was then in Warsaw, to issue a new
document for the benefit of the Jews without sufficient legal basis. The chancellor advised the *Voivode*
to endeavor, in cooperation with the Bishop of
Vilna, to effect an agreement between the Jews and
the burghers, and suggested that it was advisable for
the Jews to give way a little as the municipality had
an ancient document forbidding the Jews to live in
the city. He also added that the debts of the Jews
of Vilna to the monasteries and Christian secular
bodies constituted a weighty reason why the *Seym*
should declare in favor of the Jews living in Vilna,
and that the latter should seek to secure postponement of the court's decision.

The *Voivode*, Prince Wisniowiecki, gave the Jewish
community, on February 22, 1741, a letter of
protection, which forbade the burghers to interfere
with the Jews in their trade and work until he came
to Vilna, when the court would deal with the question. He appointed a commission, which met in
Vilna in April, 1741, to hear the arguments of the
two contending parties, and it drew up a Settlement
which, on the whole, was favorable to the Jews.

It provided that the Jews must pay the annual tax of 600 gulden for the repair of the City Hall as well as of the wall and gates; that they must not carry goods for sale to the houses of the *Szlachta* and to monasteries, on penalty of such goods being destroyed officially, although they could peddle in hides in the city; that they must not dwell or open shops too near to the City Hall on pain of punishment by the *Voivode's* office; that they could deal in woven woolen goods; and that they were forbidden to entice customers who were going into Christian shops. On the other hand, the Settlement stipulated that the municipality must respect all the privileges hitherto granted to the Jews, including the confirmatory charter of 1738; that Jewish houses should be exempt from use as lodgings for travelling noblemen or as detention cells; and that the municipality must undertake to protect the Jews from attacks by the mob.

This Settlement, which was intended to replace all previous official instruments and judgments that were in conflict with it, was accepted by the Kahal, the board of the Jewish community, despite the anti-Jewish restrictions which it contained. The municipality, however, declined to accept it and set forth its objections in writing. These were, in the main, that the Jews' payment of their annual tax was subject to conditions, that they were allowed to peddle in hides and to sell woven woolen goods in open shops, that the restrictions regarding their domicile were inadequate, that the confirmatory charter of 1738 had been wrongfully obtained, and that, so far as assaults upon the Jews were concerned, the municipality could undertake to punish only those who were under its own jurisdiction. The Municipal Council made a series of counter-proposals: that both sides should observe the Ordinance of 1633 and the court judgment of 1644, that the Jews should use only the municipality's weighing-machines and destroy their own, and that Jewish itinerant traders must sell their goods wholesale, and not retail, and pay to the merchants' guild a sum to be fixed. These counter-proposals were rejected by the Kahal, with the result that the burghers again began to interfere with the Jewish traders and to attack them. The heads of the Kahal therefore appealed to the Tribunal Court which then happened to sit in Vilna, and this court, on August 25, 1741, granted the Jews a letter of protection, warning the municipality and the merchants' guild against committing any injustice against the Jews and requesting them to take into consideration the Settlement proposed by the commission. As the letter of protection was valid only as long as the Tribunal Court was in Vilna, the Jews summoned the municipality and the merchants' guild to the Royal Court on December 15, 1741, but to no effect.

Eventually, on March 29, 1742, the Kahal was obliged to agree to conditions laid down by the municipality which were much more drastic than its previous proposals. These conditions were: that Jews who lived beyond the Jewish quarter should be punished by the demolition of their houses; that they could have little shops opening upon the street, if they did not sell woolen wares, silk, or other valuable goods; that they could possess small scales for their own requirements; and that the municipality undertook not to establish any detention cells in a house in the Jewish quarter, but only in one outside that area within its own jurisdiction. It was also provided that, if the Jews infringed any of these conditions, the municipality itself would take action; and in the case of any individual Jew being guilty of infringement, the Kahal should not be held responsible but should punish him by excommunication and any other means within its power, while the municipality would confiscate his goods, arrest him and hand him over to the proper authority. This enforced agreement also contained an entirely new clause declaring the abolition of the Kahal's monopoly in the sale of glass, tin, lead and other commodities, and prescribing, in case this clause was infringed, that the municipality should have the right to prosecute any Vilna Jews within or without the city, and even beyond the borders of the State, for instance, in Koenigsberg or Gdansk (Danzig), and to seize the offenders and their goods. The chief purpose of this agreement, which was signed on March 29, 1742, was severely to restrict Jewish trade, and, although it referred to the Jewish quarter, it did not actually define it. The Kahal also had to give the municipality a promissory note for 2,200 gulden, payable in annual instalments of 200 gulden, as legal costs (although the municipality had originally demanded 92,000 gulden as expenses incurred in the course of decades of litigation), and it now began to pay the annual tax of 600 gulden regularly.

The agreement which was thus made to satisfy the merchants' guild was not the only one of its kind, although it had been preceded by the most protracted struggle. In 1673 the tinsmiths' and needle-makers' guild agreed that there should be four Jewish tinsmiths, who should pay the guild 25 gulden a year, and should be entitled to bequeath their rights. The Jewish artisans in general had already begun to organize themselves in societies in the second half of the seventeenth century for the purpose of fighting for their existence. In 1720 the turners' guild agreed that there should be one Jewish turner, who should pay it 10 gulden a year. After the agreement was concluded with the merchants' guild, similar compacts were made with the furriers' guild and the hat-makers' guild, although details are known only of that made with the latter in 1741. It provided that Jewish married artisans, engaged in the making of fur hats, could work without restriction, but must not have more than five workmen and ten apprentices, of whom the latter must learn the trade in six years and then become workmen; that Jews were forbidden to peddle with hats but were allowed to take some to houses of the *Szlachta*; that they were also forbidden to display hats in the windows of houses, or to hang them up outside their shops. It also laid down the kinds of hat that Jews could make, and of what skins and colors, and stipulated that if a Jew infringed any of these regulations his hats should be destroyed by

the Christian guild and he should be judged by a
court consisting of two members of the Christian
and two of the Jewish guild. In case the offense was
committed more than three times, the punishment
should consist of three weeks' imprisonment and
expulsion from the guild. In return for these concessions the Jewish guild undertook to pay the
Christian guild 23½ thalers for the two years 1742–
1743, 20 thalers per annum from 1744 to 1752, and
afterwards 8 thalers per annum — the money to be
devoted to the guild's altar in the monastery of the
monks of St. Bernard.

In pursuance of the settlement reached with the
merchants' guild the Kahal threatened to excommunicate anybody who hawked goods in the street,
but the threat was without avail. Moreover, Jews
opened shops with entrances from the street, dealt
in all kinds of goods, and engaged in all sorts of
work, without any effective check being placed upon
their activity. The Settlement of 1742 did not by any
means end the battle between the burghers and the
Jews; it simply represented a stage in the conflict.
In 1750 the municipality obtained from the State
archives the document containing the decisions of
the commission of 1636, secured the affixing to it of
the royal seal, and used it for the purpose of en-
forcing the payment by the Jews of the annual
tax and limiting the number of their taverns. A
few years later the Royal Court decided to investigate whether the demands for the restrictions upon
the Jews in regard to trade and domicile were
justified, and its commission of inquiry reported in

1755 that almost all the houses in the Jewish quarter belonged to Christians. The Municipal Council now pressed for the rescinding of the 1742 Settlement and the revival of the less favorable regulations of a hundred years before. Among their many sweeping demands were the following: that the Jews should all be confined within the boundaries of the ghetto, that their open shops should be closed, that they should be limited to twelve shops without an entrance from the street and twenty places for the sale of liquor, that they should not engage in any kind of work for which there was a guild, that the Kahal should be responsible for the offenses of every individual Jew and should collect any fine imposed upon him, that Jews should not hold posts in the tax offices, that their weighing-machine and wax-boiler should be abolished, and that they should be forbidden to distill spirits, to buy before Christians had made their own purchases, and to buy cattle and horses for sale.

The Kahal pleaded that the 1742 Settlement should remain in force, and complained that the municipality had failed to discharge its obligation to attend to the water cisterns and other matters, for which it paid the annual tax. The Royal Court decided that the Settlement should remain in force and that only the weighing-machine in the Town Hall should be used, and deferred consideration of other questions. But although the Jews won their case, they did not comply with the restrictions in the Settlement, and the burghers particularly protested against their continued use of private scales.

The municipality was also indignant with the Jews
for settling in streets beyond the ghetto, for they
bought a house in 1755 in the Niemiecka Street and
rented another in the suburb of Subocz. Nevertheless, efforts to curb Jewish development were in
vain. Despite the unending conflict that the Jews
had to encounter and the sequence of calamities
which they had to endure, they succeeded, by the
second half of the eighteenth century, in securing
for themselves a position of economic stability.

Throughout their struggle with the burghers, the
Jews had the support of the *Voivode* (the governor
representing the king), who conducted his administration through his officials. The Jews were thus
thrown into greater contact with the *Voivode* and
his deputy, who expected some monetary or other
reward for their services. The *Voivode* Michael
Radziwill, who was a millionaire in Polish gulden,
therefore drew up a number of rules in 1745, to
regulate the relations between his officials and the
Jewish community. In any disputes between them,
the Jews could appeal to the *Voivode* himself; no
officials could demand from the Jews presents of
food or candles, or that Jewish artisans should work
for them for nothing; no Jew could be imprisoned
except after a proper trial — accusation by a single
person being insufficient — and no official could take
payment either at the time of imprisonment or
release; all members of the Jewish community were
subject to the jurisdiction of the *Voivode's* court,
even if they lived outside its area; Jews could be
punished by fines or imprisonment, but not by

flogging; and in return for the protection accorded by the officials, the Kahal should pay the Vice-*Voivode* two thalers and his deputy one thaler per week, but should not pay them for holding a court or give them any spirits or mead. These regulations were confirmed in 1768 by the *Voivode* Carl Radzi-will, a son of Michael Radziwill, who added some further provisions: that the Jews should deal with all their own internal affairs without interference by the Vice-*Voivode*, that they could judge any Jewish offender in their own court of law, and that if Jews had a grievance against the Kahal they could appeal to the *Voivode*.

The somewhat monotonous course of the Jews' economic struggle in Vilna was suddenly relieved in the middle of the eighteenth century by a remark-able event which lay quite outside all mundane affairs. It was the trial and condemnation to death of a Polish nobleman, Count Valentin Potocki, who had committed the heinous sin of abandoning the Christian for the Jewish faith. As a young man, Potocki had gone with his friend Zaremba, from Poland to Paris to study, and there they made the acquaintance of an old Jew whom they found poring over a Hebrew book in his wine-shop. They became so interested in his explanations of the Bible that they persuaded him to teach them the Hebrew language, and they were so impressed by his exposi-tion of the principles of Judaism that they decided to give up their Roman Catholic religion and go to Amsterdam in order openly to embrace the Jewish faith. Potocki first went to Rome, where his resolve was only strengthened, and then proceeded to Amsterdam, where he conformed with the requisite rites and became a Jew under the name of Abraham ben Abraham. After returning to Poland he wandered as a *Ger Zedek* (righteous proselyte) from place to place, until he was at last discovered in the town of Ilye near Vilna, and betrayed to the authorities. Potocki was then arrested and taken in chains to Vilna, where, after a long imprisonment, during which his mother and friends entreated him in vain to return to Christianity, and after repeated torture, he was sentenced to the stake. He was burned alive in Vilna, on the second day of Pentecost, May 24, 1749. A Jew, Leiser Zhiskes, succeeded by bribery in securing some of the ashes of the martyr, which were later buried in the Jewish cemetery.[1]

From the soil over the grave of the *Ger Zedek* there grew a vigorous tree almost in the form of a man, with outstretched branches resembling hands and feet, which drew vast pilgrimages of Jews, but the " hands" and "feet" were hacked away by some malicious hand. In order to protect the grave, the Jewish authorities, some years after the restoration of the Polish State, had an iron shed built over it, with a Hebrew inscription, enclosed with large blocks of stone joined by heavy iron rails. But Polish vandals wrought repeated damage to this protection over the last remains of the "righteous proselyte."

---

[1] See Supplementaty Note **3**.

CHAPTER V

UNDER KING STANISLAV PONIATOWSKI

WHEN the *Seym* met in Warsaw in May, 1764, after the election to the throne of Stanislav Augustus Poniatowski (1764–1795), favorite of Catherine II of Russia and the last of the Polish kings, the lower *Szlachta* of the Vilna district included a number of demands relating to Jews among the instructions that they gave to their deputies. These were that, besides dissidents, Germans, and foreigners in general, Jews should be excluded from the office of tax-collector and from positions in the customs service and frontier control; that the poll-tax imposed upon the Jewish population should be increased, for which purpose a census of all the Jews in the kingdom should be carried out, and they should remain permanently in their various places of domicile; and that Jewish trade should be so regulated as not to injure Christians engaged in trade. These demands, which were supported by the deputies from other districts, were approved by the *Seym* when imposing conditions upon the new king. At the same time the *Seym* decided to alter the taxation system pertaining to the Jews in order to increase the State revenue. According to the decisions that had been in force since 1717, the Jews of Poland (the Crown lands) had to pay a lump sum of 220,000 zloty per annum as poll-tax, and the Jews of Lithuania a sum

of 60,000 zloty. These amounts had to be apportioned among the individual communities and then
conveyed in their entirety by the Central *Va'ad*
(Council) of the Polish and Lithuanian communities
respectively to the State treasury. The government
found that the Elders of the community collected
much larger sums than their assessments and used
the surplus for communal or even private purposes.
They concluded that they could get more money
from the Jews for the State without increasing the
burden of the individual Jew, and consequently the
Seym decided that, from 1765, all Jews, without
distinction of age or sex, must pay an annual poll-
tax of two zloty. In pursuance of this new law every
Kahal was ordered to carry out immediately, in
cooperation with a controller appointed from among
the *Szlachta* by the *Starosta*, an exact census of the
Jewish population in the district.

A new phase in the struggle of the Jews in Vilna
for economic rights developed, in the reign of Stanislav Poniatowski, in consequence of the difficulties
in which many Christian artisans found themselves.
For centuries there had been a feud between them
and the burghers, whom they accused of injuring
their interests and whom they even charged with
taking bribes from the Jews. Among the burghers
were merchants who brought various precious goods
from foreign countries, which they sold at a profit
to Jews, and consequently many Christian artisans
were unable to compete against them with their own
wares. The result was that by the middle of the
eighteenth century many Christian guilds had de-

clined or ceased to exist, while the number of Jewish artisans had steadily increased. The guilds that were dissolved included those of the furriers, jewelers, gold embroiderers, glaziers, tinsmiths, bookbinders, and needle-makers. The Christian merchants, who were likewise afraid of Jewish competition, exploited the distress of the artisans by inciting them to agitate against both Jewish traders and craftsmen, and to demand that the latter be subjected to serious restrictions. The butchers' and salt-vendors' guilds also levelled complaints against the Jewish butchers on the ground that they raised prices, and against the Jewish salt-vendors on the ground that they had no right to deal in that commodity or in herring. But Anthony Tisenhaus, an official who was engaged in fostering trade and industry in Lithuania, allowed the Jews to deal in salt and herring, while he closed the shops of Christian dealers who had apparently not paid their tax. There was one guild, however, that came to an amicable arrangement with the Jews, namely, the barbers' guild, the only one that accepted Jews as members. In 1774 it allowed two Jews to practice as barbers and army-surgeons, on condition that no other Jews engaged in this occupation, that they did not attend to Christians, and that they paid two thalers per annum to the members of the guild.

In reply to the grievances of the Christian merchants and artisans, which were energetically endorsed by the Municipal Council, the Kahal retorted with a series of complaints of its own. The Jews, it declared, were harassed by the burghers, who put them into private prisons and drove them from the market with the help of the hangman and his assistants; the Municipal Council, whose business it was to effect the transfer of houses in the ghetto to Jews, allowed burghers to live there and even handed over houses of Jews in that quarter to Christian creditors without authority; and the Council, instead of applying the annual tax of 600 gulden to necessary repairs and improvements, used the money for its own requirements, while it allowed the Jews to be exposed to violent attack and even robbery. The Kahal, therefore, demanded that the Settlement of 1742 should be enforced. The unity of the artisans' and merchants' guilds and the municipality in their anti-Jewish campaign was short-lived, as the artisans' guilds, at the end of 1776, summoned both the municipality and the Kahal to court on the plea that the agreements made between these two had brought about their own decline and the dissolution of more than ten other guilds. The artisans even urged that the Jews be removed to a place about five or six miles away from Vilna — a demand which testified to their own economic distress. The only concrete result of this outburst of agitation was that King Stanislav Poniatowski, on December 15, 1776, granted the Jews of Vilna a confirmation of their privileges and added a prolongation for twenty years. In the previous year he had even issued an order to exempt from the poll-tax all Jews who undertook to devote themselves to agriculture.

A new and disagreeable development was an unfavorable change in the attitude of the upper *Szlachta* towards the Jews. The nobles had improved their own position in relation to the burghers and no longer needed to make use of the Jews against them. They therefore sought to increase the taxes on the Jews, to treat them like serfs by forbidding them to leave their various places of settlement, and to prevent them from increasing in number. They even indulged in frequent attacks upon them and robbed them, generally when they assembled for the District Diet or for legislation. One of the earliest cases was in 1724, when a nobleman, who was incensed on finding a Jew acting as a watchman in the Fortress, violently abused him and attacked him with his sword. A favorite spot for such assaults was in front of the synagogue, where impecunious nobles, servants of *Pans* (squires), and miscellaneous riff-raff would gather together and demand "tribute." An instance occurred in Vilna, in 1756, when *Szlachta* and burghers swarmed into the synagogue courtyard, and as the single soldier on guard was unable to disperse them they attacked and looted houses and shops. In February, 1765, when the *Szlachta* assembled in Vilna for the District Diet, poor members of their order, together with servants, assembled in front of the synagogue and demanded money, and after they had been appeased another crowd succeeded it with a similar clamor. The Jews refused to yield any more money, whereupon they were attacked and some of them were injured before some soldiers of the city hurried to their rescue. On September 10, 1764, two military officers, members of the nobility, seized two Jewish tinsmiths who

came to their courtyard in search of work and compelled them to eat *trefah* (ritually unclean) meat:
with the help of their servants they forced open the
mouths of the Jews and stuffed the forbidden food
into them, and when the victims refused to swallow
it they beat them and threatened to kill them. On
another occasion, a Jewish tailor was struck by
order of a priest when he called to collect a debt for
work done. In June, 1780, when a district court
was holding a session in Vilna, a nobleman with
his followers made an attack upon a house in Zydowska Street and stole some valuable girdles. The
last concerted attack took place in July, 1782, when
Christian barley vendors, with the aid of armed
soldiers, broke into Jewish houses, destroyed grind-
stones, scattered corn, and attacked and injured a
number of Jews. When the victims complained to
the court, the assailants produced their statute,
which forbade the Jews to deal in barley and prohibited members of their guild from working with
Jews.

Apart from this, however, after a relentless and
unceasing struggle of about two hundred and fifty
years, the Jews of Vilna at last secured their economic rights and the right of domicile. Their cause
was effectively championed by their *Shtadlan* (advocate, whose functions will be described later), Aryeh
Leib Meitess, and found a powerful supporter in the
humane and progressive Vice-Chancellor, Joachim
Chreptowicz. The great issue, which had assumed
increasing bitterness when the artisans joined the
burghers and the Municipal Council in the anti-

Jewish crusade, was satisfactorily settled in 1783 by the Royal Court, which displayed a combination of intelligence, tolerance and energy. The Royal Court realized that the protracted conflict, with the recurring outbreak of disorder and the constant wrangling in different courts of law, must at last be brought to an end in the interests of the peace and welfare of the city as a whole. The first partition of Poland, which had taken place in 1772 and which resulted in about one-fifth of her population and one-fourth of her territory being divided among Russia, Prussia and Austria, may have contributed a sobering influence. The valuable services that the Jews rendered in the economic development of the city, particularly in fostering trade with other countries, doubtless was another factor which weighed in their favor, for they travelled to Russia and Germany, from where they brought different sorts of goods back with them, and they exported various commodities from Lithuania, especially timber.

The Royal Court, in the first place, swept aside all the regulations and restrictions that aimed at confining the Jews within a kind of ghetto. It stated that it was impracticable to force all the Jews, who had greatly multiplied since 1633, into the three narrow streets which were assigned for their residence in that year. Even the burghers had admitted, in the Settlement of 1742, that it had been found impossible to compel the Christian landlords to sell their houses in the ghetto to Jews. The court, which based its judgment on the charters of 1593 and 1633 and the Settlement of 1742, declared that it was in accordance with justice for the Jews to dwell and buy houses throughout all parts of the city and its suburbs. It made an exception, however, in the case of two streets, those (1) from Ostrobram to the Cathedral (now Ostrobramska, Wielka, and Zamkowa), and (2) from the Troki Gate to the Monastery of St. John (now the Trocka, Domini-kanska, and Janska). If the Jews already had houses in those streets they could keep them, but they could not build any new ones there without the permission of the municipality, which should be granted in the interest of the city's improvement. Since the Jews could now live in any part of the city, save for these two, they were made liable to pay the same rates as other citizens and their annual tax of 600 gulden was abolished. In order to prevent their being taxed excessively they were allowed to appoint two repre-sentatives on the assessment commission, and if they considered that they were assessed unfairly they could summon the Municipal Council to the Royal Court. The rates payable by the Jews were so as-sessed as to cover one-third of the city's expenditure; they had to be collected by the Kahal and handed over to the municipality.

The Royal Court also decided that the Jews were henceforth free to engage in any kind of work or business, that they could open taverns without restrictions, but that they must weigh their corn on the municipality's machine. It even impressed upon the Kahal the duty of seeing that all Jews were usefully employed and of expelling any idlers from the city, and enacted a regulation that any new Jewish artisans must be examined by a board appointed by the municipality, consisting of both Jews and Christians. It furthermore enjoined upon the Jews the necessity of attending to the cleanliness of their streets and houses.

The court judiciously refrained from imposing any legal costs upon either the municipality or the Kahal, so that neither party should have a grievance, and its judgment was cheerfully accepted by both. So delighted were the Jews with what they regarded as a notable triumph that they had the following inscription made upon the tombstone of the *Shtadlan*, Aryeh Leib Meitess: "It was he who wrought the great salvation for Israel in the year 5544 (1784) and saved the city by his wisdom." The municipality, in complying with the decision of the court, appointed representatives to carry out a registration of the Jews in the city, but no record of the houses then belonging to Jews has been preserved. On the other hand, a list has been preserved of two hundred and ninety-six Jews, who were described as wandering about in the city, without any definite abode and without any permission from the Kahal to remain in the city.

Unfortunately the improvement in the position of the Jews brought about by the judgment of the Royal Court was seriously affected by one of the numerous reforms adopted by the Great *Seym*. This assembly met in 1788 and deliberated for the record period of four years in a desperate effort to check the growing disintegration of the State by devising a new Constitution. Although fully conscious of the importance of the Jewish question, it was pre-occupied too much by other affairs to devote any serious attention to that problem, which was consequently referred to a commission. There were animated and protracted discussions in the commission on the best methods of improving the social and economic position of the Jews, but without any positive conclusion being reached. A "Deputation for the Reform of the Jews" was therefore elected by the Great *Seym* on June 22, 1790, in the hope of producing a more satisfactory result. But before the "Deputation" (of which Matthias Butrimowicz, the deputy from Pinsk, was the leading member) was able to submit its report to the *Seym*, the latter adopted the Constitution of May 3, 1791, which did not mention the Jewish question, although it conceded freedom of conscience to all religions. The Municipalities Law, which was passed at the same time, declared that only Christians could be regarded as citizens; placed all the inhabitants of a city, with the sole exception of the *Szlachta*, under the jurisdiction of the municipality; and it consequently subjected the Jews to the authority of the Municipal Law Court. This reform was brought about through the influence of the burghers, who had for the first time been allowed to send deputies of their own to a parliament which was doomed to end its existence in the impending collapse of the State itself. In the session of May 24, Butrimowicz demanded an early decision on the project of the "Deputation," but owing to the objection of the deputy from Brazlaw, Cholonewski, that its proposal to extend the commercial rights of the Jews would be detrimental to Little Poland, the request of Butrimowicz was rejected and did not receive further consideration until the autumn of 1791.

The principal Jewish communities in Lithuania thereupon issued a special appeal for money, for the purpose of "intercession," and two leading members of the Vilna community, Simon ben Zeev-Wolf and Dr. Shmarya Polonus, together with delegates of other Jewish communities, submitted proposals with a view to safeguarding the position of the Jews. They even entered into negotiations with the king himself, to whom, in a solemn audience, they submitted a petition in which they asked for the grant of civil rights, especially the right to acquire land in cities, communal autonomy, and independence from the municipalities. The Jewish delegation is said to have given Stanislav Poniatowski one million gulden for the liquidation of the State's debts, in return for which he is believed to have drafted a project of his own for the solution of the Jewish question and submitted it to the *Seym*, but without achieving any success. Meanwhile Butrimowicz induced the *Seym* to reconsider the Jewish question, with the result that a statement was adopted that to improve the lot of the Jewish population the affairs of the community must be put in order, and this could not be accomplished before the heavy debts of the Kahal had been wiped out. Liquidation commissions were therefore everywhere appointed, to report to the Finance Commission by

March 31, 1792. But the scheme worked out by
the Finance Commission was never carried out.
Thus, the result of all the protracted discussions
was negative, and the various petitions of the Jews,
as well as the liberal resolutions of the Police Commission of May 24, 1792 (whereby the Jews were
assured personal security, protection against capri-
cious taxes, and other rights, including that of keeping Christian servants) remained utterly ignored.
Moreover, the request of the Kahal in 1794 to be
freed from the jurisdiction of the municipality and
to be placed under that of the *Voivode's* Court was
rejected.

The Jews were now sorely perturbed by a much
graver event, for the weakness of Poland and the
cupidity of her stronger neighbors resulted in her
Second Partition taking place in 1793, whereby the
Grand Duchy of Lithuania was annexed by Russia.
Despite the profound discontent which the Jews
felt on account of their treatment by the Polish
authorities and especially the Polish people, they
nevertheless displayed their loyalty to their native
country and rallied to its support when Thaddeus
Kosciuszko, the Lithuanian patriot, raised the standard of revolt. His army succeeded at first in recovering three-quarters of the ancient territory, including
the city of Vilna, and the Jewish community swore
an oath of fidelity to the Provisional Government.
Dr. Polonus delivered a fiery speech in the synagogue
on May 17, 1794, a Sabbath day, in which he described the cruelty of the Russians and urged his
hearers to help the struggle by giving the Polish

leaders whatever information they could glean about the movements of the Russian troops. The Jewish community provided a sum of 25,000 gulden towards the costs of the rising, which was supplemented by smaller amounts from individuals. The head of the Kahal, a merchant named Noah ben Feibusch Bloch, undertook to supply the Polish troops with gunpowder and lead and the Jewish tailors offered to furnish two hundred uniforms free. Many Jews took part and fell in the defense of the city, which, after a three weeks' siege, was again occupied by the Russians, on July 30, 1794.

In Kosciuszko's ill-fated struggle for Polish independence a notable part was played by a young Jew, Berek Joselevitch, whose martial exploits impart a note of romantic adventure to this somber period of Jewish history. Joselevitch was born about 1765 in the little town of Kretingen (in Samogitia) and was employed as estate manager by Prince Masalski, Bishop of Vilna, who took him more than once to Paris. In September, 1794, when the siege of Warsaw reached a climax, Joselevitch, together with Joseph Aronowicz, requested the permission of Kosciuszko to form a regiment of light cavalry of Jewish volunteers. The leader of the insurrection agreed in an announcement that he made on September 17th. On October 1st Joselevitch issued a fiery appeal to the Jews and within a short time recruited five hundred volunteers, who were equipped with the help of 3,000 gulden given by the national treasury and by private funds. These Jewish cavalrymen fought bravely in the defense of Praga, a suburb of Warsaw, but unfortunately, nearly the whole of the regiment was mowed down by the troops of the Russian General Suvorov. Joselevitch went into exile with the other survivors of the battle, joined the Polish Legion founded by Napoleon Bonaparte, and fought in Italy, where he was wounded. He later commanded a section of the Polish Legion in the French Army, and after the creation of the Grand Duchy of Warsaw he returned to Poland in command of an Uhlan regiment, where he was killed in 1809 by Austrian hussars, in a fight near Kotzk (in the district of Siedlec). The name of this Jewish hero, who shed luster upon his people by his patriotic devotion and military powers, is enshrined not only in Jewish history but also in Polish songs and sagas.[1]

In 1795 the remaining part of Poland was divided up between Russia, Prussia and Austria, and, after this Third Partition, King Stanislav Poniatowski resigned the Crown on April 25, 1795, and retired to St. Petersburg, where he died three years later. The Polish State was at an end, and the country was

---

[1] The newspapers printed laudatory notices of Joselevitch's death, and a representative of the Polish nobility, Stanislav Potocki, delivered a memorial address at the meeting of the Warsaw Society of Friends of Science, in which he eulogized him highly and compared him to "those warriors for whom the daughters of Zion once mourned." The gratitude of the fatherland was shown by granting a small pension to the hero's widow for the support of herself and her children and allowing her to live in a part of Warsaw closed to Jews, where she could sell liquor.

doomed to suffer in subjection until its independence
was restored a century and a quarter later.

The Russians at first sought to win the Jews over
to their side and began by adopting a friendly attitude, so that the Jews were naturally prompted to
try to liberate themselves from the authority of the
municipality. In January, 1795, the heads of both
the Vilna and the Grodno communities submitted
a petition to General Repnin, who had been appointed Governor over Poland by the Empress
Catherine II, to release them from the jurisdiction
of the Municipal Court of Law; but he replied that
their status must remain as before the revolt, although, somewhat inconsequently, he declared that
the decisions of the Great *Seym* should be ignored.
The question of legal jurisdiction, however, was
soon settled by the Lithuanian Supreme Court in
favor of the Jews. This court decided that whatever
privileges the municipality possessed, and whatever
decisions had been passed by the Royal Court in
1783 and the Great *Seym* in 1791, they did not
entitle the municipality to exercise jurisdiction over
the Jews. It declared that the Jews must continue,
as originally, to be subject to the authority of the
Fortress Court, and that, as far as their religious
affairs and internal disputes were concerned,
these fell within the province of their own *Bet Din*.
The request of the Jews that judgments relating to
them already adopted by the Municipal Court should
be cancelled was refused, but cases that had only
opened and not yet been concluded were transferred

to the Fortress Court. This decision of the Lithuanian Supreme Court remained in force until the
year 1808, when a Municipalities Law came into
effect which placed Jews exactly in the same position
as other citizens in their relation to the courts of
law.

CHAPTER VI

THE JEWISH QUARTER

1. THE GHETTO: ITS HOMES AND ENVIRONS

THE ghetto in mediaeval Vilna was not identical with the Jewish quarter, but formed only a part of it. The charter granted by Wladislav IV in 1633 restricted the domicile of the Jews to three narrow, adjacent streets — Zydowska (Jews'), Jatkowa (Slaughterers') and St. Michael; and it stipulated that the Jews must acquire all the houses in these streets within fifteen years, after which time they would not be permitted to live anywhere else. Although these three streets, or the area that they bounded, thus constituted the ghetto, the Jews never allowed themselves to be confined within those cramping limits.[1] They conducted a stubborn and incessant struggle, decade after decade, against the Municipal Council for the right to dwell in other parts of the city, until they at last achieved the Royal Court's decision of 1783 which, admitting the injustice and the impracticability of trying to pen their growing numbers within the little crowded ghetto, accorded them practically unlimited freedom of domicile. But the Jews did not wait all this time before beginning to spread abroad. They had no

---

[1] See Supplementary Note 4.

difficulty from the very outset in securing houses in
neighboring streets, belonging to nobles, priests, or
monastic orders, where they lived under the jurisdiction of the *Voivode* and the bishop and under the
protection of their respective landlords. The streets
to which they were mainly attracted were the
Niemiecka (German Street) and those intersecting
it, as that was the principal business thoroughfare,
leading directly to the Town Hall and the market-
place. Even so, the area within which they lived
was so circumscribed that they were obliged to
exploit it to the utmost. They thus created inner
streets in the courtyards behind the houses. Every
courtyard or *Hof* became a *Durchhof* or alley, which
led from one street to another, and every *Durchhof*
was flanked by little shops. Nay, every door and
every window was utilized by tradesmen and artisans for their stores or work-benches; they even
made nooks and cupboards in the walls outside,
to which they affixed doors, for the display of their
goods; while those who were unable to employ any
of these devices plied their trades or hawked their
wares in the street, courtyard, or alley. The whole
district was a hive of swarming humanity, struggling
manfully in a hostile environment for a decent
existence, yet abating not a jot of the traditional
devotion to the spiritual life.

The Jews were given, in 1633, the right, which
was converted eleven years later into an obligation,
to build gates for the ghetto, but they neither fully
availed themselves of the right nor complied with the
obligation. They feared that once the ghetto was

securely enclosed by means of gates, they would all be forced into it and be unable to leave it. They did, indeed, fix a gate at the corner of the Niemiecka and Zydowska, but there is no definite trace of any other. The arches which still span the Jatkowa and the Szklanna (Glaziers') Street are not remains of such gates, but are intended simply as buttresses to the opposing walls. The houses were, in the main, substantially built, but they were often destroyed by fire and had to be restored. They usually consisted of two or three stories, with cellars, and contained several tenements for the accommodation of different families. Some of the cellars in the Zydowska were so deep, dark, and dank, without a ray of light or breath of air, that they were called "dwellings of the devil." Each tenement mainly comprised a living-room and a bedroom, with cupboards in the walls. The street door was of iron and the windows were protected by iron shutters, as a necessary precaution against any would-be pogromists; but there was also a verandah in front of the house which was used in the intervals of peace. There were, moreover, many large houses, owned either by a single landlord or jointly by a few, which were sometimes inhabited by as many as fifteen families and, in one or two cases, even by twice that number.

There was considerable activity in the real estate market, for there was an incessant demand for dwellings, due partly to natural increase, partly to the influx from other towns or countries, and partly also, unfortunately, to the periodic destruction of houses by fire. The central authority in regard to all property transactions was the Kahal. Whoever wanted to rent a house or shop in the Jewish quarter had to apply to the Kahal and pay for the right of priority, termed *Hazakah*, which the recipient could then dispose of, if he wished, to another person. Any sale of a house or of part of one, or any division of a house for sale or letting, had to be registered in the *Pinkas*[1] (minute-book) of the *Bet Din*, and thus acquired full legal validity, although some Jews preferred to make doubly sure by registering the transaction also with a Polish court. The Kahal itself was the owner of houses in the synagogue courtyard as well as of houses and shops in adjacent streets, which it let. It also mortgaged these properties to Jews for loans, and often included in the transaction the license to open a shop, distillery, or other place of business, usually for ten years, with the option of extensions for further periods of five years. It kept a special "mortgage book," in which all such business transactions were recorded. The loan was generally obtained from the tenants themselves, who thus became the temporary owners or part owners, without any absolute right of disposal or of borrowing money from a Christian on the security of the property.

There is a wealth of local records from the seventeenth and eighteenth centuries which show the

---

[1] This word, from the Greek *pinax*, which means "board" or "writing-tablet," generally denotes the register or minute-book of a Jewish community. The word occurs in the Mishna, Abot 3.16 ("The *Pinkas* is open and the hand writes").

frequency and intimacy of relations between Jews and Christians in regard to all sorts of property transactions. So complete and continuous are some of these records that it is possible to follow the checkered fortunes of some houses for a period of a century and a half. The ownership of a house often passed from a Christian to a Jew, and sometimes continued to alternate, while there were cases of Jews and Christians at times sharing in its possession. The Jewish landlord often borrowed money from a Christian on the security of his property and continued to pay rent as interest on the loan for such a long period that the ownership meanwhile changed hands through sale or bequest so that the relations of landlord and tenant became confused and the help of the courts had to be invoked to unravel the tangle. In many cases Jews undertook to restore ruined houses on condition that they be allowed to occupy them at a small rental.

An instance of complicated relations, due to frequent change of ownership over a long period, is provided by a large house in the Zydowska, known as "Olsun's house," which the Kahal bought in 1633 for 7,000 gulden from the Monastic Order of the Holy Trinity, who administered the hospital to which the house had been bequeathed. Instead of paying the money outright, the Kahal paid only a small percentage each year. In 1664 the Kahal, which had still not paid the purchase price, sold the house to three Jews, and afterwards it was divided up among several owners. Nearly a century later a part of the house was inherited by Rabbi

Saul ben Jehuda-Leib, author of *Shevil ha-Yashar*
("The Straight Path"), who was known as Rabbi
Saul Shiskess, and there is a Hebrew document in
existence, issued by the *Bet Din*, certifying his
ownership. This document was recorded in the
Kahal's *Pinkas* in 1755, and was also registered
both in the original Hebrew and in Polish translation
in the books of the District Court of the Vilna
municipality. All might have been well but for the
heavy indebtedness into which the Kahal sank.
For in 1766, when all the creditors of the Kahal
submitted their claims to a commission appointed
by the royal treasury, the trustee of the hospital
demanded that the Kahal pay the sum of 7,000
gulden, so long overdue, or return the house. The
commission decided that the Kahal must pay within
twelve months, otherwise the house would revert
to the hospital. The Kahal could not and did not
pay, and thereupon there was a prolonged struggle
between the hospital trustee and the four Jewish
owners who would not give up possession. In 1778
the owners were obliged by the commission to pay
7,840 gulden, and they thereupon demanded the
refund of this money from the Kahal. So slowly
did the cogs of the judiciary's machinery move that
it was not until 1789 that the Royal Court ordered
the Kahal to repay the money. The owners then
declined to accept the refund, since they were
required to return the house to the Kahal. The
commission consequently decided to deposit the
money in the chancellery of the Fortress Court and
to take possession of the house, whereupon the

owners lodged a protest with the Royal Court. What the issue of the case was, the records fail to disclose; probably it was one of many cases abandoned in the upheaval caused by the Russian annexation. All that we know is that "Olsun's House," which then contained thirty-three families, comprising one hundred and five souls, remained in Jewish ownership and has so continued to the present day.

Another large house, situated between the Zydowska and the Jatkowa, that has a history, belonged in the middle of the seventeenth century to one of the famous elders of the Kahal, Eliezer ben Moses, who had secured charters for the Jews from Sigismund III and Wladislav IV. He bequeathed the house and some money to the *Va'ad* (Council) of the Jewish communities of Lithuania, but some creditors made a claim against the estate. His widow, Chwala, also put in her claim, and she was given a loan of 5,000 zloty by Asher ben Aaron, the Kahal elder, to whom the house was let (apart from other sums which she received from the *Va'ad*). In 1687 the *Va'ad* sold the house to Shmaryahu ben Yekutiel-Zalman, a rich Jew from Brest, who paid off a mortgage on it. The *Va'ad* had previously made vain efforts for three months, by public announcements in all the synagogues and houses of study in Vilna, to discover a local Jewish resident who would buy it for 13,600 gulden. In 1709 the owner borrowed 800 gulden from Dr. Aaron Gordon, giving the house as pledge. When the latter's son, Michael, gave the owner a further 16,000 gulden, he secured full possession of the house himself. In 1748 the

Gordons disposed of it to a Lithuanian dignitary, Lopota, who sold it thirty years later to Bishop Wolczacki. The Bishop let it to some Jews on condition that they carried out the requisite repairs and paid rent; it then accommodated twenty-four families comprising eighty persons. But in 1792, a certain Kreine, a female member of the Gordon family, acquired the house and afterwards disposed of parts of it. One part was sold to a tailors' society, which converted it into a synagogue which existed to this day.

At first the Jews were not allowed to live in the Niemiecka, as the burghers objected to their settling too near the Town Hall, which was situated at the end of the street; they nevertheless succeeded in securing ingress into the houses on that important thoroughfare. The first to be occupied by them was called "Slutzki's house," as the landlords were the Princes Slutzki. This house, which is connected with the synagogue courtyard, was exempt from the jurisdiction of the municipality. It remained in the permanent possession of Jews, as did the neighboring house of another Lithuanian magnate, Kishko, which was converted into a synagogue. The infiltration of the Jews into the Niemiecka went on steadily, and by the second half of the eighteenth century they already occupied most of the houses on it. They likewise settled in the Rudnicka, a by-street of the Niemiecka, which led direct to the market. By 1765 they had occupied ten houses, and in 1784 they were to be found in all. They also secured a footing in the various streets and alleys between the Niemiecka, the Rudnicka, and the wall around the city, as well as in the Troki Street, which cuts the Niemiecka at the end farthest from the Town Hall, and in the Gaon Street[1] (a continuation of the Zydowska), where they were under the jurisdiction of the bishop.

An inquiry made by the Kahal in 1645 showed that there were thirty-two houses in the ghetto, of which the Jews had acquired twenty-one. The same number remained in their possession in 1690, but, owing to the succession of calamities which subsequently overtook them, an investigation in 1755 revealed that, with few exceptions, all the houses in the ghetto belonged to Christians, including priests. By the end of the eighteenth century, however, many of these houses had reverted to Jewish possession. An inquiry conducted by the municipality in 1645 revealed that there were 262 Jewish families, or about 1,310 Jews, living within its jurisdiction, and, since an equal number probably lived outside it, there must have been a total of about 2,620 Jews in the whole of the city, compared with 12,000 Christians. In consequence of the destruction of the Jewish community in Vilna in 1655 by the Cossack marauders, the number of Jews under the municipality in 1662 was only 415. But towards the end of the seventeenth century their number was equal to what it had been before the Cossack invasion. An inquiry by the Kahal in 1690 showed that there were 227 Jewish families

---

[1] So called after the Gaon Elijah.

under the jurisdiction of the municipality. According to the Polish historian Kraszewski, the plague of 1708–10 carried off 30,000 Christians and 4,000 Jews, but these figures are probably an exaggeration. The number of Jewish victims must in any case have been large, as in 1765 the total Jewish population in Vilna was only 3,399, to which may be added the Jews in two suburbs — 150 in Shnipishok and 338 in Antokol. The Vilna community had by now become the largest in Lithuania, those in Brest or Grodno, in Pinsk or Minsk, being less than half its number. There was a further appreciable increase soon after the Russian annexation, for in 1800 the number of Jews in Vilna and its two suburbs was almost 7,000.

A census taken by the Kahal in 1784 throws an instructive light upon the vocational activities of the Jews, as it reveals the multiplicity of callings in which they were engaged. They were represented in no fewer than forty occupations. Not only were they tailors and cobblers, bakers and butchers, doctors and teachers, writers and musicians, shop-keepers and pedlars, but they were also employed in a variety of crafts indicating that they formed a self-sufficient economic organism. For they had their own masons and plasterers, glaziers and turners, tinsmiths and coppersmiths, jewelers and goldsmiths, fishermen and brewers, as well as their own drivers, night watchmen, water-carriers and chimney-sweeps. Certain manual crafts enjoyed particular favor, for there were then 135 tailors, 88 furriers, and 59 jewelers. The total number of artisans formed about fifty per cent of all those gainfully employed — sufficient testimony to the fact that they were not abnormally engaged in intellectual pursuits or as middlemen.

An insight into another aspect of the social conditions of the community is afforded by the census taken by the Russian authorities in 1800. The Mishna (Abot 5.24) prescribed eighteen as the normal age for marriage, but this was very frequently anticipated by the Jews in mediaeval times, particularly in Central and Eastern Europe. The Vilna census of 1800 showed that among 1,508 married persons there were fifty-nine Jews and eighty Jewesses of the age of 16 or less. Among the boys, seven were 14, five were 13, and one was only 12, while the girls included twelve who were 14, seven who were 13, and four who were 12. The record belonged to a married boy in the suburb of Antokoli, who was only 10. These early marriages were due to a combination of moral, material, and even mystical motives. They were prompted by considerations of chastity, upon which the utmost emphasis has always been placed in Jewish life since Bible times; by the desire to effect a marriage as soon as a dowry was available, for it might soon disappear in the prevailing turbulence; and by the belief that the Messianic era, which was so ardently longed for in periods of persecution, could not dawn until all the souls created by God had been joined to their destined mates. These child couples remained in the homes of their parents, generally in that of the girl's, until the juvenile husband, who continued his talmudic studies, reached manhood and was able to found a home of his own. There was also a professional reason for early marriage in the case of a boy who wished to become a cantor, for no bachelor was allowed to assume that sacred office.[1]

2. THE SYNAGOGUE COURTYARD

The heart of the Jewish quarter, from the time when the community first began to assume organic form in the fifteenth century until the present day, was the *Schulhof* or synagogue courtyard. It derives its name from the Great Synagogue, which was the most important of the many buildings and institutions that clustered thickly around this quaint cloistral enclosure. It was shaped like the letter L reversed, and could be approached from the Zydowska through a huge iron gate, flanked by lamps on two stone pillars, or through a short alley from the Niemiecka. It was entirely surrounded by houses of prayer and study of varied size and different degrees of antiquity, and embodied within its limited ambit more of the memories and legends, and of the aspirations and sufferings of Vilna Jewry over a period of five hundred years than any equivalent piece of earth in any other Jewish community in Europe. During the greater part of this period the *Schulhof* was the focus of all the manifold

---

[1] The famous cantor, Joel David Loewenstein (1817–1850), was called "the Vilna *Balhabessel*" ("little householder"), because he married at the age of fourteen in order to obtain his diploma for *Hazzanut* (synagogue music). See also p. 437 ff.

activities of the community — religious, administrative, judicial, intellectual and social — and even
in more recent times it continued to dominate its
religious and cutural life.

Here were formerly situated those institutions so
vital to conformity with ritual tradition — the
slaughter-house and the baths, which have long ago
been removed to more suitable locations. Here were
the offices of the Kahal, from where all the affairs
of the community were administered, and also the
courthouse of the *Bet Din*, where the judges deliberated upon the many vexing questions submitted
to their wisdom and authority. Here too, as is
recorded on a wall, was situated the well from which
the Jews of the whole adjacent area used to obtain
their water. For, although the municipality was
obliged to provide them with water as one of the
services for which they paid an annual tax, the Jews
were nevertheless obliged to procure their own
supply from the neighboring Vingari wells by special
agreement, made in 1759, with the Dominican
monks, whom they paid 200 gulden a year. These
monks, who had acquired the wells from Lithuanian
magnates, allowed the Jews to convey the water
by means of wooden pipes to the synagogue courtyard, but to no other place. Thirty years later
another agreement was made with them for an
additional supply of water through a special pipe
to the communal baths.

The *Schulhof* was thus the busiest place in the
ghetto. It was frequented not only by those who
had some particular business to transact, but also

by those in quest of the latest news or gossip. Here rabbis and scholars, romancers and poets, philosophers and ghetto politicians, would perambulate for an airing, for friendly discussion, or for solemn reflection; and here merchants, returned from an adventurous journey to Muscovy or Prussia, would eagerly relate what was happening in the outside world. It was, moreover, the object of pilgrimage of all, however mighty, who came from other lands and had heard of the *Schulhof's* fame. Napoleon thrilled the Jewish throng when, during his brief halt in Vilna in 1812, he bestrode the secluded courtyard in wonderment. Thirty-four years later, the famous philanthropist, Sir Moses Montefiore, aroused feelings of less awe but deeper veneration when he was conducted around by a galaxy of grey-bearded rabbis and savants.

The Great Synagogue, which occupies the major part of the horizontal line of the reversed L, the side of the courtyard nearest to the Zydowska, is far more impressive within than without. It was built in 1573, and, as its construction was subject to the law forbidding it to tower above the neighboring buildings, its foundations had to be dug deep so as to give it a distinguished altitude within. One has, therefore, to descend some steps to enter it. There are two portals near to one another: the door on the right, which is covered with iron, bears a Hebrew inscription: "Gift to the Lord from the Holy Society of Psalm-Sayers, 1642;" while on the left is an iron gate which, according to a memorial tablet on the wall, was presented by the Tailors'

Society in 1640. These entrances lead to the vestibule, where, until modern times, stood the pillory to which a sinner was bound, to be scoffed and spat at by all who passed by. Apart from the façade, the only part of the exterior that can be seen is the upper portion of the eastern wall, along which, not far from the roof, runs a gallery of simple design, which was added at the beginning of the nineteenth century. Beneath this are iron shutters protecting the lofty windows.

Legend hath it that when Napoleon, who was so impressed by the Jewish aspect of Vilna that he exclaimed: "This is the Jerusalem of Lithuania!" stood on the threshold of this temple and gazed at the interior, he was speechless with admiration. It has the overwhelming grandeur of an edifice in the style of the Italian Renaissance and an awe-inspiring atmosphere. Four massive, equidistant columns support the vast stone-floored pile, and within them is the ornate, rococo *Almemar*, with a beautiful cupola, which was built in the second half of the eighteenth century by Rabbi Judah ben Eliezer, the famous scribe and judge (*Sofer ve-Dayyan*), commonly known as *YeSoD*.[1] The Ark, with doors of iron, is also of very handsome design. It was restored — according to an inscription below it — by the Society *Bedek Habayit* (public works department of the Kahal) — presumably after one of the many fires in the middle of the eighteenth century. Above the Ark is a large tablet with the

[1] From the initials of the three words *Yehudah Sofer ve-Dayyan*.

Commandments supported by the conventional lion and unicorn, also a gift of *YeSoD*. The Ark is approached by a twofold flight of steps, with iron balustrades, ascending from the right and the left, and in the angle thus formed by the balustrades which meet, below the Ark, and standing on the floor, is the cantor's reading desk, its lowly position thus symbolizing the words of the Psalmist: "From the depths do I call unto Thee." Formerly there was an imposing seven-branched brass candelabrum in front of the Ark, but on the eve of the German invasion of the city during the Great War of 1914–18, it was sent off to Moscow in order to save it from destruction, only to fall "out of the frying-pan into the fire." Once there was also a "Chair of Elijah," on which the rite of circumcision was performed, in the northwest corner; but that too has gone. There is no gallery for women, but at the end of the eighteenth century a section for them was added, along the north side, consisting of two floors, and divided off from the main building by a wall with deep embrasured windows (though the ground floor is used by the men in winter as it is warmed by stoves, which could not be installed in any other part). The women's annex was built by Noah ben Feibusch Bloch, a Kahal elder, who advanced the money for the purpose, and, when the Kahal was unable to return the 14,000 gulden due, he made a present of the structure.

Perhaps the most curious feature of this venerable synagogue is a stone slab placed upright immediately on the left of the Ark. It marks the place of the

The Great Synagogue

Interior of the Great Synagogue

seat which was once occupied by the head of the *Bet Din* and serves as the memorial of an undignified dispute. For when the last occupant of that exalted office, Rabbi Samuel ben Avigdor, was deposed in 1785 owing to a bitter quarrel with the elders of the Kahal, the latter decided to abolish the office, removed his seat of honor, and replaced it with a warning tablet.[1] Hence all succeeding spiritual heads were unable to sit quite close to the Ark, but occupied seats in its vicinity.

The synagogue was designed on a substantial and massive scale, for it was also intended to serve as a stronghold within which the Jews could take refuge in time of danger. Here they not only sought shelter from any threatened attack, but also hid their money and miscellaneous valuables. But the edifice was not impenetrable, for, in 1635, after it had been enlarged, some hooligans contrived to break into it and committed assault and robbery. Many precious articles of ritual use were carried off in that and later attacks. The synagogue still treasures two fine crowns for the Torah — one presented in 1760 by the jewelers' guild, and the other in 1750 by the society *Shomerim la-Boker* (early worshippers). Over the vestibule were formerly located the offices and council chamber of the Kahal, and in an attic was a prison cell (*Arrest-Stibel*) for any delinquent deserving such punishment.

The oldest shrine in the *Schulhof* is the *Bet ha-Midrash* (House of Study) on the left of the Great

[1] See Supplementary Note 6.

Synagogue. It is commonly called "the Old Klaus." This term, which is derived from the mediaeval Latin *clusa* or cloister, was applied to a room or a house primarily used for the study of rabbinic literature and also served as a house of prayer.[1] These *Klausen* were a characteristic feature of Jewish life in Eastern and Central Europe. Their membership was generally based upon some common interest — social, religious, or economic — and in Vilna alone they were developed to such an extent that there are now over a hundred, most of them connected with various trades. An inscription over the door of the Old Klaus claims that it was founded as far back as 1440, and although there is no historic evidence of this date, its general character indicates a greater antiquity than the neighboring synagogue. Its interior is divided into two by a row of pillars, and its Ark has copper doors embellished with simple designs. On the right of the Great Synagogue is the communal library, commonly known as the Strashun Library, which, as it is a modern institution, will be more appropriately described in a later chapter dealing with contemporary conditions.

In the middle of the eighteenth century the philanthropist *YeSoD* (Rabbi Judah ben Eliezer) decided to create a permanent memorial to himself in the form of a *Bet ha-Midrash*, since there was no dearth of synagogues. The wardens of the Old Klaus were afraid that a new one would overshadow it. The *YeSoD*, therefore, agreed that a

[1] See Supplementary Note 5.

door should be made in the wall of the existing Klaus to lead into the New Klaus which was built beside it, in order that the students of the one could pass into the other. The New Klaus which had also an entrance of its own and was built in 1755–57. Its founder furnished it with generous equipment — a library of rabbinic lore; a Scroll of the Torah written with meticulous care, without flaw or blemish, by Rabbi Issar, who received 80 thaler for three years' labor; a crown and plaques for the Scroll; different curtains for the Ark for Sabbath and weekdays, and different covers for the *Almemar*; and a twelve-branched *Menorah* (candelabrum). He had set aside a fund of 1,000 gulden in 1749, the interest from which was devoted to the purchase of books for the Old Klaus. Since he now wished to transfer these books to the new establishment, while allowing the students of the old one to continue using them, the wardens of the latter objected. Agreement was soon reached on this matter, however, as well as on the question of conducting public worship. For the New Klaus proved so attractive that, in order to prevent the decline of the earlier one, it was arranged that religious services should be held in the new one only on the New Year and the Day of Atonement. The elders of the Kahal persisted in their demand for the formal amalgamation of the two institutions in respect of management and finance, and this union was proclaimed at an impressive gathering attended by wardens of both and by the president of the *Bet Din*. But the union did not continue long. In 1760 the wardens of the

Old Klaus allowed *YeSoD* to make two small windows in the north wall of the New Klaus for a period
of forty years. In pursuance of his desire to perpet-
uate his memory, the pious benefactor stipulated
that for twelve months after his death all the students in the Klaus should say the rabbinical *Kaddish*
(sanctification) for the repose of his soul, and that
they should continue to offer up prayers for his
memory on every anniversary of his death. As some
recompense for their devotion he gave the Klaus a
written promise that his heirs would provide 12 gulden a week for the students during the first year after
his death so that they might study in both Klausen
night and day without interruption. The wish of
YeSoD has been realized far beyond his anticipation,
for prayers for the repose of his soul continued to be
said on every Jewish festival to the present day.

The most sacred of all the shrines is the synagogue
on the site on which the great rabbinical luminary,
the Gaon Elijah,[1] once lived. It is the first building
on the left as one enters the courtyard from the
Zydowska, and it was erected by the Kahal in 1800
as a memorial to the sage whose fame, more than
of any other Jew born in Vilna, has conferred such
luster upon the city. Outwardly its only distinguishing characteristic is a gabled porch, but within
it is rich with individual features and pious associations. On the southern wall is a wooden tablet with

---

[1] The title of "Gaon," which means "Eminence," was first
given to the heads of the talmudical academies in Babylon after
the sixth century, and was afterwards applied to great rabbis
most distinguished for their learning.

an inscription in memory of the Gaon, extolling
his wisdom, his rabbinical erudition, his worldly
knowledge, and his spiritual grandeur; below the
tablet is a large chest to prevent any person from
sitting in that holy place. On another wall, within
a large frame, are a number of clock-faces, with
hands pointing to the times at which different
prayers are said on weekdays and Sabbaths; and
nearby are sixteen charity boxes arranged in four
rows, each labelled with its special purpose, so that
the benevolent can choose among supporting the
poor, providing bridal dowries, repairing the synagogue, keeping the Scrolls of the Torah in good
condition, and other laudable objects. On a third
wall is a printed calendar in Hebrew, indicating the
dates of the major and minor fasts and all the festivals, with a special prayer appropriate to each
occasion. There is a large table covered with lead,
on which candles for *Jahrzeit*,[1] without candlesticks,
burn to the end; and at another table are always
men absorbed in the study of the Talmud. Ten
pious scholars who have separated themselves from
their wives and families in order to achieve perfect
concentration, are always engaged here in the study
of sacred lore, to the greater glory of the immortal
sage. Whenever there is a vacancy in their ranks
it is immediately filled.

My visit to this shrine, a few years ago, was something of a distraction to these devotees. They
wished to know whence I came, how their brethren

---

[1] Death anniversary.

fared in other lands, and, above all, how they could get to the Land of Israel. One of them, thinner and more saint-like than the rest, led me up a small staircase to an attic, where, at a plain deal table, with a couple of candles, the Gaon was reputed to have studied and reflected in solitude.

"How can this be," I asked, "if this synagogue was not built until three years after the Gaon had passed away?"

"People here believe it," he replied, with calm assurance, "and you must not analyze their faith too closely."

Near the Gaon's synagogue is the Klaus of the *Kabronim*, or grave-diggers, the house of prayer and study built by the members of the society *Hebra Kaddisha*, who devoted themselves to the pious task of caring for the dying and the dead. It is a three-storied structure, with cellars, erected in 1747–8 with the aid of a loan furnished by the wealthy Rabbi Elijah Pesseles. It has a women's section which was added twenty years later. A neighboring little bethel is known as that of the "Seven Called," so named because of its strict rule that not more than seven persons shall be called up to the reading of the Law on the Sabbath — a regulation implying a protest against the practice in some synagogues of adding to the number called up in order to increase the income from offerings. It was in this building that the *Bet Din* held its sessions for a long period.

Opposite these shrines, which occupy the left side of the perpendicular of the reversed L, are various *Klausen* and *Hedarim* (Hebrew schools). On the other side some covered passages lead from the *Schulhof* to an extension called the *Durchhof*. The latter is also bordered by all sorts of *Klausen*. One belongs to workmen and occupies the site on which the Gaon Elijah's tabernacle once stood. Another is the home of the Hasidim; and a third is the meeting place of the painters, one of whom has decorated a wall with some Jewish scenes. On the buttresses of the passages are fixed clock-faces which serve an important religious purpose, for they are adorned with the Hebrew admonition: "Remember the Sabbath day to keep it holy," and indicate the times when the Sabbath begins, when the shops have to be closed, when the candles have to be lit, and when the Sabbath is ushered out. Beneath these clocks are framed notice-boards containing various kinds of announcements, mostly of a religious or semi-religious character, while on the neighboring walls of the numerous prayer-houses all around there are also little Hebrew posters conveying messages of import, mainly in regard to matters of ritual, to the denizens of this quarter. During the first World War the *Schulhof* was the principal news exchange. Here the multitudinous communiqués of the German Military Command were displayed, and here one always learned of the latest deaths, for necrologies in terms of the most lavish praise were immediately posted up for the information of the public.

CHAPTER VII

COMMUNAL ADMINISTRATION AND ORGANIZATION

THE Jewish community of Vilna, like all other Jewish communities in Lithuania and Poland, enjoyed a considerable measure of autonomy during the greater part of the existence of the first Polish State. Its sphere of competence was very comprehensive, embracing both the religious and the secular interests of the whole Jewish population. The liberty to control its own affairs corresponded to that which the German settlers possessed in the form of the Magdeburg Law, and thus did not constitute an exceptional privilege. Indeed, the Government, in allowing this arrangement, was clearly prompted less by feelings of generosity than by considerations of convenience and self-interest, for such a system greatly simplified its own task of administration and facilitated the collection of the taxes payable to its coffers. It was the duty of the community to collect from its own members the annual tax imposed upon it by the *Seym* and to hand this over to the Treasury, and it was not until the *Seym* realized in 1764 that it could obtain a much larger income by levying a poll-tax upon every Jew, irrespective of age and sex, instead of a collective tribute from the community, that the latter's powers were seriously reduced. The function of tax-gatherer, however, was only one of the many services discharged by the administrative apparatus of the community. For this was an elaborate and authoritative organization, conducted in accordance with its own accepted laws and regulations.

The government of the community lay in the hands of a body called the Kahal, which means "community." The Kahal had authority over all matters relating to religious observance and education, the relief of the poor, the healing of the sick, and the care of the orphans and the aged. It looked after the public health of the community, attended to the water supply and the cleaning of the streets, and upheld public order. It granted the right of domicile in the city, as well as the right to buy property and to engage in work. It imposed and collected taxes for the State and the municipality, for the maintenance of its own administration, and for such special or extraordinary purposes as ransoming Jewish prisoners of war, supporting refugees, or defraying the expenses of a *Shtadlan* (advocate), who went to the king, the *Seym*, or a court of law, to plead the cause of his people. The Kahal was the only body that represented the Jews in relations with the Government. It had its own court of law, the *Bet Din*, for the settlement of civil disputes as well as religious questions. Any Jew who defied its authority could be disciplined by means of the *Ḥerem*, or ban of excommunication, or, if the occasion called for it, he might be arrested by a soldier or other armed agent of the Government. The Kahal even had a jail of its own, and likewise a pillory, to which a delinquent was tied with cords and exposed to the public gaze and public shame.

The executive authority of the Kahal was vested in a board of thirteen members, as follows: (a) four *Roshe ha-Kahal*, or elders of the community, (b) two *Roshe Medinah*, or state elders, (c) four *Tuvé* (i. e., *Tové*) *ha-Kahal, viri boni*, honorary members; and (d) three *'Ikkure ha-Kahal*, active members. The *Roshe ha-Kahal* were *Parnassim* (*seniores*) or wardens, who held office in rotation for a month at a time (each thus being called *Parnas ha-Hodesh*: *senior mensis*). They exercised considerable power, especially in judicial matters, tax commissions, certifying Jewish tradesmen and artisans, fixing the communal budget, and authorizing payments and loans. The *Roshe Medinah* were the representatives of the Kahal in the *Va'ad* or Council of all the communities of the country, which met in periodical conference, and continued to be elected even after the Lithuanian *Va'ad* was officially abolished in 1764. In addition to these thirteen members there were also four auditors (whose business was to examine the Kahal's accounts), four almoners, four *Dayyanim* or judges, two *Ba'ale Takkanah* (drafters of regulations), and two *Shomre Takkanah*, whose function was to watch over the observance of the laws.

All these dignitaries and functionaries were elected from among and by members of a limited assembly called *Asefat ReHaSh*, which derived its name from the initials of the three principal functionaries of the synagogue whom it originally appointed, namely, the Rabbi, the *Hazzan* (cantor), and the *Shammash* (beadle). Membership in this assembly was open only to those who had been married at least six years, who held the honorary title of *morenu* or *haver* (a recognition of religious piety and scholarship), who were well-to-do, belonged to a family of good repute, and paid the stipulated fee. The Lithuanian *Va'ad* tried to restrict the number of the electoral assembly's members to 50, but in Vilna it consisted of 120 members in 1750, and of 196 in 1787. Five new members were admitted each year. The assembly met not less than once a quarter under the presidency of the *Roshe Asefah* (elders of the Assembly), and made decisions on important matters relating to the Kahal.

The candidates for office also were required to possess particular qualifications: they must have been married at least ten years and given a special contribution to the Kahal's treasury. According to a law of 1774, at least four of the thirteen members of the Kahal had to be men of means: two had to pay 200 gulden each and two 100 gulden each, while a minimum payment of 50 gulden was required in the case of an almoner. Family relationship played an important and rather unfortunate part in the composition of the Kahal, as father, son, and other relatives sometimes held office together and exercised a prejudicial influence. There were regulations to prevent the acceptance of office by the relatives of existing office-holders, as well as to prevent the election of relatives of the rabbi; but unfortunately these rules were sometimes violated, with the result

that there were unedifying struggles between certain
wealthy families to secure a controlling power in
the Kahal. Election to office was also based on a
system of "grades," a candidate being required to
fill a post of the lowest grade before he was eligible
for the next, the order of the hierarchy beginning
with the almoner or judge, and then rising through
the *'Ikkur ha-Kahal, Tuv ha-Kahal, Rosh Medinah*,
to the highest grade, *Rosh ha-Kahal*. Moreover,
office-holders had to pay fees, and since the Kahal,
owing to its frequent financial difficulties, was
obliged to make these fees a substantial source of
revenue, only rich men could aspire to office. The
Kahal sometimes obtained money in the guise of
a loan and promised repayment by giving the lender
either the status of a "grade" or a "ticket" entitling
him to membership of the *Asefat ReHaSh*, and the
lender was free to dispose of this "grade" or "ticket"
as he pleased.

The elections took place on the first of the intermediate days of Passover. The first stage of the
election was carried out immediately after the morning service, when the members of the Kahal, the
heads of the *Asefah*, the rabbi, the secretary, and
the beadles assembled in the Communal Council
chamber. Tickets bearing the names of the members
of the *Asefah* were put into an urn, from which five
were drawn by the beadles. The lucky five constituted the electors. They were at once brought
by two beadles to the Council chamber in order to
appoint the thirteen members of the Kahal as well
as four auditors, four almoners, and two presidents

of the *Asefah.* Before discharging their duty, the electors had to take an oath that they would faithfully comply with the regulations which prescribed whom they could choose for any particular honor, what degree of relationship to themselves would disqualify, and what offices the electors themselves could assume. They were, moreover, forbidden to re-elect the retiring *Roshe ha-Kahal* and the judges for a second year. Those who were elected had to be informed immediately by messengers, who had to wait for a reply: they were under a moral obligation to accept, but if they declined then the electors had to choose others in their places. Those who accepted office had to take an oath that they would work for the good of the community and that they would observe all its laws as well as those of the Council of the Kahal. The entire proceedings had to be completed before the end of the day. The four officers responsible for drafting laws and watching over their observance were elected before the new moon of Kislev (generally December).

The number of members of the Kahal who met to transact affairs varied according to their importance and urgency of the matter at hand. In the case of urgent business only the "Wardens of the Month" met; on more important occasions the thirteen members were supplemented by the four auditors and the two presidents of the *Asefah*; while in cases of grave emergency the entire membership of the *Asefah* was summoned.

The *Bet Din* (literally "House of Judgment") comprised twelve judges, who were elected every

year. This Jewish law-court was concerned with
all kinds of financial and business matters, as distinct
from the Kahal, which dealt with cases of breaches
of the peace. It legalized transfers of property and
registered contracts for the sale of goods, *Hazakot*
(rights of priority), seats in the synagogue, promissory notes, and similar documents. It kept watch
over weights and measures, and exercised a check
on the raising of prices. Until some time after the
middle of the eighteenth century it also dealt every
Friday with cases relating to religious matters.
Both the Kahal and the *Bet Din* did their utmost
to prevent Jewish litigants from going to a Christian
court, and if any Jew resorted to such a court without
the permission of the Kahal he was liable to excommunication and other penalties. Nevertheless, Jews
frequently did apply to Christian courts. There
was no need for them to do so for the registration
of their property, as this could be carried out by
the *Bet Din* in its own minute-book (*Pinkas*) with
equal validity, though there were instances in which
transactions were registered with both. In the case
of a purchase from a Christian, however, registration had to be made with a Christian court, and
there were even instances in which Hebrew documents were registered with a Christian court in
their original language.

The judges were divided into two groups, called
the Higher *Bet Din* and the Lower *Bet Din*, although
in important cases they sat in joint session. The
president of the entire *Bet Din* was the rabbi, who
was called *Ab Bet Din* ("Father of the House of

Judgment"). The senior group chose the *Rosh Bet Din*, who sometimes acted in the place of the rabbi. The decisions of the court were recorded in its *Pinkas* by one of its members, who bore the dual title of *Safra ve-Dayyana*, the Aramaic form of *Sofer ve-Dayyan* (Secretary and Judge), and who was also secretary of the Kahal. Although new judges were elected every year, the *Asefat ReHaSh* could also appoint judges for life or for definite periods. In 1745, for example, Rabbi Samuel ben Avigdor received an appointment for life. The judges were not given a fixed salary but divided among themselves and the *Ab Bet Din* the fees paid by the two litigant parties. In suits between Jews and Christians, if the plaintiff was a Christian, then the judge was the Vice-*Voivode* or a deputy of his, but if the plaintiff was a Jew, then he appealed to the particular court to which the defendant was answerable.

Other functionaries of the *Bet Din* were the beadles, who acted as messengers and in kindred capacities. Every month they chose by ballot a "secret informer" (*Rodef Ne'elam*), who took an oath that he would not act against anybody contrary to the law. This official, whose identity had to be kept an absolute secret, was regularly consulted by the beadles in regard to any person who failed to comply with the judgment of the court.

The Kahal, like any well-organized town council, comprised a number of departments, each of which was charged with some particular service, such as poor relief, public works, education, public health, and burials. The department concerned with poor

relief, which was called *Zedakah Gedolah* ("Great
Charity"), was directed by the wardens of the Great
Synagogue, which was the center of social life. It
distributed alms to the local poor every week and
also assisted poor persons from other towns, for
whom it provided carts to enable them to continue
their journey. It supplied flour for Passover, paid
for wet-nurses for orphan infants, furnished shrouds
for the poor who died, and helped householders in
reduced circumstances. Its income was derived
from the Great Synagogue and from other synagogues, *Bate Midrashim* (houses of study) and
Minyanim (groups for prayer). It received two-
thirds of the burial fees (in return for which it
covered two-thirds of the cost of the upkeep of the
cemetery), the other third going to the *Hebra Kaddisha*, the charitable society which looked after the
dying and the dead. It also received miscellaneous
contributions, such as a tax on the grinding of flour
for Passover, a tax of two gulden on every *etrog*
(citron) bought for the Feast of Tabernacles, and
a regular subsidy from the slaughter-house. When
the Kahal was abolished by the Russian Government in 1844, and the remnants of its autonomy
were entrusted to the wardens of the Great Synagogue, the *Zedakah Gedolah* took the place of the
Kahal.

The department called *Bedek ha-Bayit* ("House
Repairs") attended to the upkeep of the Great
Synagogue and other communal property, to the
cleanliness of the synagogue courtyard and the
Jewish quarter, and to the water-pipes, canals and

baths. It was directed by four wardens appointed by the Kahal for three years, who needed the approval of the heads of the Kahal for any important action that they took. It paid the Dominican Friars 200 gulden a year for permission to convey water from the Vingari wells to the synagogue courtyard, from where water was drawn not only by those who dwelt in the immediate vicinity but also by the tenants of houses farther off who did not have a well in their own courtyard. The baths under its control formed a sort of monopoly, as the opening of any other bath was forbidden; women were not allowed to bathe in the river and had to use the communal *Mikvah* (ritual bath). The charge payable to the Dominican Friars was covered by a water rate paid by the local consumers, a list of whom in the eighteenth century contains the name of the Gaon Elijah. Rates were also paid by the Jews living near the synagogue courtyard or in the Jewish streets for the removal of refuse.

The repair department was authorized to demand an annual tax from every householder, merchant, and artisan, who were assessed according to their annual contributions to the Kahal. A tax was also payable by the various Jewish artisans' guilds. From 1752 it was entitled to demand a contribution in respect of every wedding and circumcision in the community, and also from every dowry, and even in the case of a girl marrying a Jew from some other city the money had to be paid before she left Vilna. Beginning with the same year it also received, for a period of years, a certain amount from all properties belonging to the Kahal, equivalent to one per cent of the annual rent, and a larger sum from rentals exceeding 2,000 gulden a year. In connection with its duty to look after the structure of the Great Synagogue and its extension, the *Bedek ha-Bayit*, in cooperation with the *Zedakah Gedolah*, built a two-story synagogue for women in 1797. It also provided a new Ark for the Great Synagogue, and attended to the repair of the roof, from which accumulations of snow had to be removed whenever necessary.

The important task of caring for the dying, burying the dead, and looking after the cemetery was discharged by a body called the *Hebra Kaddisha* (Holy Society), which did not form a department of the Kahal but a separate and independent society. It had its own board of management, constitution, sources of income, and synagogue. The *Hebra Kaddisha* was usually the first society to be created in a community and sometimes even preceded the formal establishment of the community itself. There is a tradition, though no convincing evidence, that the old Jewish cemetery in Vilna dates back to 1487; but if we assume — which is more probable — that the cemetery was acquired at the end of the sixteenth century, then the *Hebra Kaddisha* must already have been in existence, as it was necessary to convey the bodies of the early Jewish settlers in Vilna to the neighboring town of Troki for burial. Its earliest extant *Pinkas*, or minute-book, dating from 1747 (an older one having been destroyed by fire), contains by-laws from 1670 and a record of unnatural deaths in Vilna which occurred between

1595 and 1665. It also includes a list of such deaths in Prague and other places, which had probably been brought by some Jews who had migrated from the Bohemian city.

It was considered a matter of religious merit to belong to the *Hebra Kaddisha*, and its membership included leading personalities in the community, such as elders, scholars, and doctors. In the middle of the eighteenth century it had 260 members (including the Gaon Elijah) and also over one hundred beadles, who were mostly artisans. Every new member had to pay an entrance fee, have his name registered in the minute-book, be "called up" to the reading of the Law, and give a feast to all the members of the society. During the first two years he had to take part in the burial rites, and it was not until some time later that he was entitled to vote in the election of officers or himself be a candidate for office. The executive board consisted of eight members — four *Gabbaim* (Wardens), two auditors, and two ordinary members, who were elected annually on the second of the intermediate days of Passover, that is, on the day after the election of the Kahal. The election was carried out by taking slips bearing names out of an urn, and nobody could be a *Gabbai* for more than two consecutive years. Every three years there was also an election of seven *Ba'ale Takkanot* (draftsmen of by-laws). Other officials of the society were a *Maggid* (preacher), who delivered the funeral discourses, and a secretary. The latter had to be a talmudical scholar, since his duties consisted not only in keeping the minute-

book and the accounts, but also in composing inscriptions for tombstones and giving addresses at
the feasts of the beadles, which were held twice a
year — on the Sabbath after Passover and on that
after Tabernacles. From 1772 the society also had
two *Dayyanim* who, in conjunction with the secretary, decided on all religious and ritual questions.
From 1781 the *Maggid* acted as one of these judges,
and in important cases the head of the *Bet Din* was
invited to assist in their deliberations.

In the eighteenth century the society was divided
into the three following sections: (1) the general
body of members, who formed the "Major *Hebra
Kaddisha*," (2) the beadles, who formed the "Minor
Hebra Kaddisha," and (3) the "pious women," who
attended to the bodies of their own sex. The beadles
had to pay an entrance fee like other members;
some were appointed permanently and others only
for limited periods; and they had their own secretary and minute-book. Their work consisted in
digging the graves and performing any other task
that might be allotted to them. They discharged
their duties gratuitously, but it is believed that they
received fees from the mourners, which they put into
a common fund for charitable purposes.

The members of the society always assembled
for religious worship in a place of their own. In 1741
they bought a site from the Kahal in the synagogue
courtyard and built a synagogue on it; but four
years later they were obliged to lease it to a group
of ten men in order to redeem a pledge from a Christian moneylender. The income of the *Hebra Kad-*

disha was derived from various sources: the weekly
subscriptions of members, entrance fees of new members, burial fees (two-thirds of which went to the
"Great Charity"), the sale of plots, and special
charges for reservations. But its expenditure —
particularly on the upkeep of the cemetery and of
the road leading to it, as well as on the feasts of
members — was generally in excess of its income,
so that it had to admit many new members and
also resort to the sale of honors. It was in 1750 that
the society first attempted to replenish its coffers
by selling positions on its executive board to wealthy
aspirants. The practice was at first sternly resisted
by the *Ba'ale Takkanot*, but in 1780 they allowed
it so that the debts of the society might be repaid.
Four years later, however, the debts had increased
to over 11,700 gulden, and the sale of honors in the
endeavor to extinguish the debts resulted in an
unfortunate decline in both the position and the
prestige of the society.

In order to stimulate the enthusiasm of the members and beadles a big feast was arranged for them
every year on the 15th of Kislev (December). On
that day they all wore their Sabbath best, and they
fasted and prayed together in the Great Synagogue,
as their own place of worship was too small to contain them all. After the morning service ten members and ten beadles, together with the *Maggid*, went
to the cemetery, where they offered up special supplications. In the evening, after the fast was over,
there was a lavish feast, to which the president of
the *Bet Din* was invited and at which the *Maggid*

delivered a talmudical discourse. The guests all
sang a special hymn composed by Rabbi Mordecai
ben Moses, who became a member in 1770. This
hymn, full of moral exhortations and reflections on
the frailty of life, was composed in the form of an
alphabetical acrostic, each letter beginning three
lines in Hebrew, followed by three in Yiddish.
Its tenor may be gathered from the following typical
strophes:

> O man, in vain hast thou thy follies sown,
> For God on high the world doth judge
>   alone,
> Where neither tears nor prayers can e'er
>   atone.
>
> With food and drink and lusts thyself dost
>   sate,
> And with thy tongue dost arrogantly prate,
> But deep below the earth will be thy fate.

The beadles had two big feasts of their own — one
on the Sabbath after Passover and the other on that
after Tabernacles. The "Great Charity" used to
provide money for the beadles' feasts, and when they
ceased to be held regularly the beadles began to
neglect their duties. Special feasts were also held
for the executive board of eight and a small number
of guests. But when the society's indebtedness became so large at the end of the eighteenth century,
these junketings had perforce to cease, and as time
went on the *Hebra Kaddisha* lost a great deal of its
importance.

The religious education of the young, especially

of the orphan and poor children, was looked after by the *Hebra Talmud Torah* (Society for Teaching Torah), which developed from what was originally a department of the Kahal. This society is believed to date from the year 1691. It engaged teachers, maintained a school in which the children were also fed and clothed, and supervised all the teachers in the city. The children were taught all subjects from the Hebrew alphabet to the Mishna, provided with books, and taken by young ushers (*Behelfer*) to pray in the synagogue. At the beginning of the nineteenth century a matron was engaged to look after the feeding of the boys, to repair their clothes, and to comb their hair. On the Sabbath there was usually a recapitulation of the lessons, and at the end of the year there was an examination. The *Talmud Torah* Society was conducted by a board of eight members and two wardens who took part in the annual examination. Its income was derived from the subscriptions of members, special donations and bequests, and contributions from teachers who had their own private Hebrew schools (*Hedarim*), amounting to about 6 per cent of their own income.

The task of looking after the poor sick people was entrusted by the Kahal to a society called *Bikkur Holim* ("Visiting the Sick"). This society maintained a hospital, called a *Hekdesh*, in which also infirm and unemployable people were lodged. There was a communal doctor who received a salary, and doctors were sent to visit the sick in their homes and give them medicine. The first hospital was

probably founded early in the eighteenth century;
in 1765 it contained eighteen patients and three
paupers. When the Russians took Vilna in 1794,
they ordered the hospital to be removed from the
center of the city, as they were afraid that it might
become the source of an outbreak of plague. The
committee of the society — a board of eight, with
two wardens — thereupon bought two plots of land
and a house some distance away, and built a large
hospital which is still in existence. The society was
supported by means of members' subscriptions,
grants from the Kahal and special gifts and bequests.

The Jews of Vilna were fortunate in possessing
many doctors. There were two families, Gordon
and Polonus, that were particularly famous for the
number of doctors they provided in the course of
some generations. The medical practitioners received licenses to carry on their profession in the
community and also letters of protection from the
bishop and the *Voivode*. In 1761, for instance,
a Dr. Gordon received from the Vilna bishop,
Sinkiewicz, a permit to heal both the Jewish and
Christian sick, and the bishop ordered the Kahal
not to appoint any fresh doctors.

The community was organized not only for religious purposes, education, and social welfare, but
also for economic affairs. The Jewish artisans were
exposed to such bitter hostility and even persecution
on the part of the Christian guilds that they created
guilds of their own for the purpose of self-defense.
There was only one Christian guild, that of the
barbers, which admitted Jewish members, who were

limited to two; but from time to time the Jewish
guilds made agreements with the kindred Christian
body for the limitation of their respective membership. The earliest recorded date of a Jewish guild
is 1674, when the Jewelers' Guild presented a
beautifully embroidered girdle for the Day of Atonement to the president of the *Bet Din*, Rabbi Moses
ben David, better known as Rabbi Moses Kraemer.
The iron door of the Great Synagogue was presented
in 1640 by the tailors, who may have already been
organized as a body, but there is no such early record
of its existence. There is a reference to a Vintners'
Guild in 1686, and the Jewish Hat-Makers' Guild
made an agreement in 1741 with the corresponding
Christian Guild. From the second half of the eighteenth century there are many references to Jewish
guilds, although some of them doubtless already
existed earlier. In a record of income of the *Bedek
ha-Bayit* Society, dating from 1759, mention is made
of societies of tailors, furriers, jewelers, tinsmiths,
goldsmiths, as well as of glaziers and candlestick-
makers. Later there were also guilds of butchers
and musicians.

Each of these trade-guilds was, like the bodies
devoted to religious and social purposes, termed a
"Holy Society." Its members had to have six
years' training and work two years as artisans
before they were fully qualified. Every member had
to pay an entrance-fee, provide a feast for his fellow-
members, and give them another feast when he
married. For the first ten years after marriage the
artisan was considered a "junior," and was restricted

as regards the number of apprentices he could take
or the workmen he could employ; but after that
period he became a "senior," although this status
could be acquired sooner by special arrangement.
Members of a guild could usually secure concessions
for the benefit of sons and sons-in-law.

At the head of each guild were four wardens and
a committee of eight, who discharged various offices, such as inspectors and auditors. According to
the constitution of the Council of the Jewish Communities of Lithuania (*Va'ad Medinat Lita*), dated
1687, only two of the wardens could be elected from
the guild and the other two were appointed by the
local Kahal. The number of members in each guild
naturally varied according to the number of qualified craftsmen in the trade. They met together not
only to discuss their common economic interests,
but also for prayer; and in the course of time they
established separate houses of prayer either in a room
or in a complete house. Their place of assembly,
called a Klaus, was used not only for public worship
but also for the study of talmudic lore. For these
men of toil did not seek immunity from the traditional obligations and customs of their people by
advancing the convenient plea: *Laborare est orare*.
However much they worked, they could not pray
enough.

CHAPTER VIII

RELIGIOUS AND POLITICAL
LEADERSHIP

THE religious head of the community was the rabbi
or, as he was always called in Hebrew, the *Rav*.
He was invested with very great authority, not
only in purely ecclesiastical affairs, but also in
secular matters. He took part in all meetings of the
Kahal, no decision of any consequence was adopted
without his approval, and he signed all important
documents jointly with the elders. He was the
president of the *Bet Din* and invariably took part
in its sittings, especially when weighty cases were
involved. His opinion was regarded as equal to the
opinions of two other members of the *Bet Din*, so
that when the court was equally divided his view was
decisive. His authority was not confined to the
community in the city of Vilna, but extended also
to the congregations in its suburbs; and he took part,
together with the rabbis of other leading communities, in the sittings of the *Va'ad* (Council) of the
Communities of Lithuania. His religious influence,
apart from the example set by his private life, was
exercised through his direction of the *Yeshibah*
(talmudical academy), where future rabbis were
trained. But he preached only rarely. He delivered
two talmudical discourses a year: on the Sabbath
before Passover and on that before the Day of

Atonement. He was usually a famous scholar, for that was one of his qualifications for the office, and his written commendation was eagerly sought by the authors of Hebrew books on religious lore. He enjoyed various honors: he was called up third to the reading of the Torah (unless he was a *Kohen* or a *Levi*) on every Sabbath and festival; if he could sing passably he could chant the "additional service" on the first day of the New Year and the concluding service on the Day of Atonement; he received the choicest citron for the Feast of Tabernacles; he officiated at weddings; and he was much sought after as godfather at circumcision ceremonies.

The rabbi was appointed, not by the Kahal alone, but by the whole assembly of *ReHaSh* by secret vote, and after the declaration of the result all the members affixed their signatures, in four columns, to the "Writ of Rabbinate" (*Ketab Rabbanut*). This document, composed in a mixture of Hebrew and Aramaic, was often couched in terms of the most extravagant hyperbole, with a liberal sprinkling of euphuistic phrases from the Psalms or the Prophets, attributing to the new incumbent the highest degree of wisdom and knowledge and spiritual powers of the loftiest order. Apart from this document, an agreement was signed with the rabbi, which set forth in detail his duties and obligations as well as his privileges and prerogatives. His election had to be confirmed by the *Voivode*, whose sanction had to be paid for very liberally, while the other officials of the Governor's Court had also to be presented with gifts. There was a period when

a certain amount of largess was distributed among
the members of the elective assembly itself, but
that abuse was suppressed by the *Va'ad* of the
Lithuanian Communities.

The rabbi generally received a fixed salary, a
residence and a fee for his two annual discourses,
besides a number of perquisites, namely, for taking
part in court sessions, conferring rabbinical diplomas
(*Semiha*), signing bills of divorce and appointing
ritual slaughterers. When the Vilna community
got into financial difficulties a rabbi was appointed
who came to its help with a large "loan," the interest
on which was paid to him as salary, or on whose
behalf a substantial sum was given by wealthy
relatives. Thus Samuel ben Avigdor obtained the
office of rabbi in 1750 with the aid of his father-
in-law, *YeSoD*, the rich philanthropist, who gave
the Kahal a sum of 24,000 gulden, besides 1,000
gulden for the *Hebra Kaddisha*. Of the principal
sum a large amount had to be paid for the *Voivode's*
approval, and 2,000 gulden was divided among the
members of the elective assembly as "signature
money." Samuel ben Avigdor also lent the Kahal
6,000 gulden to wipe out some communal debts,
whereupon his salary was increased by 10 gulden
a week. A condition attaching to the loan was that
it be acknowledged only as long as the rabbi remained in office, but if he went to another community the Kahal was not obliged either to repay
the loan or to continue paying interest. Despite
the detailed agreement made between the Kahal
and the rabbi respecting his rights and functions,

he was generally tempted to try to increase his authority, with the result that the elders tried to limit it; and a corresponding struggle took place in the *Bet Din*, where the *Dayyanim* (judges) were bent upon reducing both his influence as well as his share in the legal fees payable by the litigants.

There was no uniformity in the terms of the contract with a rabbi; for the agreement with the famous scholar Baruch Rapoport in 1708, which was limited to three years, differed considerably from that with Samuel ben Avigdor, which was for life. In the case of the former, the duty of the rabbi to attend any meeting or function at the request of the elders, "immediately and without delay," was laid down in precise and stringent language, whereas the conditions in the case of the latter were mild and deferential. Samuel ben Avigdor, who was young and immature when he was appointed, was allowed to return to his father, the rabbi at Ruszany, for another two or three years to complete his studies, while his learned father-in-law acted in his place; and it was explicitly provided that meetings or the hearing of cases could be held in the house of either of them. The agreement with Rapoport, on the other hand, contained also some uncom- plimentary clauses, namely, that he had no right "to abstain from any judgment or affair whatsoever" or "to put his head" into any of the financial affairs of the Kahal, that his sons and sons-in-law should not hold any offices connected with the elective assembly as long as he was the rabbi, that he should not try to release himself from any of the conditions

to which he had subscribed, that he had no right
to sign any decision or document without the
approval of the elders of the Kahal, and that any
signature given without their knowledge was of
no account. These stipulations were due to the
jealous vigilance exercised by the Kahal over its
authority and to its fear that the rabbi might increase his power at its expense. Such strict relations
were bound to lead to trouble, and, indeed, did so.
The first occasion for friction was in the case of
Rabbi Joshua Heschel Katzenellenbogen, who succeeded Rabbi Rapoport in 1712. As a result of a
dispute, the Kahal wanted to remove him and replace him by somebody else, but he succeeded in
obtaining a letter of protection from the king. A
far more serious controversy, however, and one that
had the most damaging consequences for the rabbinate, the Kahal and the community in general, broke
out after Samuel ben Avigdor had occupied the
position of spiritual leader for over twenty-five years.

What the real origin of the quarrel was that led
to the deposition of the rabbi, who had been appointed in such flattering terms and under such
favorable conditions, was long veiled in a certain
amount of mystery about which historians were not
agreed. Samuel Joseph Finn, the author of the pioneer history of the Vilna community[1] (whose version
is unquestioningly accepted by Schechter[2]), states
that the only specific charges brought against Rabbi

---

[1] *Kiryah Ne'emanah*, Vilna, 1915, pp. 138–143.
[2] *Studies in Judaism*, I, Philadelphia, 1915, p. 83.

Samuel ben Avigdor were that he was insufficiently
diligent in his studies, that there were nights when no
light could be seen from his dwelling after midnight,
and — a supplementary source of offense — that his
second wife did not show sufficient deference to the
wives of the elders. Finn also attributes the trouble
to the clash of personalities and temperaments and
the eruption of prejudices that had long been seething. According to Dubnow,[1] however, more serious
charges were levelled against the rabbi by his opponents, namely, corruption, drunkenness, miscarriage
of justice and perjury. The matter was first dealt
with by a board of arbitrators and then discussed
at a conference of Lithuanian rabbis. As the excite-
ment and dissensions in the community grew, the
partisans of both rabbi and Kahal agreed to defer
to the judgment of the *Voivode* Radziwill, who pronounced in favor of the Kahal. The elders took a
Scroll of the Torah out of the Ark, examined it
several times to ensure that it was flawless, and then
swore by it in their Council chamber that their decision to depose their rabbi was prompted solely by
considerations "for the sake of Heaven." Thereupon
three beadles were sent to the rabbi's house to convey
the tragic message. There they took off their shoes,
seated themselves on the ground four cubits away

---

[1] *Weltgeschichte des juedischen Volkes*, Berlin, 1928, vol. VIII,
p. 43. Dubnow gives the year of the deposition as 1785, but Finn
and other local historians give the Hebrew date as 5538, i. e.,
1777–78. Since Samuel ben Avigdor countersigned the Vilna
ban against the Hasidim in 1781, the former must be correct.
See Supplementary Note 6.

from the unhappy man, and remained silent. The rabbi understood, but spoke not a word. His relatives and friends, however, protested stormily and waged a fierce battle on his behalf, with the result that the entire community was soon rent in two. The feud was waged in synagogues and houses of study, in streets and market-place and in every home, and vehemence of language was often accompanied by violence in action. Most of the opponents of the Kahal were probably actuated less by concern for the fate of the rabbi than by bitter resentment at the load of taxation imposed upon the Jewish populace by the elders. The strife was serious enough while it was confined to the community; it became a calamity when the Gentile authorities intervened.

The *Voivode* Radziwill supported the Kahal, while Bishop Masalski — presumably as a fellow-ecclesiastic — upheld the rabbi. The *Voivode* began to persecute the partisans of the rabbi living in his jurisdiction, and the bishop retaliated by persecuting his opponents within his own. Their respective courts even went to the length of having Jews arrested and imprisoned. The consequence was that many followers of the rabbi were forced to remove to the district under the authority of the bishop, while the supporters of the Kahal sought shelter under the wings of the *Voivode*. Rabbi Samuel ben Avigdor himself fled to the suburb of Antokol, to be under the protection of the bishop, with the result that the little congregation there was also split in twain. Among those arrested by the *Voivode* was

Rabbi Simon ben Zeev-Wolf, who complained in
Warsaw about the gross abuse of power by the Vilna
Kahal and brought upon his head the ban of excommunication. The *Voivode*, who had been bribed by
the elders, had him thrown into the jail of Nieswicz,
where he is said to have been kept for two years
with fetters on his feet and forced to do hard labor.
During his imprisonment this victim of the Kahal
despots wrote a brochure[1] which was afterwards submitted to the Great Diet (1788–91), in which he
severely criticized the maladministration of the
Kahal and made suggestions for a radical reform of
its constitution.

The dispute over Rabbi Samuel ben Avigdor continued for many years, until at last the partisans
of both sides were worn out and unable to spend
any more money on lawsuits. The Kahal had
triumphed over the rabbinate, but it had damaged
itself irretrievably in the struggle; and the prestige
of both rabbinate and Kahal in all other communities in the country had likewise suffered. The Vilna
Kahal had passed a decree that the community
should never again appoint a rabbi and president
of the *Bet Din*, because it was afraid of the authority
he might develop; but its own authority had now
become discredited and undermined. As for the
cause of all this turmoil, he continued to enjoy the
respect of other rabbis; in his approbations of books
he signed himself "encamping here in the holy con-

---

[1] See the article by J. Shatzky in *Yivo, Historishe Shriften*, I,
717 ff.

gregation of Vilna." He was elected rabbi of the community of Koenigsberg, but apparently did not go there. When he died in Vilna in 1791 he was honored with such a glowing tribute on his tombstone that it was impossible to believe that there had ever been a breath of scandal about his name.[1]

One of the important functions of the rabbi was thereafter discharged by another religious dignitary, who was styled *Moreh Zedek* ("Righteous Teacher"), namely, the giving of authoritative decisions on all questions of ritual observance and practice. The first to hold that office, and who was actually appointed during the rabbinate of Samuel ben Avigdor, was Abraham Simeon ben Zevi-Hirsch Praeger, called in Vilna "Rabbi Simeon the Great." In 1773, while the latter was still alive, David ben Yehiel-Michal (also known as Rabbi David Kendess) was appointed his deputy. With him the Kahal made an agreement for three years, which was renewed five times for three years each time. At first he was given a salary of 1,026 gulden a year, which was increased in 1779 by 100 gulden for a dwelling in the synagogue courtyard. After his death the position of *Moreh Zedek* was held by a few scholars simultaneously.

Although the rabbi and president of the *Bet Din* delivered only two discourses a year, the community was not allowed to suffer from a dearth of spiritual

[1] There is a detailed study on this memorable dispute by I. Zinberg in *Yivo, Historishe Shriften*, vol. II, pp. 291–371. The fullest and latest account is by Israel Klausner in *Vilna bi-Tekufat ha-Gaon*. See Supplementary Note 6.

exhortation. A *Maggid* was specially appointed to preach regularly, and he received his emoluments jointly from the Kahal, the *Hebra Kaddisha*, and the *Bedek ha-Bayit* Society. The agreement made with him prescribed when he should preach in the Great Synagogue and when in that of the *Hebra Kaddisha*, and also what salary he should receive from each. A contract, dated 1811, with Ezekiel Feiwel ben Zeev-Wolf, of Derczyn, which has been preserved, stipulated that he should preach in the former from the first of Nissan to the first of Kislev (spring to winter), and in the latter from the first of Kislev to the first of Nissan (winter to spring).

A key-position in the community was held by the *Sofer*, or secretary, who generally combined with it the office of secretary of the *Bet Din*. He was usually also a *Dayyan*, and hence was always called by the dual title of "Secretary and Judge" (*Notarius et Judex Judaeorum*). He attended all meetings of the Kahal, recorded its decisions in the *Pinkas*, and wrote all letters, documents, contracts with officials and letters of appointment, besides recording the judgments of the *Bet Din*. Owing to the large amount of work that had to be done, a special *Dayyan* was often entrusted with the recording of decisions. Sometimes a few officials held the office jointly. Sometimes the position, which entailed both honor and authority, was given to persons who paid for it, as in the case of the *YeSoD*, Judah ben Eliezer (the father-in-law of Rabbi Samuel ben Avigdor), who obtained it in 1739 in return for various acts of public benevolence in the interest

of the Kahal and received confirmation of it both
from the Vice-*Voivode* in 1739 and from the *Voivode*
himself in 1746. In 1784, Moses ben Judah-Leib
was appointed to the office for ten years in return
for a payment of 50 ducats and a loan of 150 ducats;
but it was stipulated that if he died before ten years
the Kahal should return to his heirs the part of the
loan corresponding to the unexpired period. The
secretary received a fixed salary and a free residence
in one of the houses of the Kahal. He also derived
considerable perquisites from the writing of various
documents, such as certificates of official appointments and marriage certificates, as well as agreements between private individuals.

The beadles of the Great Synagogue enjoyed a
much higher status than do their modern counter-
parts, as they discharged a number of important
functions for the Kahal. They signed all letters,
documents and decisions of the Kahal, which were
thus given official validity. They took note of the
decisions passed by the Kahal and handed them with
their signature to the secretary for recording in the
Pinkas. They swore that they would observe the
laws of the Kahal and of the Lithuanian *Va'ad*,
and were forbidden to sign any decision in conflict
with such laws. They also acted as ushers of the
Vice-*Voivode's* Court, which dealt with Jewish cases.
The position was regarded as of sufficient importance
to be obtainable, like more exalted offices, in return
for a gift of money and a loan. In Vilna there were
four beadles of the Kahal, besides those of the *Bet
Din*, the "Great Charity," the *Hebra Kaddisha*,

and various synagogues. A record has been kept of most of their names, which indicates that they were regarded as men of importance.

A dignitary of exceptional status was the *Shtadlan*[1] (advocate or syndic), whose duty it was to look after the political and civic interests of the community and to act as the official representative in all relations with the municipal and state authorities. He had to possess qualifications not essential to those concerned only with the internal affairs of the community, such as a perfect knowledge of the vernacular and the entrée to courts, palaces, and government offices. It was his business to intervene in all cases concerning the Kahal which occupied the law-courts, to secure the suppression of "ritual murder" accusations, and to arrange the release of Jewish captives. He wrote letters and petitions in Polish and was able to translate Hebrew documents into that language. As the Lithuanian Supreme Tribunal held its sessions in Vilna, the *Shtadlan* had a large scope of activity. When the Lithuanian *Va'ad*, in 1761, decided upon the election of such advocates, it stipulated that one was obliged to reside in Vilna.

Hayyim ben Joseph, who was appointed in 1761, is apostrophized in the most eulogistic terms in his Hebrew contract, which reads more like an adulatory address than an agreement. He is described as a man

---

[1] This position existed among the Jews throughout German, Polish, and Lithuanian territories from the 16th century. It was sometimes an honorary office, held by an outstanding personality who possessed wealth, good business connections, and the power of public speech.

of wisdom and greatness, with mellifluous lips, utter-
ing the language of Torah and knowledge that
arouses deep respect, enjoying a fine reputation, fit
to stand in the palaces of kings and princes and to
speak to them in a melodious voice, chosen unanimously and accepted with perfect consent to be the
messenger of the All-Merciful and the spokesman of
the community, to be an intercessor and defender
in all the provinces in the State of Lithuania, "and
his eyes shall be open to all the needs of the State,
in order to hold impressive speeches of defense
before the king of exalted majesty, and before the
noble princes of the kingdom." After further com-
plimentary and precatory phrases, in which the hope
is expressed that he will "flourish as a date-palm in
eternal peace," the document concludes with the
dry details and terms of his appointment. Hayyim
ben Joseph was to hold office for three years at a
salary based on the rate of a half-groschen for
every gulden paid as poll-tax (which came to about
a sixtieth of the total income from this tax). He
was required to live in Vilna, and whenever the
sessions of the Supreme Tribunal began he had to
remain in the city for at least six weeks without
interruption. During his three years of office he
was exempt from all taxes imposed by the Kahal as
well as from the special meat-tax (*Korobka*), and
he had a free residence.

The *Shtadlan* was the next highly paid official after
the president of the *Bet Din*. His income amounted
to 16 to 25 gulden per week, apart from expenses
for travelling, paper, and any other official requisites.

In times of emergency he was invested with plenipotentiary powers, and he was always accorded
great honor as a man of learning and influence who
had good relations with the authorities. Other
occupants of the office in Vilna were Saul ben
Mordecai, who obtained the ratification of the
privileges of the Jews in Lithuania in 1746; Aryeh-
Leib Meitess, of Pinsk, who was highly praised for
having saved the city by his wisdom in 1784; and
Jeremiah ben Nahum (1788–1807), the last of the
series, who received the family name of Sarasohn.

The financial affairs of the Kahal were entirely in
the hands of a trustee (*Ne'eman*) or treasurer, who
had control over all monies that came in or were
paid out and who took charge of all promissory
notes, pledges and similar documents. The person
appointed to this office was generally one who
furnished the Kahal with a substantial loan; but he
received a salary which was usually 10 gulden a
week, as the post entailed not only responsibility
but a great deal of exacting work. The trustee of
the *Hebra Kaddisha*, who also obtained the position
in return for a loan, held it, as a rule, in an honorary
capacity. The other officials on the pay-roll of the
Kahal comprised a doctor who visited the sick poor
and received a regular stipend of 12 gulden a week,
ritual slaughterers, a cantor, a bass (who acted as
assistant cantor), a cantillator of the Torah, an
assistant beadle for the Great Synagogue, a care-
taker for the synagogue courtyard, and four caretakers for the houses of the Kahal in the Jewish
quarter.

CHAPTER IX

THE KAHAL'S EXTERNAL RELATIONS

1. RELATIONS WITH THE *Va'ad*

THE autonomy enjoyed by the Jewish community of Vilna and by the other communities in Lithuania naturally led to their holding periodical conferences for the discussion of their common interests and the adoption of decisions that were considered necessary to their collective welfare. These conferences were attended by specially appointed delegates, who constituted a body called the *Va'ad*, or Council. The Council of the Jewish Communities of Lithuania (*Va'ad Medinat Lita*) first came into existence in 1623. Before that date the delegates of Lithuanian Jewry used to attend the sessions of the Council of Four Lands (*Va'ad Arba' Arazoth*), which was so called because it comprised delegates from the communities of Great Poland (with its capital, Posen), Little Poland (Cracow), Ruthenia (Podolia and Galicia), and Volhynia.[1] This larger autonomous body which was established in 1581 is often referred

[1] In the earlier period of its history the Council was sometimes called "Council of Three Lands" and also, comparatively rarely, "Council of Five Lands," according to the number of provincial delegations represented, but in the course of time "Council of Four Lands" became the established designation.

to by Polish writers as proof of the tolerance and goodwill which the Jews enjoyed in mediaeval Poland. The fact is that it was organized not only with the permission of the Polish government but at its definite request, since it rendered the government considerable service in collecting and remitting the taxes imposed upon the Jewish population as well as in administering its own internal affairs. At first it provided the State with an annual income of 15,000 to 20,000 gulden; in the seventeenth century the amount was increased to 100,000 gulden, and from 1717 it was 220,000 gulden. The Council appointed an assessment commission, which allocated their respective quotas to the various provincial districts and its principal communities, and it was responsible for ensuring that the full amount fixed by the *Seym* was handed over to the treasury. Besides acting as fiscal agent for the Government, the *Va'ad* had a wide sphere of activity and competence, which embraced communal administration, religious questions, judicial matters, economic affairs, education and social questions. It not only watched over the spiritual and moral welfare of the Jews, but also over their civic and economic interests. Its deliberations ranged from authorizing the publication of an edition of the Talmud to the enactment of regulations for restraining finery among women. It usually met twice a year: in summer at Jaroslav, and in winter at Lublin, the latter city being particularly convenient on account of its commercial fairs. It had a total membership of twenty-five to thirty, including some rabbis, and their travelling expenses were defrayed by their respective communities. It was always presided over by a distinguished layman, styled *Juden Marschall* ("Jews' Marshal"), who was assisted by syndics, secretaries and cashiers.

In 1623 the Jews of Lithuania withdrew from the Council of Four Lands; but this body continued to retain the same designation, as the Council still represented four different provinces. The reason for the withdrawal was twofold: the *Seym*, from 1717, imposed upon the Jews of Lithuania a separate assessment of 60,000 zloty per annum, which they were obliged to collect themselves; and, secondly, there was a difference of economic conditions between the two countries. The Lithuanian *Va'ad* was established by the three leading communities of Brest, Pinsk, and Grodno. Of these Brest, or Brisk, at that period, was by far the most important Jewish center in Lithuania, as it embraced about thirty smaller congregations in the surrounding district, while Pinsk had only eight and Grodno seven. The founders of the *Va'ad*, in drawing up its constitution, naturally arrogated certain privileges to themselves in relation to the little communities in the suburbs of the countryside. They enacted that any member of a "principal community" had the right of domicile in a suburban or rural community in the district, but that no resident in the latter had a corresponding right in the "principal community." They also passed a law that any Jew belonging to the three main centers had the right to trade freely in the satellite communities, whereas no member of the latter could enjoy a similar right in their own midst.

As soon as the Jews of Vilna thought themselves sufficiently important in numbers and position, they applied to the *Va'ad* for admission, but they were kept waiting many years before their application was granted. In 1634 the Vilna Kahal had a certain number of little communities assigned to it for the purpose of collecting their taxes and other dues, and thus claimed to be a "principal community." The *Va'ad*, jealously guarding its prerogatives, did not fully concede this claim at first, although it gave the Jews of Vilna the right to trade freely in the townlets and villages belonging to the other main communities. It was not until 1652, after there had been an animated exchange of views between the Vilna Kahal and the original constituents of the *Va'ad*, that the Jewry in the capital of Lithuania was recognized as forming a "principal community." This act of recognition was the outcome of the labors of an arbitration court representing both sides, which, at the same time, laid down some rather cautious conditions regulating the admission of Vilna to the *Va'ad*. For the first eight years Vilna was to have in the *Va'ad* one *Rosh Medinah* (State Elder), who was a taxpayer, and after that period an additional member of similar qualifications until 1668, and in addition also a third, who might be the president of the *Bet Din* — if the other three communities agreed. If, after sixteen years, Vilna had three delegates in the *Va'ad*, it could then obtain a fourth seat if the other communities agreed; but in any case it was assured a fourth seat after the lapse of another six years. The Vilna Kahal was also consoled with the undertaking that, even before the president of its *Bet Din* became a member of the *Va'ad*, he would be consulted by the rabbis of the other communities in regard to petitions of the Kahal to the government.

The conditions laid down by the *Va'ad* proved rather slow in realization. The Vilna Kahal had to appeal, in 1670, to be allowed a third delegate, and it was not until 1683 that its rabbi secured admission with the same rights as the other rabbis. It then demanded that it should have also its own secretary and beadle in the *Va'ad*, as did the other communities; but this request was not granted until 1687. The Slutzk community had already been admitted to the *Va'ad* in 1671 without such difficulties as those experienced by Vilna, but both were treated alike in not being allowed to include within their jurisdiction any small congregation situated beyond six miles from their respective borders. In 1695 there was a dispute between the Kahal of Vilna and that of Grodno regarding some rural communities located between the two cities, and it was decided that those farther than six miles from Vilna should belong to Grodno, with the exception of Olkenik, and that those which had formerly belonged to Grodno should continue under its jurisdiction. The question of the "pertinence" of any new rural community that might arise was settled with a certain subtlety, not unmixed with grim humor, as it was agreed that this should depend upon the location of the cemetery to which its members considered that they "belonged."

Despite the chary treatment that the elders of Vilna had received from their colleagues in the *Va'ad*, they eventually played a leading part in its affairs. Situated as they were in the metropolis, where the Lithuanian Supreme Tribunal held its sessions, they were able to take the initiative in important cases, such as ritual murder accusations, as well as in other matters in other courts. In 1691 the Vilna Kahal was authorized by the *Va'ad* to expend up to 300 gulden on its behalf in the defense of any Jew exposed to serious danger, but if a larger sum were necessary the assent of the other "principal communities" must be obtained. The curb thus placed upon the Kahal's freedom of action caused it to complain that, whereas it was always ahead of the other bodies in submitting petitions to the king and other authorities, the other communities were even slow in agreeing to the necessary expenditure.

In the early part of the eighteenth century the *Va'ad* met at long intervals and only for brief sessions, owing partly to the internal rivalry among the members and the demonstrative absence of some of them. There was a short meeting in Vilna in 1714, presided over by the president of the Kahal, Dr. Aaron Gordon. When the *Va'ad* appointed a *Shtadlan* in 1761, it stipulated that he should live in Vilna so as to be on the spot when the Supreme Tribunal was in session. The *Va'ad* also delegated a special

Shtadlan to stay in Warsaw during the meeting of
the *Seym*, in order to gather information about any
proposed laws relating to the Jews of Lithuania,
especially about the amount of tax to be imposed.
The *Shtadlan* also attended the provincial Diets
where the *Seym* deputies were elected, in order to
take action in case any anti-Jewish measure were
planned.

The Vilna Kahal shared largely in the expenses
of the *Va'ad* until the disruption of the community
in 1655, after which it suffered both social and economic decline for some decades. But when it recovered, it often incurred expenditure on account
of the *Va'ad*, particularly in connection with acts
of intercession and defense measures in law-courts,
with the result that in the years 1700 and 1720 only
half of its quota was collected for the *Va'ad*, the
other half being cancelled by debts owing to the
Kahal by the *Va'ad*. In 1664 the latter owed 30,700
gulden to the Kahal, and in 1761 its indebtedness
had increased to over 93,000 gulden. In 1727 the
Vilna Kahal was in such distress that it had to borrow
the sum of 1,500 gulden from a priest named Bialosor,
for soldiers had broken into the houses of Jews to
collect the poll-tax by force, and the community
was in imminent peril.

In 1764 the Polish *Seym*, aware that the *Va'ad*
raised far more money than was necessary for the
poll-tax and that the elders spent some of it on
their inner communal needs, decided to abolish its
practice of fixing the tax payable by the Jews at a
lump sum. The *Seym* replaced the old system by

imposing a poll-tax of two zloty upon every member of the Jewish community, irrespective of sex, above the age of one, and for this purpose ordered that a census should be taken of all the Jews in Poland and Lithuania. It nevertheless placed the responsibility for collecting and remitting the money upon the Kahal, so that the latter had to pay not only for those Jews who had moved to another city without having as yet entered their names into its register, but also for the poor and even the dead. Since the main reason for the establishment of the *Va'ad* had been to act as the central tax-collecting agency and the function of tax-gatherer was now taken over by the various Kahals, and as the authorities knew from the census results the amount to be raised by each community, the *Seym* decided that it was not worth while tolerating the *Va'ad* any longer and ordered that it be dissolved both in Poland and Lithuania. Even before this dissolution, the *Va'ad* in both countries had begun to decline, partly owing to the same causes that led to the collapse of the Polish State, namely internal differences over non-essential matters and deliberate absences, and partly owing to the growing poverty of the constituent communities. Nevertheless, even after the dissolution, the regulations of the *Va'ad* continued to influence the administration of the Kahal. In 1774 the Vilna *Bet Din* actually issued a declaration that those regulations had not been rescinded. The Lithuanian *Va'ad* had apparently expired before its doom had been officially sealed, as its last meeting took place in 1761. During its career of 138 years it had held 33 sessions, at which 1,030 decisions had been adopted. Its minute-book, containing a record of all its sessions, has been preserved and forms a valuable source of information on Jewish autonomy in Lithuania.[1]

After the dissolution of the *Va'ad* the elders of the "principal communities" still found it useful and even necessary to meet at fair-times in order to exchange views and adopt decisions on matters of collective interest. Thus, when Hasidism began to spread in Lithuania, a number of elders and rabbis from different centers met in 1781, on a market-day, in Selva, where they decided to follow the example of the Vilna Kahal in proclaiming a ban of excommunication against the new sect. Moreover, when the Great *Seym* (1788–91) deliberated on the position of the Jews and issued laws affecting their rights in the towns, the five principal Kahals issued a proclamation for the raising of funds to defray the cost of intercession, with a view to averting "the evil decree." The *Va'ad* thus practically continued to function for essential purposes until the collapse of the first Polish State.

Occasionally, during the existence of both Councils, representatives of the Polish *Va'ad* met delegates of the Lithuanian Council in order to discuss matters of common interest to the Jewries of both countries, their usual rendezvous being Leczna, near Lublin.

[1] *Pinkas ha-Medina*, edited by S. M. Dubnow, Berlin, 1925.

2. RELATIONS WITH THE SUBURBS

The authority of the Kahal was not confined to the Jews in the city of Vilna but also extended to those in the two suburbs of Shnipishok and Antokol. The Jewish inhabitants in these suburbs not only paid to the Kahal the amounts due for government tax, but also recognized its *Bet Din* and appointed heads. They addressed themselves to the *Bet Din* on all important matters, and the president of the court consequently derived a certain income from them. There was a natural tendency on their part to develop and exercise their own authority: they elected a Kahal of their own and, owing to their distance from Vilna, established their own synagogue, hospital, baths and other institutions. But the Vilna community resisted these attempts at local self-government. The *Va'ad* sometimes had to intervene and arbitrate in cases of dispute, and in the "deed of settlement" the relations between the two bodies were clearly defined for the ensuing period.

The Jews began to settle in Shnipishok in the second half of the seventeenth century, and the local inhabitants soon complained of their arrival. They had to pay Prince Radziwill, the owner of the land in the district, an annual tax of 220 gulden, a land-tax of 26 gulden, and a house-tax (based on the number of chimneys) of 52 gulden. A dispute broke out in 1679 between the Kahal of Vilna and that of Shnipishok regarding their mutual relations, and upon the intervention of the *Va'ad* an agreement was reached which was set forth in a series of articles. The residents in the suburb were given the right to take part in the elections of the Vilna Kahal and also in its administration, and those who had the right of domicile in the city could act as electors and be appointed *Dayyanim*. They were also accorded the right to elect their own Kahal, but only those could take part in the election who had the right of domicile in Vilna. They were allowed to appoint a *Dayyan* of their own, who could decide all cases involving sums up to 12 gulden, but in cases where higher amounts were involved he must confer with the judges from Vilna. As for the taxes due to the Kahal, all the residents of the suburb had to go to Vilna once a year, to appear before a commission of five assessors (one of whom, with a domiciliary right in the city, was from Shnipishok) in order that their respective contributions might be fixed. Of the revenue received from those with the right to live in Vilna, three-fifths went to the Kahal and two-fifths to the suburb; but of that received from those who had no such right one-half went to each. Detailed regulations were also drawn up with regard to the killing of cattle, which the Jews of Shnipishok were allowed to do in their own slaughter-house. Every butcher had to pay on each head of cattle a fee of three gulden, of which two went to the Kahal and one to the suburb, besides smaller sums for charity.

In 1749 a serious dispute broke out between the Vilna Kahal and the congregation of Shnipishok regarding their mutual relations, and as the aged

Rabbi Joshua Heschel was ill at the time a panel of
Dayyanim representing both sides dealt with the
matter and drew up the terms of a rather elaborate
agreement, which was to be observed for the next
four years. The Jews of the suburb were to pay to
the Kahal 250 gulden each year in two instalments,
and to be exempt from all other payments; in return
for which they were free to trade in Vilna without
restriction. If the Kahal issued licenses for the
sale of candles in the city, the Jews of Shnipishok
should have the right to sell candles in their suburb
without any fee, but in the city only with the assent
of the licensees. The people of Shnipishok were entitled to kill 15 head of cattle in the course of the
year for their own needs without any payment to
the Vilna Kahal; but if any of these were found to
be *trefah* they had no right to kill more without
payment; if, however, still more were unfit to be
eaten, they could slaughter up to a total of 12 kosher
beasts without payment. The *Shohet* (ritual slaughterer) was to be provided from Vilna, and he was to
carry out his duties under the supervision of three
residents of Shnipishok chosen by the Vilna Kahal,
who had to give him their signed authority in a
special book. If more beasts were killed than the
number allowed by the agreement then the three
supervisors would have to pay a fine of 100 thaler
to the Kahal; but if the infringement was committed
without their knowledge, the slaughterer himself
was to be punished. The butchers of Shnipishok
were not allowed to sell meat in their own suburb,

but only in the Vilna slaughter-house, where a roofed annex was placed at their disposal by the Kahal, which made no charge except for keeping the place clean.

Every Jew who settled in Shnipishok after the conclusion of this agreement was treated as though he lived in Vilna, and if any Jew left the city to make his home in the suburb he could come to a private arrangement with the Kahal regarding his annual dues. The suburban congregation was also required to make a small subsidy every month to the "Great Charity" of Vilna, to provide carts for the poor Jews who came to the city from other places and who were thus sped on the way to another community; and the Kahal undertook, in return, not to send any poor wanderers to Shnipishok. The agreement further took note of the ritual requirements of the suburb for the Feast of Tabernacles, for it provided that the congregation could obtain a citron from the Kahal for the sum of 14 gulden, and a second citron at a similar price. The document ended with a solemn and rather verbose admonition that the compact was to be most faithfully observed in every detail, without the omission of a jot or tittle, for the next four years, until the New Moon of Tammuz, 5513 (1753), and that three months before it expired the elders of the Kahal were obliged to enter into negotiations with the congregation of Shnipishok for a further and final settlement. The problem of their mutual relations was ultimately solved by the growth of the city, which absorbed the suburb. In 1790 the Jews in the suburb owned 28 houses, of which two were built of stone, and all the rest of timber.

The congregation in the suburb of Antokol came into existence much later than that of Shnipishok, and in the middle of the eighteenth century was still struggling for the right to have its own independent communal institutions. The Jews were settled in two different parts: the majority lived under the jurisdiction of Prince Sapieha, and the minority dwelt in an area which first belonged to the Lithuanian Artillery and then passed under the control of Bishop Masalski. Few in number though they were (a total of 317 in 1765), there was occasional friction between the Jews in these two different areas and even a temporary rupture in 1787. The Vilna Kahal concluded with the Antokol congregation agreements similar to those made with Shnipishok. The agreement made in 1744 provided that the Jews of Antokol could hold public worship on the festivals locally, and should contribute 216 gulden a year to the Vilna Kahal as poll-tax. They were permitted to slaughter a stipulated number of cattle for their own requirements (which could be increased for festivals and weddings) without any payment to the Kahal; but were forbidden to sell any meat in Vilna under pain of a fine of 100 thaler for the benefit of the *Voivode* and Prince Sapieha. If an Antokol butcher killed beasts in the suburbs and sold them in the slaughter-house in Vilna, he had to pay a fee to the Kahal for every one that was *kosher*, but if any one was found *trefah* he could dispose of it only in the suburb or elsewhere outside the city. The Vilna Kahal had the authority to appoint a slaughterer for Antokol, but no right to enter the name of any Jews of the suburb into the "Black Book" or excommunicate him; and if the Kahal violated any of the conditions in the agreement it must pay a fine of 500 thaler to the treasury of the *Voivode* and to Prince Sapieha.

Although the Jews of Antokol were allowed to hold religious services on the festivals, they were forbidden by the Kahal to build a synagogue of their own. They therefore patiently waited for their opportunity. It came in the late sixties of the eighteenth century, when there was a change of *Voivode* and the controversy first broke out between the elders of the Kahal and the president of the *Bet Din*. They were granted permission by Bishop Masalski to build a synagogue, on condition that it was not as high as a church and did not look like one, but were not allowed to establish a cemetery; and by 1774 the synagogue had a women's section. Prince Sapieha, not to be outdone in generosity, presented the Jews in his domain with a ruined house for adaptation as a synagogue, and in 1777, with his permission, they sold the house and built a new synagogue in a more suitable locality, together with a bathhouse.

The Vilna Kahal had, therefore, now to reconcile itself to the existence of two synagogues in Antokol; but it still strove to assert its authority. In 1781 it concluded an agreement with the Jews of Antokol, providing that they should continue to pay the same annual contribution of 216 gulden as fixed in 1774, in return for which they had the right to trade in the city, though only in small quantities, and that the butchers of Antokol should have two stands in the Vilna slaughter-house, for which they should pay the Kahal at the same rate per beast as the Vilna butchers. This agreement, however, was not kept by the Jews of Antokol, as they felt strong enough to defy the tottering authority of the Kahal, which was involved in more serious preoccupations.

The dispute concerning Rabbi Samuel ben Avigdor had some repercussions in Antokol, especially as this deposed rabbi sought refuge within the domain of Bishop Masalski. The latter not only gave him physical protection and moral support, but also officially confirmed his status as rabbi within the area under his jurisdiction both in the city and in the suburb. The consequence of this development was that the Jews of Antokol in the bishop's domain adopted an unfriendly attitude towards those living under Prince Sapieha's jurisdiction, and this attitude unfortunately found expression in fisticuffs. Shortly before Passover, in 1787, there was a scuffle in the synagogue, when five Jews of the Sapieha quarter assaulted some Jews from the bishop's. This Christian prelate was drawn into a purely Jewish controversy to such an extent that, on the eve of the Feast of Tabernacles, he ordered all Jews under his jurisdiction to pray only in their own local synagogue; and when Jews who were differently minded went to the new place of worship in the Sapieha quarter, they were attacked and even injured by officers of the bishop.

After the storm over the deposed rabbi had at last died down, the Jews of Antokol became reconciled among themselves and again agreed to accept the authority of the Vilna Kahal. Four delegates were therefore sent by the latter, in 1791, to the suburb to restore relations in accordance with their views; but the arrangement lasted barely more than a couple of years, as the Jews of Antokol persisted in asserting their independence and were consequently treated by the elders of Vilna as though they belonged to another town. This feud, too, was healed when Antokol eventually became absorbed in the expanding city.

CHAPTER X

THE KAHAL'S FINANCES

IN THE history of the Jews in mediaeval Vilna —
which presents so many episodes of suffering bravely
borne and of heroism nobly sustained, which reveals
scenes of religious piety, loyalty to tradition and
unwavering hope, and which is irradiated by the
steady glow of austere yet ardent scholarship —
there is one unedifying and depressing chapter. It
is the story of the community's financial affairs.
The self-government which it was allowed to enjoy
almost from the beginning of its existence, and which
is so often characterized as a unique and enviable
privilege, proved to be anything but an unmixed
boon. Had that privilege, which was essentially
no greater than that accorded to the burghers, the
majority of whom had likewise originally been alien
immigrants, been exercised during a period mainly
of peace, it would probably have produced for the
most part beneficent results. But the life of the
community until the collapse of the first Polish
State was repeatedly disturbed by shocks and disasters, and it no sooner recovered from one calamity
that it was overwhelmed by another. The protracted
and wearisome struggle for the rights of domicile
and trade, the frequent attacks by the local populace,
the worry and expense of endless lawsuits in different
courts, the outbreaks of fire and plague, the invasion

of foreign armies, the utter destruction of the community for six years and the costly labor of its restoration, the influx of refugees from afflicted areas
and the eruption of internal discord — these were
among the major causes that hampered the efforts
of the Kahal to conduct its affairs satisfactorily.
There were also contributory causes which lay in
the system that was largely an obligarchy, and in
the abuse of power by ambitious and unscrupulous
individuals who were able to buy office and wield
it despotically. The cumulative effect of this combination of material and moral evils was that the
Kahal for over a hundred and fifty years was unable
to balance its budget and gradually sank deeper
into a financial morass, from which even government
intervention was unable to extricate it.

The Kahal certainly had many sources of income,
regular and irregular, permanent and occasional.
No Jew could settle in the city, rent a dwelling, or
engage in work or trade, without paying the Kahal
for the permission. Nobody could marry or have
his son initiated into the covenant of Abraham without buying the right to discharge these social and
religious duties. Merchants and artisans, spirit-
vendors and moneylenders, all had to render their
stipulated dues to the communal coffers. Every day,
or every other day, every Jew engaged in business
or work had to come to the office of the Kahal, declare on oath how much he had bought, sold, or
earned, and pay a certain percentage on his profit
or income. There were five assessors, appointed
annually after the election of the new Kahal, who

estimated the wealth and income of each member
of the community and imposed upon him a definite
tax, which was generally collected by weekly instalments. The assessors were closeted in a private
room which they could not leave even to go home —
except on Sabbath and festivals — to eat and sleep
until they had completed their task, for which they
received a salary; and anybody who hesitated to
appear before them was threatened with excommunication.

The Kahal derived a regular tax (*Korobka*) from
bakers and travelling merchants, from monopolies
like silks and kosher wine, gunpowder and matches,
from betrothals, dowries and circumcisions, from
the sale of citrons, fat and candles. It received four
per cent of the purchase-price of houses and other
real estate, and it had a graduated scale of charges
for the slaughter of cattle and poultry, besides a tax
ranging from 10 to 20 per cent on the purchase of
kosher meat and a statutory claim to the skins of
large beasts and three feathers from the wing of
every fowl. It also had occasional sources of income,
such as the sale of the privilege of taking part in the
meetings of the Elective Assembly (*ReHaSh*) and
of nominating others to take part, contributions or
loans free of interest from those who obtained official
positions, licenses for brokers and inn-keepers, payments from artisans' societies, rents from its own
property in the ghetto, and fees from the seats in
the Great Synagogue. Moreover, whenever some
special emergency arose that called for extra funds,
the Kahal made an express levy: for example, to

provide the Polish army with money for its hospital and principal guard, to furnish the Russian invaders with wood, candles, meat and spices, to maintain a guard for the Lithuanian Supreme Tribunal, or to defray the costs of expensive lawsuits. The total income from the regular sources amounted, in the later decades of the eighteenth century, to about 150,000 gulden a year; and if we include the sums from other sources, the total sometimes ranged from 170,000 to 180,000 gulden a year.

The expenditure of the Kahal was just as varied as its income. It not only maintained a substantial corps of officials, from the president of the *Bet Din* down to the beadles and caretakers (who all received double salaries for the weeks of the festivals), but it also had to furnish regular payments to the officials of the *Voivode* (often supplemented by gifts of meat, fish and spices). It had to pay the municipality the annual contribution of 600 gulden, and it was also responsible for the discharge of the poll-tax due to the government from all registered members of the local community, so that it had to pay for the poor and even for those who left the city. It incurred heavy expenditure in sending a *Shtadlan* to Warsaw to engage lawyers to fight its cases in the courts against the Vilna municipality, and it had many disputes in connection with the letting of its property. It also had to meet all sorts of unforeseen expenditure, as in the case of murders of Jews, which were by no means an infrequent occurrence. Thus in 1766, when two noblemen and a soldier were arrested on the suspicion of the murder of three Jews

near Vilna, and the real culprits were afterwards
discovered, the Kahal had to pay substantial damages for the wrongful detention of the innocent
trio, who had also to be provided with new clothes.
Similarly, in the following year, when three Jews
were killed near the city by two Christians, the
latter were kept in prison nearly fifteen months at
the expense of the Kahal, which had also to pay
for the judges, the prosecutor, the executioner and
even the burial. By far the largest outlay was that
involved by the invasion of the Russian army, which
cost the Kahal during the years 1773–78 a sum of
over 200,000 gulden. The total expenditure of the
Kahal in 1773 was 188,000 gulden, while in the
following year it was nearly 20,000 gulden less.

In order to solve the problem of covering liabilities
exceeding its income, the Kahal had to resort to
borrowing; and since loans given more or less volun-
tarily did not suffice, it adopted a method of compulsion. The elders would order a Jew of means to
sign a promissory note without stating to whom
it was payable; and if he refused he would be
sentenced to excommunication and his name would
be entered into the "Black *Pinkas*." Sometimes
the beadles were ordered to write the signatures of
certain persons on promissory notes and to confirm
their genuineness; and the "signatories" were obliged
to pay, as otherwise they were summoned to the
Bet Din through the medium of the "secret prosecutor." In such a case the person summoned did
not dare to ask the name of the suitor and therefore
did not appear before the *Bet Din*. But if he refused

to comply with the order of this court, the latter invoked the help of the *Voivode's* officer, who sent soldiers to collect the amount.[1] The money obtained by this method also failed to suffice, and other means therefore had to be employed.

The Kahal began borrowing considerable sums even before the flight of the community in 1655, and its debts naturally increased after the Jews returned to Vilna and devoted themselves to the restoration of their houses and institutions. The elders, in their predicament, addressed themselves to their wealthy Christian neighbors; and they met with a very ready response: noblemen, priests, and the various monastic orders were all willing to lend them large amounts at a rate of interest less than that demanded by private individuals. The result was that the debts of the Kahal began to mount, and by the year 1700 reached a total of 800,000 gulden. The Kahal was in such difficulties that it could not even pay the annual interest, and it therefore repeatedly appealed to the kings to release it from the interest and allow it to repay the principal in instalments. King Wisniowiecki was the first to grant it a moratorium. His successor, King John Sobieski, in 1687, proclaimed a moratorium for ten years, allowed repayments by instalments, and cancelled the payment of interest for ten years. In 1698 King Augustus II

---

[1] Quoted in *Toledot ha-Kehilah ha'ivrit b'Vilna*, by Israel Klausner, Part I, p. 156, from Simon ben Wolf's brochure *Ha-asir b'Nieswicz* ("The Prisoner at Nieswicz"), 1790. Klausner devotes a third of his book to a very full and detailed account of the Vilna Kahal's financial troubles.

also agreed to a ten-year postponement. The Lithuanian Supreme Tribunal, however, declared that
these various royal concessions were in conflict with
the laws and decisions of the *Seym* and insisted upon
the Kahal discharging its debts at once. But owing
to the Kahal's inability to repay the full amount,
most of the creditors agreed to accept a reduced
interest, from 2 to 5 per cent, in weekly instalments,
as they no longer expected to recover the principal.
Despite the Supreme Tribunal's judgment, King
Augustus II, in 1713, granted a further moratorium
for ten years, released the Kahal from the payment
of interest, and allowed the refunding of debts in
instalments. Nevertheless, all these relaxations were
of little avail.

The Kahal continued to borrow large sums, obtaining them despite its known insolvency, and even
tried to help itself by lending at a high interest (18
to 24 per cent) money it borrowed at a very much
lower rate. Some creditors, not prepared to wait
for a settlement indefinitely, sued the Kahal in the
courts; others stipulated that in the event of non-
payment they should have the right to close the
synagogue, the cemetery, or other communal institutions, for which authority was given by the courts.
In the *Pinkas* of the *Zedakah Gedolah* there is an
entry under the date of Ellul 2, 5466 (August 30,
1707), in the following terms: "In those days the
synagogue was closed and sealed for almost a whole
year. The cemetery also was closed." An attempt
was made on August 23, 1726, by the Deputy-
Voivode, to close the Great Synagogue for non-pay-

ment of a fine; but this was prevented by a crowd of Jews with the help of some noblemen and priests. Seven years later, when the Piarist monks threatened to seize the Great Synagogue for arrears, the Kahal was compelled to pawn the Perpetual Lamp of the synagogue, which was not redeemed until 1746. Creditors even seized the private property of the elders and had their wives and children put under "private arrest," from which the Kahal had to redeem them. And as though its burdens were not heavy enough, the Kahal sometimes intervened to settle a private Jew's debt to a Christian or to prevent property in the Jewish quarter from falling into the hands of a Christian creditor.

The memorable *Seym* of 1764, which abolished the *Va'ad* of the Lithuanian Communities, also paid some attention to the indebtedness of the Kahals — for the case of Vilna was by no means unique — and decided that a commission of the treasury should make a thorough investigation of their position and devise methods of improvement. The commission began its task the following year and completed it in 1766 by appointing a Liquidation Commission. The latter body ascertained that the total debts of the Vilna community (which then consisted of 3,206 souls) amounted to 823,000 gulden and that this was owing almost entirely to monasteries, clerical orders and priests, and comparatively little to Christian laymen or Jews. The amounts owed by the other leading communities, likewise mainly to monks, priests and nobles, were much less: the debt of Grodno (2,418 souls) was 448,500 gulden, of Pinsk (1,277 souls) 310,000 gulden, and of Brisk (3,175 souls) 119,700 gulden.

Of all the numerous creditors of the Vilna Kahal, the largest — strange though it may appear — was the Order of the Jesuits, to whom nearly half of the total was due, namely 397,600 gulden. The amount due to the Jesuits at the beginning of the eighteenth century, after remitting the interest accumulated until then, was fixed at 296,000 gulden; but subsequently, in 1736, they agreed to the reduction of interest to the abnormally low rate of 3 per cent, stating that they made this concession "out of compassion" for the Jews, on account of their poverty caused by incessant disorders and disasters. The Jesuits had, in fact, no alternative but to agree to this reduction of interest, for they knew that there was no possibility of receiving more; but the Kahal was unable to pay even this small rate or to prevent the debt from growing. The Liquidation Commission, in its efforts to put the finances of the Vilna Kahal on a sound footing, wrote down the debt to the Jesuits to 380,000 gulden. The creditors next in importance were the Dominican monks, to whom the Kahal owed 131,850 gulden. The Franciscans claimed that they had lent the Kahal hundreds of thousands of gulden over a period of one century; but as they were unable to furnish any proofs (pleading that the bills had perished with age), the Commission decided in their favor to the extent of 85,000 gulden. There were also smaller sums due to the Friars of St. Bernard, the Augustinians, the Carmelites, the Basilians, and the Penitents of the Vilna Monastery, as well as to many individual priests and noblemen.

The Liquidation Commission demanded a detailed statement of the Kahal's income so as to arrange the terms of amortization and the payment of interest; and after this was drawn up, the elders, the rabbi, the *Shtadlan*, the trustees, and the beadles all had to swear in the synagogue to its accuracy. The elders were unwilling to hand over the entire income for the liquidation of the debts, as they did not know what calls they might have to meet, and were only disposed to give the amount necessary for the annual interest, which, in 1765, came to 36,224 gulden. In July, 1766, the elders submitted a signed and sworn statement of the annual income, amounting to 34,000 gulden, and the Liquidation Commission decided that this should be applied to the payment of interest at 3 per cent, any balance to be used for amortization. As the Kahal had farmed part of its income from the taxes on silk, skins and milk, to repay certain creditors, the Commission allowed it to pay interest only for the years 1768–70 and to begin amortizing the debts in 1771. The Commission, which had the authority of a court of law, forbade the Kahal to contract any further loans or to farm out the communal taxes, and appointed an officer of the *Voivode*, the *Podstarosta* (vice-Prefect), to ensure the faithful fulfilment of its order that the Kahal hand over its entire income to the creditors and not use any of it for other purposes. Similar measures were taken in the case of other Kahals and their debts.

The Commission did not make a very thorough examination of the Kahal's finances before taking their decisions, as otherwise they would have seen that no allowance was made for the payment of the officials' salaries, of the poll-tax of the poor, the salary of the *Podstarosta*, and the annual contribution to the municipality. Nor did the Commission pay any attention to the sums due to the Kahal. The only measure that could have prevented the increase of its debts was the prohibition to make further borrowings; but this embargo was ignored by the Kahal, for, in 1773, it borrowed another 89,000 gulden. Moreover, the Polish *Seym*, in 1775, allowed the Kahals of Lithuania to raise a fresh loan of 500,000 gulden at 5 per cent in order to settle all their debts, which amounted to that sum, to the Jesuits, including the 380,000 gulden due from Vilna. The Order of Jesuits, however, no longer existed in Lithuania or Poland, as it had been suppressed by the government in 1772, and its property had been transferred to the Commission for the People's Education. The *Seym* insisted that the settlement of the debt to this body should not affect the strict observance of the decisions of the Liquidation Commission regarding the discharge of other debts. But while Bishop Masalski took steps to see that the Vilna Kahal repaid its own debt to the Jesuits, other Kahals appear to have used their part of the new loan for other purposes. The decisions of the Liquidation Commission proved utterly impracticable, for the expenditure of the Vilna Kahal for the years 1766–1772 amounted to 411,000 gulden (including

The Pulpit of the Great Synagogue

The Ark of the Great Synagogue

105,000 gulden for the Russian army), while its total income for the same period was only 196,980 gulden. So far from extricating the Kahal out of its financial morass, the Commission simply increased its burden by their own expenses to the extent of over 20,000 gulden.

The Kahal continued to administer its affairs without any proper supervision, as the *Podstarosta* proved inefficient, and imposed fresh taxes in various forms upon the distressed community. The grievances of the populace reached a climax at the time of the great dispute about the last rabbi and served to inflame the hostility of the Kahal. They were also conveyed, with concrete details, by special representatives, in 1786, to the Treasury Commission, which replaced the *Podstarosta* by a new controller and also sent a fresh commission of inquiry. The elders opposed any further investigation and in 1787 appealed to the Royal Court, which upheld the authority of the Treasury Commission. In the following year the elders were sentenced to a few months' imprisonment and damages for refusing to carry out the Commission's decisions. Moreover, the elders who had signed promissory notes themselves were obliged to repay the creditors with their own money and even to pledge their houses and shops for the purpose. During the next few years the Commission appointed a succession of controllers to keep a strict check upon the Kahal; and as these, too, proved unsatisfactory the Commission farmed the taxes of the community to a group of Jews for 60,000 gulden per annum.

Finally, the Great *Seym* concerned itself with the financial affairs of the Kahal as a serious problem whose solution could no longer be delayed, and on January 26, 1792, it appointed a number of Liquidation Courts to deal with the matter. The Liquidation Court in Vilna began its labors three months later. Owing to the internal wars it was unable to complete its task until the following summer; but it accomplished this so thoroughly and comprehensively that the results of its findings and its recommendations regarding the financial imbroglio of the Vilna Kahal filled a volume of six hundred pages. It gave a careful hearing to all the numerous claims submitted to it, including many that had remained unsatisfied since the previous attempted liquidation in 1766. After a thorough sifting of all the documents, promissory notes and verbal statements, and after rejecting various unsupported claims, the Court found that the total debts of the Kahal owing to ninety-three different creditors — Christians and Jews, priests and laymen — amounted to 1,014,200 gulden, an increase of 25 per cent upon the total debts in 1766. The amount was made up of 656,000 gulden as principal, 215,500 gulden as interest, and 142,700 gulden due to two Jewish creditors named Friedlaender. This last item is of particular interest, both as showing the relations at the time between the Jews of Vilna and their brethren in other countries, and also as illustrating how a debt of the Kahal grew like a snowball in the course of decades.

In 1760, after one of the many fires that afflicted the community, the Kahal borrowed a sum of 50,000

Polish gulden from two brothers in Koenigsberg, Seligmann and Hayyim Friedlaender, merchants and bankers, at 10 per cent. When the Liquidation Commission of 1766 inquired into the Kahal's financial affairs, the Friedlaenders declined to allow their claim to be dealt with, as they would not accept the reduced interest proposed by the Commission. They insisted on raising their interest to 12 per cent, and, as this was often not paid, the debt grew to a quite substantial sum by 1783, when the Kahal divided it into two parts (one somewhat larger than the other), giving separate bills to the two sons of Hayyim Friedlaender, David[1] and Abraham, which were guaranteed by twenty-six Vilna merchants. In 1789 the creditors applied to the courts in Vilna for repayment, whereupon the guarantors replied that the Friedlaenders had already received more interest than the amount of the loan. In 1792 the *Podstarosta* decided that the debt must be settled by the guarantors, failing which drastic steps would be taken. Two delegates were then despatched post-haste to Warsaw to submit a petition to the king, praying that he should give orders for the Municipal Council in Vilna to protect the guarantors from arrest and their shops from seizure. The delegates had to repeat their entreaty a few days later, before the king responded, with the result that the guarantors

---

[1] David Friedlaender (1750–1834), disciple and intellectual successor of Moses Mendelssohn, and famous as a writer and communal leader in Germany, whose advice was solicited by Bishop Malczewski in 1816 for improving the position of the Jews in Poland.

were saved from molestation and the Friedlaenders
were told that they could have recourse to the proper
court. At last, in 1793, the Liquidation Court decided
that the settlement of the debt of the Friedlaenders
should be given priority and that they should receive 142,700 gulden, including interest and legal
costs — nearly three times as much as the original
loan.

Among other complicated claims against the
Kahal were some which were a sort of aftermath
of the deposed-rabbi affair. The principal antagonist
of Samuel ben Avigdor was the elder, Abba ben
Wolf, who had incurred a heavy outlay, by legal
actions and by journeys to Warsaw and other places,
in the pursuit of his campaign. He had already
passed to a more peaceful world when the Liquidation Court considered the question of his expenditure on behalf of the Kahal; but his heirs were
awarded a sum of 10,600 gulden, besides damages
amounting to 8,000 gulden against some Jews who
had slandered him by accusing him of apostasy. The
Court also awarded compensation to Rabbi Ezekiel
ben Leib (called Rabbi Ezekiel "Schreiber"), who had
spent a long time in Warsaw as representative of
the Kahal in connection with the dispute. On the
other hand, the Court likewise granted compensation to two sons and a daughter of the deposed
rabbi, while the latter's son-in-law, Joseph ben Elijah
Pesseles, who put in a claim for 120,000 gulden
alleged to have been spent in connection with the
dispute, was non-suited on the ground that he was

not prepared to support his claim by an oath. Another son-in-law, Jonah ben Benjamin, demanded settlement of a promissory note for 3,000 gulden, which had originally been signed in 1766 (it was one of the numerous notes that Jews had been compelled to sign without knowing to whom they were liable) and which then passed from hand to hand in the course of years, like a form of currency.

Apart from the individual claims of ordinary creditors, the Liquidation Court had to settle the demands of various communal tax-farmers and to reorganize the Kahal's financial administration for the future (besides regulating the affairs of the Shnipishok and Antokol communities). In order to expedite the collection of its taxes, the Kahal had farmed them out to different persons, generally rich merchants or elders. Thus, one person would purchase the concession to collect the tax on silks, others the tithe on dowries or the taxes on grape-wine, fat, merchant travellers, kosher meat, poultry, and so forth. These tax-farmers, who had all paid in advance for their concessions, were prevented, in 1788, by a decision of the Treasury Commission, from continuing the ingathering of the various imposts, and were now awarded by the Court handsome compensation for their losses. As for the future fiscal arrangements, the Court calculated that the Kahal could reckon upon an income of 66,000 gulden in the ensuing year, and after that upon an income of 70,000 gulden a year, together with another 20,000 gulden from skins if the government tax on

them were abolished. It arranged that the future
income of 70,000 gulden should be farmed out, drew
up detailed instructions to be observed by the tax-
farmers, and forbade the Kahal either to lend money
or to apply the ban of excommunication. There
were, indeed, some substantial sums owing to the
Kahal — 79,000 gulden by the Lithuanian *Va'ad*
and other Kahals, and over 500,000 gulden by previous elders — but the Court came to the conclusion
that these were irrecoverable and must be written
off.

The Kahal began to collect the *Korobka* on meat
on its own account, as it needed money for the
Russian army which was still in the city; but the
Court warned it that any surplus must be applied
to the wiping out of debts. The Court also warned
the tax-farmers that they would be responsible for
the full amounts that they undertook to provide,
except in the event of what was then no exceptional
emergency, such as war, fire, or plague. Finally,
the Court authorized the new financial controller,
whom it appointed, to inform the Jewish community
that, after all its debts had been paid off, the various
Korobkas would be abolished. But all its debts were
never paid off. Some of them were certainly discharged by means of the income from the taxes
taken over by the Russian regime, but for decades
the Kahal continued immersed in debt, and the
manner of its ultimate extrication is veiled in
obscurity. It may, however, be reasonably presumed, that with the lapse of time, and in con-

sequence of the upheaval wrought by the Russian conquest, most of the successors of the original creditors gave up the fight to secure the satisfaction of their inherited claims, or were unable to prove them, and that the Russian authorities themselves had little interest in trying to remedy what they may have regarded as some of the defects of the defunct Polish regime.

CHAPTER XI

A CITADEL OF CULTURE

1. THE STUDY OF TALMUDIC LORE

HOWEVER insolvent materially the Vilna Kahal was during the greater part of its existence, the community over which it ruled never suffered from a lack of spiritual wealth. Loyalty to religious tradition, scrupulous observance of the Torah both written and oral, and diligent study of the Talmud, formed a triple rule of life, which was combined with the practice of the moral principles and social virtues transmitted and tested through centuries of persecution. The zealous pursuit of knowledge in a milieu which was disturbed only too often by alarms and disasters was remarkable enough; it was all the more notable when it is realized that the knowledge sought was of the vast rabbinic literature that related mainly to bygone times or prescribed the minutiae of rites and customs in the present. Physically, the Jews of Vilna were in a Slavic country that had been a stronghold of paganism until the fourteenth century; spiritually, they were in close daily communion with ancient Palestine or Babylon. For the tomes over which they pored, in strict fulfilment of the scriptural injunction, "Thou shalt meditate thereon day and night,"[1]

[1] Joshua, 1.8.

either originated from those Oriental lands or were based — as expositions, codes, or commentaries — upon the hallowed writings which had been composed there.

The devotion to this religious lore was not confined to the rabbi or the professional student, but was shared by the merchant and the artisan, who, when their daily work was over, would cheerfully wend their way to the *Bet ha-Midrash* or the *Klaus*, to become immersed in a page of the Talmud, a chapter of the Mishna, or a portion of some other volume on the multifarious laws and customs of Israel. Cloistered within their houses of learning, where their wits were inevitably sharpened for the battle of life, they found some solace for the sorrows of the struggle and strife without. The habit of study, which for them was invariably religious study, was inculcated from the tenderest years. While he was yet in the cradle the mother sang to her child in Yiddish rhymes of the beauty of the Torah:

> A little while together will we play
>   And then to school the child must quickly go,
> Where he will learn the Torah's happy way,
>   And good reports to us will daily flow.

The boy was taught to utter simple prayers in Hebrew as soon as he was able to speak, and when he reached the age of five he was taken by his happy father, sometimes wrapped in a *talit* (praying-shawl) to the *Heder*, a school in the humble home of a private teacher yet under the supervision of the

communal authorities. There his initiation into the
mysteries of the Hebrew alphabet was sweetened
by licks of honey or by copper coins mysteriously
dropped upon his book by some benevolent angel.
At the age of ten, when he had acquired a knowledge
of the Scriptures and its commentaries and also
been introduced to the *Shulhan Aruk*, the authoritative code of religious law, he was transferred to
an intermediate school for the advanced study of
the Bible and the Talmud. He celebrated his
religious majority at thirteen, when he became a
"Son of the Commandment" (*Bar-Mitzvah*), by
delivering a profound talmudical discourse at a
family feast, which was generally graced by the
presence of the rabbi and other communal notables;
and at the age of seventeen — or even earlier, if he
were precocious — he passed into the *Yeshibah* or
talmudical academy. While there, if he came from
another town, his material needs were looked after
by the community, and he was spurred on to achieve
distinction in his studies as the best means of ac-
quiring a bride with the twofold attraction of a
dowry and a pedigree (*Yiḥus*).[1] He married early —
at the latest, at eighteen — as prescribed in the

---

[1] The regulations of the Lithuanian *Va'ad* (1623–48) imposed
upon the rabbis the duty of receiving into their schools boys
and youths coming from other towns, providing for their support
out of the communal treasury, and placing them as guests with
rich members on Sabbaths and festivals. In 1639 the *Va'ad* took
charge of 75 wandering youths from other lands, and allotted
half to the Kahal of Brisk, and the remainder to Grodno and
Pinsk. Dubnow, *Weltgeschichte des juedischen Volkes*, vol. VI,
p. 358.

Mishna;[1] and for the first two or three years of his
new existence he lived in the home of his parents-
in-law, contributing to it the aureole of his scholar's
prestige, before he was able to found a home of his
own. His wife had received but a scanty education,
generally provided — if at all — by her father or a
visiting teacher, for learning in her case was considered unnecessary since she had fewer religious
duties to perform than a man. It was left to a later
age to make good this neglect.

The presiding genius of the community's religious
and scholastic life was the rabbi, who was not only
the president of the *Bet Din* but also the rector of
the talmudical seminary (*Rosh Yeshibah*). The title
of *Rav* was by no means the monopoly of the
ecclesiastical head, but could be obtained by any
student who, after a rigorous oral examination by
eminent rabbis, gave proof of a proficient knowledge
of talmudic lore and of the ability to decide questions
of Jewish law. There were thus many lay rabbis
who did not occupy any ecclesiastical position, but
devoted themselves to scholarship and literary activity or even to business pursuits. The simple and
unadorned title of *Rav*, however, was the lowest
in the recognized hierarchy of talmudic erudition;
the highest was the title of *Gaon*, which means
"Eminence" or "Excellency." It was not granted
by any authority, but applied by the people in
general to one whose pre-eminence was clear.
Between these two titles, and often combined with

[1] Abot 5.24.

them, were various grades expressed by laudatory adjectives or epithets, according to the different degrees of distinction or brilliance attaching to the profundity of research, the intellectual acumen, acknowledged authority, and literary achievements, in each case. A eulogistic term indicating a particularly powerful mind was "an uprooter of mountains" (*'Oker Harim*). No functioning rabbi's name was written without the prefatory words *Morenu ha-Rav* ("Our teacher the Master"), followed by a string of honorific terms, including the designation of the "holy congregation" of the *Bet Din* of which he was president; and as it was rarely given in a book or document of any importance without being particularized by the name of his father, who was generally also a rabbi entitled to some distinguishing appellations, the setting forth of his full description often occupied a number of lines. Descent from a lineage of rabbis was the most coveted of personal distinctions, and no peer of the British realm could look back upon an ancient pedigree with inherited titles with greater pride than the Jew whose forebears had each individually won fame for himself in the service of the Torah. Authorship greatly enhanced the rabbinical luster, and the book for which approbations were eagerly sought from leading rabbis was usually given a title suggested by the name of the writer, such as "Gate of Ephraim," or "Head of Joseph."

The cultivation of talmudic scholarship in Vilna began rather later than in other cities in Lithuania and Poland, such as Brisk, Cracow, or Lublin, since the community was founded later. Consequently the Jews of Vilna had at first to look to other centers and even other countries for their spiritual leaders. Of the twelve rabbis who held office during a period of less than two hundred years, until the deposition of Samuel ben Avigdor, not one can be proved to have been a native of Vilna. This, however, does not by any means reflect upon the reputation of the community, which gave birth to the most famous of talmudic luminaries in Eastern Europe, the Gaon Elijah, and to the author of the most authoritative commentary on the *Shulhan Aruk*, Shabbetai ben Meir ha-Kohen. Moreover, Vilna provided countless eminent rabbis for other communities and other countries.

2. RABBIS AND SCHOLARS

Little but his name, Abraham Segal, is known of the first rabbi in Vilna, who lived in the latter part of the sixteenth and at the beginning of the seventeenth century. He is mentioned by Rabbi Isaac ben Moses Katzenellenbogen, in his book *Toledot Yitzhak* ("Generations of Isaac"), in which he states that Rabbi Abraham Segal was his nephew. His successor was Rabbi Menahem Monash, the son of Isaac Hajes, rabbi in Prague and the author of thirteen works which exist only in manuscript. Menahem Monash Hajes, who had previously been rabbi at Turbin and Szidlow, was the author of a little work, *Zemirot le-Shabbat* ("Hymns for Sabbath"), published at Prague in 1621, of a commentary on the scriptural portion *Balak* (Numbers, 22.2–25.9), called *Derek Temimim* ("Path of the Perfect"), and of an elegy on a fire in the Jewish quarter in Posen. He held the office of rabbi in Vilna from 1617 to 1636, during which period he gave his approbation to an edition of the *Ze'enah u-Re'enah*, the homely Yiddish compilation of homiletical sections of midrashic writings composed for women by Rabbi Jacob ben Isaac, and printed in Prague in 1623. Even before going to Vilna he had conducted a learned correspondence with Rabbi Samuel Bacharach, of Worms, who died in 1615. He acquired added fame through his three sons, who were all rabbis and one of whom, the Gaon Samson Hajes, died at Belgrade in 1655, as well as through his grandsons, one of whom, the Gaon *Hasid* Rabbi Isaiah, was the author of *Bet Halevi*, printed in Venice in 1666, and lived in Ferrara, Mantua and Verona, before returning to Poland. He was followed by the Gaon Rabbi Feibush Ashkenazi,[1] who held office in the fourth decade of the seventeenth century and is described by contemporaries as "a brilliant *Rav* and great *Paskan* (decider of ritual questions)." Feibush Ashkenazi afterwards settled in Palestine, where he was *Nasi*[2] from 1650 to 1653, and his signature occurs twice in the *Pinkas* of the Sephardim in Jerusalem.

The next incumbent of the rabbinate was Moses

---

[1] This name is not mentioned by Finn, but is given by Hillel Noah Steinschneider in his '*Ir Vilna*, p. 3.

[2] A position equivalent to that of Chief Rabbi of a congregation in mediaeval Palestine who was also a supervisor of charity.

ben Isaac Judah Lima (a name indicative of Dutch
origin), who had studied at the *Yeshibah* of Rabbi
Joshua ben Joseph in Cracow, and as a young man
of twenty became rabbi and head of the talmudical
seminary at Slonim. He was called to Vilna, where
his father-in-law, Rabbi Zanvill, lived; but neither
the date of his appointment nor the length of his
tenure is known. He was certainly in Vilna in 1650,
and from there succeeded to the rabbinate at Brisk,
where he died at the age of fifty-three. He was
described by the author of *Zemah Zedek* ("Offspring
of Righteousness") as a "new bottle containing old
wine," and he established his reputation by his
commentary on the *Shulhan Aruk*, entitled *Helkat
Mehokek* ("Portion of the Lawgiver"), which was
printed by his two sons, Raphael and Lima, at
Cracow in 1670. He was followed by Isaac ben
Abraham, of Posen, who was first an assessor in the
Bet Din of Rabbi Abraham Epstein, of Pinsk, and
then held appointments at Luzk and Grodno before
going to Vilna. He is believed to have been a member of the *Bet Din* under Rabbi Moses Lima before
succeeding to his position, and he was afterwards
rabbi in Posen, where his son Jacob became *Ab
Bet Din*. He was one of the first rabbis of Vilna to
be a delegate to the Lithuanian *Va'ad*, and gave his
approbation to the "Book of Humility" (*Safra
di-Zeniut*) which was published in Amsterdam in
1669. He had four daughters who all married rabbis.
After him came Nahman ben Solomon Naphtali, of
whom nothing is known except that his signature
appears in a contemporary list of rabbis and in

commendations of some books, including *Migdal David* ("Tower of David"), by the Gaon David Lida, which appeared about 1674. His place of origin is variously given as Ladmir and Vladimir (Volhynsk).

The seventh in the line of Vilna's rabbis was a notable character, Moses ben David, a native of Cracow, and the ancestor of the Gaon Elijah. He was surnamed Kraemer, which means "shopkeeper," because, on accepting the appointment of rabbi, he declined to take a salary, being content to live on the earnings of a little provision-store kept by his wife. As he was very popular, all the members of the community made their purchases at this store. When Rabbi Moses noticed that his wife was conducting the household on a rather liberal scale, he questioned her, for he suspected that she was secretly receiving the salary he refused. But when she explained that this prosperity was due to the extensive custom which she enjoyed, he drew up a careful calculation of their weekly expenditure and told her that there was no need for them to earn more. He accordingly insisted that, as soon as she found that she had enough money for the rest of the week, she should at once close the shop, even if it was only Sunday afternoon, so that the other shopkeepers might also be able to earn enough to cover their needs. This unworldly rabbi had previously been a member of the *Bet Din* of Rabbi Abraham Epstein, at Brisk. The date of his appointment in Vilna is unknown, although it was probably some years before 1674. He was famous as a talmudic authority, but his only literary remains consist of some glosses and explanations quoted in the works of others, and of approbations of books, one of which, *Leket Shemuel* ("Gleanings of Samuel"), was published in Venice in 1694. When he died, in 1688, a space of three feet was reserved around his grave as a mark of especial honor, and his memory is held in pious and revered esteem to the present day. His repute was worthily sustained by his son, Rabbi Elijah Hasid, who was both elder and *Dayyan* in Vilna, and also by his son-in-law, Rabbi Joseph ben Jacob.

Although Rabbi Joseph ben Jacob, of Pinczow, taught in the talmudical academy in Vilna only for a short time, a few facts about his life may be recorded here as illustrating the vicissitudes to which so many Jewish scholars in Central Europe were then exposed. Three months before the death of Rabbi Moses Kraemer, Rabbi Joseph was appointed head of the *Bet Din* at Kosovi (in Russia), from where he received a call some years later to Seltz. Compelled to leave this town by the persecution which broke out under the temporary rule of the Swedes, Rabbi Joseph ben Jacob went to Hamburg, where he stayed until 1706. He then returned to Seltz, where within a few years his wife and five children died. Misfortune continued to dog him, for in 1710 the town was again visited by foreign troops as well as by plague. He thereupon fled to Berlin, where, in 1716, he published his commentary on the Talmud, *Rosh Yoseph* ("Head of Joseph"), by which he is best known.

Rabbi Moses Kraemer's successor, Samson ben Joseph Isaac, of Vizhun, does not appear to have been particularly distinguished. The only evidence of his existence consists of his signature to some decisions and letters in the minute-book of the "Great Charity" from 1678 to 1694, but there is no trace of his tombstone in the cemetery. He was followed by Hillel ben Jonah ha-Levi, who came from Chelm. This rabbi too was no writer, but his approbation was much sought after by the scholars of his day and he was one of the rabbis of the Lithuanian *Va'ad* who gave their commendation to the *Rosh Yoseph*. His opinions, too, were cited in the following terms: "I heard in the name of the late Gaon, our teacher, the Rav, Rav Hillel, who was *Ab Bet Din* in the holy congregation of Vilna." He is reported to have had a visit at his house on one occasion from a wealthy member of his community who treated him with gross discourtesy and abused him; but when this ill-bred individual returned to his home he died on the spot.

The tenth incumbent of the rabbinical office was Baruch Kahana Rapoport, who held it only for a couple of years, from 1707 to 1709, at a salary of 10 gulden per week. Apparently this satisfied his meager wants, as he was an ascetic and indulged in much fasting. From Vilna he went to Fürth (in Bavaria) to assume a similar position, and he later also received a call from Grodno. He did not accept this invitation, but in a description of himself he wrote: "his net is spread over Grodno," a conventional periphrasis which was used to indicate that the authority of the rabbi in question was recognized by another community besides his own. Rabbi Rapoport, who died in 1746, had three sons, one of whom, Rabbi Aryeh Leib, was appointed *Ab Bet Din* at Offenbach. He also had four daughters, all married to great scholars, one of whom, Rabbi Baer Oppenheim, was the religious head of the Jews in Pressburg. He was succeeded by the Gaon, Rabbi Joshua Heschel (or Hoeschel), who had held a similar position in Breslau, and was the son of the Gaon Rabbi Saul of Brisk and Cracow. The date of his appointment in Vilna is unknown, but he is believed to have been there from 1713; and he enjoyed an unusually long tenure, as he died in office in 1749. He gave his coveted commendation to many works, and maintained very friendly relations with a local Karaite scholar, with whom he loved to exchange riddles in Hebrew rhymes.

Six months after the death of the aged Rabbi Heschel, the influential secretary and *Dayyan* of the community, Rabbi Judah ben Eliezer, whose public services have already been described, sent a notice around to many cities that the position of ecclesiastical head was vacant and that anybody who thought that "by virtue of his knowledge, his qualities, and his pedigree, he was worthy to assume the rabbi's office in Vilna, should come and receive it." Rabbi Meir Ginzburg, of Vizhun, promptly sent a letter in reply, stating that he considered his qualifications entitled him to the post and that he would proceed to Antokol, where he would stay overnight, so that the elders of the community

could come there the next morning to welcome him.
The energetic Rabbi Judah immediately assembled
a meeting of a hundred and twenty of the leading
and wealthy members, urged upon them the qualifications of his son-in-law, Samuel ben Avigdor, and
secured his election to the vacancy. Early the
following morning he hastened to the expectant
Rabbi Meir Ginzburg at Antokol, consoled him with
a generous gift for his disappointment, and persuaded him to return home — a rather mortifying
anti-climax that did not prevent the crestfallen
candidate from subsequently affiancing his son,
Rabbi Benjamin Ginzburg, to a daughter of Rabbi
Judah. Although the father of Samuel ben Avigdor
was the rabbi in Vilkovishky, he himself was
originally not trained for the rabbinate, but was at
first engaged in business. It was therefore arranged
that he should return to the parental abode for a
couple of years to complete his training, during
which time his father-in-law was the acting rabbi.
To the account that has already been given in a
previous chapter of the career of the last ecclesi
astical head of Vilna, it may be added that even
after his deposition he continued to be honored
until his death. His approbation was highly prized
by scholars, and Rabbi David ben Yehiel, who in
1786 received it for his edition of the Pentateuch
with three *Targumim*, referred to him as "our master,
our king." His own literary work consisted only of
some comments on the Torah, in a book entitled
Hadrat Zekenim ("Majesty of Old Men"), and
manuscript notes on the Talmud. But such was the

esteem in which he was held despite his downfall that, according to local tradition, all who supported him lived to a good old age while those who opposed him died before their time.

Important as all these rabbis were in different degrees and in their particular generation, their contributions to talmudic scholarship cannot compare with the works of a number of savants who were, with one exception, natives of Vilna, and nearly all of whom had to suffer from the barbarous invasion of Chmielnicki. Indeed, the enforced exile of so many scholars from Lithuania and Poland proved of spiritual advantage to many communities in other parts of Europe, where they came as refugees and remained as religious leaders.[1]

Probably the earliest Jewish scholar whom Vilna could claim was Heschel Zoref,[2] a cabalist who afterwards lived and died in Cracow, the son of Rabbi Joseph Zoref, who had also been born in Vilna. Heschel Zoref, whose name is mentioned in an old *Pinkas* of the Cracow community under the date of 1551, was the author of five works, three of

---

[1] Rabbi Jacob Emden, the famous antagonist of the Shabbetian heresy, pays a glowing tribute in his *Megillat Sefer* to the high level of talmudic scholarship of the "Sages of Vilna" and to the valuable services rendered by the exiled rabbis in the dissemination of their knowledge in so many parts of Europe.

[2] Heschel Zoref (mentioned in *Kiryah Ne'emanah*, p. 291), has been identified by Dr. Gerhard Scholem with Adam Ba'al-Shem, the reputed author of the writings from which Israel Ba'al-Shem derived his ideas. [For a different date and identification of Heschel Zoref, see Scholem, *Major Trends in Jewish Mysticism*, N. Y., 1942, p. 327].

which were entitled *Sheloshet Edre Zon* ("Three
Flocks of Sheep"), the fourth was entitled *Be'er*
("Well"), and the fifth *Ayyelet Ahabim* ("Hind of
Love"). Little else is known about him except that
he was an assiduous student in the *Bet ha-Midrash*
of the cabalist and author of *Megalleh 'Amukot*
("Revealer of Profundities"), Rabbi Nathan Sha-
pira, head of the *Bet Din* of Cracow, where he wrote
his mystical works.   Another early scholar and one
of the most eminent talmudical authorities of his
age was Rabbi Joshua Heschel (or Hoeschel) ben
Joseph, grandfather of the Joshua Heschel who was
the rabbi of Vilna in the first half of the eighteenth
century. Born in Vilna about 1578, he went as a
boy to Przemysl (Galicia) to study the Talmud
under Rabbi Samuel ben Phoebus of Cracow, and
then repaired to the city of Vladimir-Volhynsk, where
he continued his studies under Rabbi Joshua Falk.
After his marriage to the daughter of Rabbi Samuel
of Brest-Litovsk, he became rabbi of Grodno,
whence he was called to the spiritual leadership
of the community of Tiktin (Tykotzin) and later
to that of Przemysl. In 1639 he became rabbi of
Lwow (Lemberg), and in the following year was
appointed head of the Cracow *Yeshibah*. At Cracow
he devoted all his time to the interests of the rabbinical seminary and to decisions in religious law,
and, as a man of means, accepted no salary for all
the services he rendered to the community. Although
he had a liking for the Cabala, he did not allow
mystical teachings to influence his *halakic* decisions.
Thanks to his profound erudition, he had a large

and constant succession of pupils, many of whom became noted rabbis themselves. His published works are *Meginne Shelomo* (Amsterdam, 1715), *novellae* on various tractates of the Talmud, in which he criticizes the strictures made by the school of the *tosafists* on Rashi's commentaries, and *She'e-lot u-Teshubot Pene Yehoshua* (Amsterdam, 1715, and Lemberg, 1860).

By far the most outstanding of Vilna's scholars in the seventeenth century was Shabbetai ben Meir Ha-Kohen, a pupil of Rabbi Joshua Heschel, who leapt into fame at the early age of twenty-six as the author of a commentary on the *Shulhan Aruk*, entitled *Sifte Kohen* ("Lips of the Priest"), in which he challenged many of the decisions of his predecessors and the opinions of his contemporaries. Born in 1621, "ShaK" (as he was called, after the initials of his name) studied in Cracow and Lublin, and when quite a young man was appointed a member of the Vilna *Bet Din* under Rabbi Moses Lima. In 1646 he went to Cracow, where, in the following year, he published his work on the second part of the *Shulhan Aruk*, which received the approbation of eighteen of the greatest scholars of his generation. He struck out on a path of his own in his interpretation of talmudic law, and although his views aroused the hostility of some of his contemporaries, such as David ben Samuel ha-Levi, author of *Ture Zahab* ("Rows of Gold"), and Aaron Samuel Koidanower, author of *Birkat ha-Zevah* ("Blessing of the Sacrifice"), the majority accepted his work as of the highest authority and applied his decisions to actual

cases as the final word on the laws in question.
"ShaK" had to flee from Cracow owing to Chmielnicki's hordes, and sought refuge for a time at
Prague, where he probably wrote his account of the
massacres, *Megillat Ayefa* ("Scroll of the Weary
Soul"),[1] and some penitential prayers, *Selihot*, for
the 20th of Sivan, in memory of Chmielnicki's victims. He soon received a call to the rabbinate of
Dresin, and was later appointed rabbi at Holle-
schau, in Moravia, where he conducted a very
friendly correspondence in Hebrew with the Leipzig
Magister Valentine Vidrich. When he died, still
comparatively young, in 1662, he left a number of
other important works, which were published later.
These included commentaries, under the same title,
Sifte Kohen, on other parts of the *Shulhan Aruk*, a
reply to Rabbi David ha-Levi, and an arrangement
of the 613 commandments according to Maimonides.

Another redoubtable scholar was Aaron Samuel
ben Israel Koidanower, whose commentary on the
Talmud, *Birkat ha-Zevah*, published in Amsterdam
in 1669, marked a new course by determining the
text according to the old manuscripts and elucidating
legal decisions in a clear and convincing manner.
Born in Vilna in 1614, "MaHaRShaK" (as he was
called, after his initials) studied in Lublin and was
afterwards appointed to the *Bet Din* of Rabbi Moses
Lima. When the Cossack invasion occurred he fled
to Langenlois, in Lower Austria, where he became

---

[1] An allusion to Jeremiah, 4. 31 ("For my soul fainteth before
murderers").

the rabbi, and from there he was called to assume a similar position, first at Fürth (in Bavaria), next at Frankfort-on-the-Main, and finally at Cracow. He died at Chmjelnik, in Little Poland, whither he had gone to attend a meeting of the Polish *Va'ad*. After his death further commentaries of his on the Talmud and Pentateuch appeared, as well as Responsa, under the title *Emunat Shemuel* ("Faith of Samuel"), which are distinguished by their thoroughness. They are signed by himself as "one of the exiles of the holy community of Vilna."

Zevi Hirsch Koidanower, the son of Aaron Samuel Koidanower, achieved a fame surpassing that of his father, thanks to the extensive popularity of his ethical work, *Kab ha-Yashar* ("The Just Measure"), which appeared in two parts in 1705 and 1706. Born about the middle of the seventeenth century, he was taken by his father on his flight to Austria and afterwards accompanied him to Frankfort, where he married. Later he returned to Vilna, where in time he acquired both wealth and esteem. Having become the victim of some slander, he went back to Frankfort and remained there until his death on March 23, 1712. With the cooperation of his father-in-law (Isaac ha-Kohen Gans) and his brother-in-law (Judah Leib Gans), he published three works of his father, the aforementioned *Emunat Shemuel* as well as *Birkat Shemuel* ("Blessing of Samuel," 1682) and *Tiferet Shemuel* ("Glory of Samuel," 1696). His own famous work, consisting of 102 chapters, deals with the most varied religious and ethical themes in a popular style. Despite its somber

mystic undertone, it enjoyed particular favor with
women. The first edition was in Hebrew, but the
work was afterwards provided with a Yiddish translation, and the two versions were published together
in 1709. Until the end of the nineteenth century the
Kab ha-Yashar appeared in thirteen editions in
Hebrew, in fifteen with the Yiddish translation, in
six in Yiddish alone, and in two editions in Ladino.
Zevi Hirsch Koidanower was greatly influenced by
his teachers, Joseph b. Judah Judel, rabbi in Minsk,
who had initiated him into the mysteries of the
Cabala and from whose work, *Yesod Yosef* ("Foundation of Joseph"), many passages are reproduced
in the *Kab ha-Yashar*. The work as a whole reflects
the sufferings and ideas as well as the social conditions of his time. He also wrote a commentary on
the Pentateuch and drew up rules for the Jewish
calendar (of which there is a manuscript in the
Bodleian Library).

A savant who — so far as the records show —
never occupied any rabbinical office was Moses
Rivkes, author of the *Be'er ha-Golah* ("Well of
Exile"), a commentary on the *Shulhan Aruk*. He
was the son of Rabbi Naphtali, secretary of the
Prague community, and his settlement in Vilna, the
date of which is unknown, was probably due to his
marrying the daughter of a wealthy resident in that
city. That he contracted a rich marriage may be
reasonably deduced from the fact that he never
occupied any salaried position or engaged in business,
that he devoted all his life to scholarship, that he
owned a large house and library, and that he left

a fortune of which he bequeathed a great part as a permanent endowment to charitable institutions in Vilna. The story of his sufferings during his flight to Amsterdam in 1655 has already been related in a previous chapter. His talmudic erudition was gratefully recognized by the religious and lay leaders of the Jewish community in the Dutch capital, and he was therefore charged by Rabbi Moses Raphael de Aguilar, Dr. Ephraim Bueno, and Jacob Castello, with the revision of the proofs of a new edition of Joseph Caro's authoritative codex. After reluctantly accepting the task, he decided to add to the text notes of his own, especially on decisions that betrayed a mutual contradiction; and these notes, under the title of *Be'er ha-Golah*, of which the first part appeared in 1661 and the second three years later, have always been printed in the margin of subsequent editions of the *Shulhan Aruk*. Rivkes lived in Amsterdam for ten years; and when he returned to Vilna, after the restoration of peace, the elders of the Dutch community, in the course of a letter to the Polish *Va'ad*, referred to him as "the veteran sage, the chief of the diligent scholars of our generation." The esteem in which he was held by his contemporaries is proved by the fact that they called him the *Hasid* (the "pious one" or "saint"), a title applied in Vilna to only one other Jew in the seventeenth century, Rabbi Elijah, the son of Rabbi Moses Kraemer, and to only one in the eighteenth century, the famous Gaon Elijah, a descendant of the latter. At Rivkes' death, in 1671 (or 1672), he left the manuscripts of two other works *Kelale Hora'a*

("Rules of Instruction") and *Keli ha-Golah* ("Vessel of Exile"), consisting of commentaries on *Halakot* (religious laws) and the Mishna, which he had been unable to complete for publication.

The *Shulhan Aruk* also occupied the critical industry of Ephraim ben Jacob ha-Kohen, whose principal work, *Sha'ar Efrayim* ("Gate of Ephraim"), consists of Responsa arranged according to the order of that standard code. Born in Vilna in 1616, he became an assessor at the age of twenty in the *Bet Din* of Rabbi Moses Lima, and held that post for about twenty years. Driven from his home by Chmielnicki's barbarians, he went to Moravia and occupied the rabbinate at Trebitsch. Later, owing to further commotion, he fled to Prague, where he taught the Talmud. He was then invited to the home of a rich relative in Vienna, Rabbi Koppel ha-Levi, with whom he stayed until he received a call to the rabbinate of Ofen (now part of Budapest) in 1666. Twelve years later an invitation reached him from Jerusalem to occupy the rabbinical post there which had once been held by his grandfather. But before acceding, he wished to publish his works. While he was engaged in the revision of his manuscripts, his eldest son, an elder of Ofen, died of the plague in 1678. He also was apparently stricken, for he died only two weeks later, after charging his other son, Rabbi Leib, to publish his works. His *Sha'ar Efrayim* was not printed until 1688, at Sulzbach, but his other book, *Mahaneh Efrayim* ("Camp of Ephraim"), a commentary on the Torah, remained in manuscript.

The vicissitudes of his son-in-law, Rabbi Jacob ben Benjamin Ze'ev, likewise a native of Vilna, may also be noted, partly because they were even more adventurous, and partly because he was the father of the famous Hakam Zevi Ashkenazi. When Rabbi Jacob, with the other members of his family, fled from the Cossacks' fury, he became separated from his wife and was in danger of being killed by some bandits; but he begged on his knees to be spared and was allowed to escape. For a week he hid among the slain, creeping out only at night into the fields in search of vegetables to keep himself alive, before he was able to get away. Some men who had seen him being threatened assured Rabbi Ephraim ha-Kohen that he had been killed, and Rabbi Heschel gave the presumed widow permission to remarry. But she refused to believe in her husband's death and rejected all offers for her hand. Six months later Rabbi Jacob was reunited to his wife, after which Rabbi Heschel refrained from granting permission to remarry to any of the numerous *Agunot*[1] at the time. Rabbi Jacob succeeded his father-in-law as the religious head at Trebitsch, then obtained a similar post at Ungarisch-Brod, and finally succeeded his father-in-law in the rabbinate at Ofen, where he founded a talmudical academy whose fame extended to Turkey. But when Ofen

---

[1] *Agunah* (singular of *Agunot*) is the term applied to a woman whose husband has either abandoned her or has not been heard from for some time; and as she has neither a bill of divorcement from him nor proof of his death her status as a wife continues unchanged.

was captured by the imperial troops, Rabbi Jacob and his wife were taken prisoner to Berlin, where they were released.   They then went to Altona, where they found their son, the famous *Hakam* Zevi Ashkenazi, at the head of the community. The last of their journeys was to Jerusalem, where, soon after the death of his wife, Rabbi Jacob passed away at the age of seventy-three.

3. THE STUDY OF MEDICINE

Although the study of the Talmud and cognate literature practically monopolized the minds of Vilna Jewry, and at least during the first century and more of the community's existence there was little or no opportunity to become acquainted with any secular subject or science, some interest began to be displayed in medicine. This was in accordance with tradition, for Jews had devoted themselves to the science of healing from the earliest times, and many of them had been distinguished physicians to kings and caliphs, popes and cardinals. Had not Moses Maimonides, whose *Mishneh Torah*, if not his *Moreh Nebukim*, was certainly pored over by the students in Vilna's seminary, also been famous as a physician? In Poland, too, the Royal Court welcomed Jewish doctors, even if they were Marranos like Isaac Hispanus, who attended three kings: John Albert, Alexander, and Sigismund.

The interest of the Jews of Vilna in medicine received a definite stimulus from the arrival in their midst, from a strange and distant land, of a rather romantic personality, a scholar of brilliant gifts, Joseph Delmedigo, who became the physician of the Duke of Radziwill. Born in Candia in 1591, the son of the local rabbi, he had studied mathematics and astronomy under Galileo at Padua, from where he used to visit that gifted but erratic scholar, Leo de Modena, in Venice, and fell under his influence. He had also made a study of medicine and philosophy, and of astrology and Cabala. But when he returned to his orthodox home in Crete, his views were found too lax, and so he journeyed to Cairo and Constantinople, in both of which he associated with Karaite scholars. He then travelled through Wallachia, Moldavia, and Poland, and came to Vilna in 1620, where the advent of such a notable visitor created a sensation. The Duke of Radziwill appointed him as his physician, and Joseph Delmedigo remained in his service for four years. Such a versatile intellect found himself somewhat out of harmony with a community dominated by the cult of rabbinic lore, and he complained of the excessive devotion to *Pilpul* (dialectics) and the lack of interest in scientific subjects. Nevertheless, he found some men after his own heart, among them Moses ben Meir, of Metz, who had come to Vilna. Another kindred spirit was a Karaite scholar, Zerah ben Nathan, of Troki, who was also staying in the city and who was one of many Karaites with whom Delmedigo fraternized.[1] Zerah ben Nathan ad-

---

[1] Finn, *Kiryah Ne'emanah*, p. 73; but Jacob Mann (*Texts and Studies*, II, 576) suggests that Zerah b. Nathan never met Delmedigo personally.

dressed a number of questions on religious and scientific subjects to him, and his answers to them are embodied in his work, *Elim* ("Palms"), which contains also seventy mathematical paradoxes and was published in Amsterdam in 1629. When Delmedigo left Vilna in 1624, he had not only aroused an interest in medicine and in the University of Padua, but had himself been infected with a love of rabbinics, for he went to Hamburg, where he served as rabbi of the Sephardic congregation, and afterwards occupied a similar position in Amsterdam. In 1630 in Frankfort, he returned to the medical profession, becoming communal physician. Subsequently he settled in a similar capacity in Prague, where he lived from 1648 until his death in 1655.

The first Vilna Jew to go to Padua to study medicine — since all the universities in Poland were closed to Jews — was Dr. Aaron Gordon, who was born about the middle of the seventeenth century. Upon returning home he was appointed physician to King John Sobieski, who was so pleased with him that he exempted him and his family from the payment of all taxes in the community and granted them and all descendants permission to dwell and trade in all parts of the city. The charter setting forth these privileges was renewed by the last Polish king, Stanislav Poniatowski, and a copy was treasured by the Gordon family until the nineteenth century, when it was lost. Aaron took an active part in communal affairs, and his signature appears in the *Pinkas* of the Lithuanian *Va'ad* in an entry dated Ab 24, 5476 (1716). He was the ancestor of the numerous family of Gordons in Vilna, although nothing is known of his antecedents. Nor is anything else known about his life, except a somewhat romantic story preserved by his descendants.[1]

According to this tradition Aaron Gordon, after completing his medical studies at Padua, took a ship to return to Poland (apparently either because he wanted to see something of the world, or a journey by land at the time would have presented difficulties). Unfortunately the ship was wrecked off the coast of Spain. On reaching land, he made his way to the nearest town. It was the day before the Feast of Passover, and he wondered how he would be able to obtain unleavened bread, seeing that the Jews had been expelled from Spain in 1492. He therefore stood in the market place to note whether any Marranos would come to buy the herbs needed for the domestic celebration in the evening. Presently a handsome carriage arrived from which a gentleman of distinguished appearance stepped out and told his servant to buy some herbs. The shipwrecked traveller then followed the carriage to an imposing mansion and asked one of the many servants whether he could see his master. When the latter came out, Aaron Gordon said to him: "I entrust my life unto you that you may entrust your life unto me. I am a Hebrew, and you too are a Hebrew, and you fear the God of Heaven like me. Today is the eve of our Feast of Passover. Pray, give me a place at your table, that I may not die of

[1] Related by Finn, *Kiryah Ne'emanah*, p. 111.

hunger." The grandee was at first angry at these words, but after Gordon assured him that nobody would know, he acknowledged that he was a Marrano and in the evening took him to a subterranean chamber, large and festive, where the table had been prepared for the ritual celebration. The host was accompanied only by his wife and eldest son, as he had not yet revealed his secret to his younger children. Gordon stayed with him for the Passover week and another month, and then the Marrano hired a ship for his return, and gave him money for his expenses and presents in addition.

About the time when Aaron Gordon was already an old man, if he was still alive, Yekutiel ben Leib, another native of Vilna, after studying the Torah and the Talmud for many years, also went to Padua to devote himself to medicine. There his interest in the Cabala brought him into contact with the mystic and Hebrew poet, Moses Hayyim Luzzatto, who, although then only a young man of twenty-two, made a deep impression upon him. Yekutiel sent some letters in the most extravagant language about his studies and discussions with Luzzatto to the rabbi of Vilna, Joshua Heschel, and also to Rabbi Mordecai Jaffe; and in one of them, dated 1729, he wrote effusively: "Nothing is hidden from him, neither great nor small."[1] Whether he received any reply is not known; in any case, Rabbi Heschel prob-

---

[1] Published in Jacob Emden's *Torat ha-Kenaot* (a polemic on Sabbetai Zevi, Amsterdam, 1752). Yekutiel b. Leib was also called Gordon (see Dubnow in *Sefer ha-Shanah*, New York, 5691, page 219).

ably shared the hostility to the Cabala so strongly manifested by his relative, Rabbi Zevi Ashkenazi. The result, however, was very harmful to Luzzatto. Yekutiel stayed on in Padua for some years, even after Luzzatto went to Amsterdam in 1733, and continued his studies of mysticism, and when he returned to Vilna as a doctor won over many followers to the Cabala. He took an active interest in communal affairs and went as a delegate for the Brisk Kahal, in 1752, to The Hague, where he was received with great honor; and although he wrote several works on the Cabala, he neither had enough money himself nor would a patron provide any for their publication.

Another child of the Vilna Ghetto who studied medicine at the University of Padua, about the middle of the eighteenth century, was Judah ben Mordecai ha-Levi Hurwitz, who, on returning to his native city after travelling through Europe, was appointed physician to the Jewish community. He was of a somewhat roving disposition, for he left Vilna to practice medicine at Ponedeli, Zhagory, and Mitau, and finally settled in Grodno, where he died in 1797. His activity was not confined to his profession, as he was a prolific Hebrew author both in prose and verse. His most important work was *Sefer ʿAmude Bet Yehudah* ("Book of the Pillars of the House of Judah"), a poetical treatise on moral philosophy (published in Amsterdam, 1765), modelled upon the *Tahkemoni* of the mediaeval Spanish writer, Al-Harizi, in which an attack upon Platonism and Aristotelianism is expressed in classic language

tinctured with humor,[1] and which received the
warm approval of Moses Mendelssohn and Naphtali Herz Wessely.[2] His other works, which were
also mainly philosophical in character, included *Zel
ha-Ma'alot*, 360 ethical sentences (published in
Koenigsberg, 1764, and reprinted in Dubno, 1796),
and *Sefer Megillat Sedarim* ("Book of the Scroll of
Orders"), on the differences between cabalists, tal-
mudists, and philosophers (published in Prague,
1793). He also published a Hebrew poem on the
occasion of the opening of the government secondary
school in Mitau in 1775. The library of this institution preserved a number of manuscript Hebrew
poems of his, chiefly translations from the German,
until the early part of this century, and it is possible,
despite the political upheavals that have since taken
place along the Baltic coast, that a kindly Providence
may have spared them to this day.[3]

[1] Franz Delitzsch, *Zur Geschichte der juedischen Poesie* (Leipzig,
1836), p. 85.
[2] Finn, *Kiryah Ne'emanah*, p. 178.
[3] An interesting reference to this medical and poetical philos-
opher occurs in Leonid Grossmann's *Die Beichte eines Juden*
(Munich, 1927) which contains the remarkable correspondence
of Abraham Uri Kowner with Dostoievski on the Jewish question.

CHAPTER XII

THE GAON RABBI ELIJAH VILNA

AMONG the host of talmudical scholars in whom Vilna so richly abounded in the seventeenth and eighteenth centuries the greatest luminary was the Gaon Rabbi Elijah. Among so many religious leaders of the period, whose erudition and authority had earned them the title of Gaon,[1] or "Eminence," he was the Gaon *par excellence*. In range of knowledge, profundity of learning, intellectual grasp and originality of research, he towered not only above all his contemporaries but also above all rabbinic scholars of five centuries before him; and he has not been surpassed or even approached since. He was a remarkable phenomenon, intellectually and spiritually, whose commanding position was based not upon any official dignity, which he never desired and never held, but upon his unchallenged supremacy as an exponent of the Torah and the Talmud. Even if Vilna had never produced any other Jewish scholar or writer, the fame of the Gaon alone would have conferred upon it eternal luster. His name is uttered to this day, by all who have a glimmer of his greatness, with a feeling of the deepest reverence.

---

[1] The term had been the regular title of the head of the Babylonian academies after the 7th century. In Europe it possessed no official meaning.

Elijah was a direct descendant of Rabbi Moses Kraemer, the modest rabbi who was head of the community in the latter part of the seventeenth century, and also of Rabbi Moses Rivkes, who spent his exile in Amsterdam in writing his commentary on the *Shulhan Aruk*. The son of Rabbi Kraemer, Rabbi Elijah, known as the *Hasid* (Saint), who was the leader of the Vilna community in his own day, had a grandson, Rabbi Solomon Zalman, whose profession was described as the study of the Torah — sufficient evidence of his humble position. Solomon Zalman and his wife, Treine, lived at first at Seltz, a little town near Brest, and to them was born, on the first day of Passover in the year 5480 (April 23, 1720), as their first child, a boy whom they called Elijah after his saintly great-grandfather. Some biographers state that Elijah was born at Seltz, but the weight of evidence seems to be in favor of Vilna. He is described as having been a very good-looking child, "as beautiful as an angel," with lovely eyes. His mental powers soon proved altogether exceptional, and he was recognized as a prodigy. At the age of six and a half he delivered in the Great Synagogue a learned talmudical discourse that he had been taught by his father; but when tested by the rabbi of Vilna he showed that he possessed sufficient knowledge and originality to be able to give such a discourse unaided. At the age of seven he studied for a time under Moses Margalith, the rabbi of Keidan and author of a commentary on the Jerusalem Talmud. He was soon able to dispense with a teacher altogether and continued his studies alone.

He is then supposed to have known several tractates of the Talmud by heart, and is said to have perplexed the rabbi of Vilna by his controversial skill in the discussion of talmudical subjects. He had such a remarkable memory that he is believed to have been able, after reading a book, to recite it by heart for the rest of his life. At nine he was acquainted not only with the contents of the Bible, the Mishna, and the Talmud, but also with the commentaries on all these voluminous works, and before he was thirteen he had not only acquired a knowledge of a number of secular subjects but also of the intricate mysteries of the Cabala. Such was his quickness of apprehension that he was credited, as a boy, with having in a single night gone through the tractates Zebahim and Menahot, comprising 230 pages, the contents of which are in part difficult enough to baffle even the veteran scholar.

However much either his own generation or later ones may been tempted to exaggerate his precocity in assigning definite dates to the various stages of his intellectual progress, there can be no doubt that as a boy he displayed astonishing mental powers, and that these developed both in strength and creative quality as he grew older. He struck out on an original course in the pursuit of his studies, which he was able to do as he was untrammeled by a teacher. He devoted himself to a systematic study of Hebrew grammar and the Bible, both of which were either neglected or regarded as subordinate in the curriculum of the *Yeshibah*. He made himself thoroughly familiar not only with the Babylonian

Talmud, but also with its congener, the Jerusalem
Talmud, which was generally treated with indifference, although both from the historical and critical
points of view it was of greater importance than the
former. He pointed out that previous Geonim, and
even Maimonides, had not paid sufficient attention
to the Jerusalem Talmud and to the *Tosefta*, the
work similar to the Mishna containing the sayings
and discussions of the *Tannaim*, which he mastered.
He furthermore assimilated a great deal of cognate
literature, such as the *Sifra*, *Sifre*, *Mekilta*, *Seder
'Olam* (a work on chronology), and some minor
tractates. Displaying a spirit of broadmindedness
rare in his country and still rarer in his generation,
he was also a diligent student of history and geography, and particularly of mathematics, astronomy
and anatomy. He would even have liked music to
be included in general education. He was prevented
by his father from applying himself to medicine, as
he might have been tempted to neglect the Torah
in his ministrations to suffering humanity, and he
was deterred from pursuing an interest in botany
by the rather uncouth habits of the Lithuanian
farmer. He did not regard the acquisition of secular
sciences as subordinate or alien to his Jewish studies,
but as helpful and even necessary to them. Many
years later a pupil of his, Rabbi Baruch of Shklow,
who had been induced by him to make a Hebrew
translation of Euclid (of which a part was published
at The Hague in 1820), wrote in the introduction
about a conversation he had had with him on the
matter in 1778. The Gaon then said that whatever

a man lacked in the knowledge of science caused a
deficiency in his understanding of the Torah, for
Torah and science were linked together. He also
wanted to see the works of Josephus translated
into Hebrew, as he was of the opinion that they
would be helpful to the study of the Talmud.

Rabbi Elijah married, probably at the customary
age of eighteen, a girl named Hannah, the daughter
of Rabbi Judah of Keidan, and lived in the home
of her parents for some time. Details about his
family are rather scanty, but we know that his
marriage was blessed with two sons, Aryeh Leib
and Abraham, who grew up to become great scholars,
and at least one daughter, who married Rabbi Moses
of Pinsk. As a young man the Gaon travelled to
various cities in Poland and Germany, as so many
students of the Talmud were wont to do in his time,
but the particulars of his journeyings are unknown.
Despite his retiring disposition, his erudition was
immediately recognized wherever he went, and he
was hardly twenty when rabbis began to submit
their difficulties in Jewish religious law to him for
decision. He returned to his home in Vilna at the
age of twenty-five, but a few years later he set out
again — this time for the Holy Land. He did not
travel beyond Germany, however. The reason why
he abandoned his enterprise has not been recorded,
but it has been suggested that it may have been due
to his inability to observe the dietary laws on board
ship. While he was at Koenigsberg he wrote a letter
to his wife (published under the title *'Alim li-Terufa*
["Leaves for Healing"], at Minsk, in 1836), which

shows him as a strict and solicitous father. He bids his wife punish their children for swearing, scolding, or speaking an untruth, advises her to live in retirement as essential to a religious life, and suggests that his daughter should read the prayers at home, as in the synagogue she might become covetous of the finer dresses of her friends and thus commit a sin. He also begs his wife to be kind to his mother, as she was a widow.

The Gaon lived the life of an ascetic, regarding such a life as a necessary means to the self-perfection which he made his dominating principle. He refused all offers of rabbinical positions, although he could doubtless have stipulated his own terms. Dr. Schechter suggested that the reason for his refusal was to be sought in the unfortunate experience of Rabbi Samuel ben Avigdor[1], but since this did not occur until the Gaon was already in the fifties, it could not have influenced his attitude which was probably due to his desire to be able to devote himself entirely to his studies. Nevertheless, even though he held no office, he was practically recognized as the spiritual head not only of the Vilna community but also of the entire Lithuanian and Russian Jewry. Throughout the second half of the eighteenth century he enjoyed undisputed authority on matters of religious law among all the Jewish communities of Eastern and Central Europe. He was so omnivorous a reader and so productive a scholar

[1] *Studies in Judaism*, I, p. 83.

that he is said not to have been able to spare more than two hours a night for sleep; and although this may be somewhat of an exaggeration, it nevertheless shows that he gave very little time to rest. Large sums of money passed through his hands, as he received about 1,400 gulden annually from the community for distribution to the poor and for educational purposes; but he maintained his family on a small weekly allowance granted to him from a legacy left by his ancestor, Rabbi Moses Rivkes, for the maintenance of any of his descendants who devoted themselves to the study of the Torah. He patterned his life according to the rule prescribed by an ancient sage: "A morsel with salt shalt thou eat and water by measure shalt thou drink, and thou shalt sleep on the earth, and thou shalt live a life of hardship, and labor in the Torah. If thou doest thus, happy shalt thou be and it shall be well with thee; happy in this world and well with thee in the world to come."[1] Even when he and his family had to suffer hunger for some years owing to the dishonesty of a minor official of the community who kept his weekly allowance for himself, he uttered no complaint, since to inform against the culprit would have brought the latter to shame, and this, according to the Talmud, would have been equal to bloodshed. He often sold his furniture to help the poor, and gave away his last meal to the hungry. Living a life of such seclusion, scholarly industry

[1] Abot 6.4.

and self-denial, it was perhaps but natural that by the time he was thirty he was already called the *Hasid* (Saint).

The greatness of the Gaon, however, lay less in his mode of life than in the use he made of it. He introduced a new method into the study of the Talmud and all rabbinic literature, and he enriched that literature with a large number of works of his own. The *Yeshibah* had for centuries cultivated the tradition of *pilpul* (dialectics) as the essential method in the exegesis of the Talmud, a practice fostered by the rivalry of the numerous competing academies, whose rectors tried to outshine one another in their novel interpretations, and by the necessity of reconciling the resulting contradictions. The Gaon sternly set his face against the extravagances of this practice. This he was able to do all the more easily as he was entirely immune from the influences and conventions of the *Yeshibah*. He contended that indulgence in casuistry was harmful both to the study of the Torah and to its observance. He insisted upon the Torah and the Talmud being explained according to their simple straightforward meaning (*Peshat*); and he applied to this method the critical apparatus of the philologist and the acumen of a well-stored mind. "With a single shaft of the light of truth he would illumine the darkness, and with a single word he would overthrow heaps of *pilpulim* hanging by a hair."[1] For him the revealing of the truth was of far greater importance than the most

[1] Finn, *Kiryah Ne'emanah*, p. 146.

subtle discussion, and if there were any obscurities
or perplexities in a passage they had to be cleared
up by a thorough examination of the text. He thus
elucidated many obscure passages in the Mishna by
reference to parallel statements in the *Tosefta*, and
he unravelled an involved argument in the Babylonian Talmud with the help of a lucid argument on
the same question in the Jerusalem Talmud. He
maintained that the exposition of the Talmud must
be based upon reason and not upon authority.

He was the first Jewish scholar to realize that
ancient documents were subject to a certain amount
of corruption in the course of successive copyings
extending over centuries. Whenever a reading appeared doubtful to him he was at pains to compare
it with the original source and amend it where necessary. He has been described as "a genius of the
first order,"[1] and as "the last great theologian of
classical Rabbinism."[2] As he knew no other language
but Hebrew, he was a more faithful representative
of rabbinic Judaism than the great theologians of
the Middle Ages, who were not uninfluenced by
Greek and Arab thinkers.

The Gaon embodied the results of his study, research and reflection in a great number of works
embracing a wide variety of subjects. Rabbi
Abraham Danzig, in his funeral oration on the
Gaon, stated that he had written seventy books,
and a similar statement was made by Rabbi Israel

[1] Schechter in *Studies in Judaism*, ibid.
[2] Louis Ginzberg in *Students, Scholars and Saints*, p. 125.

of Minsk, one of the Gaon's disciples. All these
books, according to tradition, were written before
their author reached the age of forty.[1] None of them
appeared in his lifetime; some have been lost; and
many are still awaiting publication.[2] They were
composed mainly in the course of his studies, as
notes and comments upon various ancient Hebrew
works. Other works attributed to him are believed
to have been written by his disciples on the basis
of notes taken down at his lectures. His literary
legacy comprises seven different classes of works.
On the Bible he wrote: a commentary on the Pentateuch, *Adderet Eliyahu*, giving the exact meaning
of the verses and showing that there was not a
single superfluous letter; and commentaries on the
Prophets and the Hagiographa, of which only a
few parts have been published. His works on the
Mishna include commentaries on Abot, Kodashim,
Mekilta, Sifra, and Sifre, besides commentaries on
Zera'im revised by his disciple, Hayyim of Volozhin.
Those on the Jerusalem Talmud consist of a commentary on the order Zera'im, and glosses to the
treatise Shekalim under title *Mishnat Eliyahu*; and
those on the Babylonian Talmud consist of a selection from glosses to the whole Talmud under the
title *Hagahot ha-GeRA* (i. e., ha-Gaon Rabbenu Eli-

[1] According to Finn (*Kiryah Ne'emanah*, p. 146), who adds,
"for after then writing became difficult for him."
[2] When I visited the Strashun Library in Vilna I was shown a
little book in the handwriting of the Gaon (about 6 inches by 4)
entitled *Hagahot ha-GeRA Torath Kohanim*, which was printed
at Pietrokow in 1911.

The Gaon Rabbi Elijah

המצבה הזאת להעיד שלשלמו היחסן הרב הגדול
לאחרון מהרה קדשה חלא מון הרב שמואל
בלהה מיהרי אבינר כהה מוהרור שמיאל ז'ל
נטמ גא עכך בינצה האקנא

Rabbi Samuel ben Avigdor

yahu), besides glosses to *Abot de-Rabbi Nathan* and novellae on eight treatises. His most important work was a commentary on the *Shulhan Aruk*, the four parts of which appeared at intervals between 1803 and 1858 in four different cities. He also made contributions to haggadic literature (glosses to *Pirke Rabbi Eliezer*, and to the *Pesikta*, and a commentary to the *Seder 'Olam Rabbah* and *Seder 'Olam Zuta*), and particularly to cabalistic lore, which he enriched with a commentary to the *Zohar* in eleven volumes, one on the *Tikkune Zohar* in five volumes, another on *Ra'ya Mehemna* in four volumes, besides several others. In the field of science he wrote, under the title *Ayyil Meshullash*, a treatise on trigonometry, geometry, and some principles of astronomy and algebra, besides separate treatises on astronomy and the fixing of the Jewish calendar; and finally he composed a short Hebrew grammar, *Dikduk Eliyahu*.

Although the Gaon had no liking to preside over a *Yeshibah*, he had a number of disciples to whom he used to lecture occasionally in a *Bet ha-Midrash* which he established as a house of prayer and study. He impressed upon them the importance of mastering the whole of the Bible, including its vocalization and accentuation, and the necessity of a thorough grounding in Hebrew grammar. He introduced them to the study of the multifarious pre-talmudic literature as well as of the Jerusalem Talmud itself. He taught them his own rational principles of exposition and also urged them to acquire a knowledge of secular subjects. He upheld the authority of the Talmud

as infallible and supreme, and encouraged an attitude
of criticism towards the *Shulhan Aruk* when it was in
conflict with the Talmud, declaring: "Do not regard
the views of the *Shulhan Aruk* binding if you think
they are not in agreement with those of the Talmud."[1] On the other hand, he did not disdain the
cooperation of his pupils in the unravelling of a difficult passage. Rabbi Hayyim relates that the Gaon
once sent his servant to him on a Friday, with a message that he must see him immediately. When Rabbi
Hayyim entered the house he found the Gaon lying
in bed with a bandage on his head and looking ill,
and his wife said that he had not eaten for three
days. The Gaon then explained that he was sorely
perplexed by a passage in the Jerusalem Talmud,
which he was unable to understand, and he therefore
wanted his disciple to help him. With their united
efforts they soon fathomed what had previously
seemed so abstruse, and master and disciple welcomed the Sabbath with happy hearts.

During the greater part of his life the Gaon
studiously refrained from participating in communal
affairs and also from engaging in controversies.
When he was appealed to, as a young man of thirty-
five, by Rabbi Jonathan Eybeschütz, who was thirty
years older, for his opinion on the Shabbetian
amulets which Rabbi Jacob Emden so fiercely denounced, he modestly replied: "Oh, that I had

---

[1] Quoted by Louis Ginzberg, *Students, Scholars and Saints*, p.
141, from one of the responsa of R. Hayyim of Volozhin.

wings like a dove that I might fly to restore peace,
that the strange fire, the fire of contention, might
be quenched. But who am I, from a far-off land,
that people should hearken to my words? If the
words of the rabbis, seated in authority in the holy
congregation, are not listened to, who would heed
the opinions of a young man hidden in his study?"
The humility that characterized this reply was
accompanied by the strictest and most inflexible
orthodoxy. The Gaon insisted upon the punctilious
observance of the minutiae of all rabbinical laws
and regulations, and even in cases where the *Shulhan
Aruk* was more lenient than the Talmud he insisted
upon the superior authority of the latter. On one
occasion, when he was riding in a carriage, he noticed
that it was covered with some stuff that was a mixture of wool and linen (which is forbidden in Leviticus, 19.19), whereupon he immediately got out of
the vehicle. His intolerance in regard to matters
of belief and religious conviction is more strikingly
illustrated by an incident recorded by the preacher
Abba of Hlusk (in the Minsk district). During a
visit to Berlin, where he came into contact with the
circle of *Maskilim* ("Enlighteners") associated with
Moses Mendelssohn, Abba heard that the Vilna
Gaon was a great scholar not only in Jewish lore
but also in secular knowledge, and he therefore
went to Vilna to make the acquaintance of the
savant. In the course of their conversation the
visitor happened to remark that the most popular
commentator of the Bible, Rashi, did not always

expound the text according to its real meaning and that the authors of the Midrash sometimes offended against the rules of grammar in their exegesis of the Pentateuch. The Gaon was so horrified by this heretical criticism that he immediately broke off the conversation. The sequel is related in the following letter from Abba of Hlusk to Mendelssohn:

> I returned to my lodging. But scarcely had I crossed the threshold when two evil messengers who were there waiting for me summoned me to appear before the heads of the community and their law-court. I went and found myself facing seven graybeards adorned with praying-shawl and phylacteries. Then one rose from his seat and said: "Art thou the one who scoffed and blasphemed against the sages of the Midrash and our master (Rashi) of blessed memory?" I replied: "I neither scoffed nor slandered." Then he said to me: "And what didst thou say at the Gaon's?" To which I replied: "I stated that the sages in question deviated in their explanations from the immediate sense." The old man thereupon made a sign with his hand, and the two henchmen of the evil one seized and led me out into the courtyard. Then I heard from the lips of the same old man the decision of the court, that on account of defaming the sages of olden times I was condemned to forty strokes, which the two myrmidons administered to me on the spot. But their rage was by no means assuaged by this, for I was then led to the threshold of the synagogue and my neck was enclosed

within the iron rings attached to the wall,[1]
so as thus to expose me to the people, with
a piece of paper on my head bearing the
words: "This man has been punished for
scoffing at the words of our holy teachers."
Everybody who came for the afternoon
service stopped and called to me: "Traitor
to Israel!" But even more; they spat nearly
into my face, so that the spittle really flowed
in streams. Thou knowest well that Vilna
is not Berlin, and that the people there go
to prayers in crowds. After the evening
service was over, I was conducted outside
the city and obliged to depart."[2]

The Gaon lost his wife in 1783. He found consolation among his disciples and in the good name for
scholarship and piety borne by his two sons. Rabbi
Abraham gave proof of erudition in his collection
of the smaller Midrashim. Despite unceasing toil
and many privations, the Gaon had enjoyed good
health throughout almost all his life. He first began
to feel his growing infirmity in 1791, when he called
in, not a doctor, but the famous *Maggid* (preacher)
of Dubno, Rabbi Jacob Krantz, to entertain him
with his wit and parables. In the following year the
city was besieged by the troops of Catherine II,
and the community besought the Gaon to pray for
their protection from disaster. For the second time

---

[1] This was the pillory, which was usually called by the Polish
term, *kuna*, and there was a similar contrivance in the vestibule
of the synagogue.

[2] Dubnow, *Geschichte des Chassidismus*, I, pp. 181–182.

in his life, as a graybeard of seventy-two, he went to the Great Synagogue, which was crowded with a vast congregation who had taken refuge there. He opened the Ark and then, amid the wailing of the hundreds of men, women and children, he led them in the sevenfold recital of Psalm 20, "The Lord will answer thee in the day of distress," as a means of preventing any harm to the sacred fane. His supplication was answered, for a cannon-ball fired from a neighboring castle-mount fell harmlessly upon the roof of the house of prayer, where it can be seen unto this day. The congregation trembled at the impact, but the Gaon calmed them with the assurance that the evil had been averted. And so it was, for a leader of the Polish insurrectionists opened the gates of the city to the Russians, and the siege was over. In celebration of the miracle, which occurred on the fifteenth day of Ab, that day is always observed by the local recital in the morning service of the "Hymn of Unity" and the dispensing of charity by those who have anything to give.

CHAPTER XIII

THE FIGHT AGAINST HASIDISM

The religious life of the Vilna community, which had remained unruffled for about two hundred years, was seriously and at times even violently disturbed during the last three decades of the eighteenth century by the campaign for the suppression of Hasidism. The dispute over the deposition of Rabbi Samuel ben Avigdor, which also occurred in that period, was of relatively lesser importance, since, although it destroyed the internal peace for a period, it was mainly concerned with one person and was confined only to Vilna. But the controversy in regard to Hasidism touched far deeper issues, extended over vast regions of Eastern Europe, and developed to such outrageous extremes that the government had to intervene in order to bring about a cessation of hostilities. The Hasidic movement owed its origin, among other social and religious factors, to a reaction against the intensive study of the Talmud as the principal manifestation of a religious life. It aimed at a sort of spiritual reformation by emphasizing the emotional element in man and urging the closest communion with God by means of prayer. Its followers adopted the name of *Hasidim*, which means "pietists," as an indication of their specific conception of Judaism. But although at first idealist in character, the movement

gave birth to what were regarded as heresies, it
evolved along unedifying lines and degenerated into
abuses and excesses. The result was that a campaign for its suppression was undertaken, primarily
by the rabbis of Lithuania, in which the lead was
taken by the Vilna community under the zealous
and authoritative direction of the Gaon Rabbi
Elijah.

The movement was founded by Israel ben Eliezer
(1700–1760), whose early life is veiled in obscurity
and adorned by legend. Born in the little village of
Ukop, on the border between Podolia and Wallachia,
of parents who were said to have been already old
at the time, he was left an orphan at a tender age
and was brought up by kindly neighbors. He spent
more of his childhood wandering in woods than
attending the *Heder*, though it was believed that in
his youth he studied the Talmud and other rabbinical lore in seclusion at midnight. While still in
his teens he was believed to have felt a call to a
sacred mission, and was reported to have received
some mystical writings that had been entrusted by
a certain Rabbi Adam, before his death, to his son.
At the age of twenty he married the sister of Rabbi
Abraham Gerson Kutower, of Brody, and for the
next sixteen years lived a simple, austere life in
various places — as a lime-quarrier at the foot of
the Carpathians, as a teacher, and as the owner of a
little countryside inn, which was kept by his wife,
while he meditated the whole week in the solitude
of a woodland cottage, from which he returned home
only for the Sabbath. Not until his thirty-sixth year

did he reveal the miraculous powers that he was credited with exercising through the name of God, and by virtue of which he was given the title of *Ba'al Shem Tob* ("Master of the Good Name"), commonly abbreviated to "Besht." He then wandered about in the service of his movement and attracted a gradually increasing following, which included not only simple, God-seeking folk, but also a number of scholars and a band of disciples, whose conversion was in many cases explained by some legend. He finally settled at Miedzyboz in Podolia, which thus became the citadel of the movement and the bourn of ceaseless pilgrimages.

The Ba'al Shem had doubtless been influenced by a study of the *Zohar*, the cabalistic work of Moses de Leon, a Spanish Jew of the thirteenth century, but he could certainly lay claim to originality. He never expounded his teachings in writing, but communicated them only by word of mouth. His cardinal doctrine was that God was present in all things and hence that there was good in all things. He taught that everybody could be reclaimed and that intimate communion with the Godhead could be achieved by such a degree of devotion and ecstasy in prayer that one became unconscious of one's own existence. He laid little stress on the study of the Torah except for the purpose of learning the true service of God. The three principal virtues that he preached were humility (*Shiflut*), cheerfulness (*Simhah*), and enthusiasm (*Hitlahabut*). He was a friend of the common people, opposed every kind of asceticism or depression, and proclaimed that

religious enthusiasm would lead to a daily advance
in the knowledge and love of the Divine Master.
He sought to infuse joyousness into the religious
life of the Jewish masses, whose surroundings were
so drab and whose outlook was so bleak; he instituted
ritual ablutions and the wearing of white garments
on the Sabbath; he indulged in prophetic visions
and gesticulations in prayer; he wrote Hebrew
amulets and professed to effect cures by herbs. But
although his creed was pure and lofty in its
idealism, it rapidly became perverted and corrupt
after his death owing to the exaggerated importance
attributed to a relatively minor article of his gospel
— the honor due to the divine in man. For a man
who reached the highest level of holiness was regarded as a sort of God-man; such a chosen spirit
was called a *Zaddik* ("just" or "righteous") and
became a local leader, and it was only through
veneration of the *Zaddik* that one might win God's
grace. This doctrine of the intermediary became
the distinguishing feature of Hasidism. Pushing
every other principle into the background, it even
supplanted the primacy of the belief in the Imma-
nence of God, and led to an idolatrous devotion to
the living leaders, which gradually and inevitably
engendered a state of corruption.

After the death of the Besht the mantle of leadership was assumed by his chosen successor, Rabbi
Dov Baer of Meseritsch (born 1710 in Volhynia,
and died 1772 at Anapoli), a distinguished talmudist
and cabalist who had been converted to Hasidism,
so legend relates, after receiving proof from the

founder himself of his intimacy with the higher
spheres of existence. He was styled "The Great
Maggid" (preacher) and was the first real teacher
of Hasidism. He attracted three hundred disciples
from many quarters, many of whom afterwards dispersed to spread the new teaching. They founded
Hasidic centers, some in secret. These, however,
encountered the most determined resistance of the
traditional orthodox, who were called *Misnagdim*
("opponents" or "protestants"). His most important disciples, who afterwards became *Zaddikim*
(or *Rebbes*) were Menahem Mendel of Vitebsk, Levi
Isaac of Berditchev, Jacob Isaac of Lublin, Aaron of
Karlin (near Pinsk), Israel of Kozienic, and, above
all, Schneur Zalman ben Baruk of Ladi.[1] The
Hasidim withdrew from the communal synagogues
and retired to *Klausen* of their own, where they
could observe their own ritual and pray in their own
fashion. They adopted the Sephardic prayer-book of
Isaac Luria, the chief cabalist, excised many old
prayers and inserted new ones, and disregarded the
prescribed hours of worship on the ground that no
set time could be fixed for communion with the
Creator any more than for children who wished to
speak to their parents. Many of them punctuated
their prayers with shouts and shrieks, and worked
themselves up to such a state of exaltation that they
even danced and sometimes turned somersaults.

---

[1] Commonly called "the Rav of Ladi." He was born at Liosna
in 1746, settled at Mohilev in 1772, moved to Ladi in 1777, subsequently returned to Liosna, and died near Kursk, in 1812,
a fugitive from the French Army.

Their little bethels were often the scene of jollity and junketings, in literal fulfilment, as they maintained, of the Psalmist's precept: "Serve the Lord with rejoicing." They esteemed it an honor and privilege to spend the last hours of the Sabbath and to eat the final meal at the table of their *Zaddik*, who held a sort of court, where they sang special hymns with ecstatic fervor. They were generous in gifts to their leader, for they believed they could thus win his grace and blessing; and he, in turn, had an interest in securing a large band of followers of his own, from whom he could draw an undivided and unceasing revenue.

The movement made unimpeded progress in Podolia, Volhynia, Eastern Galicia, and the southwestern provinces of the Ukraine, but had some difficulty in penetrating Lithuania, where there was a higher standard of education and intellectuality and where rabbinism was so strongly entrenched. After the dissolution of the Lithuanian *Va'ad* in 1764 and the consequent weakening of a central control over the local communities, as well as owing to the internal political unrest, the secret Hasidic societies began to establish their own houses of prayer and to disseminate their views among all strata of the Jewish population. As soon as the rabbis in Lithuania realized what was happening, they began to consider what measures could be taken to combat the movement. The communal authorities in Shklow summoned the sectaries to the Jewish law-court for an inquiry into their practices, and sent their writings, which they had seized, to the rabbinical authorities of Vilna. The Gaon Elijah found in these manuscripts unmistakable evidences of heresy. Mendel of Vitebsk, anxious to arrange a disputation with the Gaon for the purpose of proving that there was nothing heretical in the new doctrine, came to Vilna in 1771 for the purpose. The Gaon, however, refused to see him. The Hasidim in Vilna used to meet in a house called "the Klaus of the Karliner" (as they at first mainly belonged to the particular school founded by Aaron of Karlin), and their leaders were Rabbi Issar, a recognized talmudical scholar, and Rabbi Hayyim, the preacher of the community. That two such important persons should take part in these meetings was particularly distressing to the rabbinical authorities.

Official action in Vilna was precipitated by a serious epidemic in the city at the end of 1771, which caused the deaths of several hundred children. The rabbis discerned the cause in the Divine wrath at the neglect of the Torah and the departure from traditional customs in the conventicles of the Hasidim. They examined the writings of the sectaries, found that these contained dangerous heresy, and deemed their conduct offensive. Rabbi Hayyim had actually said in public that the Gaon Elijah was "full of lies, his teachings were lies, and his faith was a lie." The *Bet Din*, consisting of two panels of judges and the elders of the community thereupon met in the intermediate days of Passover, 1772, and decided to close the Klaus of the Karliner, and to order Rabbi Hayyim to beg pardon before the Ark of the Law in the Great Synagogue for violating the honor of God, of the Torah and of the Gaon. When the preacher, accompanied by ten witnesses, appeared before the Gaon to seek his personal forgiveness, Rabbi Elijah said: "The defaming of my honor is forgiven you, but as for the honor of God and the honor of the Torah, your sin will hardly be forgiven to you and such as you until your death." So Rabbi Hayyim could not ascend the pulpit any more, remained ostracized by all, and had to leave the city.

Soon after Passover an investigation was conducted into the case of Rabbi Issar. The books and writings that he used were examined and some remarkable documents were discovered. Admissions were secured from the Hasidim that objectionable practices took place in their house of prayer: that they interspersed their Hebrew prayers with Yiddish supplications, and that some of them turned somersaults. When the Gaon was informed of the results of the inquiry he voiced the opinion that it was their duty "to prosecute the Hasidim and drive them out of the land." The law-court then held a special session, with the communal rabbi, Samuel ben Avigdor, participating, and pronounced the following judgment: (1) The writings of the sectaries should be burned, on the eve of the Sabbath, at the pillory at the entrance to the synagogue; (2) Rabbi Issar must, during the Sabbath morning service, mount the highest step of the *almemar* in the Great Synagogue and deliver a confession of repentance formulated by the court, whereupon the beadle should pronounce a ban of excommunication against the heretic and all his adherents; (3) All the principal communities (i. e., Brest, Grodno, Pinsk, and Slutzk, as well as those of Shklow and Minsk) should be informed of all this by circular letters. When the Gaon, who had been at Antokol, was apprised of the judgment, he summoned the elders of the community to him and said that if it had been in his power he would have done with the sectaries as the prophet Elijah had done with the prophets of Baal. He wanted Issar to be exposed at the pillory; and the elders, though not agreeing to this, sharpened the sentence by subjecting him to flagellation in the office of the Kahal. Issar spent the Sabbath night there as a prisoner, and on the following morning he, together with his fellow-sectaries, ascended the *almemar* to listen to the ban. Circular letters were then sent to the most important communities in Lithuania and White Russia, requesting them to excommunicate all Hasidim. The letter to the Rabbi of Brest, Abraham Katzen-ellenbogen, was signed by the Gaon as well as by Rabbi Samuel ben Avigdor and sixteen judges. It ran as follows:

> Our brethren in Israel, you are certainly already informed of the tidings whereof our fathers never dreamed, that a sect of the "suspects" (*Hashudim* instead of "Ha-sidim") has been formed ... who meet to-gether in separate groups and deviate in their prayers from the text valid for the whole people ... They are the same who, in the

middle of the *Shmoneh-'Esreh* prayer, inter-
ject obnoxious alien words (Yiddish) in a
loud voice, conduct themselves like madmen,
and explain their behavior by saying that
in their thoughts they soar in the most far-off
worlds ... The study of the Torah is neglected
by them entirely, and they do not hesitate
constantly to emphasize that one should
devote oneself as little as possible to learning
and not grieve too much over a sin committed ... Every day is for them a holiday ... When they pray according to falsified
texts they raise such a din that the walls
quake ... and they turn over like wheels, with
the head below and the legs above ... Yet
all this is only a little fraction, only a thou-
sandth part of their disgusting practices ...
as the aforesaid *Hashudim* have themselves
admitted to us ... Praised be God that that
which has been committed by them has, with
the help of heaven, been brought to light here
in our camp, for by the most careful inquiries
and investigations they have had to make a
complete confession ... Therefore do we now
declare to our brethren in Israel, to those near
as well as far: ... All heads of the people shall
robe themselves in the raiment of zeal, of zeal
for the Lord of Hosts, to extirpate, to destroy,
to outlaw, and to excommunicate them. We
here have already, with the help of His name,
brought their evil intention to nought; and,
as here, so should they everywhere be torn up
by the roots ... Do not believe them even if
they raise their voices to implore you ... for
in their hearts are all seven horrors ... So

> long as they do not make full atonement of
> their own accord, they should be scattered
> and driven away so that not two heretics
> remain together, for the disbanding of their
> associations is a boon for the world.

The circular letter, sent to all communities, contained some further details about the results of the
investigation. It stated that the head of the sectaries was a certain *Issur* (which means "forbidden,"
an intentional corruption of "Issar"), that a manuscript had been found in his possession which
pointed to misdeeds, that he had already made a
full admission and been ordered to utter a confession
of atonement in all synagogues and houses of study
in the community, and that "soul-snatchers such as
these were destroyers in a double sense, as they not
only beguiled people to forsake the Torah but sought
to seize the money of their youthful followers, whose
dowry (i. e., of their wives) was squandered in
wandering from town to town and in orgies." The
document concluded with a request to persecute and
disperse the Hasidim everywhere, so that they
should not be able to form a quorum of their own
for prayer. A special letter was sent to the heads
of the community of Brody, in May, 1772, reporting
on the steps which had been taken in Vilna and
calling upon them to take similar measures. The
Brody authorities accordingly issued a strong manifesto, on Sivan 20, which was market-day when
Jews were gathered from all the surrounding districts, culminating in a "great, terrible *Herem.*"

The drastic measures thus taken for the suppres-

sion of Hasidism resulted in a considerable dwind-
ling of its conventicles in Lithuania. Solomon
Maimon (1753–1800), who left Lithuania for Germany a few years after 1772, could not have been
correct in the statement which he made in his autobiography that the movement vanished completely,
though it disappeared from the surface, at least for
some years. All the circulars and manifestos issued
against the Hasidim were printed together in a
book entitled *Zemir 'Arizim v'Harbot Zurim* ("Up-
rooting of Tyrants and Flinty Swords"), at Olek-
siniec, in 1772, by order of the Gaon Elijah and
several Lithuanian and Galician rabbis. The editor
was Aryeh-Leib ben R. Mordecai, the secretary of
the Brody community. This publication, which the
leaders of Lithuanian and Galician Jewry did their
utmost to distribute, produced the profoundest
impression. Among the Hasidim it aroused such
alarm that they bought up and burned all the copies
they could. In Grodno copies were committed to
the flames at the instigation of Hayyim Haikel
Amdurer, a disciple of Baer of Meseritsch and of
Aaron of Karlin, and a bitter foe of the Gaon Elijah.
Many leaders of the sect considered it prudent to
transfer their activity to other towns, especially in
the northern parts of White Russia. In this province
the principal supporters of the Gaon were the rabbis
of Shklow (which lay close to the Russian-Polish
border), who persecuted the Hasidim relentlessly.
Rabbi Mendel of Vitebsk and his friends of the
school of the *Maggid* of Meseritsch, talmudical
scholars who revered the Gaon Elijah, felt deeply

hurt that they were denounced in his name and
wished to prove to him that there was no ground for
the accusations. Accordingly Rabbi Mendel, accompanied by his younger friend, Rabbi Schneur
Zalman, went to Vilna to see the Gaon; but the
latter would not receive them. They called again
and were again ordered away. The elders of the community urged the Gaon to receive the two visitors
and confute them, so as to bring peace to Israel,
but Rabbi Elijah was adamant; he disappeared
from the city and returned only on the day of their
departure. The Hasidim also tried to arrange a
disputation with their opponents at Shklow, but the
latter would not hear of it. Thereupon Mendel,
together with his friends, Israel of Polozk and
Abraham of Kolusk, and their families, with many
other Hasidim, a company numbering altogether
three hundred, emigrated to Palestine and settled
in Safed for the purpose of founding a new center.
There, too, they could not escape persecution, which
was meted out to them by some Ashkenazi rabbis,
admirers of the Gaon.

A new phase of the struggle opened in 1776, when
the Hasidim, who previously had had only manuscript writings, began to print their works. Of
these the most notable was the *Toledot Jacob Joseph*
by Jacob Joseph of Polonnoie, which appeared in
1780. Incensed by this bold propagandist move on
the part of the sectaries, the Gaon and his friends
decided to take fresh action. A ban was again
proclaimed on Sabbath, Ab 20, 1781, in the Vilna
Great Synagogue and several other synagogues. It

expressed regret that despite the previous bans the "epidemic" had broken out again; it invoked all the curses and imprecations in Leviticus and Deuteronomy upon the sectaries, who were to be excommunicated and banished from the House of Israel. In signing this *Herem*, which also bore the signature of Chief Rabbi Samuel ben Avigdor, the Gaon wrote: "Although it is not my custom to trespass beyond my province, yet I also give my signature, mindful of the saying: When the Torah is being made void, it is time to act." The sectaries belonging to the Vilna community were ordered to abandon their homes and wander forth with wives and children, and all Jews subject to the authority of the Kahal were forbidden to let dwellings to the Hasidim either in Vilna or its suburbs, on pain of being liable to the ban themselves.

The Vilna authorities, having taken action in their own community, appointed two delegates, Rabbi David (a member of the local rabbinate) and a certain Joshua Segal, to travel throughout Lithuania and warn all other communities against "Satan's brood," as the Hasidim were called. The delegates were furnished with a long manifesto signed by all the members of the local rabbinate and all the elders as well as by the Gaon. There was no need for them to visit Brest, Grodno, Pinsk, and Sluzk, as the rabbis and lay heads of these principal communities held a conference at Selva (in the Grodno district) on the occasion of the annual fair, in place of the previous meetings of the *Va'ad*, for the very purpose of discussing the question of the Hasidim. The conference unanimously decided to pronounce a ban on the spot in the form of a joint declaration against the Hasidim, and to address separate appeals in the names of the representatives of each community to the districts subordinated to it. The *Herem*, which was proclaimed in the market-place before a dense throng, prescribed that the Hasidim should have no prayer-houses, that no lodging should be let to them, no business should be done with them, nobody should intermarry with them, and their dead should be denied burial. The heads of the four communities sent letters to their respective districts requesting them to follow the example set at Vilna and Selva; and the Vilna community, in accordance with the Selva decision, again imposed a ban upon the Hasidim (Ellul 13, 1781).

Despite all interdicts and threats, however, the sectaries in Vilna made a desperate fight for their existence. They belonged to two *Klausen*, that of the "Karliner," who followed the teachings of the *Zaddikim* of Karlin,[1] Stolin, and Liachowicz, and that of the *Habad*[2] school founded by Schneur Zalman of Liosna. At the head of the latter conventicle was an audacious leader, Meir Raphael, who braved the wrath of the generally feared Gaon and

[1] See *Der Karliner Chassidismus*, by Wolf Rabinowitsch (Tel-Aviv, 1935).

[2] From the initial letters of the words, *Hokmah* (wisdom), *Binah* (understanding), and *Da'at* (knowledge), a trinity indicating the intellectual element of the system, which was opposed to the adoration of the *Zaddik*.

even tried to secure the election of some of his
followers to the council of the Kahal with the help
of the Russian authorities.

After twenty years of futile effort to suppress the
new doctrine the Gaon Elijah, who was now in the
seventies, had become rather passive. But at the
urgent request of the rabbi of Pinsk, Avigdor ben
Hayyim, he gave instructions that a book popularly
attributed to the Besht, the *Zavaat ha-Ribash* ("Testament of the Besht"), published in 1793, should be
burnt in front of the Great Synagogue in Vilna, an
act that was carried out on the eve of Passover,
1794. The Gaon then relapsed into silence, and the
Hasidim took advantage of this to spread the
report that he had changed his views. Such false
reports were circulated particularly in certain cities
in Germany — Koenigsberg, Breslau, and Hamburg
— with which Vilna had commercial relations, and
the Hasidim even devised a cunning trick to further
their propaganda. In May, 1796, it was learned that
a Hasidic delegate was travelling about in Germany
with a young attendant, who was saying that his
master was a son of the Gaon Elijah. When the
latter was asked what were the views of his father
on the new movement, he replied that the Gaon had
now repented of his previous attacks and that if he
were young enough he would fast and pray to the
Almighty for forgiveness. The rumor thus spread
that the son of the Gaon was leading a wanderer's life
to atone for the sins of his father and to proclaim
his repentance. An elder of the Vilna community,
R. Zundel, who happened to be in Breslau, heard

of the story of the swindler and assured everybody
that the Gaon had recently burned the *Testament
of the Besht* and that both of his sons were in Vilna.
The Jews of Breslau therefore immediately sent
letters to other communities to inform them of the
trick, so that when the impersonator arrived in
Hamburg and called upon Rabbi Raphael Cohen
(formerly of Pinsk) he was at once seized and sentenced to flagellation. The leaders of the Hamburg
community at once advised the Vilna Kahal, and
the fight against the Hasidim was consequently
resumed with renewed ardor.

After thorough deliberation the elders of Vilna
Jewry decided that the Gaon should write a letter
to the communities of Lithuania and White Russia,
exposing the machinations of the Hasidim and
urging them to start a fresh campaign. In this letter,
which he signed on Sivan 28, 5556 (June 22, 1796),
the Gaon indignantly repudiated the lie about his
recantation and called upon everybody to persecute
and expel the Hasidim because "in their breast lies
sin and they (may their name be blotted out!) are
like leprosy on the body of Israel." The document
was entrusted to two local notables, Rabbi Hayyim
(of the rabbinate) and Rabbi Saadyah (of the council), who were delegated to visit all communities,
which were requested to help them with advice and
money. When a copy reached Minsk the Hasidim
there were so alarmed that they said the Gaon's signature was forged. As their opponents also doubted
the genuineness of the signature, they sent two representatives to Vilna with a letter, signed on October

8, 1796, to make a personal investigation. The
Minsk delegates reached Vilna shortly before the
Day of Atonement, and immediately after the fast
the Gaon instructed one of his sons to write a reply
in the form of a circular letter to all the principal
communities in the whole of the Russian Empire.
In style and contents this is the most remarkable
document composed on the initiative or with the
approval of the Gaon. When printed, it was headed,
"Response of the zealot Elijah, zealous for the Lord
of Hosts," and contained the following passages:

> They transgress the Torah, change the laws,
> and explain the Holy Writings in a new per-
> verted sense ... They are a generation whose
> spirit has become faithless to God ... There
> clings to their hands the blood of poor inno-
> cent souls, who in their simplicity allowed
> themselves to be led like lambs to the
> slaughter ... Satan has forced his way among
> the scattered flock of Israel and caused con-
> fusion among them ... These dolts who have
> sown so much evil should be chastised before
> the assembled people with whips and scor-
> pions and brought to reason. No man shall
> have pity upon them and take their part,
> but rather shall they be cast out from all the
> tribes of Israel as evil-doers.

This letter, countersigned by the court of the
Vilna community on Tishri 11, 5557 (October 14,
1796), was taken by the two representatives to
Minsk, where it was read in all synagogues, and

the Hasidim, whose conventicle was closed, were obliged to attend the public reading. A conference of the district Kahal was also held, at which resolutions were adopted for curbing the activities of the sectaries, and a vigilance committee of three was appointed to watch over the strict observance of the resolutions. Moreover, in order to protect the honor of the Gaon from attacks by the Hasidim, a declaration of the Kahal was made in the synagogues, that if anybody dared to defame the honor of Elijah Hasid[1] "our master and teacher, the great, pious, true, and godly head of all children of the Diaspora, celebrated for his learning in the domain of the revealed and secret Torah and for his unshakeable fear of God," he should fall under the ban in this and in the next world. The Minsk Kahal also sent copies of the Gaon's statement to the smaller communities throughout the district and claimed to have authority from the Governor-General (with whose chancery they had friendly relations) to deal with the Hasidim as they thought necessary.

When the Vilna delegates, Rabbis Hayyim and Saadyah, in the course of their mission through Lithuania and White Russia, reached Shklow, they conferred with the local elders on the measures for combating the heresy in White Russia, where it was being stimulated by the publication of Rabbi

[1] The term used in reference to the Gaon had, of course, a totally different meaning, signifying "Saint."

Schneur Zalman's book, *Tanya* ("It Is Taught!").[1]
The followers in Vilna of this scholarly leader begged
him to come to the city to have a disputation with
the Gaon, in order to prove that the suspicions of
the latter were unfounded. They hoped the Gaon
could be convinced that the *Habad* teachings did
not affect the traditional views of Judaism about
the Creator and the creation, nor disparage the
study of the Torah or antagonize the Hasidim
against rabbinism. Schneur Zalman declined to act
upon this suggestion, certain, because of his previous
experience, that such a step would be futile. Nevertheless, he set forth his views in a letter, which he
hoped that the Gaon or his supporters would see,
and that this would lead to an exchange of correspondence with him. But the Gaon never saw the
epistle, since it reached Vilna just before he passed
away.

The Gaon died on Tishri 19 (October 9), that is
in the middle of the Feast of Tabernacles, 1797.
"The joy of the festival was turned into mourning,
and all the streets of Vilna resounded with lamentation."[2] Not only the community of Vilna, but
hundreds of other communities throughout Eastern
and Central Europe were plunged into grief, for
the "light of the exile" was extinguished. All the
rabbis, the elders, and other notables, at the head of

---

[1] This work had a sub-title, *Likkute Amarim* ("Selected
Speeches"). The first two parts appeared anonymously in 1796,
a third part was added in 1806, and a new edition with a fourth
part appeared in 1814.

[2] *'Aliyyot Eliyahu*, p. 74.

a sorrow-stricken multitude with rent garments, followed the bier to the last resting-place. All the talmudical scholars of the day delivered funeral orations, in which they extolled the learning, the wisdom, and the saintliness of the Gaon, and bewailed the irreparable loss that had befallen his generation. But the Hasidim regarded the death of their principal opponent as the design of Providence. Far from mourning, they indulged in the customary festivities of Tabernacles to the full. They even held a special banquet, at which they ate, drank and danced to the music of fiddlers; and as the night's carousal advanced, there was an outburst of violence, which was said to have resulted in three men being killed and five arrested on the following morning. Whatever embroidery the story of that orgy may have received through rumor or hostility, there can be no doubt that the Hasidim conducted themselves on the Gaon's death with gross impropriety. His followers, therefore, infuriated with indignation, vowed vengeance at the funeral.

The heads of the Vilna Kahal, lay and religious, immediately held a meeting at which they appointed a committee of five to carry out all resolutions. On the seventh day of Tabernacles a "great proclamation" was made in all the synagogues of the city, amid the sounding of the ram's horn and the extinguishing of candles. It recalled the measures taken in 1772 to combat the Hasidim, who had now renewed their activities, and declared that anybody who belonged to the sect should not only cease to be reckoned a son of the people of Israel and hence be disqualified to hold any office in the Kahal or any other Jewish body, but should lose his right of domicile and be expelled from the community for ever. It was characteristic of the grave view of the movement taken by some rabbis that, when Elijah ben Mordecai (also called R. Elijah Hindes), who died in 1829, heard that his son had become an ardent supporter of Hasidism, he mourned for him as dead for two weeks — one week for his body and the other for his soul. In addition to the vigilance of the committee of five, the Kahal also appointed a "secret prosecutor," whose instructions were to be carried out by the secretary. By way of retaliation, the Hasidim resorted to individual acts of violence in the streets after dark, in which more than one rabbi was severely and shamefully mishandled.

The struggle now assumed a more acute and scandalous development in consequence of the approaches made to the Russian authorities by each side in order to secure the discomfiture and defeat of the other. In October 1798, a certain Hirsch ben David (presumably a pseudonym for a collective informer) lodged with the public prosecutor in St. Petersburg a denunciation of Rabbi Schneur Zalman. The Hasidic leader was accused of anti-State activities on the ground that he was sending money every year to Turkey for some suspicious purpose, although the informer must have known quite well that the money was for the relief of poor Jews in Palestine. Rabbi Schneur Zalman was taken under armed escort to St. Petersburg and imprisoned.

The examining judges thoroughly investigated the charge and, of course, found it baseless, so that on Kislev 19 (December) the prisoner was released and allowed to return to Liosna. The governor of White Russia signed an order, on December 15, 1798, that Schneur Zalman and his adherents were henceforth not to be molested. The Hasidim, for their part, interpreted the government's favorable attitude as authorizing them to spread their doctrine and to assert their rights in the communities. Since they had been driven out of all positions in the Vilna Kahal and even excluded from the annual elections, they determined to have their revenge. Their leaders in Vilna therefore bribed the local officials, disclosed to them that the elders had handed over to the State treasury only part of the collected taxes, retaining the rest for the expenses of their vigilance committee, and promised that if they were elected as elders of the community they would discharge their duties in a more honorable manner. Accordingly, on February 4, 1799, the police arrested all the elders and confiscated all documents in the Kahal's office. Some government officials, accompanied by Hasidim, made their way into the Great Synagogue, where one of them announced that the Kahal had been dissolved and new elections would be held. The result was that eight Hasidim secured seats on the Council of the Kahal, and their most influential member, Meir Raphael, became head of the community. The defeated elders lodged a protest with the public prosecutor and demanded the rein-

statement of the old Council. But the reply from
St. Petersburg was that the Hasidim must be tolerated in all communities and that the Jewish court
had no authority to deliver judgment except on matters of religious law.

The next move in the battle was taken by a leader
of the *Misnagdim*, Rabbi Avigdor ben Hayyim,
who had been deprived of his ecclesiastical office in
Pinsk by the victorious Hasidim. He not only
demanded compensation for his dismissal, but went
to St. Petersburg, early in 1800, and delivered to the
Imperial Chancellery a document accusing the Hasidim of being followers of the heresy of Sabbetai
Zevi and charging Rabbi Schneur Zalman with sending the money collected for the poor in Palestine
to Salonika, the center of the Sabbetian cult. An
inquiry made by the authorities in Lithuania showed
that this charge was baseless. But later in the year,
on October 26, the Russian Senator Dershawin, who
had been making a study of Jewish conditions in
White Russia, and who was doubtless influenced
by Avigdor ben Hayyim, presented a lengthy report
to the public prosecutor in St. Petersburg, alleging,
among many other matters, that the money sent
by Schneur Zalman to Turkey was intended for
Napoleon, who had promised the Jews the restoration of the holy city of Jerusalem in return for their
assistance in his campaign. Since France was then
on a war footing with Russia, such a charge was
very serious, and the accused rabbi was therefore
arrested and imprisoned in St. Petersburg for a

second time. His principal accuser was Avigdor
ben Hayyim, who drew up an elaborate indictment.
But the prisoner's detailed rebuttal of all charges
and a favorable letter from the governor of White
Russia resulted in his being released, on November
27, after three weeks' arrest, though he was required
to remain in the capital until the Senate adopted a
final decision in his case. It was not until after the
Emperor Alexander I ascended the throne, and a
spirit of liberalism began to prevail, that Rabbi
Schneur Zalman was granted complete liberty, on
March 29, 1801, and allowed to return home. The
Senate then proceeded with its leisurely examination
of the dispute between the irrepressible Avigdor ben
Hayyim and the sorely tried Schneur Zalman. Two
successive petitions addressed by the latter to the
Emperor for an order to the *Misnagdim* not to
molest the Hasidim any more remained unanswered.

The Senate, as well as a "Special Commission for
Jewish Affairs," deliberated on the Jewish question
for three years and enacted the Jews' Statute in
1804. With that the fight against the Hasidim was
formally brought to an end. By virtue of this
Statute every sect in a Jewish community received
the right to build a separate synagogue and choose
its own rabbis, provided the Kahal administration in
each city retain jurisdiction over all the separate
congregations. The Statute likewise forbade the
rabbis to pronounce a ban for offenses of a purely
religious character. Thus were the religious and
lay heads of Vilna Jewry and of all other commu-

nities in Russia deprived of a weapon that had been used for the suppression of divergent views and that had been the cause of so much violent disturbance to the peace of Israel. The Hasidim had won their right to existence and were henceforth free to continue their activities without fear or hindrance.

CHAPTER XIV

UNDER RUSSIAN RULE

1. FROM CATHERINE II TO NICHOLAS I

THE transfer of the Grand Duchy of Lithuania and of a large part of Poland to the Russian Empire involved the Jews of Vilna, like those in all the rest of the conquered territory, not only in a change of government but, what was much more serious, in a change of treatment. It inaugurated a period during which the Jews were seldom left in peace by the government. Thereafter they were subjected to alternating policies of cultural reform and physical oppression, until, after more than a century of tyranny and misrule, tsarist Russia itself was brought to an end by the first World War. There was a fundamental difference between the attitude of the kings of Poland towards the Jews and that of the tsars of Russia. The kings, with insignificant exceptions, were sympathetic, tolerant, and benevolent, doing their utmost to protect the Jews from the hostility and violence of their Christian neighbors. The tsars, apart from ephemeral instances, were reactionary and intolerant; not content to embitter the lives of their Jewish subjects by barbarous edicts, they permitted their officials to instigate the Christian populace to chronic violence. The kings respected the religion and culture of the Jews, favored their separate communal organization, and showed some solicitude for their economic welfare. The tsars were, in the main, fanatical foes both of Judaism and the Jewish people, resolved to stamp out the one and either to annihilate the other or else by various so-called reforms to bring about their gradual amalgamation with the general population. The kings were humane defenders of Jewish rights; the tsars were vindictive creators of Jewish wrongs.

Another consequence of the change of regime was that the political history of Vilna and its Jewish community was no longer as distinctive as it had been until then. Although not enjoying the same rights, Jews and burghers soon became subject to the same laws and to the same local administration, for the Magdeburg Code was not permitted to survive under Muscovite rule. The Jews of Vilna, too, were the objects and victims of the same ukases that were enacted by the Russian government for the benefit, or the martyrdom, of all the Jews who languished under its yoke. Hence the story of their vicissitudes on the political plane becomes, in the main, identical with that of the Jews in Russia in general. It is principally in the sphere of intellectual and literary activity, in which they displayed a striking leadership and fertility of creation, as well as in the part that they played in the Jewish national and labor movements, that the history of Vilna Jewry henceforth presents an individual character. But these internal developments can only be explained and appreciated against the somber political background.

The new regime began somewhat mildly and promisingly under Catherine II (1762–96). In a manifesto issued on October 30, 1794, she announced her forgiveness of the "rebel" people and assured them of her good will. Despite the malevolence displayed by her predecessors, who would not allow the Jews to settle within the Muscovite dominions unless they accepted baptism, she issued an order giving them the right to live and trade in a number of cities (such as Minsk, Mohilev, Kiev, Plotzk, and a few others) if they paid double the ordinary amount of poll-tax, failing which they could leave the country. This condition did not apply to Lithuania, where the Jews were only required to pay the same State tax as their Christian fellow-citizens. The enumeration, however, of particular territories accessible to Jews marked the initiation of the policy which was afterwards developed and solidified in the Pale of Settlement. The new subjects of Russia were all assured of their religious liberty and of their personal and property rights, and the Jewish system of communal organization was expressly acknowledged. In 1796 the Kahals were legally confirmed in their former status, not only as religious corporations, but also as judicial bodies and fiscal agencies. The city of Vilna was made the capital of the "government" or province of Vilna, but the seat of the provincial government and of the Supreme Court was established at Grodno. All the printing presses of the country were consequently transferred in 1794 to Grodno, where an official censorship for all books was set up, and the first Hebrew printing press of the Jews of Lithuania was thus founded there in that year.[1]

The policy of Catherine II was continued by her son, Paul I (1796–1801), whose brief reign, disgraced by tyranny and madness and ending in assassination, was not marked by any particular enmity towards the Jews. On the contrary, he allowed a Hebrew printing press to be established in Vilna; and he appointed two Jewish censors, Moses Heckel and Ezekiel David Levy, for Hebrew books from foreign countries, which were examined in a censorship bureau in Riga. He would probably have taken no interest in the Jews at all, but for the agitation provoked by the marshals of the Lithuanian nobility, who blamed the Jewish innkeepers for the wretched condition of the peasantry. These autocratic landowners, who treated the peasants as serfs and employed the Jews for the sale of liquor for their own profit, were anxious to see the communal organizations of the Jews broken up and the Jews themselves merged in the general population. The governor of Vilna, Friedel, who is described by historians as "an educated German," discovered that the "root of the evil" in the Jews consisted in their distinctive dress and religious customs; and he urged various reforms for their improvement. He proposed that the Jews should use Polish instead of Yiddish in their business correspondence, that they should wear European dress instead of the mediaeval Polish costume to which they clung, that they should not marry before

[1] See also page 328 ff.

twenty, and that their children should attend public schools.

A more elaborate series of proposals was made by the poet, Dershawin, a member of the Russian Senate, who submitted a memorandum to the tsar for "curbing the avaricious pursuits of the Jews" and for their transformation into an element "useful to the government." He proposed that the Jews should be made to adopt family names and be registered under four categories — merchants, urban burghers, rural burghers, and agricultural settlers. Their religious life should be under the control of the synagogues, their rabbis and teachers being under the authority of a supreme ecclesiastical tribunal in St. Petersburg. The Jews, Dershawin urged, should be evenly distributed over various parts of White Russia and any surplus should be transferred to other provinces. They should be forbidden to take part in municipal government or to keep Christian domestics, and they must abandon their distinctive dress and peculiar speech. Jewish children should attend their own religious schools up to the age of twelve, when they should begin to attend public schools. Finally, the poetic senator, who was apparently apathetic about the illiteracy of the overwhelming majority of the tsar's Christian subjects, recommended the establishment by the government of a special printing press for the publication of Jewish religious books "with philosophic annotations." These proposals are hardly likely to have received any serious consideration on the part of the tsar, for he was much more concerned about the continuation of his own life, which was brought to a sudden and violent end by a number of his officers and courtiers.

Even before the days of Paul the Russian government had given the Jews in Poland the right to participate in municipal government as electors and as members of the municipal councils and the municipal courts, hoping that they would thus give up their traditional autonomy, although this had been reduced to a shadow of its former substance. The Jews readily availed themselves of the right to vote in the elections to the councils, but they still clung to their Kahals. Both Russians and Poles strongly opposed the election of Jews, and thus even in towns in which the Jews formed the great majority they were limited for some years to one-third of the membership of the councils. In Vilna, however, where the antagonism of the burghers had not abated with the turn of the century, the Jews were excluded altogether. When the ukase of the Senate in favor of Jewish membership was made known in that city in 1802, the Christian burghers addressed a vehement protest to Alexander I (1801–25). In their petition they stated that such a measure would be a violation of their old privilege, whereby in Lithuania "Jews and other dissidents are forbidden to hold any office," that the participation of the Jews in the municipality of the Lithuanian capital would be a danger and a disgrace, "as they have no idea of morals and the nature of their education makes them unsuitable for judicial dignity," that "the Christians would be robbed of any pleasure in the public service," and that the admission of the Jews to the Municipal Council, even though limited to one-third of the members, would undermine the confidence of the people in the civic administration of the municipal court. The Christians of Kovno objected to the Jews as judges on another ground: they pointed out that on the judge's table there was always a crucifix for administering the oath, that a Jew would turn his eyes away from this and entertain evil thoughts about it, and thus instead of serving Christian justice he would hold the Christian law in contempt. The government acknowledged these objections, and the Senate thereupon withdrew the ukase for the communal suffrage of the Jews in these two Lithuanian provinces.

Alexander I was doubtless influenced by the terrible fate that had overtaken his erratic and despotic father to devote himself to improving the condition of his subjects. Although Jews formed only an insignificant proportion, he appointed a commission in 1802 to make proposals for ameliorating their position in Lithuania and the other provinces annexed from Poland. All the Kahals were invited to send deputies to St. Petersburg, to take part in the deliberations of the commission. But the Jewish members did not agree with some drastic proposals of this body, and their request for a prolonged postponement was ignored. The only member of the commission who pleaded that the best solution was for the Jews to have the maximum of liberties and minimum of restrictions was the statesman, Speranski, who believed that if the Jews were left to

themselves they would work out their own salvation.
Other counsels prevailed. In 1804 the government
approved a statute, which represented its firm determination to reorganize and restore the lives of the
Jews, but in which some favorable reforms were
counterbalanced by repressive restrictions. The
statute was based on the principle of excluding the
Jews from Russia proper, stimulating them to acquire a Russian education, and encouraging them
to engage in agriculture. They were to be confined
to thirteen provinces, including five of Lithuania and
White Russia, and forbidden to lease lands or to
keep inns in villages; but they might buy unoccupied
lands or settle on the Crown lands for the purpose
of cultivation. They were to be removed entirely
from the villages, a policy diametrically opposed to
that observed under the Polish regime, and the
application of which threatened about 60,000 families
with disaster. The double tax was not to be exacted
from manufacturers and artisans; and merchants
and burghers were to be left in peace. The rabbis
and elders of the community were to be elected for
three years, subject to confirmation by the governor;
and the authority of the rabbis was to be confined
to religious matters and should not include the right
to excommunicate. Both rabbis and lay leaders,
whether in the Kahal or the Municipal Council, were
required to speak and write either Russian, Polish,
or German; and members of the Council had to
adopt European dress. The Kahals were made
responsible for the regular payment by all Jews of
the State taxes. Neither Hebrew nor Yiddish was

to be used in any public or communal documents. The Jews were allowed to establish their own schools, with either Russian, Polish, or German as the obligatory language, while the public schools, both elementary and higher, would also be open to them.

Despite the attempt to curtail the jurisdiction of the rabbis, Jews continued to bring their civil disputes before them, and those litigants who were refractory were liable to the *Ḥerem* (ban) as before. The most revolutionary of Alexander's enactments was that permitting the settlement and purchase of land by Jews in New and Southern Russia. He presented them with 80,000 acres in the province of Kherson as a nucleus for agricultural settlements and granted them exemption from military service to induce them to go upon the land. By 1810 several Jewish colonies were established, comprising 1,700 families, in Kherson. Alexander was influenced in his treatment of the Jews by the action of Napoleon in France. He had a suspicion that the purpose of the Assembly of Jewish Notables in Paris, in 1806, and of the Grand Sanhedrin in the following year, was to win over the Jews of Prussia, Austria and Russia. Alexander even entertained the strange fear that his Jewish subjects might secure the intervention of the French conqueror through the Grand Sanhedrin. He therefore ordered his governors to convene provincial assemblies of Jewish representatives, so that they might submit their views on the various proposed reforms. Moreover, the threatened expulsion of Jews from the villages, which was to take effect, after three years' grace, on January 1,

1808, was suspended, so as not to embitter Jewish feeling at such a delicate juncture in the international situation.

Soon after the signing of the Peace of Tilsit (1807), however, when the Russian and French emperors came to a temporary understanding, a peremptory order was issued to the local authorities to carry out the decree of expulsion — one-third of all those affected to be driven out of the villages in each of the next three years, and the total evacuation to be completed by the end of 1810. The sufferings inflicted upon the tens of thousands of Jews who were forcibly expelled, and the distress and congestion resulting in the urban community to which they were compelled to flee, led to the appointment of a further commission (in January, 1809), to inquire into the operation and effects of the decree. After three years the commission reported to Alexander I that the expulsions had not been of any benefit to the peasants, whose sorry plight was due in no way to the Jewish liquor-vendor, but that it had merely aggravated the ruinous condition of the Jews themselves. The commission accordingly recommended that the decrees forbidding the Jews to dwell in villages and to keep inns should be dropped; and the government agreed, less on account of the commission's criticism than because the Grand Army of Napoleon was now on its way to Russia and its defeat called for the mobilization of all the country's forces, including those of the Jews.

Napoleon's invasion immediately affected the Jews in Lithuania and White Russia, for the towns and villages which they so thickly populated in those regions formed the principal theater of war. The Jews displayed a remarkable loyalty to the Russian cause and rendered whatever practical services they could to the Russian troops. Far from being impressed by Napoleon's Jewish policy as exemplified by the Grand Sanhedrin, they distributed Yiddish circulars calling upon their brethren to pray for the victory of the tsar. They were deterred by the prospect of a political change which might undermine their religious orthodoxy, and preferred to preserve their traditions under a government that would alleviate their lot without risk to their souls. They proved far more reliable than the Poles, who hoped for a restoration of their independence by the invader; indeed, in Grodno, where the Polish officials were suspect, the Kahal had to be entrusted with the police administration. Napoleon made his headquarters in Vilna for eighteen days, from June 28th to July 16, 1812, and the palace in which he lived during that period has a memorial tablet on the façade recording that fact. The Russian governor of the city testified that "the Jewish people during the enemy's occupation showed particular attachment to the Russian government."[1] All these evidences of patriotism were brought to the cognizance of Alexander I, who acknowledged them with satisfaction and promised that, after the return of peace, he would take steps to ameliorate the position of the Jews.

[1] See Supplementary Note 7.

After his spectacular victories over Napoleon, the conclusion of the Vienna Congress, and the formation of the Holy Alliance, Alexander I returned to his capital a totally different man. He had abandoned whatever liberal outlook he had hitherto cherished, was obsessed by a spirit of Christian mysticism, and became a religious reactionary. In 1817 he entrusted Prince Alexander Golitzyn, his new Minister of Religious Affairs, with the settlement of the Jewish question. This pious statesman, who was president of the Russian Bible Society, was much more interested in the spiritual salvation of the Jews than in their material welfare. He was given the assistance of a Jewish advisory board, consisting of six deputies, who were to be elected at a conference of twenty-two delegates representing the Kahals of eleven provinces. This conference, which was held in Vilna in August, 1818, circulated an appeal to all the communities to raise a special fund from their well-to-do members in order to defray the expenses of the advisory board during their stay in St. Petersburg. The members of this board were certainly not lacking in energy and vigilance; but unfortunately their repeated representations to the Ministry of Religious Affairs were fruitless, and the board was dissolved in 1825.

Alexander I, influenced by the English missionary, Lewis Way, had conceived the idea of at least a partial solution of the Jewish question by having the Jews converted to Christianity. He therefore issued an ukase, in March, 1817, for the establishment of a "Society of Israelitish Christians." The promise he had made for improving the conditions of the Jews was forgotten. He now was interested only in those Jews who had "convinced themselves of the truths of Christianity" and who were ready "to join the flock of the Good Shepherd and the Savior of Souls." The new Society, founded under his imperial patronage, was to assist apostates by granting them free plots of land and other privileges. But this attempt to lure the Jews from their faith proved a complete fiasco; the Society, despite persistent propaganda, failed to secure any members. Prince Golitzyn therefore proposed to the Emperor, in 1824, that it should be abandoned, but Alexander stubbornly clung to his creation. It lingered on uselessly until 1833, when it was dissolved by his successor, Nicholas I.

Not only was Alexander disappointed by his failure to win the Jews over to Christianity, but he was mortified by the success of a contrary movement. In the same year in which he founded his missionary society, an extensive conversion of Christian peasants to Judaism began in the governments of Voronezh, Saratov and Tula, and spread over vast regions of Central Russia. These converts, who observed the seventh day Sabbath (*Subbotniki*) and professed Jewish beliefs, aroused the indignation of Alexander and his government. The peasants were subjected then to the most ruthless punishment, including banishment to Siberia. Moreover, the Jews were held responsible for this movement, although there were none in the provinces where it developed. The result was a revival of anti-Jewish legislation. Harsher measures were adopted against the Jews upon the outbreak of famine in White Russia in 1823, when 20,000 of them were expelled from a number of villages and driven into the towns. Many, suffering from cold, hunger, and disease, came to Vilna and were helped by the Kahal as well as by individual Jews.

Intolerant as Alexander I had proved to be in the latter part of his reign, he was altogether surpassed by his brother, Nicholas I (1825–55), who was notorious for his autocracy, obscurantism and inhumanity. Several years before his accession, this "Iron Tsar," as he was named, had stigmatized the Jews as "the leeches of the country," and he inaugurated his anti-Jewish policy in 1827 by an ukase that spread consternation throughout the Jewish communities of his Empire. Decreeing that the exemption of the Jews from military service must now cease, he made no secret of the fact that he wanted them for the army not in the interest of the country's defense, or because they were to be given rights in return for additional duties, but because he wished to win fresh souls for the Greek Orthodox Church. The usual age for military service was eighteen, but the age for Jews was fixed at from twelve to twenty-five; and although Christian soldiers had to serve for twenty-five years, the period of service in the case of the Jews was to count only from the eighteenth year. Thus a Jewish conscript was doomed to remain in the army for over thirty years.

Every Kahal was required to provide a certain number of recruits each year. Certain classes, however, were exempt from conscription: merchants, artisans, mechanics, agricultural workers, rabbis, and the small number of graduates from Russian educational institutions. Owing to these various exemptions and the attempts to escape conscription, the Kahal often had difficulty in supplying the requisite quota. It therefore employed official "catchers," who were simply salaried kidnappers. Not only boys of twelve, but many as young as eight or nine were torn away from their homes, often in the middle of the night, or were tracked down in woods where they were hiding, and dragged to the "recruits' prison" of the Kahal, to be handed over to a military officer. The recruits had to go through a solemn swearing-in ceremony in the synagogue, as prescribed in the decree. Wearing praying-shawls and phylacteries, they had to stand before the Ark of the Law, their faces made more pallid by the light of candles, and amid the awe-inspiring blasts of the *Shofar* they had to utter a long formula of allegiance and obedience. Thereupon, they were separated from their families and all the community, placed for a time in Christian houses, and then transported to some remote eastern province. Some of these juvenile recruits succumbed to the rigors of the journey. Those who reached their destination were exposed to fresh torments.

Boys under eighteen were placed in military training schools, called "cantons," where, apart from the general ill-treatment by the officers, they were subjected by priests to more refined tortures in order to force them to accept baptism. They were aroused in the middle of the night and compelled to kneel

until they either yielded or collapsed; they were fed
with salt herrings and denied any water; or they
were flogged, so as to break down their resistance.
Only the strongest and sturdiest were able to remain
steadfast in these religious torture-chambers. In
the long annals of Jewish martyrdom there are few
calamities so barbarous in conception, so prolonged
in operation, or so demoralizing in their effects as
this training in Muscovite culture.[1] Galling as were
the sufferings, both physical and mental, of these
child-soldiers, the agony of their parents and their
families, who mourned them as lost, was only less
poignant. Moreover, after the completion of thirty
or more years, these "cantonists," as they were
called, were not allowed to live in the district in
which they had discharged their military service,
but were obliged to return to the Pale of Settlement,
from which they had become utterly estranged.
The elders of the Kahal were also affected, for the
doubts sometimes thrown upon their fairness in the
selection of recruits made them an easy prey to
Jewish informers (*Mosserim*), who levied blackmail
under the threat of denouncing them to the authorities.

This system of conscription led to the opening of
many *Yeshibot* in Vilna and other cities, to which
Jewish boys flocked in the hope that their industry
in talmudic study would save them from being taken
by the Kahal for recruits. One such academy in Vilna,

[1] Written before reports were received of the German atrocities
in Eastern Europe.

called *Reb Maila's* or *Ramaila's Yeshibah*,[1] was established in 1831 and existed until 1909, when it collapsed owing to age and decay. There was also organized a group of forty talmudical students belonging to families of means, who outdid all others in their diligence and made it a principle to pore over the ponderous tomes both day and night. This group produced several well-known rectors of *Yeshibot*, such as Rabbi Mordecai Meltzer and Rabbi Jacob Pieskin, as well as scholars like Zevi Hirsch Katzenellenbogen and Abraham Baer Lebensohn.

The conscription ukase was followed in 1835 by another statute, much more comprehensive in its oppressive effect. When the Vilna Kahal learned that the State Council in St. Petersburg was devising new laws for the Jews, it submitted a suggestion that Jews should not be liable for military service before the age fixed for the rest of the population. But although the State Council approved this suggestion the emperor brusquely rejected it. The Vilna Kahal also forwarded a petition, as did other communities, begging permission to send delegates to the capital who might explain their views on the Jewish question. Such requests were also in vain. The Statute of 1835, which was to remain in force for decades, was a codification of all the restrictions and disabilities enacted since 1804, with a certain tincture

---

[1] So called because it was situated in the courtyard of Rav or Reb Maila, a well known personality of the middle 18th century who is mentioned several times in the *Pinkas* of R. Judah b. Eliezer (*YeSoD*). Cf. H. N. Maggid Steinschneider, *'Ir Vilna*, p. 119.

of "cultural reform." It limited the Pale of Settlement to Lithuania, the Ukraine, White Russia, Little Russia (the provinces of Tchernigov and Poltava), New Russia (excepting the naval ports of Nikolaiev and Sebastopol), the province of Kiev (with the exception of the city of Kiev), and the Baltic provinces. Jews were not permitted to settle within a 50 kilometer zone along the western frontier; nor had any except merchants the right to visit the interior provinces. They were forbidden to have Christian domestics in permanent employment, and those temporarily engaged had to live in separate quarters. They must use Russian or some other language of the country, but not Yiddish, in their commercial correspondence. Only those able to read and write Russian could be elected to the Kahal; and only those with this linguistic qualification could be elected to the city councils, except in the case of Vilna, where Jews were wholly excluded from the municipal administration. Synagogues must not be built near churches; and the barbarous recruiting law was to remain in force. On the other hand, Russian educational institutions of all grades would be open to Jewish children, who would not be subjected to conversionist attempts.

An attack was next made against Jewish books, in 1836, by a drastic censorship crusade. Not only had all books printed by the Jewish presses in Vilna and elsewhere, whether Bible or prayer-book, talmudical tractate or cabalistic volume, to be submitted to a preventive censorship, but all books in the numerous Jewish libraries, public or private, which had been printed mainly in Poland or some foreign country, also had to be examined, lest they contain passages obnoxious to the Russian government. Since the transport of so many thousands of books to the capital would have entailed great difficulties, the tsar agreed that they could be examined locally, that all objectionable works should be burned under the supervision of "conscientious officials," that a report upon every such auto-da-fé should be sent to him, and that a copy of every "destroyed" work should be forwarded to the Minister of the Interior. The censorship authorities not believing that the rabbinical censors could be trusted, the latter were placed under official control. All books permitted by them had to be sent to Vilna or Kiev, where the censorship committee either stamped them with the official seal of approbation or else consigned them to the flames. Train-loads of Hebrew and Yiddish literature were thus transported to the two cities to undergo searching scrutiny, and years passed before their fate was decided.

Not content with the progress made with the Russification of the Jews, the government devoted itself anew, in 1840, to devising measures for expediting the process. The State Council came to the conclusion that there would be no "improvement" in the position unless the "evil" were attacked at the roots, unless the religion and separateness of the Jews were undermined by their being lured into Russian schools, unless they were estranged from the Talmud and its teachings, and the remnant of autonomy still enjoyed by the Kahals was abolished.

The tsar, after receiving a memorandum from the State Council, appointed a "Committee for determining the Measures for the Radical Transformation of the Jews in Russia." The Committee first addressed itself to the question of "enlightenment." A leading part in the deliberations of this Committee was taken by Count Uvarov, the Minister for Public Instruction, who pointed out that other governments in Europe had abandoned the policy of trying to solve the Jewish question by means of persecution or violence, and that a new era should likewise be initiated in Russia. He argued that the Talmud exercised a pernicious influence, which educated Jews themselves admitted, and that the only way to counteract this and "to purify the religious conceptions" of the Jews was to provide them with education on modern lines. He therefore proposed that the largest possible number of Jewish elementary schools should be established, in which instruction should be given in "religion according to Holy Writ" and in Hebrew, as well as in Russian and general subjects, that the teaching should be conducted in Russian or temporarily in German, and that teachers with a modern education should be engaged either from Russia or Germany.

In order to make the proposed reform palatable to the Jewish leaders, the government appointed a Jewish director, Dr. Max Lilienthal. It was expected that he would tour the principal communities in the Pale of Settlement, and emphasize the advantages of the new scheme, thereby dispelling whatever suspicion the Jews might have as to its ulterior purpose. Dr. Lilienthal, who was born in Munich in 1815 and educated at a German university, was the principal of a modern Jewish school in Riga, which impressed Count Uvarov as the model upon which all Jewish schools should be based. When he addressed a Jewish meeting in Vilna early in 1842, his speech was received with undisguised distrust. He was asked by the spokesmen of the community whether he did not realize that the government's motive was ultimately to lure them into the Christian Church. In his reply he tried to dissipate the prevailing fears and gave his word that if he found that the government had any such sinister intention he would abandon his mission. The Kahal, thus reassured, appropriated 5,000 roubles for school purposes and promised more if necessary. The advocates of modern education in Vilna, the *Maskilim* ("Enlighteners"), gave him their support, and Nissan Rosenthal, who had been instrumental, in 1841, in opening the first two schools in Vilna for teaching Jewish and general subjects, discussed with him the details of the curriculum.

After visiting Minsk and paying a second visit to Vilna, where distrust had meanwhile increased, Dr. Lilienthal returned to St. Petersburg and reported the result of his tour to Count Uvarov. The latter thereupon issued an ukase, on June 22, 1842, which placed all Jewish educational institutions, including the *Heder* and the *Yeshibah*, under the authority of the Ministry for Public Instruction. It was announced that there would be a special Jewish commission in St. Petersburg to assist the government in effecting the reform. Dr. Lilienthal returned to Vilna once more and published a Hebrew manifesto, *Maggid Yeshu'a* ("Herald of Salvation"), in which he appealed to the leaders of the Jewish people for their cooperation. This provoked a rejoinder from the Vilna writer, Mordecai Aaron Guenzburg, who, in his *Maggid Emet* (Leipzig, 1843), sharply criticized the proposed reforms as too radical. The commission which met in St. Petersburg consisted of two rabbis: the head of the *Misnagdim* and rector of the talmudical seminary at Volozhin, Rabbi Isaac Izhaki, and the head of the White Russian Hasidim, Mendel Schneerson; and of two laymen: the Berditchev banker, Halperin, and the principal of the modern school at Odessa, Bezalel Stern. The rabbinical members insisted that the *Heder* be not placed under official control, and the government agreed to allow it to continue for the time being as before, side by side with the new schools which were projected.

The result of all these discussions and negotiations was that the tsar, on November 13, 1844, signed two decrees: an ukase, which was made public, for the reform of Jewish education; and a secret order to the Minister for Public Instruction. The ukase prescribed the establishment of Jewish elementary schools and two Rabbinical Seminaries. The schools were to be staffed by both Jews and Christians; the pupils who attended them were promised a reduction of military service; and joint committees of Jews and Christians were to supervise the institutions. The secret rescript, however, disclosed that the object of "the education of the Jews was to bring them nearer to the Christian population and to eradicate the prejudices inculcated by the talmudic teaching." It demanded that the closing of the old schools (*Hedarim*) should keep pace with the opening of the new ones, that only Christians should act as inspectors, and that, after twenty years, only those Jews who had the certificate of a State Rabbinical Seminary should be allowed to hold positions as teachers or rabbis. The Jewish leaders, scenting the ultimate aim of the government, adopted a policy of non-cooperation. It was thus some years before the new institutions, which were opened in 1845, got into proper swing. Of the two Rabbinical Seminaries one was founded at Vilna and the other at Zhitomir. The former, which was opened in 1845, existed until 1873 and developed a high reputation. As for Dr. Lilienthal, as soon as he realized that the fears expressed by the spokesmen at the Vilna meeting were justified, he kept his promise by resigning his office and leaving Russia in 1845 for ever. He emigrated to the United States, where he occupied the position of rabbi in New York and Cincinnati. He died in the latter city in 1882.

After depriving the Jews of their cultural autonomy, the government proceeded to destroy the remaining shreds of their communal self-government. An edict was issued on December 19, 1844, for "the abolition of the Kahals and the subordination of the Jews living in the towns and the country to the general administration." The Kahals were stripped of all their administrative functions, which were transferred to the police authorities, while their

economic functions were assigned to the Town
Councils and the municipalities. Two categories
of communal officials, however, were allowed, or
rather required, to continue their activity, not in
the interest of the Jewish community but in that
of the government. One was the "Conscription
Elders," who were responsible for providing the
annual quota of recruits; and the other was the
tax-gatherers, who had to collect not only the
customary levy (*Korobka*) on the sale of meat, but
also a new tax on the candles used for the Sabbath
eve ritual. The proceeds of the meat-tax had to be
placed at the disposal of the provincial authorities
to cover any deficit in the State taxes payable by the
communities, while the rest was used for the maintenance of the State schools, for the furtherance of
agriculture among the Jews, and for social welfare
purposes. The income from the candle-tax went
entirely to the Ministry of Instruction.

Scarcely had the Jews recovered from this decree
than another was issued, ordering not only those
in the villages but also those living in the towns and
townlets within 50 *versts* (about 35 miles) of the
frontier bordering on Germany and Austria to leave
within two years. The catastrophe that thus threatened many thousands of Jewish families in Lithuania and the Ukraine aroused such alarm that
another two years' grace was allowed. Indignant
protests and petitions came from Jewish communities in Western Europe; Tsar Nicholas, on a visit
to London, was asked by British statesmen to show
more clemency to his Jewish subjects. Only when

it was found that the proposed expulsion would result in the desolation of whole towns and damage the interest of the state, the decree was allowed to lapse. Ever inventive in oppression, the government now proposed to divide all the Jews in Russia into two classes: the "useful" and the "useless." The "useful" category was to comprise the merchants, artisans, farmers, and small property-owners; and the "useless" category was to include petty traders and persons without means. The petty traders were afterwards withdrawn from this class and described as "performing unproductive work." The rest, those living from hand to mouth, became a helpless prey to conscription and to all sorts of disabilities.

The increasing gravity of the Jewish situation in Russia, which had aroused serious concern in all Jewish communities in the western world, prompted the distinguished Anglo-Jewish humanitarian, Sir Moses Montefiore, to pay a visit to that country in 1846. His repeated attempts to secure an audience with the tsar when in London had been fruitless; but in St. Petersburg he was received in the imperial palace with every courtesy by the Autocrat of all the Russias, to whom he made "the strongest appeal . . . for the general alteration of all laws and edicts that pressed heavily on the Jews under His Majesty's sway." Sir Moses also had interviews with Count Nesselrode, the Russian Prime Minister, Count Uvarov, the Minister for Public Instruction, and Count Kisseleff, the minister in charge of Jewish affairs, with all of whom he firmly pleaded for just

treatment for the Jews. In accordance with a suggestion made by the tsar, and with the assistance
provided by government officials, Sir Moses undertook a visit to the Jewish communities of Vilna,
Kovno and Warsaw, and was received by the governors and other authorities in these cities with
every mark of honor.

In Vilna, Sir Moses Montefiore was welcomed
by the Jewish community with the utmost enthusiasm as a long-awaited deliverer. He was in the city
for eleven days, from April 30 to May 10. During
this time he had talks with all the leaders, visited
all the principal Jewish institutions, and made a
study of the local conditions. A special memorandum
had been prepared for him by the Hebrew poet,
Abraham Baer Lebensohn, who attributed the plight
of the Jews to lack of education and of skill in handicrafts, too early marriages, the ignorance of rabbis
and teachers, and to extravagance. Lebensohn proposed relief through the intervention of the government. The Jews were particularly impressed by
the sympathetic interest which the English aris-
tocrat, whom Queen Victoria had delighted to
honor and who was the only Jew who had spoken
to the "Iron Tsar," showed in their religious life
and scholastic activities. They were moved by the
sight of the Hebrew word "Jerusalem" on the banner
forming part of his coat of arms on the carriage that
he had brought with him from London. Montefiore
visited the synagogues not only to see but also to
pray; he went to the *Yeshibot* not merely to look
around but also to listen; he spent some time in the

Talmud Torah schools, the Hebrew printing works
and the hospital, and was conducted through the
two Jewish cemeteries. In Ramaila's *Yeshibah*,
the learned rector, Rabbi Mordecai Meltzer, gave
a short discourse in his honor, and Sir Moses
Montefiore's secretary, Dr. Louis Loewe, the Orien-
talist, replied with an address, in which he exhorted
the students to pay heed to their master, and the
elders to encourage the study of Russian.

Sir Moses also called upon an aged and blind
scholar, Rabbi Isaiah ben Judah Ashkenazi, popularly named "Reb Yeshayele," who was reputed to
know the whole of the Talmud by heart, and received
from him a Hebrew blessing. Throughout his stay,
which was observed by the Jews of Vilna as one long
festival, he had the help and advice of Rabbi Zevi
Hirsch Katzenellenbogen, a wealthy talmudical savant and author, who, it was said, conversed in Latin
with Dr. Loewe. At all the institutions that he visited, particularly the *Yeshibot*, the great-hearted philanthropist made generous gifts. When he left the
city, after a week and a half of crowded experiences,
he was accompanied not only by the blessings of
a grateful multitude, but above all by the hope that
his mission would be crowned with success. After
his return to London he sent memoranda on his
impressions to Count Uvarov and Count Kisseleff,
and in dignified terms repeated his appeal for the removal of the disabilities of the Jews and for their
just treatment. The ministers courteously acknowledged these memoranda, which they said had been

"placed before the emperor," but the position became no better; on the contrary, it became worse. What else could one expect from a crowned bigot who expressed the belief that there was a Jewish sect which practiced ritual murder?

The last seven years of the life of Nicholas I were marked by further measures designed to humiliate and torment his two million Jewish subjects. The passionate movement for emancipation and progress which seized upon so many countries in Europe in 1848 was not allowed to penetrate beyond the frontiers of Russia. An era of intensified reaction began; anybody who spoke or dreamed of liberty was banished to Siberia; and the Jews were again the principal victims of the government's fury. No device was too mean to harass them in pursuit of the policy of Russification. In 1850 a decree was issued forbidding them, from the following year, to wear their traditional garb (the *Kaftan*) or to retain their earlocks, although old men could secure exemption on payment of a fee. In 1851 the Autocrat of all the Russias had nothing more important to think of than the hair on the heads of Jewish women, which they were wont, in accordance with religious custom, to shave off and replace with a wig on the eve of marriage. He issued an edict prohibiting this practice under pain of a fine of five roubles and ordering any rabbi who allowed it to be put on trial. As these petty decrees were ignored, all the myrmidons of the State, instigated by governors-general and governors, were mobilized to en-

force them. Women were taken to police-stations
to have their heads examined, and men were stopped
in the street to have their *Kaftans* cut off or their
ear-locks shorn. The unjust and obnoxious scheme
for dividing the Jews into "useful" and "useless"
classes was now rigorously put into effect. All who
claimed to belong to the four categories of merchants,
farmers, artisans, or townfolk with a fixed domicile
had to bring documentary proof in support of their
claims to the local authorities by the autumn of
1852; otherwise they were relegated to the category
of "townfolk without a fixed domicile," and were
thus a prey to all manner of disabilities and especially to conscription.

It was in connection with the inhuman requirements of military service that the Jews had to drink
of the cup of misery to the dregs. The sufferings
which the "cantonists" had to undergo, and their
prolonged absence — often amounting to total dis-
appearance — from their homes, led to all sorts of
attempts to escape the clutches of the imperial
army. On the eve of the annual muster many youths
and boys would flee to the next town or the neighboring woods, or mutilate themselves by cutting off
a finger or a toe, with the result that most of those
left were either too old or infirm. Owing to the
shortage of recruits, the tsar ordered that for every
Jew who was missing the Kahal must provide three
others under 20, and that for every 2,000 roubles
of taxes in arrear a further recruit must be given.
In 1851 an edict was issued that those trying to

escape should be flogged, that the community con-
niving at an escape should be fined, and that the
places of those who failed to appear must be taken
by their relatives, even by fathers and the elders
themselves. The elders were thus obliged, to quote
a contemporary comment, to act either "as robbers
or as martyrs."

As the government was still not satisfied with the
number of soldiers provided by the Jews, and the
outbreak of the Crimean War in 1853 demanded
further large contingents, a new device was conceived to make good the deficit. An order was
published that any Jew who was found outside his
own town without a passport could be seized either
by the Kahal or any private individual and handed
over to the military authorities as a substitute for
a missing recruit. The consequence was that many
a Jew who wished to secure exemption either for
himself or a relative was tempted to take advantage
of this regulation. Gangs of Jewish footpads sprang
into being for the purpose of waylaying a fellow-Jew
at night on a country road or near an inn, robbing
him of his passport, and then seizing him for the
conscription officials, from whom they obtained a
receipt which they could sell to anybody in quest of
a substitute. Such was the degree of demoralization
that was created among the Jews in the reign of
Nicholas I, a period of ever-increasing tragedy and
despair, which had begun with one "ritual murder"
trial and ended with another. No wonder they
heaved a sigh of relief when he died in 1855.

2. FROM ALEXANDER II TO NICHOLAS II

The accession of Alexander II (1855–1881) brought a spell of relief. Educated by the poet Zhukovski, who had been influenced by western thinkers, and sobered by his country's defeat in the Crimean War, the new tsar adopted a liberal policy as compared with his predecessor. He did not go so far as to liberate his people, but introduced several reforms in the first years of his reign which alleviated their lot considerably. He abolished the serfdom of the peasants, created a modern judicial system, and granted self-government to the rural communes. He put an end to the outrageous evils under which the Jews suffered in connection with military service, and accorded freedom of movement in limited measure. In his Coronation Manifesto, in 1856, he announced that recruits would henceforth be taken from the Jews on the same basis as from the rest of the population, though mainly from those without a fixed domicile and not engaged in productive work; that they would be liable only from the age normal for the whole country; that "penal" substitutes would no longer be exacted; and that the regulation for the seizing of Jews without passports was rescinded. He declined, however, to allow Jewish soldiers, upon their discharge after twenty-five years, to settle in the place beyond the Pale where they had served. Not until 1867 did he agree to this reasonable demand; and then the privilege was made hereditary.

Animated by the same desire as his predecessors to merge the Jews with the general population, Alexander II instructed a new "Jewish Commission" to revise all existing enactments "so as to harmonize them with the ultimate aim of amalgamating this people with the native population, so far as the moral condition of the Jews permits it." The Commission pointed out that this object was impeded by the restrictions to which the Jews were subjected. It was therefore decided, after a discussion lasting two years, to select certain categories possessed of financial and educational qualifications, and to separate them from the mass of their fellow-Jews. The ukase, issued in 1859, permitted Jews who were members of the first merchants' guild to leave the Pale and to settle, with their families and a limited number of servants and employees, in any part of the empire. It also gave Jews who had received a university education the right to live in any part of the country, but on condition that they first submit an inaugural dissertation or emerge successful in a learned disputation. The privilege of escaping from the Pale was supplemented later by the right to be admitted to the bar (though not, except in rare cases, to any judicial office) and likewise to participate in rural self-government.

After nine years of lucubration by the Commission, Alexander II, in 1865, issued a further edict permitting Jewish artisans, mechanics, distillers, and artisans' apprentices to live in any part of the empire. But the right was subject to certain restrictions: all the persons belonging to this category had to furnish a certificate from the police as to their good conduct; those who gave up their occupations had to return to the Pale; and artisans and mechanics could only sell things of their own manufacture. Not until 1879 was the privilege of living outside the Pale bestowed upon all Jews of academic education, irrespective of their degree, as well as upon pharmacists, dentists, army surgeons, and certificated midwives. The total number of Jews who benefited by these various relaxations was comparatively small and probably included a mere fraction of the 30,000 Jews then living in Vilna. Those not belonging to any of the authorized categories who wished to dwell outside the Pale could do so only by bribing the police: a process which, to be successful, needed periodical repetition.

In pursuance of his policy of assimilation, Alexander, soon after his accession, renewed the decree of Nicholas I which, after the lapse of twenty years, limited appointments of rabbis and teachers to those who had been trained in the State Rabbinical Seminaries or in some other higher grade institution. Strict supervision was exercised by government inspectors over the *Hedarim* and their teachers, and Jewish merchants were obliged to send their children either to the general schools or to those established for the Jews by the government. But, as time elapsed, the government abandoned its faith in the assimilatory powers of its special schools and in 1873 closed them all, together with the Rabbinical Seminaries in Vilna and Zhitomir. In their place were opened about a hundred Jewish elementary schools, while the Rabbinical Seminaries were replaced by Teachers' Seminaries. On the other hand, the reform consisting in allowing Jewish merchants to settle in the interior provinces had succeeded to such an extent that the Russian merchants raised a clamor about suffering from Jewish "exploitation."

There was no consistent policy regarding settlement on the land, although the general and final tendency was negative. In 1862 the Jews were given the right to buy rural land, and were also permitted to settle freely in those cities and parts of cities previously barred to them. But two years later, after the suppression of the Polish insurrection, the government applied itself to the Russification of the western provinces and forbade both Poles and Jews to acquire rural land. It was actuated in this, as in all other matters, not by any regard for the interests of the Jews, but solely by its own advantage. As the cooperation of the Jews was no longer so necessary in the development of the southern provinces, the government, in 1865, prohibited the creation of any further Jewish agricultural settlements after 371 had already been established. Another antiliberal measure forbade the use of Hebrew and Yiddish in business correspondence, contracts, wills and similar documents. Moreover, in the 'seventies the government took nearly 90,000 acres away from the Jewish colonies in the provinces of Volhynia, Kiev, Podolia and Tchernigov.

The Jewish problem to which the tsar and his advisers devoted so much time, and which they

could easily have solved by abolishing all Jewish
disabilities, underwent further aggravation by reason
of the part played by Jacob Brafmann, a Jewish
apostate, in traducing his own people. A native of
Minsk, he, as a youth, had found refuge from conscription in the Russian Church. He sought to
wreak revenge upon the Kahal's "kidnappers" by
inventing a false denunciation against the Kahal
itself. A memorandum which he submitted to
Alexander II in 1858 caused the Holy Synod to
appoint him, a couple of years later, as teacher of
Hebrew at an Orthodox Theological Seminary. He
was then instructed to find means of propagating
Christianity among the Jews. When the government was engaged on its Russifying crusade in the
middle 'sixties, Brafmann went to Vilna to impress
upon the authorities that the Kahal, which had
been abolished in 1844, still existed as a powerful
secret organization. He declared that by means of
the *Herem* (ban) and the dispensing of *Hazakah*
(priority rights), the Kahal exercised despotic sway
and fomented hostility against the Christian world
and the government, and that this "secret government" would disappear only if all Jewish separate
organizations were dissolved and merged into the
general community. He based his charges upon
material that he had obtained through the poorest
pupils of the Rabbinical Seminary — extracts from
old minute-books, and passages from the Talmud
and the rabbinical codes. After publishing his
alarmist views in a series of articles in the official
Vilna Messenger, he wrote a Russian work in two

volumes, *The Book of the Kahal* (1869–1871), in
which, by his perverse elucidation of documents,
he tried to prove that the Jews formed a "State
within the State."[1] He bolstered his libels against
the Kahal by linking it with the philanthropic
Alliance Israélite Universelle in Paris, as a body
alleged to be looking after the interests of the Jews
throughout the world. The government printed
this work at its own cost and distributed it among
all its offices as a handbook in the war against the
"internal enemy." Jewish scholars promptly re-
acted by refuting the venomous libels. They wrote
articles and pamphlets to expose Brafmann's ignorance. They showed that his documents about the
Kahal were mutilated, distorted, or misconstrued,
many of them — dated on the Sabbath — obviously
being falsifications. At the request of the Vilna
rabbi, Jacob Barit, a commission was appointed, in
1869, by the governor general of the district to
discuss the apostate's proposals, but although the
Jewish representatives did their utmost to discredit
his theses and arguments, their efforts were in vain.
The authorities believed that they had secured
definite proof of the dangers of Jewish separatism
and shaped their policy accordingly. *The Book of
the Kahal* was a sinister instrument in the dissemination of anti-Semitism in Russia and a forerunner
of the more notorious *Protocols of the Elders of Zion*.

[1] A German edition, translated by Dr. Siegfried Passarge,
and published by the Hammer Verlag in Leipzig in 1928, has
played a part in Nazi anti-Semitism.

Under the influence of these "revelations," the State Council appointed a special commission in 1870 to draft proposals "for loosening as much as possible the social ties holding the Jews together." Composed of representatives of various departments, the commission devoted itself for about ten years to the study of two main questions: the reformation of the religious life of the Jews, so as to stamp out the fabled power of the Kahal, and the extension of the overcrowded Pale of Settlement, so as to lessen the competition existing within its borders. Without awaiting its conclusions, however, the government introduced an important improvement for Jews in military service. Its statute of 1874, which reduced the period of service to six years, prescribed exactly the same conditions for Jews as for all other subjects. The statute applied equally to all classes, abolished the principle of communal responsibility, and made each recruit personally liable. But the Jewish merchants, so long privileged, could not easily reconcile themselves to their new obligation, and complaints were loud about Jewish shirkers. In 1876–78 the War Office therefore issued supplementary orders: that unfit Jewish recruits must be replaced by other Jews, that Jews of sub-normal height and chest-measurement could be accepted, and that, if necessary, only sons, who were otherwise exempt, must also be conscripted.

The measures adopted by the government for encouraging the Jewish youth to devote themselves to modern education had one unforeseen effect. Attendance at Russian schools and the study of

Russian literature and periodicals introduced the
Jewish students to the ideas and ideals of radical
writers and political agitators like Herzen, Cherni-
shevsky and Pissarev, who yearned for the overthrow
of the tsarist autocracy and the dawn of an era of
liberty. The attempts at revolution, which had begun
in the reign of Nicholas I, were revived in the late
'sixties by a new generation of students, who were
fired by the new doctrine of "Populism," which
meant going straight to the people to rouse them
to revolt. This doctrine found enthusiastic support
among a section of the Jewish youth in Vilna,
especially — strangely enough — among those who
had passed through the *Heder* or were still at the
Yeshibah. Their sympathies in most cases were
aroused less by the disabilities and sufferings of
their own people than by the enslavement of the
Russian masses, and they began to take a keen
part in revolutionary propaganda among workers
and peasants.

The only attempt by Jews to form a revolutionary
organization of their own was undertaken, in 1875,
by a small number of students of the Teachers'
Seminary and other educational institutions in Vilna,
who worked in secret conjunction with similar
Russian circles in St. Petersburg and Moscow. The
members of the Vilna group included Aaron Zundelevitch, Vladimir Jochelson, and Aaron Lieberman,
all talmudical students, as well as a young woman,
Anna Epstein, who, in the course of her medical
studies at the St. Petersburg University, became
associated with such leading revolutionaries as

Prince Peter Kropotkin and Nicholas Tchaikovsky. They acted as a liaison between the secret organizations in the Russian capitals and friends in Western Europe, facilitated the escape abroad of members who were hunted by the police, and arranged the smuggling of forbidden literature from the other side of the Russian frontier. Suddenly the police swooped down upon the Teachers' Seminary, made a search of the premises and of the students' homes, and effected several arrests. Lieberman, who was among those who escaped, fled to London, where he got into touch with the revolutionary scholar, Peter Lavrov, and founded in 1876 the first Jewish Socialists' League in England. This League, consisting of workmen and students, discussed social problems and composed Yiddish manifestoes appealing to the workers to unite. When, after a brief existence, the league was dissolved, Lieberman went to Vienna, from where, in 1877, he issued a Hebrew Socialist periodical *Ha-Emet* ("The Truth"), of which the first two numbers entered Russia but the third was seized by the censor. Arrested and expelled from Austria and Prussia, Lieberman returned to England, and then migrated to the United States, where at the age of forty, he died by his own hand, at Syracuse, in 1880. As for the revolutionaries who were captured by the Vilna police, they were sentenced to various terms of imprisonment or banished to Siberia.[1]

---

[1] Zundelevitch, who spent twenty-six years in various prisons and in banishment to Siberia, died in London, in poverty, in 1923. Jochelson took the opportunity of his exile in northern Siberia to

The discovery of this illegal activity in Jewish student circles came as a shock to the government, which had looked upon them as a pioneer agency in the cultural reform of the Jewish community. The disappointment found an echo in the discussions of the special commission appointed to deal with the Jewish question. In 1880, shortly before this body was dissolved, two members, Nekhliudov and Karpov, submitted a memorandum urging the government to solve the problem in accordance with the principles of morality and justice and to abandon the policy of treating the Jews on the basis of their utility to other elements of the population. They pointed out that the congestion of the Jews in the Pale and the oppressive discriminations and disabilities to which they were subjected caused the profoundest discontent among them, which sought an outlet in a revolutionary channel. They therefore recommended that the Jews should immediately be granted the right to live in all parts of the empire.

Whatever hopes had been entertained of an improvement in the position were shattered by the assassination of Alexander II on March 13, 1881—a victim of his own dilatory and niggardly reforms. His son and successor, Alexander III (1881–1894), was utterly opposed to any thought of progress. He was completely dominated by his former tutor,

study the life of the aborigines, discovered two Yukaghir dialects, became recognized as an ethnologist, and was appointed to a chair at the Leningrad University, by the Russian government, in 1919. Many of his works were published by the American Museum of Natural History. He died in 1937.

Pobiedonostzev, an arch-reactionary, whom he appointed Procurator of the Holy Synod. Hostile to all occidental institutions, which he considered fundamentally bad and inapplicable to Russia, Pobiedonostzev manifested a special malevolence towards the Jews. His solution of the Jewish question in Russia was a mixture of cynicism and cruelty: that one-third of the Jews should be absorbed into the Orthodox Church, one-third should emigrate, and the remaining third should perish. It was not long before an impetus was given to the two latter points in his program. Eastertide in 1881 ushered in the first of those pogroms, which became a monstrous feature of Russian policy for the next twenty-five years and turned the country into a veritable inferno for the Jews. Beginning in the southern provinces, where the Jews in Elisabethgrad, Kiev, and Odessa were the first to be looted, assaulted, and massacred, these blood-orgies continued at intervals of ten years and broke out in over 200 places. The simultaneity with which they started in different districts and the similarity of their genesis and characteristic features pointed to a central organization; while the passivity of the police and the laxity shown to the marauders and murderers left no doubt as to the attitude of the authorities.

The government pretended that these disorders were due to an outburst of popular indignation against the Jews, who were accused of "exploitation." The minister of the interior, Count Ignatiev, ordered the provincial governors to submit reports on the measures to be taken in the future. Governor-

General Totleben, of Vilna, was resolved that this city should not be made the scene of a massacre; for the plague had spread to Poland, and the Jews of Warsaw were the helpless victims of a two-days' saturnalia. The only advice that he proffered was that the Jews should be restrained from settling in rural localities. The various reports were considered by a "Committee for the Revision of the Jewish Question" but its proposals were merely a repetition of previous attempted measures, including the expulsion of the Jews. Dissatisfied with this result, Count Ignatiev, in May, 1882, promulgated a series of so-called "Temporary Laws" (also known as the May Laws), which confined the Jews to the towns and townships of the Pale and forbade their settling in the villages. The carrying out of these Laws entailed all sorts of difficulties and hardships, and the law-courts were engaged in solving countless problems. The government tardily suppressed the massacres which it could easily have prevented; but it heaped further disabilities upon the Jews. The number of Jewish surgeons in the army was reduced to 5 per cent of the total number, and an order was issued to the military district of Vilna (as to all other districts in the Pale of Settlement) that no further Jewish surgeons should be accepted until the proportion had fallen to 5 per cent. The Jewish technical school at Zhitomir, after twenty-three years of useful activity, was closed down in 1884 on the ground that the artisans it trained "exploited" the Russian population. The policy of encouraging the Jews to acquire a modern education and to enter

the liberal professions, which had been favored by
Alexander II, was deliberately reversed. The number of Jewish students at the secondary schools and
the universities in the Pale was limited to 10 per
cent, although Jews formed from 30 to 80 per cent
of the urban population in many parts of that region.
Outside the Pale it was limited to 5 per cent, and
in St. Petersburg and Moscow to 3 per cent. The
consequence was that thousands of young Jews and
Jewesses were ruthlessly denied the opportunity of
obtaining a higher education, and only those whose
parents could afford it wandered forth to Germany,
France and Switzerland to obtain the academic
qualifications upon which they were bent.

The commission under Count Pahlen, after studying the Jewish question for nearly five years, pointed
out that there were 650 special laws which restricted
the rights of the Jews, that it was impossible to expect
any good from such a system of injustice, and that
a policy of gradual emancipation should be adopted.
But although that was the view of the majority,
it was the reactionary minority who triumphed.
Expulsion became the order of the day. Repeated
raids were made upon Jews in towns and villages
in which they had lived for generations, and from
which they were now brutally driven out at short
notice without regard to the material sacrifices entailed or elementary considerations of humanity.
The only way to avert such a disaster was to bribe
the police, who took full advantage of the opportunity. So determined was the government not to leave
the Jews in peace that the governors issued an order

to the police authorities in 1890 to insist upon the Jews showing respect to officials in the street by taking off their hats. Kachanow, the governor general of Vilna, replying to an address of welcome delivered to him by the heads of the Jewish community, inveighed against the Jews for their "disorderliness" in the streets in gathering together in crowds. But these were mere pinpricks by comparison with the pogroms that again broke out in 1891 and the following year. Imposing demonstrations of protest against this continued persecution were made in London, Paris and other cities; but all in vain. The Muscovite Pharaoh and his counsellor-in-chief, Pobiedonostzev, whom Mommsen called "a resurrected Torquemada," hardened their hearts, with the result that a powerful impetus was given to emigration. The exodus of the Jews to the lands of liberty in the West, especially to America, had begun in the previous reign; but from the pogroms of 1881 it assumed ever growing dimensions and poured forth in different directions, including the Holy Land. To this steadily swelling tide of refugees the Jews of Vilna also contributed their fair proportion, as witnessed by the hundreds of congregations and societies named after the city, which sprang up in many different parts of the world.

Intolerable as the Jewish position was at the end of the reign of Alexander III, it was aggravated still further under that of his son, Nicholas II (1894–1917), whose twenty years of misrule before the World War were punctuated by insistent demands for political reform and outbursts of revolutionary agitation, which finally swept him and the whole tsarist regime out of existence. Although most of the provincial governors took their cue from the capital, there was occasionally an official who evinced a humanitarian tendency. Thus the governor of Vilna, in his report, in 1895, suggested that the Jews be allowed to migrate from his district, which was overcrowded with refugees from neighboring town-lets and villages, into the interior of the empire. But the tsar, prompted by Durnovo, his Minister of the Interior, wrote on the margin of the report: "I do not at all agree with the view of the governor." The reactionary policy of the government stimulated Jew-hatred among the population, which found vent in further pogroms in 1897 and 1899. Vilna was fortunate in being spared such a visitation, but in March 1900 it was the scene of a trumped-up "ritual murder" trial. The Polish servant girl of a Jewish barber, David Blondes, became the willing tool of some malevolent mischief-makers. She suddenly rushed out into the street one night, crying that her master wanted to draw her blood for Passover bread. As she showed some scratches on her arm and throat, the mob attacked Blondes, who was taken to prison and put on trial. The court rejected the imputed religious motive and sentenced Blondes to imprisonment for physical assault. But in order to dispose entirely of the suggestion of "ritual murder," Oscar Grusenberg, an eminent lawyer, induced the Senate to grant a retrial by a different court in Vilna. The jury was convinced by the state-ments of experts and the speeches of defending coun-

sel that the charge was utterly devoid of foundation,
and Blondes was acquitted in February, 1902.

Soon after the accession of Nicholas II the growing
resentment and discontent of the Russian people
at the lack of any prospect of political liberty led
to the formation of two large parties: the Social
Democrats and the Social Revolutionaries. The
Jews who espoused the socialist cause joined either
the Social Democrats or else the Bund, a purely
Jewish organization which was founded in Vilna
in 1897. Many Jews joined the Social Revolutionaries and played important parts in this as in
other political parties. In energy, courage and self-
sacrifice they were no whit inferior to their Russian
comrades, nor did they recoil from acts of terrorism.
A notable instance of such daring was presented in
May, 1902, by Hirsch Leckert, a twenty-two-year-
old shoemaker, a member of the Bund, who had
previously been imprisoned for political offenses.
Incensed by the brutality of Von Wahl, the governor
of Vilna, who had ordered the flogging of a number
of Jews and Poles for taking part in a May Day
demonstration, Leckert fired several shots at him
one evening as he came out of a circus, but injured
him only slightly. The young Bundist was tried
by a military court, frankly declared that he had
intended killing the governor, and was sentenced
to death. His execution, on June 10, aroused furious
indignation in the ranks of all the socialist and
revolutionary parties, and his reckless act — committed without the consent of his party, but was

afterwards lauded as a deed of heroism — has formed the theme of at least three Yiddish dramas.

The participation of a number of Jews in the revolutionary movement, which had been provoked by their systematic persecution, was seized upon by the government as a convenient pretext for threatening further calamities upon the Jews in general. "The Revolution will be stifled in Jewish blood!" was the slogan formulated by Von Plehve, the new minister of the interior, and secretly communicated to the provincial authorities. In the following spring, 1903, the whole world was shocked by the three-days' massacre at Kishinev, which had been officially organized by the vice-governor of Bessarabia, with the cooperation of a high official from the St. Petersburg Department of Police and a fanatical journalist, named Krushevan. A young member of the Zionist-Socialist party, Pinchas Dashevski, made a futile and harmless attack upon Krushevan and was sentenced to five years' penal servitude. The political consequence of this act was a secret order to all governors to take energetic measures against Zionist propaganda, which was conducted by the Zionist Central Committee from their office in Vilna. This repressive step prompted Dr. Theodor Herzl, the Zionist leader, to pay a visit to St. Petersburg, in order to ask Von Plehve to refrain from suppressing the Zionist societies. Herzl utilized the opportunity to try to induce the Russian government to influence the Ottoman government in favor of Zionism. Von Plehve declared that he was

willing to tolerate the movement as long as it was
concerned with the creation of a Jewish settlement
in Palestine and with mass emigration from Russia,
but that any attempt to make nationalist propaganda, which he considered detrimental to Russian
national interests, would be quashed. Within about
a year both men were dead — the Jewish leader
mourned by millions, and the Russian oppressor
blown to pieces by a bomb. Sviatopolsk-Mirsky,
the governor-general of Vilna (the change of these
administrators was significantly frequent), who was
reputed to have liberal views, was appointed in Von
Plehve's place and declared that he would try to
restore confidence between the government and the
people. He had previously told a Jewish deputation
in Vilna that he intended to be guided in the Jewish
question by considerations of justice and benevolence; but he found himself powerless against the
forces of barbarism surrounding the tsar.

Early in 1905, the Jewish community of Vilna,
acting in concert with thirty other communities,
addressed a petition to the government, requesting
the abolition of the crushing burden of disabilities,
so that the Jews, "in possession of freedom and
equality, can work hand in hand with the other
citizens of the great empire for its welfare and prosperity." A radical group in Vilna wanted to add:
"As a civilized nation we claim the right to national
cultural self-determination, which must be conceded
to all peoples composing the Russian Empire." In
April, a meeting of Jewish leaders of all parties from
all the principal communities was held in Vilna, and

there formed a "Union for the Attainment of Complete Emancipation for the Jewish people in Russia." An executive committee of twenty-two members was elected, which had its seat in St. Petersburg and included Dr. Schmarya Levin and Boris Goldberg as the representatives of Vilna. The program envisaged by this body was not limited to civil and political rights, but also included the right of national and cultural self-government in all its manifestations, particularly in communal administration and education. The Union also undertook to fight against the terrible menace of the anti-Semitic forces banded together in the "League of Genuine Russians" in the cities, and as "Black Hundreds" in the provinces, who surpassed all previous exhibitions of butchery by organizing the pogroms of October, 1905, when as many as 725 places were the scenes of riot, rape, bloodshed and looting.

The Duma, the parliamentary assembly wrung from the unwilling and purblind emperor, which met in the spring of 1906, included twelve Jewish deputies, who lost no time in opening a discussion of the Jewish question and particularly in denouncing the policy of pogroms. Among those who distinguished themselves by the energy and eloquence with which they pleaded the Jewish cause in that assembly was Dr. Schmarya Levin, who held the position of preacher in Vilna (at the Taharat ha-Kodesh Synagogue). But the efforts of the Jewish deputies to end the enslavement of their people were in vain. The Duma had to fight for its own existence. There were more pogroms even while it was in session, and it was summarily dissolved after a couple of months by imperial decree. The Parliamentary Opposition then drew up the Viborg Manifesto calling upon the Russian people not to pay any more taxes or to provide any more recruits until their political rights were restored. As the signing of this document, in which all the Jewish deputies took part, entailed imprisonment, Dr. Levin and others left the country. Stolypin, the Minister of the Interior, wished to abolish some of the less important disabilities, but the tsar declared: "As long as I rule, the emancipation of the Jews in Russia is not to be thought of." In each succeeding Duma, thanks to government manipulation and "Black Hundred" intimidation, the number of deputies of the liberal parties diminished, while that of the reactionaries increased. In the third Duma (1907–10), which contained only two Jews, the deputy Friedmann complained that his people were now treated worse than in the days of Von Plehve; and, although his colleague, Nisselowitch, with the aid of the signatures of many liberal Christians, secured the presentation of a petition for the abolition of the Pale of Settlement, nothing happened beyond a fruitless committee discussion.

The concluding years of Nicholas II were a period of rank reaction, in which the throne fought desperately against the revolutionary movement, while all the evil elements of the population were incited against the champions of liberty. Among those who took part in the bloody struggle were many Jews, who were imprisoned, banished, or hanged. Even those who confined their activity to the "self-defense corps" formed for the protection of their people against pogroms were arrested and sentenced to long terms of imprisonment. The crowning and culminating incident of a troubled reign was the "ritual murder" trial at Kiev (1911–13) of Mendel Beilis for a crime that was known to have been committed by a gangster. However, although both judges and jury had been carefully selected by the government, the evidence of Beilis's innocence was so overwhelming that he was acquitted. The sufferings of the Jews, nevertheless, were doomed to continue and to enter upon a new phase with the outbreak of the first World War.

CHAPTER XV

RELIGIOUS AND LITERARY ACTIVITIES

THE devotion to religious tradition and the pursuit of talmudic study, which had distinguished the Jews of Vilna throughout the existence of the Polish State, continued to characterize them under the less tolerant regime of the tsars, despite the persistent efforts of successive statesmen to bring about their Russification. So far from proving successful, these attempts, except in a few individual cases, had the very opposite effect. They fortified the Jews in their attachment to their faith and customs and made them regard any deviation from the ancestral mode of life as heresy. Not only were those who indulged in the reading of a modern book or the study of any secular science exposed to persecution by their ultra-orthodox brethren, but even the wearing of modern garb or the trimming of the beard was frowned upon as a Gentile practice. Ignorance of the rabbinic law could not serve as an excuse for its violation, as there were popular compendia of the two parts of Joseph Caro's standard code, the *Shulhan Aruk*, most applicable to daily life. These works, entitled *Hayye Adam* ("Life of Man") and *Hokmat Adam* ("Wisdom of Man"), were compiled by Abraham ben Yehiel Michel Danzig (1748–1820), who had migrated to Vilna from his native city, to which he owed his name, and were afterwards translated into Yiddish by Mordecai Plungian. They are marked by a strong ethical undercurrent; and their author, in his introduction, justified their compilation on the ground that people did not have enough time for study either because of their material distress or because they lived in luxury. He was a man of strong principles himself, for he served as a member of the Vilna *Bet Din* in an honorary capacity from 1794 to 1812, and consented to accept a salary only when his modest fortune was destroyed by an explosion.

The spiritual influence that had been exercised by the Gaon Elijah, both as regards the rational exposition of the Talmud and the combating of the Hasidic movement, was continued, though in a modified degree, by his various disciples. The most important of these, Rabbi Hayyim ben Isaac Volozhiner (1749–1821), was recognized as the religious leader of orthodox Jewry in Russia. He founded a *Yeshibah* at Volozhin in 1803, which played a decisive part in the spiritual and cultural life of Russian Jewry for nearly a century. He endeavored, by applying the methods of the Gaon, to attract the Jewish youth to the study of the Talmud and to ward off the allurements of Hasidism. In furtherance of the latter purpose he wrote an ethical work on the Cabala, *Nefesh ha-Hayyim* ("The Soul of Life"), which was not published until three years after his death. His brother, Solomon Zalman (1776–1809), known as "Reb Shlemele Vilner," whose early death prevented the fruition of his intellectual

powers, was one of the most gifted disciples of the
Gaon. One of the most ardent followers of the Gaon
was Saul ben Joseph Katzenellenbogen (1770–1825),
whose annotations to the Talmud are printed in the
Vilna edition and who was known for his asceticism.
Another disciple was Moses ben Mordecai Meisel,
who was both beadle and scholar, and the author
of *Shirat Moshe* (a commentary in verse on *Ha'a-
zinu*), which appeared at Schklow in 1788. After
the death of the Gaon, Moses Meisel feared that
his friendly relations with the Hasidim might expose
him to danger and consequently fled to Germany,
where he became connected in some obscure manner
with Napoleon's army. But after the defeat of the
French conqueror he returned to Russia, which he
left in 1813 for Palestine and settled in Hebron,
where he died at an advanced age in 1838.

After the death of the Gaon Elijah and the
departure of Rabbi Hayyim ben Isaac for Volozhin,
the leading rabbinical authority in Vilna was Abraham Abele Posweler (1763–1836), who derived his
name from the town where he had been *Ab Bet Din*
as a young man. He settled in the Lithuanian capital
in 1802, and was the President of the *Bet Din* and
Moreh Zedek for about thirty years. Not only did
he enjoy extensive fame on account of his learning,
wisdom and critical intellect, but he was also popular and beloved because of his tolerance and kind-
liness. All the scholars of his time submitted questions to him for elucidation and were eager to profit
by his erudition, but unfortunately his literary remains are confined to only a selection of his *novellae*

and responsa printed in the works of contemporary rabbis.[1]

The Vilna rabbinate was strongly opposed to any criticism of orthodox doctrine or practice, even when advanced by a sincere follower of the Talmud. Thus Manasseh ben Joseph Ilier or "Ben Porat" (1767–1831), who, as a disciple of the Gaon, had acquired a knowledge of modern languages and of mediaeval Jewish religious philosophy, aroused a storm by the publication in the city, in 1807, of a book, *Pesher Dabar* ("Explanation of the Matter"), in which he sought to broaden the outlook of orthodoxy and complained that the rabbis showed no proper grasp of the realities of life. Some fanatics tried to prevent the publication of the work; and when it appeared they did their utmost to stop its circulation and in many places even burned it. Ten years later, when he was in Volhynia, he wished to publish his religio-philosophical work, *Alfe Menashe* ("Thousands of Menasseh"). But when the printer realized the contents of the first sheet he burned it together with the manuscript, and it was with the utmost difficulty that the author rewrote the book and secured its publication in Vilna in 1822. Before it was printed, however, Rabbi Saul Katzenellenbogen, hearing that the book recognized the right of spiritual leaders to revise ritual prescriptions in accordance with the requirements of his time, warned him that such a work would be burned

[1] Particularly in *Minhah Belulah* (1832) of R. Simeon of Slonim, *Bigde Yesha‘* (1834) of R. Samuel Halevi, *Dayyan* of Bialystok, and *Yehege Hokmah* of R. Dov Baer Nieswicz.

in the synagogue courtyard without further ado,
whereupon the harassed critic was obliged to insert
in it explanations contrary to his own convictions.
Another work of his, *Shekel ha-Kodesh* ("The Holy
Shekel"), written in 1823, although containing
nothing more heretical than a deprecation of early
marriages, was likewise strongly resented, and nearly
every copy was committed to the flames by his
opponents. The hostility to his views continued
long after his death, for when Mordecai Plungian
(1814–83), the Yiddish translator of the *Shulhan
Aruk*, published a monograph on Menasseh Ilier,
in 1858, under the title of *Ben Porat*, he provoked the
bitter enmity of orthodox circles.

   Dissatisfaction with the exclusive study of the
Talmud, on the one hand, and revulsion at the
crude superstition and ecstatic orgies of the Hasidim, on the other, prompted Rabbi Israel Lipkin
(1810–83), also known as Salanter,[1] to emphasize the
importance of self-knowledge and self-perfection.
He looked upon joy and happiness as sinful and
exhorted his disciples to repentance and moral
reflection. As head of *Ramaila's Yeshibah*, in 1840,
he founded a movement for the study of *Musar*,
or ethical literature, such as the works of Bahya,
Gabirol and Moses Hayyim Luzzatto, in which he
sought to combine the fundamental ideas of Rabbinism and Hasidism. Groups of his followers, *Musar-*

   [1] From Salant, the little town near Kovno in which his wife
was born.

nikess,[1] met in a special conventicle, *Musar-Stübel*,[2] where, in the evening, they would indulge in silent introspection. Rabbi Israel displayed a remarkable spirit of broadmindedness, for when Vilna was afflicted by the cholera in 1848 he declared that one might profane the Sabbath in the interests of health. He even announced that it was permissible on that account not to fast on the Day of Atonement, and set a public example by ascending the *Almemar* in the synagogue after the morning service, pronouncing a blessing aloud on a piece of cake and eating it.[3] In the same year he was appointed by the government as head of the new Rabbinical Seminary; but as he was doubtful about its utility he declined the honor and secretly moved to Kovno, where he established another *Musar-Stübel*, which formed the pinnacle of the moralist movement. After living in Kovno for about twelve years he spent the rest of his life in Memel and Koenigsberg, apart from a brief stay in Paris. He wrote several Hebrew works expounding his views and principles (including *Imre Binah*, "Words of Understanding," 1878, and *Eben Israel*, "Stone of Israel," 1883), and died in Koenigsberg, greatly honored and widely mourned.

[1] A term, meaning "moralists" or "moralizers," compounded of a Hebrew noun and a Russian suffix. For a fuller account of this moralist movement see Louis Ginzberg's essay on Rabbi Israel Salanter in *Students, Scholars and Saints*.

[2] *Stübel* — a little *Stube* (room).

[3] See David Frischman's story, "Three who Ate," in Helena Frank's *Yiddish Tales* (J. P. S., Philadelphia, 1912).

Despite the successive generations of orthodox leaders, who gloried in the name, the "Lithuanian Jerusalem," by which Vilna was known, and sought to strengthen its claim to that title by their zealous activity in the production of religious literature, the spirit of progress could not be stayed. The quest of secular knowledge was stimulated by Phineas Elijah ben Meir Hurwitz, a native of Vilna, the dates of whose birth and death are unknown. His principal work, *Sefer ha-Berit*, was encyclopaedic in range, embracing sections on various sciences, such as chemistry, physics, anatomy and cosmography, as well as theology, ethics, metaphysics and mysticism. This work, which was begun at Buczacz (Galicia), finished at The Hague, and published anonymously at Bruenn in 1797, exercised a profound influence upon the *Haskalah*. As it was alternately attributed to the Gaon Elijah and Moses Mendelssohn, Phineas Hurwitz issued an enlarged and annotated edition under his name, and a third revised edition appeared in Vilna in 1818.

The first call to the modern way of life was made by Isaac Baer Levinsohn (1788–1860), whose work, *Te'udah be-Israel* ("Testimony in Israel"), printed in Vilna in 1828, virtually inaugurated the *Haskalah* movement in Russia. Founded in Germany by Moses Mendelssohn in the latter part of the eighteenth century, *Haskalah* aimed not only at introducing the Jews to the culture of the western world but also at modernizing them in speech and dress. It was a sort of intellectual reformation, which sought to overthrow the all-embracing hold of rabbinic tradition and to create a synthesis between the Jewish mode of life and thought and that of the modern world. Levinsohn, who had become an adherent of the movement in Galicia, under the influence of Joseph Perl[1] and Nachman Krochmal,[2] was the spiritual father of the *Haskalah*. He published his book with a grant of 1,000 roubles from the Russian government, who regarded it as a contribution to their policy of assimilation. He urged that the study of the Bible should be combined with that of Hebrew grammar, that the use of the vernacular and the study of foreign languages and literature was not forbidden by Jewish law, that the acquisition of secular sciences was not harmful to Judaism, that Jews should devote themselves in larger numbers to manual crafts and agriculture, and that they should refrain from early marriages. These theses, which seem so obvious and commonplace nowadays, were then regarded as revolutionary and aroused the bitterest opposition. They were

[1] Joseph Perl (born 1774 at Tarnopol, where he died in 1839) founded the first modern Jewish school in Poland and built a synagogue with a modernized service, in 1815, at his own expense. He wrote a scathing satire, *Megalleh Temirin* (Revealer of Secrets), against the Hasidim under the pseudonym of Obadiah ben Petahya. It was published in Vienna in 1819.

[2] Nachman Krochmal (born 1785 at Brody, died 1840 at Tarnopol), who exercised a profound influence upon the Jewish thinkers of his time, was the first scholar to proclaim the importance of the historic factor in Judaism. He wrote a critical work, *Moreh Nebuke ha-Zeman* ("Guide of the Perplexed of the Time"), in which he combined historical research with philosophic speculation.

reaffirmed by Levinsohn in his chief work, *Bet Jehuda* ("House of Judah"), published in 1839, the same year in which he wrote his refutation of the ritual murder libel under the title of *Effes Damim* ("No Blood"), which played a part in the Damascus Affair.

The *Haskalah* was vigorously fostered in Vilna by a literary circle called the "Berliners" (an allusion to the Mendelssohnian school), founded in 1830 for the cultivation of Hebrew literature and the advancement of humanism. Its foremost figures were two writers of outstanding ability, Mordecai Aaron Guenzburg (1795–1846) and Abraham Baer Lebensohn (1794–1878). Guenzburg, born in Salant and settled in Vilna in 1829, was the first master of modern Hebrew prose to make borrowings from the Talmud and modern languages for the vocabulary he found necessary for his fifteen volumes. He created a sensation by his translation of Campe's *Entdeckung Amerikas*, which appeared in 1823 and opened a new world to his generation. He exercised a profound influence and achieved wide popularity through his historical works; his collection of model letters, *Kiriat Sefer* ("City of Books," 1835) and his literary miscellany, *Debir* ("Sanctuary," 1849), laid the foundations of modern Hebrew style. His brief autobiography, *Abiezer*, vividly reflects the conditions of his time.

Abraham Baer Lebensohn (whose pseudonym was "Adam ha-Kohen"), a native of Vilna, was the first to give passionate utterance in nervous Hebrew to the misery of his people, to paint the tragedy of

their history and the irony of their internal bondage.
A student of the Talmud at the age of seven, married
at thirteen, he was first employed in business, then
became a private Hebrew teacher, and later was
appointed lecturer in Hebrew and Aramaic at the
Rabbinical Seminary. Inspired by Wessely's *Mosiad*,[1] he soon surpassed that work in purity of
language, brilliance of style and originality of
thought. In his *Shire Sefat Kodesh* ("Songs of the
Holy Tongue"), of which three volumes appeared
between 1842 and 1869, he poured forth his thoughts
and feelings in a strain of almost unrelieved pessimism regarding the life around him. He gave
expression to his doleful philosophy in the lines:

O world, abode of grief and vale of gloom,
Thy rivers sadly flow with human tears,
The fabric of thy earth a mound of ash:
And o'er thy face the ceaseless mournful march
Of men in silence to the hungry tomb.

He rose to the supreme height of passionate despair
in a passage of striking imagery:

If I but thought that with my voice of wrath
I could destroy in one resounding crash
The swarming earth and all the hosts of
heaven,
Then would my voice go hurtling through the
air

[1] Naphtali Hartwig (Herz) Wessely (1725–1805), one of the
most prominent members of the Mendelssohn circle, was a distinguished Hebrew poet, whose *Mosiad* was an epic of five books on
the Exodus, written under the influence of Klopstock's *Messiad*.

And raise a roar of thousand thunder-bolts,
As I bawled forth the words: "Let all things
    cease!"
And so, through wild abysmal chaos hurled,
I'd sink with all mankind to nothingness.

The Vilna circle included a number of *Maskilim*,
as the votaries of the *Haskalah* were called, all of
whom were distinguished in their respective spheres
of intellectual work and literary achievement. Samuel Joseph Finn (1818–91) was brought to Vilna
in boyhood from his native Grodno and is best
known by his history of the Jews in Vilna, *Kiryah
Ne'emanah* ("Faithful City," 1860), in which he
describes in laudatory detail the lives of the city's
long roll of rabbis and scholars and reproduces the
florid inscriptions on their tombs. His principal
works are *Ha-Ozar*, a Hebrew-Aramaic dictionary
of the Bible, Mishna, and Midrashim; and *Keneset
Yisrael*, a biographical lexicon of Jewish scholars
and famous men (1886–90). He also edited *Sofre
Yisrael* ("Scribes of Israel," 1871), a collection of
letters in Hebrew from Hasdai ibn Shaprut until
his own time. To Finn, too, belongs the distinction
of having founded the first Hebrew weekly in Russia,
Ha-Karmel, which was published from 1860 to
1881, although during its last ten years it appeared
as a monthly. Finn was a wealthy scholar and owner
of a brick-kiln, of whom a wit once said: "His
Hebrew is as hard as brick, and his bricks are as
soft as butter." Even before the publication of
Ha-Karmel, however, there appeared in Vilna two
numbers of the first Hebrew review, *Pirhe Zafon*

("Blossoms of the North"), in 1841 and 1843, to which all the modern Hebrew writers in the country, who were spoken of as the Russian *Meassefim*, contributed articles and poems, but which had no successors owing to the intolerance of the government.

Matthias Strashun (1817–85), who wrote an introduction and notes to Finn's history of Vilna, besides contributing to the *Haskalah* journals, was a talmudical scholar. He devoted his fortune to the creation of a large private library, which, with considerable additions, has been preserved under his name to this day, as the communal library of Vilna Jewry.[1] Isaac Benjacob (1801–63), the bibliographer, who lived in Vilna from 1848, issued an edition of the Bible in seventeen volumes with a German translation (in Hebrew letters) and the commentaries of Mendelssohn's disciples. This work enabled the Jews of Eastern Europe to become acquainted with the German language and to find their way to western culture. His principal work, *Ozar ha-Sefarim: Thesaurus librorum hebraeorum tam impressorum quam manuscriptorum*, a critical bibliography of the whole range of Hebrew literature up to 1863, recording 17,000 works, was published after his death by his son Jacob (died 1926), who devoted all his. life to the enlargement and improvement of this scholarly achievement.

Although similar in its motives and initial character to the Mendelssohnian movement, the *Haska-*

---

[1] This library was reported to have been destroyed by the Germans in 1942.

lah in Russia developed along fundamentally different lines. The leaders of .the movement in Germany frankly advocated assimilation, in which Hebrew was relegated to ,secondary importance; while those in Russia earnestly devoted themselves to the renaissance of Hebrew literature and prepared the way for the Jewish national movement. A new and powerful impetus to Russian *Haskalah* was given by Kalman Schulmann (1819–99), who, though not born in Vilna, became associated with the *Maskilim* there and wrote and translated a number of scientific and belletristic works which helped to propagate general knowledge among Russian Jewry. He popularized Hebrew literature among the masses by his history of the world in nine volumes and his geography of the world in ten, by his biographical handbook, *Toledot Hakme Yisrael* ("History of the Scholars of Israel") in four volumes and his translation of the works of Josephus. His great achievement was the founding of the Romantic movement by a translation, in 1847, of Sue's *Mysteries of Paris*. This movement was the greatest event of the kind in Hebrew literature since the days when the mediaeval singers of Spain invented a Hebrew prosody, for it inaugurated a new era and a new genre in literary expression. Its first exponent was the son of Abraham Lebensohn, Micah Joseph Lebensohn, who has been called the Keats of Hebrew literature; while in prose it gave birth to the novel through the art of Abraham Mapu.

Micah Lebensohn (1828–52), who attended the lectures of Schelling in Berlin on natural philosophy, became an early prey to consumption and pessimism. After translating Homer and Virgil, Horace and Goethe, Heine and Mickiewicz, he revealed the wealth of his powers in his principal works: a rendering of Schiller's *Destruction of Troy*, and a series of six historical poems based on biblical episodes and themes of national import, entitled *Shire Bat Zion* ("Songs of the Daughter of Zion"). Gifted with a rich imagination, a lyrical soul and a beautiful style, he occasionally drew a contemporary moral from an ancient story, while in his tragic compositions on Moses and Jehuda Halevi — both doomed to die as they hoped to enter the Promised Land — he gave moving utterance to his private sorrow. After his death his father published a number of his other poems, under the title of *Kinnor Bat Zion* ("Harp of the Daughter of Zion"), lyrics displaying further evidence of genius cut off all too soon.

A more dominant figure was Abraham Mapu (1808–67). His historical romance, *Ahabat Zion* ("Love of Zion"), published in 1853, was the first prose work of creative imagination in the language of Isaiah. Born at Slobodka, a suburb of Kovno, Mapu was a learned Talmudist at thirteen. He was employed by a rich Jewish farmer as teacher to his children, and there made the acquaintance of a Polish priest who taught him Latin classics and modern languages. He was only twenty-two when he conceived his romance, and it was not until twenty-three years later that, under the stimulus of Schulmann's translation of *The Mysteries of Paris*, he presented his epoch-making work to the Jewish

world. He lived in Vilna only a short time, but his
book was printed in that city, and it produced a
profound and almost revolutionary influence upon
his generation. Written in the style of the Bible,
this idyllic story of the love of Amnon and Tamar,
set amid the beauties of bounteous nature, in that
golden age when the son of Amoz was in the vigor
of prophecy and King Hezekiah ruled over a peaceful
Judaea, immediately captured the imagination of the
ghetto readers hitherto bent over the folios of the
Talmud. They devoured its delights in secret —
in some secluded wood by day and by a flickering
candle in the dead of night. *Ahabat Zion* went into
four editions within twenty years and became the
favorite reading of the Jewish youth of Eastern
Europe until the beginning of the present century.[1]
Mapu soon left the world of romance for that of
realism, when he wrote his big novel, *'Ayit Zabu'a*
("The Hypocrite"), of which three parts appeared
in Vilna between 1857 and 1864 and the first complete edition in Warsaw in 1869. In this work,
which presents a portrait-gallery of types of Lithuanian Jewry, he scourged Kahal despots and bigoted
rabbis alike, while presenting a sympathetic figure
of the *Maskil* struggling between religion and
science. He also wrote another romance of Bible
times, *Ashmat Shomron* ("The Sin of Samaria,"

---

[1] *Ahabat Zion* has been translated twice into English (London,
1887; New York, 1903), seven times into Yiddish, and also into
Arabic (1908). A German version by Salomon Mandelkern was
published in 1885, under the title of *Thamar*, without any mention
of Mapu's name.

1865), depicting the conflict between the two king-doms of Palestine, and a novel dealing with the life of Sabbetai Zevi, of which only a small fragment appeared under the title of *Hoze Hezionot* ("Seer of Visions").

All these writers were soon overshadowed by a greater figure, Judah Loeb Gordon (1830–92), a native of Vilna, and the greatest poet in Hebrew literature since the Middle Ages until his own time. Distinguished as a Talmudist and Hebraist at the age of fourteen, he naturally became a teacher. He was strongly influenced in his earliest work by the two Lebensohns and by Schiller. His first productions were poems on biblical themes, such as *Ahabat David u-Michal* ("The Love of David and Michal," 1856) and a collection of fables, *Mishle Jehuda* ("Fables of Judah," 1860). But he quickly developed into a revolutionary poet who used his artistic genius and literary craftsmanship in a series of passionate protests against the intolerance of the rabbis and the corruption of communal leaders, as well as against the general conditions which made life so hard and harassing for the Jew. "Be a Jew at home and a man outside," was his maxim. Whether the poem is inspired by the Bible, like "King Zedekiah in Prison," or by mediaeval history, like "In the Depths of the Ocean," which treats of the Spanish expulsion, or by the misery of modern life, like "The Two Josephs ben Simon," it always forms the stage from which Gordon fulminates against rabbinical despotism or contemplates the tragic panorama of his people's history. He spoke

from his very soul when, in the poem dealing with
the Judeo-Roman wars ("In the Lion's Jaws"), he
thus addressed his generation:

> Full many hundred years have countless
>   guides
> Instructed thee and founded schools of lore,
> But whither has their teaching carried thee?
> Alack, all counter to the path of life
> Have they thy footsteps led, and fast confined
> Thy tender soul in lonely dreariness,
> Within the gloomy walls of massive codes.

After settling in St. Petersburg in 1872 as secretary
of the Society for the Propagation of Knowledge
among the Jews, Gordon published a series of
"Modern Heroic Poems" in the monthly *Ha-Shahar*,
in which he gave full vent to his indignation against
the rigidity of rabbinic legalism. His bitterest
invectives were hurled at the narrow interpretation
of scriptural texts, as in his *Kozo shel Yod* ("Point
of the Yod"), in which he depicts the wretched
plight of a poor woman condemned to a loveless
life:

> By cords of precepts are we all enchained,
> By fetters of inane and galling rules.
> No more do strangers persecute our lives,
> But our own kin. Our hands are bound no
>   more,
> But shackles clog our soul.

Gordon's most poignant outbursts were those evoked
by the sorry condition of his people among the
nations. In "The Two Josephs ben Simon," in

which he describes with satirical power the roving
life of the poor Jewish student, he exclaims:

> And what is thine, O people Israël,
> Except a wand'ring beggar student's lot?
> To roam among the nations ceaselessly
> And seek a grudged pittance bought by tears.
> For all mankind hast thou the light divine
> Enkindled, but for thee the world is dark:
> And thou art now become the slave of slaves,
> O Nation, mocked by all, and sick to death.

The poet experienced the bitterness of disillusion
when political reaction set in under Alexander II,
culminating in the horrors of 1881. Then he realized
the futility of the *Haskalah* as the road to emancipation. He noted that Jews were deserting the fold
and becoming estranged from the national language
in which he wrote, and he poured forth his doubts
and fears in a poem entitled: "For Whom Am I
Creating?" He therefore welcomed and supported
the idea of the return to Palestine, which began
to be advocated, but he was too intimately bound
up with the *Haskalah* movement to throw himself
wholeheartedly into the new cause. When Lilienblum[1] unfurled the Zionist banner and Pinsker[2]

[1] Moses Loeb Lilienblum (born 1843 at Keidany, died 1910
at Odessa), was a critical Hebrew writer, who, after advocating
religious reforms and furthering the *Haskalah*, became, under
the influence of the pogroms of 1881, an ardent apostle of the
Jewish return to Palestine and published a Russian pamphlet on
The Rebirth of Israel on the Land of his Fathers, which had very
wide repercussions.

[2] Leon Pinsker (born 1821 at Tomashov, died 1891 at Odessa)
was at first a champion of assimilation, but was converted by

issued his famous pamphlet, *Auto-Emancipation*, Gordon replied:

> What are we, do ye ask, and what our life?
> A nation like the nations of the world
> Or but a brotherhood made one by faith?
> Nor brotherhood nor nation, but a flock:
> The flock of God, a holy flock are we,
> And all the earth is but an altar vast,
> And we the victims for the sacrifice
> Are marked and bound, yea, marked from day
>   of birth
> And bound by priestly precepts all our lives.

Despite this implied reflection upon Jewish nationalism, however, which must be regarded in the light of a poet's license, Gordon composed some moving "Songs of Zion," in one of which he gave pathetic utterance to his misgivings:

> Perchance I am the last of Zion's bards
> And ye the last who hearken unto me.

The course of events belied his doleful forecast, for he was followed by other bards who lived to see and acclaim the rebirth of Zion.[1]

the political reaction in 1880 to the view that the only solution of the Jewish question was the concentration of the Jews in a land of their own. He became leader of the *Hobebe Zion* ("Lovers of Zion") movement and convened the historic Kattowitz Conference in 1884.

[1] The complete poetical works of Gordon (who was called, after his initials *YeLaG*) were published in six volumes in Vilna, in 1898. His *Tales* appeared in Odessa in 1889. His *Letters*, numbering 536, from 1858 to 1892, were issued by J. Weissberg,

A powerful stimulus to literary activity in Hebrew was subsequently provided by a daily newspaper, *Ha-Zeman*, which was published in 'Vilna and had a splendid though somewhat checkered career for over ten years. It was founded by Feiwel Margolin, a *Hobeb Zion* from his youth, and his rich father-in-law, Jacob Elijah Rivkind, who invested in it a capital of 60,000 roubles, all of which was eventually lost. It was published by the firm of Romm for a time with weekly and monthly editions. Its editor was Ben-Zion Katz (born 1875 in the Vilna district), who lived mainly in St. Petersburg, from where he contributed regular political articles, and frequently travelled to Vilna; and it had a brilliant staff, including Hillel Zeitlin, its dynamic force; I. A. Trivush, chief assistant; and I. Berschadski, acting editor; apart from younger writers, like S. Tcherno-vitz, Ben-Eliezer, and I. D. Berkovitz. *Ha-Zeman* was not associated with any particular political party; it was a progressive organ devoted to the fight for political freedom and equality, published contributions from all the leading Hebrew writers of the day, and was on a level with the best of the Russian papers. Its first number appeared on December 6, 1904, when the struggle against tsarist

1892–95. Especial interest attaches to his *Diary* (printed in the journal *He'Abar*, I–II, St. Petersburg, 1918), to his *Notes* on his brief imprisonment due to a false accusation of revolutionary activity (in *Pereschitoje*, IV, 1–45), and to his memoirs, *Al Nehar Kebar* (in *Reshumot*, I, 69 f., and V, 61 f.). A complete edition of his works, including his memoirs, has been issued by the Debir publishing company (Tel Aviv).

tyranny was growing ever stronger and both courage
and cunning were needed to defeat the censor.
Ben-Zion Katz was a dauntless editor, who printed
everything of public interest even at the risk of
imprisonment. He was wanted by the authorities for
over a year before they succeeded in arresting him
for the offense of publishing the Draft Constitution
submitted by the Minister Bulygin to Nicholas II
after the Russian Revolution of 1905. He was in
jail for twelve months, but even from there continued
to contribute articles to *Hed ha-Zeman*, to which
the name of the paper was changed in consequence
of the prosecution. But in 1911 the name *Ha-Zeman*
was restored, and the paper continued to appear
until April, 1915, when it succumbed to the effects
of the first World War.

The *Haskalah* found expression also in Yiddish
and would probably not have exercised so much
influence among the masses but for the literature
produced in that language. In this sphere, too,
Vilna played a very notable part throughout the
nineteenth century. Apart from Yiddish writers
who were born there, others were attracted to this
literary metropolis for longer or shorter periods,
and all kinds of Yiddish works first saw the light
in that city, including many (from 1872) by "the
father" of Yiddish literature, Mendele Mocher
Seforim. Novels, realistic, romantic, and historical,
plays and satires, lyrics and ballads, collections of
legends and folklore, as well as works of an educational, religious, or ethical character, appeared in
almost ceaseless spate, revealing a wealth of creative

energy, imaginative fancy, and critical faculty, and providing intellectual sustenance for hundreds of thousands. The first Yiddish work of a purely instructive kind was the translation by Mordecai Aaron Guenzburg of Campe's *Entdeckung Amerikas*, for, after having published that work in Hebrew at a financial loss, he also produced a Yiddish version in the following year, 1824, in order to recoup himself; and his enterprise was rewarded by a succession of editions.

The most eminent and popular Yiddish writer born in Vilna was Eisik Meir Dick (1807–93), who taught at a government school for a time and showed his ability as a Hebrew satirist in a talmudical parody, *Masseket Aniyyut* ("Tractate Poverty"). His mastery and versatility as a Yiddish storyteller are abundantly displayed in about four hundred booklets which he wrote in the course of his long life. They are all distinguished by remarkable powers of observation and description, and helped to educate the people and free them from superstition. The stories are very varied in character — historical, realistic, sentimental, and humorous; they reflect the hopes, ideals, and struggles of the time; and they played an important part in the cultural development of Lithuanian Jewry. In 1865 he contracted with the printing firm of Romm to provide a booklet of short stories every week, an undertaking he faithfully kept for years; and every Jewish housewife, in making her purchases for the Sabbath, also bought Dick's latest work for the family's edification.

Two other authors of popular novels and novel-
ettes were Ozer Blaustein (1840–98), who wrote
about a hundred works of fiction largely for the
masses, besides Russian, Hebrew, German and Yiddish dictionaries; and Abraham Isaac Buchbinder
(1860–97), who produced some historical romances.
Zevi Hirsch Reicherson (1857–92) translated all of
Krilov's fables into Yiddish and also published a
collection of talmudical proverbs and parables.
Michel Gordon (1823–90) owed his popularity to his
poems in the Yiddish language, although he also
composed in Hebrew and exercised a powerful influence over his brother-in-law, Judah Loeb Gordon.
One of his best known poems is *Steh oif, mein Volk*
("Arise, My People," 1869), in which he urged the
acquisition of modern education and denounced
Hasidism and fanaticism.

A writer of much greater originality and artistic
craftsmanship was Perez Hirschbein, who was born
in the Grodno district in 1880, and settled in Vilna
in 1900, residing there for several years. He first
attracted attention with a Hebrew drama, *Miriam*,
in 1905; but in the following year appeared his
first original work in Yiddish, *Auf jener Seit Teich*
("Beyond the Pond"), which in its symbolism betrayed the influence of Maeterlinck. A number of
Yiddish dramas which he wrote earned him recognition as the first Yiddish playwright of literary
importance, though he also translated some of them
into Hebrew. In 1911 his play, *Die Puste Kretchme*
("The Empty Inn"), which was successfully performed later by the Vilna Troupe, marked his

transition from sentimentalism and symbolism to realism. In that year he migrated to the United States, where his plays have greatly contributed to the advancement of the Yiddish theater.

A unique place in the intellectual life of the community was occupied by Eliakim Zunser (1840–1913), who united in his person the varied gifts of poet, wit and minstrel. He was commonly known as "Eliakim Badhan," as he was a professional *Badhan* or jester, who entertained people at weddings, in inns, and at social gatherings generally, by reciting poetic compositions on themes mostly taken from daily life or singing them to his own melodies. He began his career as a minstrel in 1861, when he published his first collection of songs. For the next twenty-eight years he contributed to the entertainment of the Jews, not only of his native city but of the greater part of Russia, with the products of a fertile mind. He also enjoyed popularity in Rumania and Galicia. He is estimated to have composed in all about 600 songs and ballads, published in some sixty booklets, and varying from the humorous to the serious, from the satirical to the dramatic. He dealt with religious and literary themes as well as with questions of the day; and after the pogroms of 1881, when the idea of the Jewish return to Palestine began to be ardently advocated, he composed many songs of Zion and gave literary evenings in support of the cause. His melodies represented a transitional stage between the music of the synagogue and that of the theater. Thanks to the thoughtful element in his compositions and the moral they generally conveyed, he was as popular with rabbis and other intellectuals as with the unlearned members of the community. He had various imitators, but no equal. In 1889 he migrated to the United States, either because he was unable to make a decent living by his recitals, or because the authorities resented his references to pogroms, and in his new home he composed many new songs dealing with American themes. But he had passed his zenith and had to turn to business for a livelihood. A complete edition of his works in three volumes, with his autobiography, appeared in 1921. Another folk-singer born in Vilna, though of the old-fashioned type, was Moses Chaskes (1830–1906), who wrote songs and satires on Jewish life not only in Yiddish but also in Hebrew.

An important part in the development of Vilna as an intellectual center was played by various Jewish printing and publishing concerns, the earliest of which was the printing press founded there in 1799 by a bookseller named Baruch ben Joseph Romm. Originally, some ten years earlier, he had set up his Hebrew press in Grodno, under special authorization from King Stanislav Poniatowski. As the first such press in Lithuania, its establishment was regarded as a significant landmark in Jewish history. From the time of its transfer to Vilna the business soon made rapid progress, which greatly increased after 1845, when, owing to the action of the censorship, the house of Romm practically enjoyed a monopoly in Russia and Poland. The press was of peculiar advantage to Vilna's cultural life.

In the centuries before Vilna had its own Hebrew press, many a Jewish scholar, anxious to get his work published, would wander to some other city, where he was often induced to settle, perhaps with the reward of rabbinical office. When Baruch Romm died in 1803, the press was conducted by his son Menahem. In 1835, he began, in partnership with Simhah Zimel, of Grodno, the ambitious publication of a new edition of the Talmud. The first volumes of this edition bear the imprint "Vilna and Grodno," but the later ones show only the name of Vilna. After Menahem's death in 1841, he was succeeded by his only son, Joseph Reuben, who reorganized the business in 1847; and when the latter died in 1858 the concern was carried on by his three sons, David, Hayyim Jacob, and Menahem Gabriel. David, who was the head of the firm, died suddenly in 1860, while on his way to St. Petersburg where he had obtained a practical monopoly of the Hebrew printing and publishing business in Russia. But after his death the monopoly came to an end and many printing firms were founded in various parts of the empire. The business was then conducted by his widow and two brothers, and hence, in 1863, the present name, "The Widow and the Brothers Romm," was adopted, which has become famous not only in Eastern and Central Europe but also among Jewish communities throughout the world. The firm existed until the outbreak of the second World War, although it no longer included any representative of the founder's family. In the course of its hundred and fifty years' exist-

ence it had produced not only prayer-books for
all sorts of occasions, but also editions of the Talmud,
the Mishna, the *Shulhan Aruk*, and all other works
of Jewish religious lore, as well as a large number of
secular works, which made the name of Romm
famous throughout Jewry.

The long reign of the house of Romm was largely
due to the devotion and qualifications of its compositors and proofreaders, who had necessarily to
be good Hebrew scholars themselves to be able to
deal with the texts of the Talmud, the Bible, the
Midrashim, *Shulhan Aruk*, and other rabbinical
works. One of them, Abraham Z. Rosenkranz
(1815–1901), who came to Vilna as a child from the
province of Minsk and was a compositor at Romm's
for many years, in 1862 founded his own business,
in partnership with a younger brother and Samuel
J. Finn, under the name of Rosenkranz and Schrift-
setzer. This firm published both religious and
secular works, among them being an edition of the
Bible with a Yiddish commentary by David Notik
and others, and over a hundred novels and storybooks, each in editions of 5,000 copies. Isaac Baer
Chones, born in Vilna in 1840, entered this concern
as a proofreader when it was established, but in
1870 transferred his services to Romm, where he
corrected works both of rabbinical and *Haskalah*
literature. He settled in the United States in 1891
and there published part of a biblical concordance
with a Yiddish translation (A–B) and a talmudical
reference-book with 8,000 titles. Another leading
publisher was Boris Kletzkin (1875–1937), who came

to Vilna as a boy and devoted himself from early manhood to the distribution of good Yiddish literature, especially among the working classes. He was an active member of the Jewish socialist organization, the Bund, from its creation in 1897, and helped to organize and establish its legal press, *Der Vecker* and *Die Volkszeitung*, as well as its publication department. He founded his firm in 1910, published books by all the leading Yiddish writers (Sholem Asch, David Einhorn, David Bergelson, Naumburg, and Abraham Reisen), and also textbooks and other works, as well as a weekly, *Literarische Bletter*, and a monthly journal, *Die Iddische Velt*.

The literary circles of Vilna Jewry contained few who made names as Russian writers, for Yiddish was the language spoken by all, while Hebrew was zealously fostered as a literary medium. The community's best known Russian author was Abraham Uri Kowner (1842–1909), who began his literary career with two Hebrew works, *Heker Dabar* ("Criticism of the Matter," 1865) and *Zeror Perahim* ("Bunch of Flowers," 1868). In these works he scathingly criticized contemporary Hebrew literature as devoid of a realistic sense of the needs of life, and provoked indignant rejoinders from the *Maskilim*. At the end of the 'sixties he settled in St. Petersburg and wrote for the Russian press, particularly feuilletons, modelling himself upon the Russian publicist, Pissarev. Unfortunately distress drove him to commit a bank fraud, which resulted in his imprisonment in Moscow (1875–77) and subsequent banishment to Siberia, where he adopted

Christianity. On his return from exile he engaged in correspondence with Dostoievski, whom he challenged to justify his unfriendly attitude to the Jewish question; and the novelist, in his reasoned replies, while trying to vindicate himself, denied any hostility. Kowner's writings included *Memoirs of a Jew*, *Recollections from Prison*, and an unpublished comedy (written in jail) which was awarded second place among over sixty entries.[1] A writer of far higher moral principle was Judah Leo Lewanda (1835–87), who was employed at the chancery of the governor-general of Vilna as expert on Jewish affairs. He wrote a number of Russian novels and sketches, in which he envisaged the complete cultural intermingling of Jews and Russians and forecast a new era in Jewish history. The terrible events of 1881, however, made him abandon his enthusiasm for assimilation and take an active and ardent part in the movement for the return to Zion.

[1] An excellent critical biography of Kowner is given in *Die Beichte eines Juden*, edited by Leonid Grossmann (Munich, 1927), which also contains the text of the correspondence exchanged with Dostoievski.

CHAPTER XVI

SOCIAL AND POLITICAL DEVELOPMENTS

1. COMMUNAL EXPANSION

THE prolific activity displayed by the Jews of Vilna in the spiritual and literary domain throughout the greater part of the nineteenth century surpassed, both in importance and variety, that of the Jews in any other city in Russia. This was, in part, a natural consequence of the extraordinary growth of the community. In 1765, when the Gaon Elijah was already a man of forty-five, Vilna's Jewry represented only a small settlement of 3,887, including those in the suburbs of Antokol and Schnipishok. By the end of the eighteenth century it had increased to only 6,971. But the subsequent expansion of the community was truly remarkable. In 1832 it already had 20,706 souls; by the year 1875 it numbered 37,909; and the official census of 1897 showed that it had multiplied to 63,841 souls, forming as much as 41.3 per cent of the total population. There was a still further advance, to 77,533, by the year 1912, although the Jewish proportion of the population declined to 33 per cent.

This increase was out of all proportion to the ordinary growth of the urban population. It was due to the May Laws of 1882, which prohibited Jews from living in rural districts and thus brought a large number to Vilna as to other urban centers. A city in which every third inhabitant was a Jew had an unmistakably Jewish character; and this was enhanced by the fact that, according to the census investigators, 98.9 per cent of the Jews in the Government or Province of Vilna used Yiddish as their ordinary medium of intercourse. There were only three other cities in Russia — Warsaw, Odessa and Lodz — which had a larger Jewish population. But Vilna could claim to be, not only the "Jerusalem of Lithuania," but the cultural capital of Russian Jewry. Its reputation had been developed and sustained not only by a succession of notable rabbis, writers and scholars, but also by the important part it had played in providing education.

The first modern Jewish school in Vilna is believed to have been founded in 1810 by Naphtali Herz Schulmann, who was probably an uncle of Kalman Schulmann; but orthodox opposition brought its career to an early end. The first private Jewish school was established in 1841 by the writers, Mordecai Aaron Guenzburg and Solomon Salkind; but that, too, does not seem to have been fortunate in its development. In 1847 the famous Rabbinical Seminary was opened under the direction of Hirsch Katzenellenbogen (1796–1868), author of *Netibot 'Olam* ("Ancient Paths"), who had the competent assistance of such scholars as Salkind and Samuel Joseph Finn. This Seminary produced many rabbis, scholars and writers, prominent among whom was Judah Loeb Kantor (1849–1915), the eminent Hebrew writer who at one time belonged to Lieberman's group of socialists, subsequently founded and edited the first Hebrew daily, *Ha-Yom* (St. Petersburg, 1886–87), and later became Crown Rabbi in Vilna. The Seminary was converted in 1871 into a Teachers' Institute which, as the only establishment in Russia for the training of Jewish teachers, enjoyed a great reputation. There were attached to it four subordinate elementary schools for Jewish children, and some twelve to thirteen students graduated every year. The cost of upkeep, about 30,000 roubles per annum, was appropriated by the government from the municipal meat-tax, the burden of which fell mainly upon the poor section of the Jewish population, since members of the liberal professions and college students were exempt from the tax and the well-to-do class were more or less indifferent to the use of kosher meat. Towards the latter part of the nineteenth century there were twenty other elementary schools for Jewish children, called "people's schools;" but neither in these nor in the Teachers' Institute and its subordinate schools was instruction given in specifically Jewish subjects. Thanks to the Zionist movement a girls' school, with Hebrew as the medium of instruction, was established in 1893 under the name of *Yehudiah*, and ten years later a parallel institution for boys under the name of *Heder Metukan*, which will be described more fully in the third section of this chapter.

Among the other social welfare institutions of the community were a hospital, a home for the aged needy, and a soup kitchen. The last-named, which was supported by voluntary subscriptions from Jews,

provided free meals for about 30,000 persons a
year — a good proportion being non-Jews. It was
used very largely by the Jewish soldiers stationed
in the city, of whom the community alone provided
about 112 recruits a year. The Province of Vilna,
however, furnished a far larger number of Jewish
soldiers, and one greatly in excess of the Jewish
ratio of the population. Thus, in 1891–92, although
the Jews formed 12.3 per cent of the total male
population in the province, they furnished 8,871
out of 51,575 soldiers, that is, 17.2 per cent; and
in 1903, when they were 12.47 per cent of the population, they provided 739 out of 4,639 soldiers, or
nearly 16 per cent.[1]

The Jews continued to engage in all the manual
and mechanical occupations which had distinguished
their economic life under the Polish regime. Many
had made sufficient progress to establish their own
workshops and factories; they practically monopolized the hosiery, leather, boot, tobacco and paper
industries, giving employment to thousands of
Jewish workers, and finding markets in the remotest
parts of the Russian Empire. They were also largely
engaged in the export of lumber and grain, and many
had shops, which were more notable for their number
than their size. The liquor trade, in which a considerable number of Jews had been previously engaged, was barred to them by the government
decree at the beginning of this century, causing

[1] *The Legal Sufferings of the Jews in Russia*, edited by Lucien
Wolf, London, 1912, pp. 3–4.

increased competition among the shopkeeping class. Outside the city many devoted themselves to agriculture, and the number who were so employed in the Province of Vilna was close to 4,000. Despite their industry and frugality, however, the majority of the Jews failed to reach even a low standard of comfort. Poverty, prevalent throughout Russian Jewry, was particularly marked in Vilna, involving insistent claims both upon charitable organizations and well-to-do individuals. Although no detailed statistics are available, it was commonly said that fully four-fifths of the Jewish population in the city did not know in the evening where they would be able to obtain a meal the next morning. An investigation conducted in 1898 in 1,200 places in Russia showed that, at Passover, 19 per cent of the Jewish population had been assisted by public contributions; but in Vilna it was 37.7 per cent.[1] The city could thus lay claim to the title of "Jerusalem of Lithuania" not only on the ground of its spiritual and cultural distinction but also on that of its material distress and desolation.

The attitude adopted by the Russian government, during the last forty or fifty years of the tsarist tyranny, to the Vilna Kahal as to most Jewish communities, was somewhat anomalous. It neither recognized the Kahal as a public body with legal rights, nor did it deny that it had such rights. The Senate issued all sorts of inconsistent orders, and

[1] Ibid., p. 56.

the Kahal complied whenever there was no alternative. The executive organ of the community,
for instance, was liable to collect and remit the
taxes from the Jews to the government. But although its legal status left much to be desired, its
financial position was satisfactory, as the special
taxes, the *Korobka* and candle-tax, provided an
adequate amount for defraying Jewish religious and
philanthropic needs as well as certain social welfare
and cultural requirements. The administration of
the community was in the hands of a few elders
called *Gabba'im* (literally, alms or tax collectors)
who, thanks to their mode of election, were able to
act as petty autocrats. Every year a number of well-
to-do Jewish citizens, whose names were entered
on a special list at the municipal office, were called
there to elect the elders for the new period. The
list was drawn up in accordance with the advice of
the *Gabba'im* themselves, and anybody who proved
refractory at the election was summarily removed
from the list. For the mode of election was extremely
simple: there was neither a secret ballot nor a choice
of candidates, but a pre-arranged list was adopted
by acclamation. This corrupt system was but a
reflection of the general conditions in the Russian
bureaucracy and was preserved by bribing the officials. Nevertheless, in the 'eighties and early 'nineties
of the last century the Vilna community had a very
capable president in Muni Solz, who reorganized
the principal charitable organization, the *Zedakah
Gedolah*, and also introduced a proper system of
accountancy. In the last decade of the century

there was formed a "Society of Brotherly Love,"
which included all the leading communal and intellectual workers. It was able to perform useful service
in the social, cultural and political spheres, and to
act as an effective curb upon the *Gabba'im*. But
the status of the Kahal was seriously weakened by
the developments in the political world, for the
formation of Jewish parties inevitably resulted in
the extinction of its political commission.

2. THE SOCIALIST MOVEMENT

The revolutionary ferment, which had first manifested itself in the middle 'seventies, had been
checked but not suppressed. Owing to the continuance of government tyranny it was gradually revived, stimulated by the discontent due to the bad
conditions in the workshops and factories — long
hours and low wages — in which a goodly proportion of the Jewish population were employed.
Secret circles of Jewish workers began to be formed
in Vilna in 1886. They were then limited to between
five and ten, for they could meet only in private
dwellings, but there were about twenty such circles.
They discussed their economic wrongs, studied the
"illegal" literature brought to them from Western
Europe, and imbibed the ideas of thinkers like
Robert Owen, Lassalle and Plekhanov. They composed and distributed Yiddish bulletins and pamphlets, organized secret meetings for the propagation
of their views, and fomented strikes for an improvement of their lot. The first strike, carried out by

thirty compositors at Syrkin's printing works in
1888, proved successful and was followed at intervals by strikes at other and larger concerns. The
first May Day demonstration in the city was organized by Jewish workers in 1892 and was savagely
dispersed by the police with their *nagaikas*; the
ringleaders, who were arrested, were "bloody but
unbowed." The struggle was extremely difficult
and dangerous, not only because of the rigorous
measures of suppression adopted by the authorities, of which banishment to Siberia was the most
common, but also because of occasional treachery
on the part of comrades who were intimidated or
seduced by the police to act as informers. The Jews,
however, were not the only people in Vilna engaged
in such activity. The Poles, despite previous abortive attempts to shake off the Russian yoke, were
still bent upon regaining their independence, and
an underground agitation was carried on among
workers and students both there and in many other
cities in Poland. The leader of the Polish revolutionaries in Vilna was Josef Pilsudski, destined to rebuild and rule the Polish State, who had close relations with the Jewish leaders and brought them copies
of manifestoes and other forbidden literature from
abroad. There was no agreement between them,
however, on their ultimate objective, for, while
Pilsudski and his Polish Socialist Party (commonly
called "P.P.S.") were primarily concerned with the
revival of an independent Poland, the Jewish workers,
who feared that their condition would be no better

under such a regime, were mainly anxious to see the Russian Empire converted into a socialist republic.

After a decade of preparation and organization, during which the Jewish workers' circles in Vilna had kept in constant communication with similar bodies in many other cities in the Pale, a conference of delegates was held for the purpose of forming a united organization. The gathering took place secretly in a little wooden house, in a quiet narrow street, in an obscure part of Vilna, near the Lukiska jail, on three days, October 8th to 10th (September 25th to 27th of the old Russian calendar), 1897. It was attended by only eleven persons, including two women, for many domiciliary searches and arrests by the police had recently taken place and made attendance at such a meeting extremely dangerous. The delegates from Vilna were Alexander Kraemer, Vladimir Levinsohn (Kossowski), and David Katz. The others came from Warsaw, Minsk, Bialystok, and Vitebsk. There were representatives also of the *Arbeiter Stimme*, the organ of the movement, produced by a secret printing press in Vilna, which began to appear in the preceding August. They held their deliberations in a small ill-furnished room, with a bare table in the middle and only a few chairs, so that some delegates had either to stand or to squat on the floor. The proceedings were conducted by Alexander Kraemer, the leader of the local Jewish Social Democrats, and culminated in the unanimous decision to found the *Allgemeiner Juedischer Arbeiter Bund in Polen und Russland* (General Jewish

Workers' Union in Poland and Russia). It was not long before this organization, briefly and popularly termed "the Bund," became known for its energy, audacity and success, not only throughout Russia but in all parts of the world. Its title became amplified later by the inclusion of "Lithuania." The Bund comprised sixteen district committees in various parts of the Pale, all under the control of the Central Committee, which issued a new and popular paper, *Der Bund*, for the working masses.

Originally economic in its aims and aspirations, the Bund soon changed its program to a revolutionary character, since the leaders reflected that even with the achievement of all their demands regarding hours of work and wages, the Jews would still be the helpless prey of Muscovite oppression. Hence, as soon as there was an organized agitation among the Russian people for political liberty and constitutional government, the Bund began to cooperate in a systematic and conspicuous manner. The difficulty of arranging a propaganda meeting, in view of the risk of arrest and imprisonment, was got over by holding it in a synagogue, in the guise of a religious service, or in a cemetery, under the pretense of a funeral, or sometimes in the secluded depths of a forest, with patrols on the outskirts to give warning of any approaching police. Leaflets were distributed broadcast during a May Day demonstration or showered down from the gallery of a theater during the performance. Agitation was also conducted at military recruiting centers and even in prisons. Adherents were won over not only from the working class but also from student circles, and even from pious scholars of the *Yeshibah*, who could be induced to abandon the Talmud for the teachings of Karl Marx.

The Bund joined the Russian Social Democrat Federation when this party was formed in 1898. But, as it was not allowed to exercise as much autonomy as its leaders demanded, the Bund seceded in 1903 and continued an independent existence. It was opposed by the Polish Socialists, who wished all efforts to be directed solely towards the restoration of the Polish State. It was opposed by Jewish employers for economic reasons, by the rabbinical authorities for religious reasons, and by the Zionists for Jewish national reasons. At its fourth conference, held at Bialystok in 1901, the Bund did indeed acknowledge Jewish nationality, but only in theory. It adopted a resolution declaring that Russia, being composed of a number of different nationalities, should in future "be organized on federative principles, each nation enjoying complete autonomy, irrespective of the territory occupied by it," and adding that "the idea of nationality is also applicable to the Jewish people." Nevertheless its leaders did not consider the time opportune for including national autonomy among their demands, and they qualified their conception of Jewish nationality by confining themselves to the use of Yiddish and opposing that of Hebrew. Despite the antagonism which the Bund encountered from different quarters, it secured over 30,000 members throughout the Pale, carried on extensive propaganda by means of its press and pamphlets, helped to organize many self-defense committees as a protection against pogroms, and suffered many casualties through the loss of members by imprisonment, banishment and death.

For a brief period, thanks to the limited liberty wrung from the government at the end of 1905, the Jewish socialists in Vilna were able to conduct their press legally. The first socialist daily in Yiddish, *Der Vecker*, began to appear in the city on January 7, 1906 (December 25, 1905, in the old Russian calendar); but after thirty-two issues it was suppressed by the censor. It was succeeded a few days later by the *Volkszeitung*, which ran for a year, followed by *Die Hoffnung*, whose brief career was ended by the arrest of the entire editorial staff. An attempt was then made to publish a weekly paper, *Der Morgenstern*; but after three issues, edited by Vladimir Medem, the office was closed by the police. Altogether, the Jewish socialist press enjoyed only two years of legal existence; and when it was no longer possible to issue a paper, the Bund began to publish a series of miscellanies, under various titles, such as *Die Naie Zeit*, edited by Medem.

3. THE ZIONIST MOVEMENT

Parallel with the growth of socialist and revolutionary agitation began the development of the movement for the realization of a far more ancient ideal — the return to Zion. That enthusiasm for this cause should have been aroused in a time of acute oppression, in a community which for generations had been devoutly praying for its fulfilment, was but natural. As early as 1870 David Gordon (1826–86), a Hebrew writer born near Vilna, had contributed a series of articles to *Ha-Maggid*,[1] in which he expounded the principles of Jewish nationalism in connection with the rebuilding of Palestine. The latent sympathies of Vilna Jewry were stirred to eager action by the pogroms of 1881, and a society called *Ohabe Zion* was formed early in 1882 to work for the Jewish resettlement in Palestine. Its directing spirits were the author and communal leader Samuel Joseph Finn, who was the president, and Judah Leo Lewanda. Since both held official positions and the attitude of the Russian government was certain to be antagonistic, the name of the society was changed to *Tikvat 'Aniyim* ("Hope of the Poor"). In October, 1883, Leon Pinsker, whose *Auto-Emancipation* had made so profound an impression upon Russian Jewry, convened a meeting at his home in Odessa of representatives from various cities who were in favor of resettlement in Palestine, and the committee then formed immediately secured Finn's collaboration. From that time Vilna took a leading part in the furtherance of the *Hibbat Zion* movement: it was largely due to the pressure exercised by Finn and Lewanda that the memorable Kattowitz Conference took place in 1884; and, although circumstances made it impossible for the Vilna community to be represented there, Finn was

[1] A Hebrew weekly published at Lyck (East Prussia) from 1857 to 1892.

elected one of the three joint treasurers whose signature was necessary for any expenditure incurred by the central committee.

The *Maskilim*, realizing the futility of their ideas as a solution of the Jewish problem, gave increasing support to the movement. It also found poetic championship, not only in Judah Loeb Gordon, but also in bards of lesser renown, such as Izhak Goldman (1839–1905). The celebration of Finn's seventieth birthday in 1888 took the form of a veritable demonstration in favor of the restoration of Palestine. The idea attracted enthusiasts from many communities; and the important part that Vilna played in the furtherance of the cause was recognized by its being selected as the venue of the third conference of the *Hobebe Zion*, held in 1889. This gathering, which was attended by 38 delegates from 35 societies, was mainly concerned with the problem of securing government approval for the "Society for the Support of Jewish Agriculturists and Artisans in Palestine and Syria," as the organization was called, since without such approval it was forbidden to raise any funds for the practical work in Palestine. The statutes of the organization received official sanction the following year, with the result that greater progress became possible.[1]

Six years later Theodor Herzl published *Der Judenstaat*, and the movement entered upon a new and more active phase. The "Lovers of Zion" be-

---

[1] See Supplementary Note 8.

came political Zionists, and Vilna sent three delegates — Isaac L. Goldberg, Arkadi Naischul, and A. Perlis — to the first Zionist Congress, which took place at Basle on the last four days of August, 1897. Henceforth Vilna Jewry constituted one of the strongholds of the Zionist movement and provided leaders for its various parties, each of which stoutly advocated its views in its own particular organ. The leaders of the General Zionists were the brothers Isaac and Boris Goldberg and Arkadi Naischul, and Dr. Schmarya Levin was their prominent and eloquent colleague during his two years' sojourn in the city, as preacher in the Taharat ha-Kodesh Synagogue, 1903-05. The more orthodox members of the movement founded the Mizrahi party in Vilna, in 1902, under the leadership of the eminent talmudical authority, Rabbi Isaac Jacob Reines (1839-1915) and the historian, Wolf Jawitz (1847-1924). The latter had already lived a few years in Palestine and now became the editor of the party organ, *Ha-Mizrah.* They chose the "Jerusalem of Lithuania" as the place in which to emphasize the part the Torah should play in the restoration of Zion, by reason of the wealth of spiritual tradition associated with the city and the influence they believed it would exercise. But despite the scrupulous fidelity of the Mizrahi leaders to rabbinic doctrine there were some ultra-orthodox members of the community who regarded the aim of Zionism as incompatible with a belief in the coming of the Messiah and organized fanatical opposition. The antagonists, who were commonly spoken of as the *Lishkah ha-Shehorah* ("Black

Cabinet"), conducted their campaign through the medium of a journal, *Ha-Peless* ("The Scale"), which appeared in Berlin, under the editorship of Rabbi Akibah Rabbinowitch of Poltawa, and were also instrumental in causing the temporary closure of a Zionist library which had been opened in Vilna in April 1902. Other societies were formed by different sections of the community: the *Po'ale Zion* by the workers, the *Degel Zion* by commercial employees, *Ha-Tehiah* by students and scholars, *B'not Zion* by women, and a Literary Circle by the intelligentsia.

Although the Zionists could not reasonably have been suspected of any subversive activity, Von Plehve, the Minister of the Interior, issued a secret circular on June 24, 1903, to all governors, city prefects, and chiefs of police, ordering them to forbid all Zionist meetings and all collections for Zionist purposes. The reason given was the supposed impossibility of realizing the Zionist program except in the distant future. More probably the ban was a reprisal for the attack made by a Zionist socialist upon the Jew-baiter Krushevan, as well as in order to prevent Jewish socialists from making use of the Zionist platform for the propagation of their views. This blow at the movement, as well as a desire to secure the Russian government's influence at Constantinople in favor of the cause, prompted Theodor Herzl in the following August to visit St. Petersburg and to have interviews with Von Plehve and the Finance Minister, M. Witte. The diplomatic purpose of the mission proved unattainable; but as for the movement in Russia, Von Plehve declared that he was willing to tolerate it as long as it was concerned only with the creation of a Jewish center in Palestine and with mass emigration from Russia, though any attempt to carry on nationalist propaganda, which he considered harmful to Russia's national interests, would be suppressed.

The Zionist leader felt that he could not leave Russian soil without seeing for himself the great Jewish community of Vilna, which so strikingly typified the urgency of the cause to which he had dedicated his life. The ovations with which Herzl was overwhelmed by the Jews in Vilna were worthy of a king, though the Russian police did their utmost to reduce ceremonial functions to a minimum and to subdue the public enthusiasm. The local authorities were apparently frightened by the vast excited crowds which had assembled at the railway-station and in the streets to welcome the Jewish leader, and issued strict orders that he must on no account be taken to see the Great Synagogue or the synagogue courtyard. In his Diary Herzl describes the day he spent in Vilna, August 16, as "unforgettable." He writes:[1]

> I then drove through excited Jewish streets to the community office, where the elders and deputations awaited me in a dense throng. There was a tone in the greetings which moved me so deeply that I was only able to restrain my tears with the thought of the

---

[1] *Theodor Herzls Tagebücher*, vol. III, pp. 487–9. An account of Herzl's visit to Vilna was also given by Boris Goldberg in *Die Welt*, May 20, 1910, although he assigned to it a wrong date.

newspaper reports. The many speeches over-
rated me mightily, but the misery of these
sorely oppressed people was genuine.

In a scene charged with emotion, rendered more
tense by the smallness and stuffiness of the dingy
chamber in which the ceremony took place — sym-
bolic of the ghetto itself — the *Gabbai* Naischul,
on behalf of the community, tendered the Zionist
leader a Hebrew address inscribed on parchment;
the historian Jawitz presented him with a scroll of
the Torah; and the senior rabbi, the venerable Reb
Schleimele (Rabbi Solomon ha-Kohen), with trembling palms outstretched, pronounced the priestly
blessing. In awed silence Herzl expressed his thanks
in thoughtful words that thrilled his hearers and
inspired them with hope and comfort for the future.

As the police restrictions rendered a festive gathering in Vilna impossible, Herzl was driven in the evening to the outlying village of Werki where, at the
summer house of Jacob Benjacob, some fifty guests
sat down to dinner and many glowing toasts were
drunk. He was more deeply impressed, however,
by the uninvited guests who suddenly appeared
before the veranda, poor youths and girls who had
trudged all the way from the city, a two hours'
journey, to see him feasted. He writes:

> There they stood outside, looked on as we ate
> and listened to the speeches. And they
> provided the dinner music by singing Hebrew
> songs. Benjacob, a real generous host, was
> good enough to feed these uninvited ones too.
> And one of the young workmen, who had

struck me by his hard determined features,
so that I took him to be one of the revolutionary "Bundists," surprised me by calling for a
toast to the time when *"Ha-Melech* Herzl"[1]
would reign.   But this ridiculous outburst
produced a remarkable effect in the dark
Russian night.

Herzl left the city for Vienna after midnight in a
scene characteristic of the conditions of the time
and place. For the police, with their perverse conception of maintaining order, lashed out with their
nagaikas against the crowds of Jews who had assembled in the streets to see him off and refused to
permit any people except those with luggage to
enter the station. Within a few minutes over fifty
Zionists sped home, returned with hand-luggage, and
were admitted to the platform. Thus were the
requirements of the police loyally observed and
Herzl was given a moving farewell.

Passionately as the Zionists in Vilna, like all
their brethren in the Russian Pale, yearned for an
early deliverance from their bondage, they were
not prepared to exchange the ancestral homeland
of their aspirations for any other territory. Hence,
when the British Government made an offer of a
Jewish autonomous settlement in East Africa, the
great majority were opposed to its acceptance. A
conference of 47 delegates, representing the Zionists
of Russia, was held in Vilna on January 14, 1905.
It was there resolved that "as regards the view which

[1] "King Herzl."

considers it possible to realize the ultimate aim of Zionism in a country other than Palestine, it is agreed that such a view is opposed to both the historic ideal of Zionism and the Basle Program."

The leading part which the Zionists in Vilna increasingly played in the movement in Russia resulted in the transfer to that city from Kishinev, in October 1905, of the seat of the Central Committee for the entire country, the members being Isaac L. Goldberg, Schmarya Levin, Bezalel Joffe, Yehiel Tschlenow, and Simon Rosenbaum. To further the cause a new paper, *Dos Yiddishe Folk*, began to appear in 1906 under the editorship of Dr. Joseph Lurie (many years later Director of the Education Department of the Jewish Agency in Palestine), with the active collaboration of Shmarya Levin. The discussion of measures for advancing the movement was attended by danger, for on one occasion, when there was a meeting of about twenty leading workers in the house of Levin (including Isaac and Boris Goldberg, Leo Motzkin, Rosenbaum, and Lurie), the police made a sudden raid, arrested them all, and put them in jail; and it was not until telegrams had been sent to the Zionist President, David Wolffsohn, in Cologne, and the latter despatched an urgent telegram to the Russian premier, Stolypin, that the Zionists were released after a few days' detention.

The continuance of propaganda activity, however, was by no means easy. The suppression by the government of the attempted revolution was followed by a ban upon public meetings of all kinds.

Wolffsohn, therefore, visited St. Petersburg where, on July 10, 1908, he had an interview with the Russian Premier, Stolypin, to whom he explained the general aims of the Zionist movement, the activity of its institutions, and the nature of its work in Russia. The result was that the premier expressed his fullest sympathy with the cause and declared that the government had no intention to prevent the Zionists from carrying on the work for the realization of their program. After Wolffsohn had also had an interview with the Foreign Minister, Iswolsky, he went to Vilna, where he was enthusiastically welcomed not only by the Central Committee and the local Zionists, but also by deputations from Warsaw, Kovno, Grodno, Minsk, and several other cities.[1] The imperial government had telegraphed instructions to the local authorities in Vilna not to make any difficulties in connection with the gathering in honor of the Zionist leader. It was therefore possible to hold a public dinner at the Grand Hotel, lasting from 10 in the evening until 3 in the morning, at which numerous speeches were delivered, including one by the humorous author, Shalom Aleichem, who addressed Wolffsohn as "President of the disunited Jewish States." The influence of the Russian Central Committee was greatly strengthened by the transfer later in the year of *Ha-'Olam*, the official Hebrew organ of the World Zionist Organization, from Cologne to Vilna. But its responsibilities and risks were likewise in-

[1] *Die Welt*, July 17 and 24, 1908.

creased, for charges were more than once brought
against its members and the editor, that they had
committed some acts against the interests of the
country. Their "crimes" consisted of nothing more
serious than urging the sale of *shekel* vouchers, but
they were sufficient to bring upon their heads
sentences of imprisonment, which, after appeals were
lodged, were usually quashed.

Enthusiasm for the Jewish national revival also
found expression in the establishment of schools for
the purpose of making Hebrew a living language.
The first such school, originally opened in 1890,
was for girls. Owing to an "information" lodged
with the governor by the old-fashioned Hebrew
teachers (*Melammedim*), who were opposed to the
new method, the school was closed for a couple of
years. It was reopened in 1893 by the *B'not Zion*
under the name of *Yehudiah*. As it had no official
license, the teaching had to be conducted secretly in
ten private houses in different parts of the city. The
curriculum consisted of the Hebrew language, the
Bible, Jewish history, and general subjects. The
first teachers were the founders, who taught volun-
tarily. But in 1897 the management was taken over
by Mrs. Isaac L. Goldberg, who had the active cooperation of David Notik (one of the authors of a
popular commentary on the Bible) as inspector.
Qualified teachers were engaged, including many
well-known writers, such as I. Z. Anochi, Hirschbein,
Mukdoni, and others. Thanks largely to the personal
devotion and generosity of Mrs. Goldberg, *Yehudiah*
secured an official permit in 1905, after which it

was housed in one large building. Ultimately the school received so many pupils that branches had to be opened in the suburbs and other towns. The reasons why such a school was first opened for girls reveal the spirit of that generation. It was thought that it would not encounter such determined opposition on the part of the old-fashioned teachers, and that the mothers of the future should be educated in a Jewish national spirit.

The project was so successful that in 1903 a similar school was opened for boys. It was founded by Jacob Heilprin (formerly a Russian teacher at Raduszkowitz), with official permission, under the name of *Heder Metukan* ("Improved School"). It proved so attractive (beginning with 140 paying pupils) that it aroused opposition among the *Melammedim*, who feared that their own little schools would be deserted. Not only did these reactionary teachers send in forty-four letters of denunciation to the local authorities, but, by collecting one kopeck a week from each of their pupils, they gave 100 roubles to the "informer" of the community, who undertook to secure the closing of all the schools of the new type, of which there were thirty-two in the Vilna district. A meeting of the local government inspectors decided to suppress the schools. Heilprin, however, went to St. Petersburg to invoke the support of Baron Horace de Guenzburg, an ardent friend of Jewish education, and thanks to the latter's intervention with the minister of education the schools were reopened and resumed activity with increased vigor. Both the *Yehudiah* and the *Heder*

Metukan existed until 1915, when they succumbed to the effects of the first World War.

Between the Zionist ideal and the Bundist program there was an unbridgeable gulf. Nevertheless various attempts were made in Vilna to form a synthesis of the different principles that they embodied. In the years 1901–05 these attempts developed into three distinct currents of thought, which led to the founding of three separate parties. The first consisted of the Po'ale Zion (Workers of Zion), who, under the leadership of Ber Borochow (1881–1917), aimed at the fusion of nationalism and socialism in Palestine and seceded from the parent movement. The second party was the Zionist Socialists (popularly called "S.S."), founded in 1904, under the leadership of Dr. Nahman Syrkin (1867–1924) and Jacob Lestschinsky. In contradistinction to the Po'ale Zion, they declared that the solution of the Jewish workers' problem must be sought by a concentrated settlement in some other territory than Palestine. The third party, also called a Jewish Socialist party, was that of the "Seymists," whose program envisaged a *Seym* (or Diet) as the highest organ of Jewish self-administration in their present domicile. Their leading theoretician was Dr. Chaim Zhitlowsky. All these parties expounded and propagated their views in their respective organs: the Po'ale Zion in *Proletarischer Gedank*; the Zionist Socialists in *Unser Weg*, *Das Wort*, and *Der Neue Weg*; and the Seymists in *Die Volksstimme*. They all indulged in mutual discussion and recrimination, passionately defending their principles against the slightest criticism, and frequently attacking, either singly or in combination, the ideals and doctrines of the other parties — the General Zionists, the Mizrahi, the anti-Zionist Orthodox (the *Agudas Yisroel*), the Bundists, and the Social Revolutionaries. They formed a veritable medley of mutually warring groups and grouplets, each firmly convinced that its own program was wisest and alone would lead to the salvation of Jewry. They caused an incessant ferment and seething turmoil that kept life throughout the community and beyond at fever-heat, all alike heedless of the shadow of the great catastrophe which was to break upon them and upon the world in the summer of 1914.

CHAPTER XVII

WAR'S TRIBULATIONS AND AFTERMATH

1. THE RUSSIAN EVACUATION

THE World War which broke out at the beginning of August 1914 ushered in a period of suffering for the Jews in Russia, of which those in Vilna were doomed to bear more than a proportionate measure. However harassing their plight had been under the tsarist tyranny, it became aggravated under the succession of calamities which began to befall them and which continued with cumulative agony for several years. They not only experienced increased barbarity on the part of the Russian government and gross maltreatment on the part of the German invaders, but were also exposed to outrageous assaults by the Polish troops who celebrated the recovery of their country's independence by an outburst of savagery. Within the small space of eight years, from 1914 to 1922, the Jews of Vilna tasted of the blessings of nine different governments and suffered from a combination of other evils even more noxious. They became a prey to economic depression, military requisitions, unemployment, famine and disease; thousands of them were subjected to forced labor, imprisonment, plunder and brutal attacks; and physical and material deterioration inevitably engendered a certain degree of social demoralization. All the variegated differences of principle, of religious outlook and sociological doctrine, were now forgotten in the inferno created by the common foe. The long protracted fight for civil and political rights had to yield to the more primitive and desperate struggle for mere existence.

The Jews in the western provinces of Russia were the first to suffer, for they lived in one of the principal theaters of war. Before their torments began, however, the Jews of Vilna were called upon to supply comforts to the trainloads of wounded Russian soldiers. These were welcomed at the station by women and girls with milk and food, and by talmudical students with Red Cross armlets, who helped to carry them into ambulances. The Jewish community gave up a hospital for their special use. But since the Jews in the western districts, like all their brethren in the Russian empire, had been treated for over a century as enemies of the State, the government would not credit them with any sentiment of loyalty, although it summoned 600,000 Jews to its defense; and since they spoke a language of German origin, it was thought but natural that they would fraternize with the invaders and help them. Hence, soon after the outbreak of hostilities, the commander-in-chief, the Grand Duke Nicholas Nicholaievitch, ordered the evacuation at short notice of the entire Jewish population of those districts. Tens of thousands of fugitives were thus driven from the provinces of

Kovno, Grodno and Suvalk into the province of Vilna, swelling the swarms of refugees who had previously streamed from the war-troubled zone, so that, by the summer of 1915, the city of Vilna already contained several thousand homeless Jews and Christians. This enormous addition, mostly of needy humanity, to the local population made exacting claims upon the community for relief, which was cheerfully rendered. The Jews were lodged not only in private dwellings and public institutions but also in synagogues and *Klausen*, in prayer-rooms and houses of study.

The Vilna community, as the nearest large center to the war-front from where relief could be organized, had to provide succor not only for the victims in its own midst, but also for those who crowded into the neighboring townlets, which were unable to help with their scanty resources. Fortunately, the Vilna Central Committee, which had been formed soon after the outbreak of war, received financial aid from the Jewish Relief Committee, "Jekopo,"[1] created in St. Petersburg. The difficulty consisted in securing adequate supplies. Hundreds of dealers had come from other parts of the war-zone to buy up whatever foodstuffs and manufactured goods they could get, causing prices to rise and supplies to shrink. Moreover, the Poles in Vilna, who received generous support from a Polish Relief Fund organized in Switzerland, managed to obtain con-

---

[1] Abbreviated from the Russian name, *Jewrejskij Komitet Pomoschtschi.*

trol of most of the staple commodities, so that the Jewish committee was baffled in its efforts to satisfy both the large host of local poor and the multitude of refugees. Such was the position in the summer of 1915, when the military situation of the Russians became increasingly perilous, compelling them at last to evacuate the city. Along with the Russians went also a large number of Jews, particularly those with means. The "presidium" of the Jewish Central Committee likewise fled, leaving a disorganized office, and a new committee was formed under the chairmanship of Dr. Jacob Wygodzki.

2. THE GERMAN OCCUPATION

The German troops entered Vilna on September 18, 1915, which was the Day of Atonement. The Jews were all assembled in their synagogues in prayer and repentance; but they had less need to pray for the forgiveness of their sins than for mercy on the part of their new oppressors. The hope they had entertained that the arrival of the Germans would mean an alleviation of their distress soon gave way to disillusionment, for General Ludendorff's alluring promises in his famous manifesto to *Meine lieben Juden* turned out to be nothing but a monstrous deception. For a short time there was a Citizens' Committee, including four Jewish representatives (Dr. Jacob Wygodzki, Dr. Zemah Shabad, Littauer, and Joseph Izbicki), for the purpose of conferring with the invaders on matters of food, health, and questions of administration. But it was soon dissolved, as all authority was concentrated in a hierarchy of German military and civil authorities. Official notices were at first posted only in German, Lithuanian and Polish; but at the urgent request of the Jewish leaders they were issued also in Yiddish.

The new authorities were solely concerned with their own interests, to which those of the local population were rigorously subordinated. They made extensive requisitions for their troops as well as for export to the Fatherland, for the people in Germany had already begun to feel the shortage of food. The problem of provisioning the inhabitants of the city became increasingly difficult, since the number of Jewish refugees had swollen to 22,000 and that of the Christians to 10,000, while available supplies were greatly reduced. To facilitate the task, nearly a hundred communal kitchens were opened for the Jews alone, at which not only the poor but the impoverished middle class could get half a pound of bread and some soup each day; but as the supplies, which were strictly controlled by the German Food Department, diminished, the number of kitchens was reduced and the rations were cut down. Communal shops, which obtained supplies when available from the German authorities, were also opened both for Jews and Christians. A census was carried out three times, at intervals of some months, to check the issue of bread-cards, and in December, 1916, the Germans reduced the bread ration by one-eighth for every portion of soup given to the poor.

The entreaties and protests of the Jewish leaders were unavailing, and it therefore became necessary to reduce the number of mouths to be fed. Permission was obtained for the refugees to return by free trains to the neighboring townlets and villages, where there was more food available and living was cheaper. Gradually all but about 1,000 Jews left. The Germans were also induced to allow a number of Jews with means to emigrate to America; but after about 2,500 had gone, by the end of 1916, the invaders prohibited all further departures, as they wanted those who still had any money to share in the burden of maintaining the rest. The situation was further aggravated by the general economic collapse, partly due to the restriction of movement enforced by the military authorities. Business people were forbidden, except in rare cases, to travel to other towns either to buy materials or to sell goods. Industry was thus brought to a standstill, trade was paralyzed, and unemployment was rampant. After only a year of the enemy's occupation, over 50 per cent of the Jewish population, 32,000 out of 60,000 were dependent upon charity for mere sustenance, and the position of the Christian inhabitants was not much better. Fortunately some funds had begun to come from the Jews of America (through the Joint Distribution Committee) early in 1916, but then the municipality withheld its own support on the ground that the Jews were receiving "so much money." Even with the help from abroad, however, it was impossible to satisfy the hunger of thousands of families. Many mothers, in their despair, abandoned their little children in the streets, knowing that they would be rescued and placed in orphanages, where they would receive better care than in their homes.

The Germans were not content to requisition foodstuffs and other commodities, including Sabbath candlesticks and Hanukkah menorahs, but also decided to conscript labor. They were influenced by the additional motive of eliminating from the large number of recipients of relief those able to work, and they used the bread-cards as a means of achieving their purpose. An entry was made on each card to show whether its holder was able-bodied. He was then given ten days in which to find employment, and if he failed he was compelled to join the labor battalions or forfeit his card. Thousands of Jews had already been deported from Poland and Lithuania, including Vilna, to work in the coalmines of the Ruhr and Upper Silesia and in the docks of Tilsit and other harbors. But as the bread-card trap did not yield the required number, the various national committees in Vilna — the Poles, the Lithuanians, the White Russians, as well as the Jews — were requested to furnish further contingents. The Jews were dealt with more harshly than the others, and were largely excluded from the factories and other works under German control.

The Jewish Central Committee, in the summer of 1916, tried to secure a minimum wage of 90 pfennig (about 24 cents) a day as well as tolerable conditions for the laborers they were to recruit. The Germans, however, would not offer more than 30 pfennig and

A Street in the Jewish District of Vilna

A Street in the Jewish District of Vilna

were evasive about the other conditions. Bullied by the authorities on the one hand, and constrained to reduce the number of hungry mouths on the other, the Committee appealed to the Jewish workers and raised a battalion of 5,000. These men were taken by the military authorities, locked up for a fortnight in jails and military camps, and then sent in batches, under armed guard, to work on the making of roads and the clearing of forests. They were herded in wooden barracks outside the city, where they had to sleep on planks in tiers; they were clad in shabby clothes, with a colored patch bearing a number; they were given the miserable and scanty fare of convicts, compelled to trudge three miles and more to the scene of their toil, constantly kept under strict watch, and if anyone seemed not to work hard enough during the twelve-hour day he was brutally flogged. Dr. Wygodzki and Rabbi Isaac Rubinstein urgently pleaded for the release of these men, who had been captured under false pretenses; but only a few dozen, broken by their grinding task, were liberated. A few hundred escaped; the rest remained captive. The Committee ceased recruiting and ignored all further orders of the Germans.

At the end of the autumn of 1916 the invaders began seizing men, mostly Jews, in the streets, in the early morning. The captives were locked up in a jail and then sent to join the other battalions. The Jewish leaders again intervened and obtained the release of those who were certified as sick, or who were already employed, or who had at least two children. Not content with the yield of these "catches," the *Stadthauptmann* (City Prefect) issued an order on November 6, commanding all males between the ages of 17 and 60, whose passports bore numbers from 1 to 45,000, to present themselves in groups of 3,000 at fifteen specified centers. Members of the clergy, talmudical students, doctors, dentists, pharmacists and teachers were exempt. Other persons with means or who were unfit to work could gain immunity on payment of 600 marks each,[1] which, so the official announcement stated, would be used to provide clothing for the conscript laborers and relief for their families. Those who failed to present themselves without any legitimate reason were threatened with imprisonment up to three years and a fine of 10,000 marks. This new decree caused alarm and furious resentment among the working masses. Secret meetings of the Jewish leaders were held with representatives of the three other nationalities, and a joint memorandum of protest was sent in to the local commander, Prince Leopold of Bavaria. The advice given by the leaders to the workers was to ignore the order; those who had means promised that they would not pay to be exempted; and bills in Yiddish and Polish were posted on the walls before daybreak, strongly protesting against the decree and threatening to inform neutral countries. Hundreds of men hid in cellars

[1] *Pinkos far der Geschichte fun Vilna in die Yohren fun Milchomo un Okkupazie*, article by Dr. J. Wygodzki, page 71. But Dr. Z. Shabad, in the same work, page 6, gives the amount as 600 gold roubles.

or sought sanctuary in houses of prayer. Not until after three days did a small number of workers present themselves for the muster, while of the majority who boycotted it many were imprisoned and others were fined.

A month later the authorities issued another order for workmen to present themselves, but met with even less success than on the previous occasion. They therefore resorted again to the seizure of men on the streets, not only in Vilna but throughout Lithuania. The objection to serving in the labor battalions, from which some men indeed bought exemption, was due to the harrowing stories of ill-treatment which reached the families of the captives. The conditions became quite unbearable in the severe winter when the men had to toil in the frost and snow in tattered clothes and, in many cases, even without boots, with the result that hundreds fell ill and died. The leaders of the four nationalities pleaded earnestly with the authorities, who at last agreed to provide footwear and better clothes, to carry out a strict medical examination, and to improve the living conditions a little. But the slave wage of 30 pfennig a day was left unchanged. The Germans maintained that they could not raise it. On the other hand, they had the cynical effrontery to demand that the people of Vilna should furnish them with a loan of one million marks (about $250,000.) of which the Jews should provide three-fourths, although most of the Jewish charitable institutions were facing ruin. This monstrous request was obviously im-

practicable, and Dr. Wygodzki, who resisted it as
bravely as he had fought against other oppressive
exactions, was sent to an internment camp in
Germany for over a year.

The conscription of labor was not the only means
by which the demands upon the city's food supplies
were reduced; death also played a notable part.
Owing to undernourishment, exposure to cold, and
lack of proper medical attention, sickness was widespread. The Russians had left a legacy of cholera,
which was stamped out by November, 1915; but
the physical privations of sixteen months led to an
epidemic of typhoid, which raged from the beginning of 1917 for nine months and was accompanied
for a time by dysentery. In the summer of that
year there was hardly a house in Vilna which did
not display a red ticket warning the public that the
plague had entered there.[1] Urgent cases usually
had to wait two or three days before the ambulance
could call to remove them to the isolation hospital,
and in many instances it arrived too late. People
had to queue up for coffins. The hearses were unable
to cope with the demand, so that coffins were
ranged along the pavements to await the wagons
upon which they were piled. Vilna became a city
of the dead, and those who still moved about felt
that they were mere ghosts.[2] All schools were closed

[1] Houses in Vilna consist mostly of numerous apartments or
flats, containing anything from eight to a dozen families or more.
[2] Vivid and detailed accounts of the afflictions suffered in 1916-
17 are given in the *Pinkos* edited by Zalman Reisen and in H.
Lunski's *Me-ha-Getto Ha-Vilnai*.

for over six months, and when the authorities at last allowed them to reopen they made the condition that German be taught for six hours a week, as though that would serve as a prophylactic against a return of the plague. The death rate of the Jewish population at the end of March, 1917, when its total numbers had fallen to 55,000, was 97.5 per 1,000, or nearly five times as high as the rate before the war. It meant that every tenth person was doomed. Fortunately, from that time there was a slow and steady improvement.[1]

Famine, plague, and death were not the only evils that marked the devastating regime of the Germans; there were moral evils too. Hunger drove many women and girls, in a city swarming with an army of occupation, to forsake the paths of virtue. The sight of lascivious streetwalkers and the sounds of roisterous orgies floating from shady restaurants after midnight caused a shudder among the

[1] The number of deaths among the Jews in Vilna rose from 1,088 in 1913 to 2,165 in 1915, and, after a drop to 1,649 in 1916, mounted to 3,649 in 1917. In the first half alone of 1917 there were 2,251 deaths, nearly as many as in the two years 1912 and 1913 together. The rate of mortality, which had varied from 20.4 to 22.6 per 1,000 shortly before the war, rose from 34.4 in March, 1916, to 41.5 in the following December, and reached its peak at 97.5 in March, 1917. For the whole of the year 1917 it was 68.2, after which it fell to 39.6 in 1919 and 25.8 in 1920. The number of births fell from 1,502 in 1913 to 489 in 1917, after which it gradually recovered to 1,014 in 1920. (See article by Dr. Z. Shabad in *Pinkos far Geschichte fun Vilna in die Yohren fun Milchomo un Okkupazie*, pp. 133–204).

pietists as they hurried home from their talmudic studies.[1]

Another social sore, which affected the entire community, consisted of the "smugglers" or "speculators." These were unscrupulous individuals who bought up from the peasants in the neighboring villages whatever foodstuffs they could, and smuggled them into the city, where they sold them to dealers at high prices. This form of "free trade" was strictly forbidden by the authorities, as it diminished the supplies over which they could keep control. But most of the officials and soldiers who had to watch on the roads traversed by the smugglers were easily bribed, especially with food, though they occasionally made a capture to satisfy their suspicious superiors and ease their conscience. The inflated prices demanded for the coveted provisions forced many Jews to stay their pangs with horse-meat and radishes, and provoked a repeated outcry against the profiteers, who were denounced as vampires. Services in the synagogues were often disturbed by famishing men and women, who demanded drastic action. Begging in the streets for bread, especially by children, became a daily spectacle. Moreover, the number to be fed was vastly increased by the return of hundreds of Jews from the interior of Russia after the signing of the German-Soviet peace treaty at Brest-Litovsk on March 3, 1918,

[1] A vivid glimpse of this phase of life in Vilna in war-time is given in *Hawdoloh und Zapfenstreich*, by Sammy Gronemann (Berlin, 1925), who was attached to the German Eastern Command (*Ober-Ost*) as a Yiddish censor.

causing a shortage of dwellings, the raising of rents, and many evictions.

Since the Germans failed to suppress the smuggling scandal, the rabbis decided to exercise their dreaded power of declaring a Ḥerem (ban of excommunication) against the sinners — an act which had not taken place in that city since the Gaon Elijah had inveighed against the Hasidim over a hundred and twenty years before. The solemn ceremony was enacted in the Great Synagogue, on August 26, 1918, when, after candles had been lit, three graybearded rabbis stood before the open Ark, holding scrolls of the Torah, and the most patriarchal of them, the "Lukischer Rav," clad in a white shroud and *Tallit*, pronounced in a trembling voice the maledictions that should befall those who caused so much misery to the community. The *Shofar* was blown, the candles were extinguished, and the awed assembly, which contained some of the smugglers themselves, believed that the evil would now cease. But the effect was only transitory. Three months later the ceremony was repeated, on November 26, 1918, this time as a measure against those who carried on secret distilleries, or allowed them on their premises, or provided them with corn for the making of whisky.[1]

Amid all the sufferings and anxieties, the privation and oppression, that the community had to endure throughout the German rule of over three years, its leaders faithfully and bravely adhered to its tradi-

[1] See Supplementary Note 9.

tional ideals. They kept alight the lamp of learning, fostered the love of culture, and furthered the knowledge of handicrafts. They not only maintained most of the schools previously existing but, despite the scanty funds available, opened many new ones. The Zionists founded Hebrew schools, and the votaries of Yiddish opened others for educating their children in what they regarded as the national tongue. So zealous were the teachers that they even defied the German prohibition to carry on their work during the epidemic. The Society "Help through Work" did particularly valuable service by rescuing hundreds of children from the streets, caring for them in special homes, and teaching them useful manual occupations. The Talmud Torah institutions and *Hedarim* continued without interruption. There were evening classes for adults as before the war, and courses were started in technical subjects, such as electrical engineering. The Strashun Library was always crowded, and an impetus was given to various literary and kindred enterprises. The workers formed their "Society for Culture and Art," and the students organized their own associations. Hundreds of concerts were held, partly for the benefit of needy institutions, partly to dissipate the prevailing gloom. Perhaps the most remarkable product of this period of suffering was the theatrical company of gifted players which came into existence in February, 1916. It performed both Yiddish plays and works of European dramatists in the Vilna Municipal Theater, and thus strikingly exemplified Jewish enthusiasm for the dramatic art.

Owing to the poverty of the general public the company played in Vilna only twice a week; but it also performed in other cities of Poland, and afterwards earned fresh laurels as the famous "Vilner Truppe" far beyond that country.

Internal political life received a powerful stimulus, partly as a result of the British Government's declaration in November, 1917, in favor of a Jewish National Home in Palestine, partly as a result of the Bolshevik revolution in Russia which had just preceded it, and partly because of the inevitable discussion about the fate of Vilna itself. The Zionists greatly increased in number and influence. Their well attended public meetings were graced by the presence of eminent rabbis, who made passionate avowals of their sympathy with the cause. The Bundists lost many members through the conscription of labor and departures to other districts; but although their influence had declined their gatherings too were crowded. The ultra-orthodox, who fulminated against both Zionists and Bundists, were organized as the *Agudat Israel* under the energetic leadership of Rabbi Hayyim Ozer Grodzensky; while there were also the *Volkists*, who wanted Jewish autonomy in the Diaspora, Socialists who did not agree with the Bundists, and Democrats who shared some of the principles of one or two parties but differed on others. The conflicting standpoints of all these parties, and the friction caused by internal shades of difference, and other views opposed to them all, found expression in the non-partisan *Letzte Naies*, the only Yiddish daily allowed by the German military command, under strict censorship, to appear in Lithuania, which enjoyed the cooperation of a galaxy of writers who helped to sustain the Jewish spirit during a period of trial and tribulation.[1]

Such was the position when, in consequence of the collapse of the Kaiser's army on the western front, the German troops, with all the panoply of their bureaucratic machinery, were compelled ingloriously to vacate the city and retreat home at the end of the year 1918.

3. INTERLUDE OF CONFUSION

There followed a time of confusion, in which both Lithuanians and Poles tried to gain the upper hand. The Lithuanians quickly democratized their national committee as a *Taryba* (parliament) and invited the Poles and other nationalities to join it. They proposed that half of the seats in the Municipal Council should be occupied by Poles and the other half divided between Lithuanians, Jews and White Russians; but they stipulated that the president must be a Lithuanian and the Council subject to the authority of the *Taryba*. Both Poles and Lithuanians courted the support of the Jews, who mediated between them, but conciliation or collaboration proved impossible. The Poles absolutely refused to recognize the *Taryba*; and, as they already had a semi-legal military organization, which procured arms from

[1] These writers included S. An-ski, S. L. Zitron, Z. Reisen, Dan. Kaplanowitch, E. Olschwanger, and many others.

the retreating Germans, they soon seized control
of the municipality. All the employees, who had
served under the German command and who included a good percentage of Jews, went back to their
posts, and the Polish members of the Council re-
appeared on the scene. Suddenly there emerged a
"Soviet Government of the White-Russian Lithuanian Republic," which posted notices in the city
that nobody should take over the municipality
except the government of Soviet Russia. A Workers'
Council was formed, in which the "Presidium" consisted of Communists; but the Polish and Lithuanian
national committees held strictly aloof.

In the midst of the general commotion and excite-
ment, in which all sorts of political meetings, conferences and demonstrations took place, the Jews
held a communal election, which lasted three days,
from December 25 to 27, 1918. It was the first
election on a real democratic basis, and ten parties
competed for 80 seats. The result was that the
Zionists and the Bundists secured 24 seats each,
the *Volksvereinigung* (People's Association) 9, the
Artisans 7, the Democrats 5, while the remaining
eleven seats were divided among the five other
parties (United Socialists, Orthodox groups, and
Merchants). The Bundists and the Po'ale Zion
declined to sit with the Zionists and other bourgeois;
but their withdrawal had little effect upon the
Kehillah (community) since it was in any case
unable to do much. Scarcely had the Jewish community recovered from the turmoil of this electoral
contest, than Polish announcements appeared in the

streets, on January 1, 1919, that the city had been taken by Polish legionaries and that "the dream of centuries"— the reunion of Vilna with Poland — would at last be realized. But the Polish regime was short-lived; five days later the city was taken by surprise by the Russian Red Army.

4. THE BOLSHEVIK OCCUPATION

The Bolshevik rulers seized control of all branches of the administration, and created such a multitude of bureaus that many of them had nothing to do. They made numerous arrests, changed the occupants of public offices, nationalized factories, and collectivized big businesses. The civil service had many young Jews in the departments for economic affairs, food and requisitions, as well as in the courts; but the military offices and the departments for posts, railways, lands and forests were mainly in the hands of the Poles. The Bolsheviks forbade any work to be done except under their authority; they interfered with the "Ort," which had begun to form cooperative workshops for which both machines and materials had been bought from the Germans. As a result of their regime, the vast majority of the Jewish population was reduced before long to an even lower degree of poverty than before, and unemployment became more widespread.

Although they promised that each nationality would be able to foster its own culture, the Bolsheviks betrayed a strong preference for Russification. All previously existing papers were suppressed, and the majority of the Bund became Communist. The education department tried to gain control of all schools, libraries and other cultural institutions, and its Jewish section issued a new monthly, *Die Naie Welt*, and a pedagogical journal, *Volksbibliothek*. The teachers of Yiddish schools were paid regularly; those of Hebrew schools poorly; and those of Talmud Torahs not at all. The *Kehillah* was reduced to a "collegium" of seven, minus the Socialists, and unable to attend to any but petty affairs. The work of all Jewish charitable institutions was paralyzed, and the swarms of homeless and refugees would have been in a terrible plight but for the formation of a local branch of the "Jekopo." In three and a half months the Bolsheviks succeeded in ruining whatever had survived the regime of the Germans. They had totally undermined the economic position, brought trade and industry to a standstill, caused a serious upheaval in social life, accentuated the class conflict, and split the ranks of the workers. On April 19 they fled almost as quickly as they had come, scared by the sudden appearance of the Polish legionaries.

5. THE POLISH LIBERATION

The arrival of the new "liberators" opened a fresh chapter of Jewish agony. The Bolsheviks, before retreating, made their last stand from the old Jewish cemetery at Shnipishok. This circumstance, together with the fact that some Jews had sided with them, although many Poles had likewise

done so, sufficed to make the Polish legionaries see
a Bolshevik in every Jew. After a couple of days'
fighting the Bolsheviks were driven to flight, whereupon the legionaries defiled and desecrated the
cemetery, smashed the tombstones, and opened the
graves (including some of Vilna's earliest rabbis) in
the belief that they would find in them arms and
money. Disappointed in their search, the Poles
transferred their attentions from the dead to the
living and ran amuck in the Jewish quarter. For
three days they seized Jews in the streets, dragged
them out of their homes, bludgeoned them savagely,
and looted their houses and shops. About eighty
Jews were shot, mostly in the suburb of Lipuvka,
where some were ordered to dig their own graves;
others were buried alive, and others were drowned,
with their hands tied, in the Vilia. On April 21
a detachment of soldiers fired at a house from which,
they said, Jews had been shooting through a window.
They drove out all the occupants, who included the
writers A. Weiter, Leib Jaffe and Samuel Niger.
Weiter was shot dead on the spot; the two others
were seized and imprisoned for several days. All
sorts of outrages were committed in those days by
the Poles in their celebration of victory. They tied
a Jew to a horse and dragged him through the streets
for three miles. They took a sadistic delight in
cutting off the beards and earlocks of pious Jews.
They even arrested, assaulted and humiliated Rabbi
Rubinstein and Dr. Shabad. Altogether thousands
of Jews in Vilna, as well as in Lida and Bialystok
were imprisoned in various concentration camps

where they were ill fed and beaten, and where they suffered from hunger and typhoid. Moreover, the total loss due to the destruction and pillaging of Jewish people in this pogrom, in Vilna alone, was estimated at about 20 million roubles (about $10,000,000.).

The indignation of the Jewish community was voiced in a resolution of protest adopted by the Council of the *Kehillah*, which, after an interval of some months, reassembled on May 25, 1919. The meeting, which was attended by 77 members (the three Po'ale Zion representatives having absented themselves), elected a "presidium" of seven, which included Dr. Shabad (Democrat) as president, Dr. Wygodzki (Zionist) and Solomon Kleit (Bundist) as vice-presidents, as well as Rabbi Rubinstein (*Volksvereinigung*). The majority of the "presidium" divided the various departments of the *Kehillah* among themselves, since the Left parties declined to take any part in the administration. Their task was by no means enviable. There were thousands of prisoners whose liberation had to be secured. There were over 30,000 Jews who had to be fed and whose wants were proclaimed by the crowds who invaded the Great Synagogue during the service to beg for bread. The leaders of the *Kehillah* fought desperately to replenish their empty coffers; they tried in vain to secure some of the blessings promised to them as a national minority, as envisaged by the designers of the Peace Treaties.

The ill-treatment of the Jews, which created a sensation throughout the world, evoked a declaration from the Chief of the Polish State, General Pilsudski, that the legionaries had expelled the Russians only to give the local population the opportunity of self-determination. The first step was to hold a democratic election for the City Council, in July. The result of the election was the return of 34 Poles and 14 Jews, to hold office for three years; but as the majority of the Poles were National Democrats, the party of fanatical anti-Semites, the Jews were unable to obtain any material support for the needs of their own community. Fortunately, however, communication was established with the Warsaw community, and a steady stream of relief began to come from America, both from the Joint Distribution Committee and the numerous relatives of Vilna Jewry.

The outrages by the soldiers, however, continued; they were, indeed, by no means confined to Vilna, but occurred for months in all parts of Poland. The suppression of the scandal, which was in such ironic contrast to the country's liberation from the Russian yoke, called for intervention on the part of the victorious democratic Powers. On June 13, 1919, Mr. Hugh Gibson, the American ambassador in Warsaw, paid a visit to Vilna and drew up a report on the position, which the Jews rejected as a travesty. The legionaries continued their hooliganism; they broke open coffins in search of money, they attacked a Jewish agricultural colony in the suburbs, they planted cartridges in houses and shops so as to have an excuse for their accusations. On July 19, there arrived an Inquiry Commission sent by President Wilson, and headed by Mr. Henry

Morgenthau, a former American ambassador to Turkey. The purpose of the commission was to ascertain the facts about the atrocities and to find a means of bringing about the conciliation of the Poles with the Jews. It proved a failure, for, although it heard a few hundred witnesses and took 1,500 "protocols" of cases of looting, assault and murder, its report, which was published in January, 1920, utterly failed to give an adequate account of the extent and character of the disorders or to express unqualified condemnation of those responsible.[1] On November 13, 1919, a British government commission, headed by Sir Stuart Samuel, arrived. Although its report aroused less controversy than that of Mr. Morgenthau, it proved equally futile. The Polish government did not conduct an inquiry of its own, nor did it punish anybody guilty of the misdeeds. On the contrary, the soldiers continued their persecution. They seized Jews for forced labor so as to secure money as ransom; they searched the Great Synagogue for arms; they raided Jewish institutions and clubs; they extorted 400 marks from the Lida rabbi to spare his beard. On May 14, 1920, an inquiry commission of the Second Socialist International, consisting of M. Renaudel and Dr. Oskar Cohn, arrived; but their efforts had no more success than the previous missions. The attacks upon the Jews continued at intervals; many were arrested under the pretense of being Bolsheviks and sent to a concentration camp.

[1] See Supplementary Note 10

The climax came in July, due partly to the Poles' adventurous advance against the Ukraine. The Russians and the Lithuanians had signed an agreement at Moscow, on July 12, 1920, whereby the district of Vilna as far as Grodno was ceded to the latter. Both then marched against the city of Vilna again. The Poles at first compelled the Jews to help in the work of defense; but when they realized that their position was untenable, they made a final assault upon the Jews, breaking open their shops, looting their goods, destroying what they could not carry or cart away, and left behind a trail of desolation. Thousands of Jews remained in hiding for a week, equally afraid of the retreating Poles and the returning Russians.

6. BOLSHEVIKS AND LITHUANIANS

The Bolsheviks recaptured Vilna on July 14, 1920, and repeated their previous program: numerous arrests of Poles and Jews, changes in offices, requisitions and nationalization of factories. The Russian commander declared that he handed over the beautiful city to the Lithuanians; but for a time the Russians continued in control. Both Bolshevik and anti-Bolshevik papers appeared simultaneously, although the latter betrayed evidence of their tolerated position. But on August 28, after a six weeks' stay, the Bolsheviks, by order of the Moscow government, withdrew, leaving the Lithuanians in possession.

A Provisional City Council was formed, representing the four nationalities, and the Jews began to indulge in the hope of better times. The Jews in Lithuania had been accorded a ministry for their own affairs in the Kovno government, and those in Vilna believed that the blessings of national cultural autonomy would now be extended to them too. Delegates of the Jewish ministry came to Vilna for conferences, and Rabbi Rubinstein was appointed the city's temporary representative. The education department of the City Council promised that all Jewish schools would be supported, and economic conditions slightly improved through the resumption of communications with Kovno as well as with Germany. There were, however, language difficulties, as the Lithuanian authorities insisted on publishing notices in Lithuanian, which only less than 5 per cent of the population understood. The Lithuanians hoped to revive their ancient glories, with Vilna as the capital of a Great Lithuania. But on October 9, 1920, two days after signing an armistice convention with the Poles at Suvalki, they were driven out by the troops of General Zeligovski, who violated the pledge made by Poland to the League of Nations, to respect the neutrality of the territory east of the Curzon line.

7. THE STATE OF "MIDDLE LITHUANIA"

General Zeligovski's action was nominally disowned by the government in Warsaw, but it was afterwards disclosed that it had been taken with the authority of General Pilsudski. A Provisional Government Commission was formed, which announced

that the army had occupied Vilna in order to let
the population decide whether they wanted to join
Poland or Lithuania. It created a new State, called
"Middle Lithuania," which was said to be independent of either country, and the government offered
the Jews one or two posts as assistant-commission-
ers. They declined to take part in what they regarded as a revolutionary regime. The Polish government soon entered into relations with "Middle
Lithuania," provided it with money and soldiers,
and began to assert its authority. The process of
Polonization was fostered through the university
and high schools, but Jewish cultural institutions
were not interfered with. Jewish schools increased,
and seminaries were opened for both Hebrew and
Yiddish teachers. The material position was relieved with the aid of funds from America and
England, as well as from the "Jekopo" and the
Jewish Colonization Association. The "Jekopo"
opened a Cooperative People's Bank and furnished
support for the homeless; the "Oze" established a
nurses' training institute, and the "Ort" founded a
technical school.

General Zeligovski cultivated friendly relations
with the Jews, as he was anxious to gain their support in determining the city's fate. He therefore
had an inquiry commission appointed, including
Rabbi Rubinstein and Advocate Gordon, to investigate the anti-Jewish excesses, with a view to
punishing the culprits. Two methods of deciding
the future of Vilna were proposed: one was by a
plebiscite under the auspices of the League of Na-

tions; the other was by a Diet (*Seym*) specially elected by the citizens. The Polish government was opposed to a plebiscite, since one of the conditions was
the withdrawal of General Zeligovski's troops. They
insisted that the question be determined by a Diet,
and replaced the military commander by a civil
official, Mejstowicz, as president of the Provisional
Governing Commission. The Polish Democrats
wanted the Jews to enter the Diet, so as to strengthen
the forces against the reactionary "Endeks" (National Democrats), and the Polish government, too,
was anxious that they should participate, so that
the decision arrived at might impress the world as
a faithful reflection of the wishes of the entire
population.

The leaders of all the Jewish parties, however,
after mature deliberation, decided not to take part
in the elections to the special Diet. Rabbi Rubinstein, Dr. Wygodzki, and Dr. Shabad were thereupon
invited to Warsaw to explain their reasons to the
government, which was represented for the occasion
by M. Skirmunt, the Foreign Minister, M. Dovnaro-
wicz, the Minister of the Interior, and other ministers and high officials. They stated their case fully
and cogently. They regarded Vilna just as much a
part of Lithuania as Kovno; they looked upon
Lithuania not as the state of one nationality but as
a state of various nationalities, in which all were
entitled to equality; they were of opinion that Vilna
should belong to a Great Lithuania; but as the country was too small to exist independently and was
closely connected with Poland historically, econom-

ically, and culturally, they considered that the best
solution would be that it should be federated with
Poland. Since, however, the one and only question
on which the Diet was to vote was formulated as
"For Poland or Lithuania?" and no alternative or
qualification would be allowed, there would be no
possibility whatsoever for the Jews to record their
views. Moreover, although forming nearly 15 per
cent of the population of the Vilna province, they
would be unable to secure the election of more than
two or three deputies, which was less than the proportion to which they were entitled.

Not only the Jews but the Lithuanians and the
White Russians abstained from putting up any
candidates. The elections, in which only two-thirds
of the population voted, took place on January 8,
1921. The Diet opened on February 1, and on
February 20 it unanimously adopted a resolution
for the incorporation of Vilna into Poland. The
Vilna Diet and the State of "Middle Lithuania"
thereupon ceased to exist. Two years later, on
March 5, 1923, the action of the Diet was endorsed
by the Conference of Ambassadors in a decision
which assigned to Poland the whole of the Vilna
province which had been seized by General Zeligovski. The ambassadors had been empowered to
deal with the question by the principal Allied and
Associated Powers, in virtue of the provisions of
article 87 of the Treaty of Versailles and on account
of a request addressed by both Poland and Lithuania. The Lithuanian government was naturally
profoundly disappointed by the decision and re-

quested the Council of the League of Nations to submit the question to the Permanent Court of Justice at The Hague, but the Council unanimously decided that there was no occasion to accede to such a request. The culminating act took place on December 14, 1925, when a bill was passed by the Polish Diet, whereby the Vilna province was incorporated within the Polish Republic.

CHAPTER XVIII

UNDER THE POLISH REPUBLIC

1. POLITICAL CONDITIONS

THE friendly attitude towards the Jews in Vilna that had been carefully cultivated by the authorities of "Middle Lithuania" immediately vanished with the liquidation of this State and was replaced by the policy of the government in Warsaw. The desire to conciliate them had been prompted solely by political expediency, and the change of attitude was again due to the subordination of all other interests to those of the Poles themselves. In its efforts to help the population to recover from the ravages of war, the government gave preferential consideration to the dominant group, although the other peoples were equally in need of its aid and constitutionally entitled to it. On regaining her independence, Poland was the first of a number of states which were required by the Allied and Associated Powers to sign a Minorities Treaty, specially conceived and designed to secure for her racial and religious minorities the same civil and political rights and the same economic opportunities as those possessed by the majority. This precaution was all the more necessary in the case of the Jews owing to the widespread excesses with which the Poles had celebrated their national liberation. The victorious Powers hoped

that a friendly understanding would soon prevail
between the Jews and their fellow-citizens. Unfortunately this hope proved illusory. Scarcely had the
ink of the signatures to the treaty become dry before
the government betrayed indifference to its provisions, with the result that the Jews had to wage
a persistent struggle to secure their observance.

The incorporation of the province of Vilna within
the Republic thus made the sorely-tried Jews of
that district subject to the policy of illegal and unjust
discrimination to which all the other Jews were
exposed. The question of citizenship was a matter
of immediate concern to a great many. According
to the treaty all Russian (as well as German,
Austrian, and Hungarian) nationals habitually resident, at the date when it came into force, in territory recognized as part of Poland, were declared to
be "Polish nationals *ipso facto* and without the
requirement of any formality." But on January
20, 1920, only ten days after the treaty went into
force, the government passed a law requiring those
who claimed Polish citizenship to show that their
names were inscribed in the local official registers
or submit proof of their *Heimatsrecht*, a civic status
dependent upon several years' continuous residence
in the same commune. Owing to the removal of
the official records to Moscow, it was practically
impossible, especially for those Jews who had returned from the interior of Russia, to comply with
this regulation. Thus thousands of them were denied
Polish citizenship and were rendered "stateless."
The effect of this disability was that, while they

had to discharge all duties, they were refused all rights. They were unable, for instance, to obtain a passport and were prevented thereby from travelling abroad. Those who received the so-called Nansen passport could not obtain a visa for a foreign country, as they would not be permitted by Poland to return if the country to which they emigrated refused them permission to stay. The Jewish members of the *Seym*, who included Dr. Wygodzki, as well as Rabbi Rubinstein, who had been appointed a member of the Senate, repeatedly demanded the abolition of the disability;[1] but it was not until August 1926, that the government issued instructions to the local administrative authorities to facilitate the acquisition of citizenship, though even then many were left "stateless."

The other grievances under which the Jews in Vilna suffered were common to all the other Jewish communities in the country. Before the incorporation of the city, its Jewish schools at first received a small subsidy from the local administration. Afterwards the education department announced that free elementary schools would be opened for the Jews, with Polish as the medium of instruction, but that they would be closed on Saturdays in deference to Jewish religious requirements. In consequence of strong Jewish protests, the education committee of the City Council recommended that the schools of the Jews use their own language, as was the case with the other nationalities; but the recommendation

---

[1] Another Vilna deputy was M. Stuczynski.

was rejected by the full Council on August 3, 1922. According to the Versailles Treaty the Jews had not only the right, in towns in which they formed a considerable proportion, to give instruction in their primary schools through the medium of their own language, but were "assured an equitable share in the enjoyment and application of the sums which may be provided out of public funds under the state, municipal, or other budget for educational, religious, or charitable purposes." The amount so allotted to them, however, although the Jews in Poland formed a tenth of the total population, was quite insignificant. They were thus obliged to maintain their schools and other educational establishments by their own efforts, with aid from Jews abroad. Nor was a more generous attitude shown as regards admission to institutions for higher education. In the State technical schools Jews were limited to 5 per cent of the students, and in the municipal establishments to as few as 2 per cent, so that in Vilna they had to provide their own technical institute, which was opened in 1921. At the Vilna University, which was reopened by the Poles in 1920, after having been closed for political reasons since 1832, a *numerus clausus* was applied to the Jews (as at all other universities in Poland). The restriction was enforced with especial rigor in the medical faculty.[1] Many Jewish students were thus com-

[1] In 1932, when there were about 75,000 Jews in a total population of 200,000 in Greater Vilna, there were 1,100 Jews among the 4,000 students at the University, the great majority being in the faculties of law, philosophy, and the humanities.

pelled to wander forth to other lands in quest of
more hospitable seats of learning.

There were also other regulations and practices
that placed the Jews at a serious disadvantage.
They were driven out of all state monopolies, including the tobacco factories in Vilna, in which they had
formed 95 per cent of the workers before the first
World War. Only very rarely could they obtain
any contracts, concessions, licenses, or credit from
any state institution. They were employed in the
public services of the city only to the extent of 2.8
per cent of the total, which was merely a tenth of
their ratio of the population (while the percentage
of Jews so employed in other cities was still less).
They did not hold a single post in any of the state
or communal schools or in any of the post office
savings banks. They were subject to exacting regulations which made it difficult, if not impossible,
for them to qualify as master artisans. Moreover,
they had to comply with the severe Sunday closing
law, which was passed at the end of 1919 ostensibly
to protect the Poles from undue Jewish competition,
but which inflicted grave hardships upon Jewish
employers and employed, who mostly observed their
Sabbath. For in consequence of their having to rest
two days a week (or nearly two and a half in winter,
when the Sabbath begins on Friday afternoon), as
well as on the numerous Jewish and Christian holy-
days, they were compelled to idle 137 days, or over
one-third of the year — a crushing handicap in a
country suffering from economic depression. And

despite all these disabilities, the Jews were invariably taxed higher than their Gentile neighbors.

The only way in which the Jews in Vilna could seek to defend their interests, with some measure of satisfaction though with varying success, was by taking part in the affairs of the Municipal Council. But even here they were unable to assert themselves to a degree commensurate with their numbers, in consequence of an administrative trick employed by the authorities. For in order to reduce the proportion of the seats which the Jewish population of the city would normally have secured, the authorities created a Greater Vilna by incorporating a number of suburbs in the environs which contained a preponderance of Gentiles. Moreover, the Jews themselves seldom presented a united front. Not only were there fights for seats between the Zionists on the one side and the Bund and the *Volkspartei* on the other, but also between these and the different trade organizations. Nor was there unity in the Zionist camp, for the Po'ale Zion and the Revisionists strove against the General Zionists and the Mizrahi. In those districts in which the Jews were too few to have any chance of electing their own candidate, they voted for a progressive Pole. They were generally represented by fourteen members on the Municipal Council, and as a result of the last election, which took place in April 1939, over half of them were members of the Bund.[1] The Jewish

[1] Among the prominent Jewish members were Dr. Wygodzki, Dr. Z. Shabad, Dr. H. Globus, A. Klebanoff, Adolf Gordon, Eliezer Kruk, and J. Czernichow.

members on the Council had to watch unremittingly over the interests of their community; and in the stand they made against the dominant majority, who often betrayed a tendency to racial discrimination, they combined vigor with dignity.

2. COMMUNAL REORGANIZATION

The council of the Jewish community, or the *Kehillah*, had to cope with an enormous burden. Its sphere of responsibility embraced not only religious institutions but also educational and cultural work and various branches of social welfare. Its task would have been difficult enough even if it had funds; but it had no legal right to raise any until it had proper authority to do so, and that could not be obtained until the political status of the city was definitely settled. At the end of the war the only body possessing assets and enjoying an income was the Great Charity (*Zedakah Gedolah*). After the Vilna *Seym* of 1921, the authorities wished to apply to the Jews in the city the decree issued by General Pilsudski on February 7, 1919, whereby every community was required to elect a council to administer its religious affairs. Only male Jews over twenty-five years of age and paying an annual subscription were qualified to vote in the election of the Council, which thereupon appointed an executive committee, of which the rabbi was a member *ex officio*. The Jews of Vilna, however, strongly objected to this law being applied to them. They wished to have a *Kehillah* which would truly represent them as a

national minority, a body whose scope would not
be limited to religious affairs but comprise all aspects
of communal activity; and they also wanted a more
democratic system for their elections. They submitted repeated petitions to the government to this
end, but in vain.

On October 28, 1925, the government adopted the
decision that the law concerning Jewish communities
must be applied also to Vilna. This decision evoked
protests both from the politically-minded Jews as
well as from the purely religious section; but after
two and a half years of further discussion, the
Minister of Public Worship issued a fiat, on April
11, 1928, ordering the election of a Council in accordance with the terms of the Pilsudski decree. Since
the *Kehillah* had not yet been recognized as a public
corporation it had no right to receive subscriptions,
and there could therefore be no list of voters with
the necessary financial qualification. There was,
indeed, a comparatively small number who paid
subscriptions, but they formed only a minute fraction of the Jewish population. The difficulty was
therefore overcome by a relaxation of the decree,
permitting those who had not yet paid to vote on
condition that they gave a written promise to pay
in future. All the parties thereupon became busy
and secured signed promises from 7,500 persons, but
only 4,700 actually voted in the election, which took
place on July 29, 1928.

Eleven parties or groups put up candidates for
25 seats, with the result that the Zionists (including
1 Mizrahi) obtained 5; the Artisans, 4; the Bund,

Ahdut (non-political religious), and Merchants, 3 each; the *Agudat Israel*, Retail Traders, and Democrats (*Volkists*), 2 each; and the Property-Owners, 1. Two smaller groups failed to elect a candidate. As no single party was strong enough to take control, the four "economic" groups, with a total of 10 seats, combined with the Zionists to form a majority and elected Dr. Wygodzki as president. The Council elected an executive committee of 12 *Parnassim*, representing seven parties: 3 Zionists, 2 each for the Artisans, Merchants and *Ahdut*, and one each from the Retail Traders, *Agudat Israel*, and Bund. The rival principles of the Hebraists and Yiddishists were satisfied by the decision that the two languages should enjoy equality in official transactions. All stationery had to be printed in Hebrew and Yiddish, besides Polish, and all official announcements had to be made in all three; but in case any special expense were involved, only Yiddish and Polish were to be used for the text, with Hebrew also for the headings. The *Kehillah* now had the right to enforce the payment of a communal tax for the upkeep of the religious institutions, but it needed a fund to start with. The prefect (*Starosta*) of the Vilna district accordingly gave the Council a letter of guarantee for 8,000 zloty (about $1,750.), on the strength of which the local Jewish bank of Bunimowicz furnished it with a loan to carry on its work.

The *Kehillah*, as a public corporation, had the legal right to take over all property belonging to Jewish religious institutions and to be the sole controller of the cemeteries. It had previously demanded that the Great Charity should hand over to it all the properties that it administered, which included the Great Synagogue and adjoining buildings, the Strashun Library, the ritual baths, cemeteries, and properties in other parts of the city; but it was not until after it was reconstituted in 1928 that the *Kehillah* was able to insist upon its request. Since, however, the *Gabbaim* of the Great Charity were mostly members of the *Agudat Israel*, they naturally objected to handing over such influential assets to a body in which they were a minority. A bitter conflict, for over three years, consequently raged between the *Kehillah* and the Great Charity, until the *Starosta* energetically intervened in favor of the former and addressed an official letter to Rabbi Rubinstein, the senior *Gabbai* of the Great Charity, requesting him to hand over all its properties, assets, and liabilities to the *Kehillah*. This transfer was completed on September 1, 1931, whereupon the *Zedakah Gedolah*, which had played so important a part in the history of the community, was finally liquidated.

There was a special difficulty in connection with the building at 7 Orzeszkowa Street, which housed the offices of the *Kehillah*, the Hebrew Teachers' Seminary, the An-ski Museum, the Jewish Nurses' Training Institute and a school for defective children. Originally this property had been acquired by the Russian government, in 1873, for 55,000 roubles out of the fund collected from the Jews by the Ministry of Education for establishing a Jewish Institute and an elementary school. The German

authorities requisitioned it during their occupation,
and it was afterwards taken over by the Bolsheviks.
In April 1919, when the Poles secured control of the
city, the *Kehillah* obtained permission from Jan
Pilsudski (a brother of the General), who was then
commissar for the city, to take the building for its
offices; but in 1923 the Polish authorities demanded
the return of the building as their property. The
matter was brought before the law-courts, which
declared that the building was legally the property
of the State, but that, as it had originally been purchased with Jewish money, the *Kehillah* was justified
in applying for permission to use it for communal
purposes. Successive petitions were submitted to the
government to this end. It was not until 1933 that,
thanks to the energetic intervention of Rabbi
Rubinstein, then a member of the Senate, the
Council of Ministers passed a special bill through
both Houses of Parliament formally transferring
the property to the *Kehillah*. In the same year the
Kehillah also took over the so-called "cheap houses"
at 37 Subocz Street, which had been built in 1898
by the Jewish Colonization Association to provide
cheap accommodation for the poor. No rent had
been paid for many years by the destitute tenants,
and as the property had fallen into serious decay
the authorities insisted upon the *Kehillah's* assuming
possession of it, with the liabilities that it entailed;
otherwise it would have been handed over to the
municipality.

The total value of all the properties acquired by

the *Kehillah*, apart from the synagogues, the ritual bath, and the cemeteries, was 950,000 zloty (about $200,000.). Thus, the executive organ of the community, entirely devoid of means in 1928, developed into a financially sound corporation. Its expenditure in 1935 amounted to about $125,000. The scope of its activities and obligations was all-embracing. It was not only responsible for all religious institutions and affairs, including *Shehita*, but also maintained the staff at the Strashun Library, purchased books for three other Jewish libraries, provided kosher meat for hospitals, and furnished subsidies for a variety of institutions and purposes, including the Hebrew Teachers' Seminary, the Technical School, *Ramaila's Yeshibah*, the Talmud Torah, Hebrew and Yiddish secular schools, the Historical and Ethnographical Society, the Yiddish theater, the Students' Association, summer schools for poor children, a cheap soup-kitchen, and emigration to Palestine.[1]

According to its constitution the *Kehillah* was bound to elect a chief rabbi and several deputy rabbis. The *Agudat Israel*, however, was opposed to such a system and wished the Council to divide the city into several districts, each of which should have a separate rabbi; but neither the majority of the Council nor the government was in favor of this. The two principal candidates for the office of chief rabbi were Hayyim Ozer Grodzensky, leader

[1] See Supplementary Note 11.

of the *Agudat Israel* and widely famous as a talmudical authority, and Isaac Rubinstein, who, in addition to his rabbinical learning, had distinguished himself by his courageous leadership of the community from the beginning of the German occupation. A keen controversy between their partisans lasted for two years, until it was ended in 1928 by the appointment of Rabbi Rubinstein as chief rabbi and the creation of a special status for his rival as "rabbi of the *Kehillah*," while a number of others were designated as deputy rabbis. In practice Chief Rabbi Rubinstein acted as the representative of the community in relations with the authorities, and his office dealt with all matters concerning births, marriages, and deaths. Rabbi Grodzensky was looked upon as a leading religious authority. His decisions were sought even by rabbis in other cities, and he devoted himself particularly to the maintenance of *Yeshibot* in Vilna and other parts of Poland. But whatever rivalry may have existed between the two rabbis ceased with the simultaneous termination of their functions after the annexation of Vilna by Soviet Russia on June 15, 1940, for they, like all other rabbis, were divested of all authority. Rabbi Grodzensky died only two months later (August 11).

When the Council of the *Kehillah* completed its five years' term of office, the community wished to have a new election. But the government, which had meanwhile assumed a semi-dictatorial character, was afraid that public elections of any kind might be used for political agitation. The question hung fire for two years, and as the government adhered to its standpoint it dissolved the Council and appointed a Jewish commissar and a small Council, consisting of persons least opposed to its policy. All the parties previously represented on the Council thus lost control over communal affairs. This condition continued until 1938, when, owing to the strength of public opinion, a new election was held, in which all parties took part. The result was a shift to the left, with the election as president of Dr. Milkonowicki, a representative of the Po'ale Zion. This Council continued in office until Lithuania, to which Soviet Russia had restored Vilna in October, 1939, was retaken by the Russians eight months later, when the *Kehillah* was dissolved as a religious corporation.

3. SOCIAL AND ECONOMIC CONDITIONS

The dominating character of the social conditions was one of want and depression. The policy pursued by the Polish government and the municipality would of itself have sufficed to obstruct the material recovery of the Jews. Recovery was prevented even more effectively by the general economic decline which the city experienced during and after the first World War. Before 1914 many industries, such as timber, paper, books, leather, hosiery and gloves, had been entirely in Jewish control, with Jews forming from 75 to 100 per cent of the employees. After the war all these industries dwindled to a half and even less of their former compass. Previously there had been 1,000 Jewish tailoring workshops, many of which employed 40 men and more; but after the war they were reduced to 700, and few employed even five workers. The position was much worse in the hosiery trade, which had been built up by the Jews of Vilna and once employed over 3,000, mainly Jews, but had now become a mere shadow of its former self. Similarly, in the glove trade, which had once kept 100 workshops busy, more than half were now closed. This progressive paralysis of industry, bringing ruin upon thousands of Jews, was largely due to the severing of Vilna from Russia, whose markets it could no longer supply, to its being cut off from Lithuania, with which Poland did not have even diplomatic relations until 1938, and to its inability to compete in the home market with such manufacturing centers as Lodz and Warsaw.

The economic plight of the Jews was aggravated by the increasing influx into the city of Poles from the neighboring townlets and villages, all anxious to improve their own sorry lot. These newcomers, helped both by the state and the municipality, succeeded in forcing their way into many of the industries formerly dominated by Jews, and also in supplanting them in business, for they not only entered factories and workshops but also opened a multitude of stores and shops. The ethnical composition of the population consequently underwent a radical change, to the detriment of the Jewish element, as shown by the following figures:

Year	Total Population	Jews	Jewish Percentage
1897	154,532	63,996	40.9
1916	140,840	61,263	43.5
1923	167,454	56,168	33.5
1931	193,337	55,007	28.5

Thus, while the general population increased after the war by over 27,000, the Jews declined not only numerically but still more proportionately. In 1920 the Jews formed 74.5 per cent of the artisans of the city, but by 1932 they diminished to 47.7 per cent.[1]

The diminution of factories and workshops, both in number and size, resulted not only in widespread unemployment but also in a deterioration of labor conditions. The sweating system came back in full vigor. Workers were content to·toil as long as sixteen hours a day for a miserable wage, and were afraid lest a strike deprive them even of this wretched pittance. Another effect was the vast multiplication of little shops, for most of the big ones were now secured by the Poles. Without free loans from the Jewish credit cooperatives most of even these shops, and many workshops, would have been unable to survive.[2] Gone were the days when Jewish stores prospered on the custom of Russian officers and officials who studiously avoided Polish shops. Now the

[1] *Vilna: A Zammelbuch*, edited by E. N. Jeshurin, article by Dr. J. Lestschinsky, pp. 374–5.

[2] Over two-thirds of the Jewish population in Vilna depended upon free loans from the credit cooperatives and communal loan funds (called *Kassen*), largely financed by the American Joint Distribution Committee.

Poles were in possession; and they patronized only
their own people. "*Swoj do Swego*" ("Buy of your
own kin")! was their slogan. It would be an exaggeration, indeed, to apply the term "business" to
most of the Jewish concerns, as they consisted, to a
very large extent, merely of a little heap of old
clothes or rusty iron, or of decaying fruit, black
bread, or herrings, sold either from some gloomy
cavity in a wall, illumined by a lamp at night, or
from a little hand-cart, basket, or the pavement
itself. Yet thousands of men and women, middle-
aged and old, shabbily clad and half-starved, patiently offered their shoddy wares day after day to a
public as poor as themselves, and depended upon
their puny profit to keep body and soul together.

Nor were many of the members of the educated
class in any better case. They were excluded from
the public services, which were open only to the
Poles; and those who qualified for the liberal professions found them so overcrowded that hundreds—
engineers, lawyers, and even doctors — were glad
to get any kind of clerical work for a living. They
formed an intellectual proletariat, whose only hope,
like that of the unemployed workers, lay in emigration. Every year numbers of young men and girls
sought admittance to the *He-Halutz* centers, to be
trained on a farm or in a workshop with a view to
obtaining the coveted certificate for settlement in
Palestine. The lot of the idle intellectuals was even
more pitiable than that of the swarm of Jewish cab-
drivers who, after waiting for hours, at least got an
occasional fare, and hardly more enviable than that

of the street-porters who, with a look of resignation on their faces and a coil of rope around their necks (with which to hold or secure packages), stood hoping for a job that could not yield more than half a zloty.

So widespread was poverty within the Jewish community that it was commonly estimated that at least three-fourths were dependent upon some form of relief — either from local philanthropic societies or from Jewish organizations or relatives abroad. According to the official figures, at Passover, in 1938, the number of Jews who applied for relief was 25,000 out of a total of 60,000. Unable to exist on the doles they received, hundreds were compelled to beg in the streets and haunted the doors of restaurants and cafes.[1] Out of 122 philanthropic societies in Vilna 72 belonged to the Jewish community. One that particularly distinguished itself for its constructive aid was the Jewish Women's Society, founded in 1924 to provide girls with a useful occupation. It trained them in all forms of needlework, millinery, and domestic economy; opened a crèche for the young children of working mothers; tried to find the husbands who had deserted their wives and families; and arranged lectures and social evenings.

Even in the narrow gamut of social life in Vilna Jewry there were scales, ranging from the merchants

[1] Once, when I sat at the open window of a café, I was approached within ten minutes by six persons in turn — from an old man to a young child — all appealing timidly for bread.

who had their modest club, the doctors who had their medical circle, and the students who had their academic and athletic societies, down to the paupers who had only their hovels. Of all the districts in the city the poorest was that which saw the birth of the community — the ghetto. There the houses, once inhabited by well-to-do merchants and manufacturers, had degenerated into slums that swarmed with the destitute, the beggars and the underworld. Wretched as the dwellings were above ground, without an indoor water-supply or proper sanitation, they were nevertheless more habitable than the cellars that existed beneath many of them. From a frowsy, evil-smelling courtyard one descended by a steep, rickety, wooden staircase to find a large cavernous chamber, dank and gloomy, sparsely furnished for living and sleeping, and sometimes occupied by a family that even took in lodgers. There were some cellars with other subterranean chambers beneath them, which were likewise inhabited by human beings.

4. CULTURAL LIFE AND INSTITUTIONS

In marked contrast to the economic depression was the robust vitality that continued to distinguish the cultural life of the community. There was, indeed, no repetition of the literary efflorescence that had adorned the middle and latter part of the nineteenth century, or of the dazzling display of rabbinic scholarship that had illumined both the seventeenth and the eighteenth. But there was an

impressive cultivation of Jewish lore in all its
branches, and the publication of books, both creative and critical, on a variety of subjects. The
spirit animating this intellectual activity was that
of a community which felt itself wholly Jewish.
Conflict of opinion existed as to whether Hebrew or
Yiddish was the national tongue — the former
championed by the Zionists, who conducted a vigorous propaganda in support of the Jewish National
Home in Palestine, and the latter by those who
believed that the destiny of their people would
continue indefinitely in the Diaspora. In no community in Poland, however, was this conflict less
acute, and the intelligentsia and the members of
all liberal professions — lawyers, doctors, engineers — all spoke Yiddish and had their stationery
printed in that language, as well as in Polish. Moreover, both Hebraists and Yiddishists were agreed
in safeguarding the national integrity and treasuring
the spiritual legacy of Israel. They were both, like
all other Jews in the republic, perfectly loyal to the
state and ready to make sacrifices in its defense;
but, like the Lithuanians and the White Russians,
they would not give up anything of their ethnic
individuality. They had experienced too many
changes of political overlordship to be disposed
to be, or to become, assimilated to the Lithuanians
one day and to the Poles the next. True, they were
called *Litvaks* by their brethren in other parts of
Poland, whom they in turn called *Polaks:* these
were, however, designations of geographical rather
than of national import. They regarded themselves

as Polish citizens not only of the Jewish faith but
also of the Jewish nationality, claimed that they
could combine the scrupulous fulfilment of their
civic duties with all the requirements of Jewish
tradition, and maintained that they were entitled
to all the rights that Polish citizenship conferred
as well as the guarantees assured to them by the
Versailles Treaty as a religious, racial and linguistic
minority. This stressing of their ethnic identity
may have provoked political controversy at home
and misunderstanding abroad; but it was a fact
which, with their teeming numbers, their social
and religious life and their characteristic culture,
could not be argued away. Their national conscious-
ness was fostered in their schools, their libraries and
their cultural societies; it found expression in their
theater and their press, their music and their folklore.

The majority (over 4,000) of the children attended
the Hebrew or Yiddish secular schools, which first
came into existence soon after the beginning of the
German occupation. The Yiddish schools were
maintained by the Central Education Committee,
and the Hebrew ones by the *Tarbut*, the organization founded in various countries for the promotion
of modern Hebrew culture by means of schools,
publications and other agencies. The maintenance
of both systems entailed difficulties, financial and
pedagogical; nevertheless both thrived. The teachers
found it easier to devise terminologies and compile
textbooks in their respective tongues than did the
managers to provide the funds; but they were ani-

mated by a love for their work, in which they often
had to seek compensation for unpaid salaries. The
schools were mostly of the elementary grade. They
were under government supervision and had to devote a number of hours to the teaching in Polish of
the Polish language and of Polish history and geography. Both educational systems included a teachers'
seminary and a secondary school, though only the
Yiddish secondary school, popularly called *Real
Gymnasie*, was accorded by the Ministry of Education, in 1935, full recognition as a public school from
which students could be admitted into the Vilna
University without any special examination. There
were two other kinds of schools — those of the
Mizrahi, at which the teaching was in both Hebrew
and Yiddish and in which religion formed an important part of the curriculum; and the ultra-
orthodox and Talmud Torah establishments, which
were managed by the Javneh Education Committee.
There were, moreover, several elementary schools
for Jewish children provided by the Polish Government, at which all subjects were taught in Polish,
including the Jewish religion (for two hours a week),
and at which there was attendance on Sundays instead of Saturdays. Finally, there were two private
secondary schools, attended by about 1,500 pupils
of both sexes, from provincial towns as well as Vilna,
whose entire curriculum was in Polish, and which
were accorded by the government the same status
as public schools.

The community also possessed a few technical
training institutions. The most important were the

establishment founded by the "Ort" in 1920–21 and the manual school which was started by the Society "Help through Work" during the German occupation. The Jewish students who attended the Vilna University came from all parts of the country. They had their own Union (with refectory, health insurance scheme, etc.) which played a notable part in the cultural life of the community. It was the only academic organization to which they could belong, as Jews were rigorously excluded from Polish students' unions.

Of the various libraries in the community by far the largest and most important was the communal or Strashun Library. Founded in 1893, with a legacy of 7,000 volumes bequeathed to the community by Matthias Strashun (1817–85), who also left some property for its maintenance, it was transferred in 1902 to the building it occupies in the synagogue courtyard. Strashun was a wealthy and childless scholar, whose distinguished public services earned him two medals from the Russian government, and whose literary output consisted chiefly of notes to several tractates of the Talmud and to Finn's *Kiryah Ne'emanah*. He had inherited a good collection from his father, increased this by judicious purchases made during frequent visits to foreign countries, and acquired many works and manuscripts of interest and value. His collection, which consisted mainly of rabbinical literature and of 1,000 volumes of Judaica in German, was substantially increased by subsequent gifts until the library ultimately contained 35,000 volumes.[1] About half of these consisted of rabbinical literature, 8,000 belonged to the category of *Haskalah*; 5,000 were in Yiddish, and the remainder were Judaica in modern languages. The library was the fortunate possessor of a few incunabula, including the *'Aruk* of Rabbi Nathan ben Yehiel of Rome (printed in 1477), *Mibhar ha-Peninim* of Solomon ibn Gabirol (Soncino, 1485), and some *Mahberot* of Immanuel of Rome (Brescia, 1492). Among its treasury of manuscripts were a Spanish commentary on the Pentateuch in Hebrew cursive script, written by Mattathias Hayizhori in 1415; the faded *Pinkas* of the Lithuanian *Va'ad* (Synod) for the years 1623–1761; a minute-book of the "Society of Grave-Diggers" over a century old, with the names of persons buried, rules of interment, and prayers; and a little book in the handwriting of the Gaon Elijah, consisting of notes on the *Sifra*. The library, which had seats for a hundred readers, was always crowded and occasionally had to be closed to prevent an uncomfortable crush. Its visitors' book, which was specially prepared in 1903 in anticipation of the

---

[1] The principal additions were several hundred books from Samuel Joseph Finn, nearly 1,000 from the library of the scholar, Rabbi Judah Behak (1820–1900), many with his own notes; 3,600 (mainly *Haskalah* literature) from Hayyim Leib Markon (1848–1905); over 2,000 from the collection of Dov Baer Ratner, (1852–1917), the author of 12 volumes of commentaries on the Talmud; 1,000 from Rabbi Mordecai Epstein (1844–1916); and a few thousand Hebraica and Judaica from the bibliographer, Jacob Benjacob.

arrival of Theodor Herzl, who was forbidden by
the Russian authorities to visit any of the institutions in the synagogue courtyard, contains the
signatures of many men of fame.[1]

The Jewish Historical and Ethnographical Society,
founded in 1919 by S. An-ski (1863–1920), author
of *Der Dibbuk*, organized a very valuable collection of Jewish materials, originating particularly
from Vilna, in the varied spheres of history and
folklore, literature and drama, music and art. Its
library contained the original manuscripts of many
famous Hebrew and Yiddish writers, ancient records of the community, and Tatar prayers in
Hebrew characters. Its archives included the records
of the old Rabbinical Seminary, which existed from
1847 to 1873, and of its successor, the Teachers'
Seminary, which existed until 1915. Its museum,
which was begun in 1913 and once possessed many
valuable objects, which were despatched to Moscow
in 1914, still housed an interesting collection of
exhibits. Among these were the parchment charters,
with the royal seals, granted to the Jews by the
Polish kings, Augustus II, Augustus III, and John
Sobieski III; a traditional portrait in oils of the
Gaon Elijah, said to have been painted by an unknown Polish artist, who, from a concealed position,
studied the sage's lineaments as he sat at his window;
a legendary portrait of Maimonides, remnants of

[1] The Strashun Library is reported to have been destroyed by
the Germans in 1942.

scrolls of the Law destroyed in pogroms, and personal souvenirs of celebrated writers.

In striking contrast to the dusk that seemed to settle over the realm of Hebrew letters in the "Jerusalem of Lithuania" was the lurid light made to play upon the world of Yiddish. It was here that the Yiddish Scientific Institute (commonly called "Iwo"[1]) was founded in 1924. Its purpose was to collect and classify all sorts of publications — books, pamphlets and periodicals — that had appeared in Yiddish, to publish works and to promote research. It occupied a modern three-story building in a fine part of the city, and had extensive cellarage for archives and old newspapers, equipped with up-to-date mechanical contrivances for protection against fire and water. It contained large collections illustrating all the main aspects of Jewish life and thought, arranged in four principal divisions: history, sociology, philology and pedagogics, and culture, the last embracing several sub-divisions, such as art, drama, music, and folklore. Jewish newspapers from all over the world were filed, and a card-index was kept of all their important contents, especially signed articles. There was a most interesting collection of portraits of Yiddish and Hebrew actors, of playbills and dramatic notices, and likewise a veritable treasury of Jewish music. There was a room full of literary curiosities and

[1] From the initials of "Iddischer Wissenschaftlicher Institut," the last word beginning with *Aleph*.

rarities displayed in showcases, such as Yiddish revolutionary pamphlets of the pre-war period in the guise of the Passover *Haggadah*, booklets on the history of Socialism in different countries, and photographs of Jewish politicians who had attained any fame. The library, which was not confined to works in Yiddish, comprised 20,000 volumes, mainly presented by publishers and authors, and also possessed numerous manuscripts of eminent writers. There was a special room for research, in which students explored various fields of Yiddish lore. Within the grounds of the Institute there was a little house containing guest-rooms for distinguished scholars from other cities or countries. With such forethought was the main building planned that another story could easily be added in the future.

The creative spirit was fostered by several publishers, who complemented Romm's activity in the religious sphere by their enterprise in the secular. The most prominent among them was Boris Kletzkin, whose firm, established in 1910, did a great deal to popularize good Yiddish literature among the working classes, published the works of such leading writers as Perez, Asch and Einhorn, and issued various periodicals. The press played a very active part under the Republic; over two dozen journals of different kinds appeared throughout the period, and at its close there were five Yiddish dailies (*Vilner Tog, Ovend Kurier, Die Zeit, Vilner Radio,* and *Vilner Express*), besides several periodicals, including a children's illustrated fortnightly magazine,

Grininke Beimelech, and the monthlies, *Iwo Blaetter, Volksgesund,* the socialist *Baginnen,* and the orthodox *Dos Vort.*

5. CEMETERIES

A Jewish cemetery, in the traditional parlance of
orthodox Jewry, is a *Bet 'Olam,* a "House of Eterni-
ty," a term that may be said to combine a love for
euphemisms with a belief in immortality. Vilna
has two such "houses," situated at a considerable
distance from one another. The old cemetery, which
lies beyond the River Vilia, a couple of miles from
the city, has been in disuse for over a century. It
stretches over a very large area, looking for the
most part like a deserted field, with grass growing
wild; for the number of gravestones is comparatively
small. There are only a few conventionally upright,
most of them being merely shapeless stones or
boulders, though there are some in the form of
little Gothic structures with Hebrew inscriptions,
on which the names have been painted over in yellow
to facilitate identification.

Most famous of all is the tomb of the Gaon
Elijah, who lies in the company of a few other
pietists, including his mother, on a spot covered
by a modest mausoleum which is entered by an
iron-barred door. Over the graves are two large
concrete slabs, separated by a small space, and on
that of the Gaon is a little heap of moldy notes
and petitions, in Yiddish and in Hebrew, entreating

the saint to intercede on behalf of the suffering supplicants. The names of the Gaon and of his honored companions are inscribed on the wall opposite their respective resting-places; and a solitary visitor, wrapped in prayer and meditation, may often be seen in the dim interior. The tombstones, with long eulogistic epitaphs, are not enclosed within the mausoleum, but stand at the back of it, in close juxtaposition and closely protected by a thick growth of shrubs and bushes. A little distance away is the grave of the "righteous proselyte," Count Valentin Potocki, the Polish nobleman who was burnt at the stake in 1749 for his conversion to Judaism. The communal authorities did their utmost to ensure his remaining at peace, by having an iron shed built over the grave, enclosed with stone blocks and iron rails; but some Polish vandals persistently damaged the enclosure.

The modern cemetery, which was opened a hundred years ago, extends over a vast area, and is intersected with fine long avenues lined with trees. A multitude of tombstones faces every direction. They are closely huddled together, with epitaphs in Hebrew, Yiddish, and Russian. Some are adorned with framed photographs. The inscriptions are not all of a conventional character, for the tombstone of a famous *Marshallik* (jester) bears the legend: "Stop and look! You are still a visitor; I am at home." In the center of the cemetery is a large mortuary, with separate sections for men and women, whither the dead are brought for the last rites; for here all are buried on the day they die. On the opposite side of the avenue is an elevated platform, reached by a flight of steps, from where the funeral oration is delivered. The speaker stands before an iron lectern, flanked on either side by lamps in large glass shades, which are necessary in cases of burial after nightfall.

Here may be seen the graves of the writers Lebensohn and Kalman Schulman, and of all the other luminaries who irradiated the firmament of Hebrew culture in the nineteenth century. Here too may be seen the graves of the victims of various riots and outrages. Nineteen members of the Bund, killed in the revolutionary rising of 1905, are laid to rest together, their sepulcher marked by a stone column from where a memorial address is delivered on every anniversary. The Jews killed by the Polish troopers in 1919 also lie together, some of the graves being marked pathetically "Unknown." And over the tomb of the Yiddish writer, A. Weiter, who was shot in that outburst of lawlessness, is a striking piece of sculpture — an eagle with a broken pinion.

Among these graves, before the city was retaken by the Russians, a stentorian voice could be heard every day offering up the prayer for the dead, and rending the air with heart-breaking grief in every note. Scarcely had the sound died away when, from an opposite quarter, the same moving, piercing chant rose again, uttered with even more poignant anguish of spirit, as though seeking to give expression to the infinite tragedy of the Jewish people.

These were the voices of poor cantors, unable to
find a pittance among the living, and trying to earn
twenty groschen a time from those visiting the
graves of their dead.

6. THE CONCLUDING PHASE

The last few years of Polish rule in Vilna were a
period of increasing reaction, in which the evils of
economic oppression and political discrimination
were aggravated by a campaign of anti-Jewish terrorism. From the spring of 1935 there was an almost
continuous reign of violence throughout the country,
not only against Jewish lives and property, but also
against synagogues and even cemeteries, in which
the weapons used were knives and pistols, stones
and clubs, iron bars and bombs. Those mainly responsible for this outburst of savagery were members
of the two political parties, the "Endeks" (National
Democrats) and the "Naras" (National Radicals),
who constantly boasted of their determination to
drive the Jews out of Poland, and who made no
secret of the fact that they had been incited by the
example of the Nazis. "Germany's success," wrote
the *Gazeta Warszawska* (April 19, 1935), "teaches
us in Poland to adopt the same policy, which will
force the Jews to organize their own mass emigration. We can do that only by making the Jews
realize once and for all that there will be no stopping
until not a single Jew is left in Poland." And in
pursuance of this barbarous policy the same brutal
methods were employed that had been used by

Hitler and his henchmen for years in order to enable them to rise to power. The "Endeks" and the "Naras" likewise struck at the Jews in order to discredit the government and to replace it. Their fanatical campaign was fomented not only by the anti-Semitic newspapers previously in existence, but also by a large number of new ones launched with German money. They achieved not only the destruction of Jewish lives and property and the sowing of internal dissensions, but also the disintegration of the political fabric of their country, which now became an easy prey to Nazi aggression.

The Jews of Vilna were by no means immune from this reign of terror. As early as February 1935, a bomb exploded under a synagogue. In the following years there were attacks on the Jews, in which many were severely injured and one died. An economic boycott was conducted against them with the utmost rigor. But nowhere was hostility waged against them so relentlessly and unremittingly as at the universities. The crusade against the Jewish students in Poland, as in other parts of Central and Eastern Europe, had been carried on intermittently for many years, and it was greatly intensified after the Nazi revolution in Germany. In the ancient seats of learning of Vilna and Cracow, and in the more modern ones of Warsaw and Lwow, the corridors and lecture-rooms often re-echoed with the cries and groans of Jewish students of both sexes, who were assaulted by bands of "Endeks" and bludgeoned into such a state that they had to be taken home or to a hospital. The object of these outbursts of hooliganism was to enforce segregation of the Jews, who were required to sit in the lecture-rooms on the benches on the left. Since they refused to occupy what they called "ghetto benches" and were not allowed to sit on the right, they were obliged to stand throughout the lecture or to squat on the floor.

At the Vilna University, which was attended by about 1,000 Jews, the "Endeks" tried to institute a "Jew-less" day. They stationed pickets at the entrances, with the result that those who succeeded in getting past were beaten up and seriously injured. The rector, who was powerless to maintain order, carried out an inquiry by ballot among all the students to ascertain whether the "ghetto" system should be introduced, and, when he found that the majority were against it, he resigned. During a lecture by Professor Rudnicki, the "Endeks" one day attacked the Jews several times, whereupon the professor asked them why they did not leave the Jews alone. They replied: "Because we are Christians," to which he retorted: "If Christ had been alive today he would have taken his seat with the Jews on the left side of the lecture room." On another occasion (February 9, 1937) a Jewish student was stabbed by an "Endek" comrade and was taken to a hospital in a grave condition.[1] In order to enforce their demand the "Endeks" presented an ultimatum to the rector and barricaded themselves in the University buildings, from which they had to be ejected

[1] *The New Statesman*, March 20, 1937 (article by the author).

by the police. The University was thereupon closed for a time. The helpless Jewish students, in order to make an impressive protest against their persecution, undertook a twenty-four hours' fast; but their self-imposed privation was in vain. In the autumn of 1937 the Ministry of Education authorized the rectors of all universities to issue orders for the "maintenance of peace" and to assign separate seats to the students. The Jews were allotted benches on the left of the lecture-rooms; but, as a matter of honor, they strictly refrained from sitting there and preferred to stand for hours or to lean against the walls.

The attitude of the government towards this anti-Jewish crusade was a grave disappointment and the measures it took quite inadequate. The "Endek" party was dissolved in various districts, its offices were raided by the police, and hundreds of culprits — a mere fraction of the guilty multitude — were arrested and imprisoned. But the sentences imposed were too lenient and the Jew-baiting continued. The current of reaction was stimulated by the "Camp for National Unity," which was organized in 1937 for the purpose of "consolidating the national forces of Poland." It was a transparent imitation of the party system in Nazi Germany and Fascist Italy both in organization and mentality. It declared that the Jews were a foreign element in the Polish body-politic, pressed for anti-Jewish legislation, and proclaimed that the only solution of the Jewish question was planned emigration. The Camp enjoyed the patronage of the president and the support of practically all the members of the cabinet. In a speech in the *Seym* on January 24, 1938, M. Skladkowski, the premier, even declared that the conflict between the Jews and Poles must be supported by the government because of "economic necessity." It was futile to make any appeal to the League of Nations, whose duty was to watch over Poland's observance of her pledge to respect the rights of her racial minorities, for the government, in 1934, had formally repudiated the right of the League to intervene.

But this and all other internal problems were soon swept aside by the scourge of war. The Polish Republic, which had made it so difficult for the Jews to live within its frontiers, and even questioned their right to live there, had now to fight for its own existence. Hitler was determined to destroy it and let loose his invading hordes on September 1, 1939. The Jews, persecuted though they had been, immediately gave proof of their loyalty and of their readiness for sacrifice in the peril that threatened their country. Now at last they were welcomed into the "Camp for National Unity;" but it was the military camp for national defense and was of no avail. For within a month Poland lay bleeding and battered, her armies defeated, and her government in exile. The western half of the country had been bombarded and conquered by the Nazis, and the eastern half was overrun, with little opposition, by the Russians, who had signed a non-aggression pact with Germany on August 23. The Russian troops took Vilna on September 19, and for a few weeks the fate of the city hung in the balance. But on October 10, after the Soviet and Lithuanian governments had signed a mutual assistance pact, the city and district of Vilna were transferred to Lithuania, and seventeen days later Lithuanian rule was re-established there once more. The name of the city, which had been "Wilno" under the Polish flag, was now changed to "Vilnius."

CHAPTER XIX

NOTABLES AND CHARACTERS

THE Jewish community of Vilna has produced an imposing host of celebrities, who, each in his respective sphere and in varied degree, have contributed to the wealth of its culture, to its historic importance and to its great renown. Any attempt to give an adequate account of their lives and activities would need not a chapter, but a volume, and indeed, two such attempts have been made: in the *Kiryah Ne'emanah* by Finn, and the *'Ir Vilna* by Noah Maggid Steinschneider. Both these volumes contain indispensable material for any history of the community; both are somewhat encyclopaedic in character, the fruits of years of laborious research and inquiry. Steinschneider's book in particular is a veritable thesaurus of detailed information, not only about the achievements of the notables, but also about their pedigrees unto the third and fourth generation and, in some cases, even unto the ninth and tenth. Both authors reproduced, with meticulous fidelity, the eulogistic inscriptions from hundreds of tombstones. These works, however, deal mainly with those who occupied official positions in the religious life of the community or whose literary creations were primarily concerned with rabbinic lore. There were, however, a very large number who toiled in other fields and attained distinction — in secular scholarship and the arts, and in social and political life; and there were also many who were characters in their way, whose quaint and peculiar personality gave birth to legends that enriched the fascination of the city for those who had come under its spell. Not all of these celebrities, however, were natives of the city. Some came to it early in life but lived there long enough to be regarded as inextricably associated with it; others again left it in their youth and achieved in other lands the fame that also reflected upon their birthplace. Neither Finn nor Strashun was born in Vilna — the former was a native of Grodno and the latter of a village from which he derived his patronymic — yet to the Jewish scholar Vilna would be unthinkable without either of them. The great majority of those who have played a part in its vicissitudes and its glories have already been noted, but there still remains an impressive phalanx, from whom only the most outstanding, or those typical of varied walks of life, can be selected here for special mention.

The records of a few more rabbis, famous for their scholarship and spiritual leadership, must be added. Prominent among these is Rabbi Moses Meltzer, who was born in 1797, the year of the Gaon Elijah's death, and who died at the advanced age of eighty-six. He was a son of Rabbi Asher Klatzki, derived his surname from his father-in-law, Rabbi Judah Leib Gordon, who was a maltster (Mälzer), and claimed descent from "Maharam" of Padua (R. Meir Katzellenbogen, who died in 1565). Rabbi Moses' distinction lay not only in his profound talmudical erudition, before which all the scholars of his time bowed in deference, but also in the fact that he was a spiritual leader for long periods in three communities. He presided over *Ramaila's Yeshibah*, from its foundation in 1831, for about twenty years,[1] but was absent for one year (1839–40) owing to the appointment of Rabbi Israel Salanter as his assistant, with whom he was unable to work amicably. During that year he established his academy in the *Bet ha-Midrash* of the chimney-sweeps, to which all his pupils followed him. After Rabbi Salanter vacated his post and founded a new house of learning in the suburb of Zaretzie, Rabbi Meltzer returned to his former place and was also appointed *Moreh Zedek*[2] and preacher. When Sir Moses Montefiore, during his stay in Vilna in 1846, visited his *Yeshibah*, Rabbi Meltzer delivered a special discourse in his honor, and the great humanitarian showed his appreciation by giving largess both to the staff and the students, besides presenting a sum of money for the teaching of Russian. In 1851 Rabbi Meltzer accepted an appointment as rabbi at Kalvarie, and in 1863 he went to assume a similar position at Lida, which he retained until his death twenty years later. In his old age he indulged in the study of the Cabala and gave his approbation to many books on mysticism and rabbinic lore. Rabbi Meltzer left many notes

[1] Steinschneider, *'Ir Vilna*, p. 124, but according to the inscription on his tomb, as given ibid. on p. 127, R. Meltzer held office in Vilna for about 30 years.

[2] See chapter VIII, p. 141, above.

on the Talmud and Responsa, which were published after his death under the title of *Tekelet Mordecai*. He was exceptionally honored by the erection of a mausoleum over his grave, and an iron box with a slot was fixed in the wall so that all who came there to pray could drop coins into it. Thereby, in the course of years, a large amount was obtained for the benefit of Talmud Torah schools.

A later rector of *Ramaila's Yeshibah* was Rabbi Jacob David Pieskin (1796–1875), who combined the activity of a prosperous merchant with talmudical scholarship until 1857, when he was elected to the academic office. He was the author of two books, *Yad ha-Hazakah*, a commentary on the Passover *Haggadah*, and *Tumat Yesharim*, rules for a religious life. His writings on other themes are still in manuscript.

Another distinguished talmudical scholar was Rabbi Jacob Barit, who was an exact contemporary of Rabbi Meltzer, his span of life being likewise from 1797 to 1883. Born at Zimno, in the province of Suvalki, he settled in Vilna in 1822, where he dwelt until the end of his days. He devoted the earlier part of his manhood to the study of secular subjects and modern languages and to business pursuits. In 1850 he was appointed head of the *Yeshibah* founded by Hayyim Nathan Parnas, an esteemed pietist and director of the Great Charity, who was honored by a visit from Sir Moses Montefiore. Rabbi Barit held that position for twenty-five years, training many students who themselves became eminent rabbis, and from the 'forties on, all

sections of the community recognized him as their
representative in dealings with the outside world.
He it was who helped Sir Moses Montefiore draft
a petition to Nicholas I for the amelioration of the
Jewish position. Thanks to his knowledge of Russian — a rarity among rabbis in those days — he
enjoyed the favor of Governor General Nazimov,
and was appointed a member of the Jewish delegation to St. Petersburg (1852) as well as chairman
of three rabbinical commissions (1856, 1862, and
1868). In a petition to the governor general for the
betterment of Jewish conditions, he recommended
the abolition of the Pale and permission for those
who had discharged their military service, as well
as for artisans and merchants of the second and
third guild, to settle in the principal cities. It was,
moreover, on his initiative that a commission was
convened to investigate the charges brought against
the Jews by the convert Brafmann, charges whose
falsity he had no difficulty in proving.

Second in importance only to the dignity of rabbi
was that of the *Maggid* or *Darshan*, the preacher,
who not only had the duty to impart instruction but
also the right to reproach and reprove as well as
to console and exhort. The earliest recorded occupant of that position was Rabbi Moses Darshan, a
son of Rabbi Hillel ben Naphtali Hertz (1615–91).
He was born at Brisk, was a member of the *Bet
Din* of Rabbi Moses Lima in Vilna from 1651 to
1664, and, after occupying rabbinical office in
various places in Lithuania, Altona, and Hamburg,
was appointed head of the *Bet Din* for Lwow, with

his seat at Zolkiew. Rabbi Hillel left copious notes on the *Shulhan Aruk,* which were published soon after his death by his son, Moses, with additions of his own, under the title of *Bet Hillel.* Rabbi Moses, who was born in Vilna about 1661 and accompanied his father to the various places where he held office, studied at Kalisz, and became head of the *Bet Din* at Kempne. In 1709 he returned to his native city, where he was both preacher and president of the *Bet Din* until his death in 1726. He left in manuscript comments on various talmudical tractates, under the title of *Torat Asham* ("Law of Offense"). Occasionally a son was found worthy to succeed his father in this office. Thus, Rabbi Solomon Zalman, who was preacher for about ten years, until his death in 1766, was followed by his son Rabbi Hayyim, who adorned the position until his death in 1795.

A more remarkable instance of son succeeding father as preacher occurred more than half a century later. Rabbi Ezekiel Feiwel, born at Dretschin in 1757, was not called to the position of *Maggid* in Vilna until 1811. He had already long enjoyed the reputation of a powerful preacher and profound scholar. As a young man of nineteen he had travelled to Hungary to seek a cure for some ailment, and on the way preached in the synagogues of Lwow and Brody, where he evoked the admiration of all talmudical savants. He wrote two books, *Musar Haskel* ("Discipline of Wisdom"), comments on religious laws, which appeared in 1790, and *Toledot Adam* ("History of Man") a scholarly miscellany, which

was published in two parts, in 1801 and 1809. He
visited Vilna occasionally before he received his
appointment there, and, since the fame of his erudition had reached the Gaon Rabbi Elijah, the latter
sent for him in the last year of his life, when, it is
recorded, Rabbi Feiwel held converse with him five
times. Rabbi Feiwel continued as *Maggid* until
his death in 1833, and his son, Rabbi Zalman Wolf,
was proclaimed his successor on the day of his
funeral, even before his burial.

It happened in this wise. The aged Rabbi Abele
Posweler and the elders, who accompanied the
entire congregation to the cemetery, called one of
the sextons attending to the interment and said to
him: "When you call us to robe the departed with
his cerements and we all stand around his bier,
then, as is customary, ask forgiveness from him
for us and all the men of our congregation. After
you have made this request, call out aloud: 'Our
master, *Mazzal Tob!* Your son, our master, Rabbi
Zalman Wolf, has just been raised to the position
of *Maggid* in place of your honor,' and we shall
answer after you: '*Mazzal Tob!*'" And so it was
done.[1]

Rabbi Zalman Wolf was consulted by Sir Moses
Montefiore on the occasion of his visit to Vilna.
In the visitor's honor he delivered a discourse,
which was published many years later under the
title of *Tiferet Moshe* ("Glory of Moses"); and, upon
the death of Lady Montefiore, he wrote a tribute

[1] Steinschneider, *'Ir Vilna*, p. 88.

to her memory under the title of *Alon Bakut* ("Oak of Weeping"). He composed a special address to celebrate the escape of Alexander II from an attempt on his life and received a letter of thanks from the imperial palace. He died in 1867, in his seventy-eighth year, three days after he had fainted in the course of a sermon before a thronged congregation in the Great Synagogue. Throughout his life, despite the esteem and popularity that he enjoyed, he was poor. The society of carpenters subsequently bought the dwelling in which he had lived many years and dedicated it as a house of prayer and study in the name of "The *Maggid*."

In the field of *Haskalah* the most important Vilna writers have already been mentioned; but at least four more, even though not of the very first rank, must be noted. They are David Gordon (1826–86), Joshua Steinberg (1830–1908), Zevi Nissan Golomb (1853–1934), and Benzion Alfes (born 1851). Gordon, after spending seven years in England in early manhood, entered the editorial office of the Hebrew journal *Ha-Maggid*, at Lyck in 1857, and after twenty-five years became the owner of the paper and made it the leading organ of the *Hibbat Zion* movement. In its columns he expounded the fundamental principles of Jewish nationalism in connection with the restoration of Palestine as early as 1860, and afterwards secured the cooperation of the most eminent Hebrew writers of the day in support of his views. Steinberg was an educator and philologian, who acted for a number of years as Crown Rabbi in Bialystok and Vilna (1860–66), and

later as censor of Hebrew and Yiddish publications.
He helped to open several Jewish schools in Vilna
in 1863, was appointed four years later lecturer on
Hebrew and Aramaic at the Rabbinical Seminary,
and when this was converted into a Teachers' College he became an inspector. In this capacity, in
which he continued until 1904, he visited the
Volozhin *Yeshibah* in 1887 and insisted upon the
teaching there of Russian. His works include *Sefer
ha-Millim* (Hebrew-Russian and Russian-Hebrew
Dictionary, 1878–80), a *Manual of Hebrew Grammar*
(1884), and a *Manual of the Aramaic Language*
(1872). Moreover, he enjoys popularity among Hebraists because of his *Fables* and other works in
Hebrew.

Golomb was a very versatile and scholarly
writer, who was born at Podzelve, a few miles from
Vilna, and settled in the city in 1872. He began his
literary career as a proofreader for the firm of
Romm. Since the latter were the publishers of
Dick's Yiddish stories, which were written in an
illegible script and had to be read first by the censor,
Golomb used to take them home and copy them
during the night in a clear hand. As a result he
began to write stories himself. Among his varied
productions were a Yiddish translation of *Hilkot
De'ot* of Maimonides (1876), a manual of Hebrew
(1883), a Hebrew-Yiddish dictionary, various works
on Jewish music (including compositions by the
Vilna *Balhabessel*), and a book on women's rights
(*Mishpat ha-Banot*, 1890). He was a pioneer in the
collection of Yiddish folk songs and folk melodies

and also wrote on economic questions. Though obviously an industrious and tireless scribe, he nevertheless had to eke out a living by giving Hebrew lessons. The last of the quartet, Benzion Alfes, went to Palestine in 1871, and after living there a few years returned to Vilna and became a proofreader at the works of Judah Leib Matz. He worked there for fifteen years, correcting Steinberg's dictionary and works of rabbinical literature. He revised Moltschan's *Life of the Gaon Elijah*, translated into Yiddish Jonah Girondi's *Sha'are Teshubah* and other works, and published a series of storybooks interspersed with moralistic parables.

A far more illustrious scholar was Daniel Chwolson, born in Vilna in 1819, who, although he forsook the faith of his people, became the champion of their cause and made valuable contributions to the "Science of Judaism" in Russia. The *Heder* and *Yeshibah* failed to satisfy his thirst for knowledge. A poor, tattered student of twenty-two, he wandered into Germany, where he received help and encouragement from Abraham Geiger. He devoted three years to the study of classics; then entered the Breslau University, where he specialized in Semitic languages; he received his degree at Leipzig. Upon his return to Russia, the Imperial Academy, at its own expense, published, in 1856, his first work of profound research on *The Sabaeans and Sabaeism*, which at once established his authority in the field of Oriental scholarship. He had been baptized in the previous year, and there was thus no obstacle to his appointment to the chair of

Hebrew and Syriac at the newly opened Oriental
Faculty of the St. Petersburg University. This post
he retained until shortly before his death, in 1910,
even after he became blind. For twenty-five years
he was also Professor of Hebrew and Biblical
Archaeology at the Greek ' Orthodox Theological
Seminary in St. Petersburg and for a similar period
at the Roman Catholic Theological Seminary (an
impartiality probably due to his religious origin).
The most important of his works were *Corpus
Inscriptionum Hebraicarum* (tombstone inscriptions,
especially from the Crimea, 1882); Syrian-Nestorian
tomb inscriptions from Semiretschie (1897); and
Christ's Last Supper and the Day of his Death (second
edition, Leipzig, 1908), which deals with the relations of the Jewish parties to Jesus and constitutes
a vindication of the Pharisees. Although a convert
to Christianity, he maintained friendly relations
with many Jewish scholars, such as Kalman Schulman, and even corresponded with the Kovno Gaon,
Rabbi Isaac Elhanan, who urged him to defend the
Jewish cause.

Professor Chwolson proved a redoubtable champion of the Jewish people, particularly in connection
with "ritual murder" accusations. When a charge
was brought against the Jews of Saratov in 1857,
and the government convened a commission of
scholars to see whether any passages could be found
in Jewish literature recommending the use of Christian blood for ritual purposes, he was appointed an
honorary member. The investigation extended over
nine years. In the meantime, in 1861, he was allowed

to publish his memorandum disproving the accusation. A fresh charge was brought in 1877 against the Jews at Kutais, in Transcaucasia, at the same time that Russian anti-Semitic writers were waging a campaign against the Talmud and reviving the libel that it contained blasphemies against Jesus. Chwolson thereupon republished his memorandum with many additions (St. Petersburg, 1880). A German edition of this work appeared later under the title, *Die Blutanklage und sonstige mittelalterliche Beschuldigungen der Juden* (Frankfurt, 1901). He also defended the Jewish people in a pamphlet which was translated into English under the title, *The Semitic Nations* (Cincinnati, 1874). Numerous works in Russian, German and English, were the product of his learned pen. In 1899 his literary jubilee was celebrated by the publication of a presentation volume containing articles written in his honor by many leading scholars.

Another child of the Vilna ghetto who forsook the faith of his fathers, though without any subsequent atonement, was Julian Klaczko, born in 1825. At the age of seventeen he had already published a collection of Hebrew poems. Later the spirit of enterprise drove him abroad. In 1849 he settled in Paris, where he subsequently became the librarian of the Parliamentary Library Corps Legislatif and a regular contributor to the *Revue des Deux Mondes*. He had been so profoundly influenced by his study of Polish literature in his youth that he not only became a prominent spokesman of Polish nationalism and an enthusiastic historian of Polish literature, but also adopted the dominant religion. In 1870 he was elected to the Galician Diet, but, owing to political disappointments, he went to Italy for a few years, returning in 1875 to Vienna, where he remained until his death in 1908. His works include *Etudes de Diplomatique Contemporaine* and *Rome et la Renaissance*.

Still another Vilna Jew who became a Christian was Henry Gersoni (1840–97). He had attended the Rabbinical Seminary and afterwards studied philosophy in St. Petersburg. He soon repented of his baptism. From Paris, in 1868, he wrote a full confession of his conversion and a declaration of his return to Judaism, which appeared in *Ha-Maggid*, the Hebrew journal published at Lyck (East Prussia). He then went to the United States, where he was a rabbi and preacher in New York and Chicago, published a Hebrew translation of Longfellow's *Excelsior* (1872), wrote *Sketches of Jewish Life and History* (1873), founded a monthly paper, *The Maccabean* (1879), and established a Hebrew-speaking society.

Moses Rosensohn was another curious character who lived in Vilna during the latter half of the nineteenth century. He advocated the amalgamation of all religions and was therefore called a missionary. He was a wealthy property-owner who wrote many booklets in Hebrew on his favorite idea, and persistently annoyed the members of the community by trying to foist his tracts upon them.

Among the eminent writers born in Vilna, of whom the most important have already been noted, there are three who in their youth left their native city for America, where they have rendered the most valuable services to the Jewish press and, each in his particular domain, achieved high distinction. Abraham Cahan, who arrived in New York in 1882 and was a pioneer in the Jewish labor movement, helped to build up the Yiddish press on modern lines. His capable direction of the *Jewish Daily Forward* over some decades richly contributed to the Americanization of the Jewish masses. Peter Wiernik followed Cahan three years later. For about forty years he was prominently associated with the *Jewish Morning Journal*, in whose columns he displayed an amazing versatility. He also wrote in English a *History of the Jews in America*. Isaac Hourwich (1860–1924), who emigrated still later, after doing five years' penance in Siberia for revolutionary agitation, wrote extensively on social and economic questions in both the English and Yiddish press and was the author of a number of books, of which the best known is *Immigration and Labor* (New York, 1913).

Not only in the field of scholarship, sacred and secular, and in literature and journalism, did the Vilna community produce men of mark, but also in the varied domain of the arts. Music was one of the few arts that could be practiced without infringing any religious injunction, and not a few Vilna Jews achieved celebrity through its medium. The most romantic was the *Hazzan*, Joel David Loewenstein, better known as the *Vilner Balhabessel*, possessor of a phenomenal voice and the hero of legend. Born in Libau in 1816, he was a boy of ten when his father was appointed principal cantor at the Great Synagogue in Vilna. The boy had already impressed critical connoisseurs with his melodious voice as well as with his brilliant playing of the violin at the age of five; but it was not until one Sabbath morning, when he was eleven, that the community realized the wonderful quality of his vocal gifts. After the conclusion of the reading of the Law, his father stood him on a stool before the reading-desk and asked him to sing the prayers *Yekum Purkan* and *Ab ha-Rahamim*, and the boy sang with such sweetness, such pathos and such power, that the entire congregation were swept off their feet and insisted upon his chanting the service to the end. Since nature had obviously decided that he should be a cantor, he had to acquire the necessary social qualification in order to obtain a position. Thus, at the early age of thirteen, shortly after he was *Bar Mitzvah*, he was married to Hannah, the elder daughter of R. Mordecai Strashun, a local magnate. His opportunity soon came. His father died in the following year, and he was appointed to succeed him. Henceforth he was called the *Balha-bessel*,[1] or "little householder," to emphasize the fact that the principal precentor at the Great Synagogue, although a boy in years, was not a bachelor. His rendering of the prayers was of such enchanting beauty that the Synagogue and its fore-

---

[1] Yiddish diminutive of the Hebrew *Baal Habayyit*.

court were always thronged, not only with Jews, but also with Christians of high degree.

The fame of his voice reached the ears of the composer, Professor Moniuszko, of the Warsaw Conservatoire, who took the warmest interest in him, urged him to go abroad to be trained for the operatic stage and predicted for him untold wealth and world renown. So the *Balhabessel* was persuaded to go to Warsaw to give a concert, the proceeds of which would cover the cost of his training. The concert, a brilliant and sensational success, attended not only by Jews but by the Polish aristocracy and Russian official circles, proved the beginning of a tragedy. For among those present was the beautiful daughter of Count Paskewicz, who was also a singer, and she conceived for the cantor a deep admiration. The *Balhabessel* became a frequent visitor at the Count's palace and fell in love with the girl. He remained in Warsaw so long that his wife and the elders of the Vilna community had to go there to fetch him back. Henceforth he was no longer the same. Torn between the sense of duty to his religious office and of loyalty to his family and people on the one hand, and the dazzling attractions of an operatic career and the beautiful countess on the other, he fell into a state of profound melancholy, from which he never recovered. He was unable to sing as he used to; his brief contact with a wider world had made him discontented with his narrow lot. He left his wife; he lost his children; and his search for healing in travel was in vain. So he longed for death, and as he lay on his bed, murmuring the prayer of confession, his golden voice came back, rising and vibrating through the air in notes of dulcet splendor, yet charged with an undertone of such ineffable contrition that the vast multitude who were gathered around the house in hushed and awed silence were moved to tears.[1]

Vilna has produced other musicians of greater fame, though without the aureole of legend. Pre-eminent among them is Jascha Heifetz (born in 1901), who received his first lessons in the Vilna Royal School of Music at the age of five, and is recognized throughout the world as one of the most brilliant violinists of the day. Another instrumentalist as well as composer was Leopold Godowsky (born in 1870), who began to perform in public at the age of nine, toured America at the age of fourteen, and for three years was successor to Busoni as teacher of music at the Imperial Academy of Music in Vienna (1909–1912). Joseph Vinogradoff, who began his musical career as a chorister in the Vilna synagogue, became one of the leading baritones in Russia, and after singing Russian and Italian opera both in that and other countries, returned to the service of his people by becoming a *Hazzan* in America. Another once famous opera singer was Michael Michailov (born in 1858), who sang at the Imperial Opera in St. Petersburg in 1884–86 and

---

[1] There are various versions of the romantic career of the *Balhabessel*. Two are given in Jeshurin's *Zammelbuch*; and a third is related by Dienesohn in *Das Buch von den Polnischen Juden*. He died in Warsaw at the age of thirty-four.

was a favorite of Alexander III. He abandoned his Jewish name, Moses Silberstein, at the outset of his career, and after he had acquired a great reputation he also abandoned his Jewish faith. Soon afterwards his star began to sink. The father of modern Yiddish operetta and musical comedy, Joseph Rumshinsky, also first saw the light in the Vilna ghetto. He came to America in 1904, greatly improved the standard of music in the Yiddish theater by the quality and influence of his own compositions, and is one of the most important figures in the Yiddish theatrical world.

Although the plastic arts were always frowned upon by the rabbis as an infraction of the Second Commandment, and the Vilna ghetto was hardly a milieu in which to develop the aesthetic sense, it was the birthplace of a sculptor who ranks as one of the greatest artists of Russia. Mark Antokolski (1842–1902) was the son of a poor innkeeper, who buffeted him about in his boyhood, scolded him for his "clumsy hands," and intended making him a chimney sweep. But from the moment that he was apprenticed to an engraver, young Antokolski began to give evidence of the artistic genius which afterwards found world-wide recognition. His early wood-carvings aroused the admiration of the wife of Governor General Nazimov, who helped him, at the age of twenty, to enter the Art Academy in St. Petersburg. There he studied for six years, during which wood-carving earned him a grand silver medal and a bursary. In 1869 he returned to St. Petersburg and modelled his *Ivan the Terrible*, which at once made him famous. He was honored by a visit from Alexander II, who climbed up to his fourth-floor studio and was deeply impressed by the masterly creation, which he bought and placed in the Hermitage Museum. In 1872 the sculptor married a daughter of "Yudel" Opatov, one of the richest merchants in Vilna, and lived the latter part of his life abroad, partly in Rome but mainly in Paris. In Rome he created the colossal statue of *Peter the Great*, besides *Christ* and *John the Baptist*. After settling in the French capital, where he exhibited in 1878, he produced, among other important works, his *Socrates*, *Spinoza*, and *Mephistopheles*. Although much sought after in artistic and fashionable circles, he remained faithful to Jewish tradition throughout his life. He never worked on the Sabbath, and he gave expression to his Jewish feeling in such compositions as *A Talmudic Disputation* and *Nathan the Wise*. But he was also ardently attached to Russia, as shown in his correspondence with Turgenieff, and he had the satisfaction of contributing to his native city a monument of Catherine II. Nevertheless, his work was savagely attacked by the anti-Semitic press in St. Petersburg. After his death, Vilna and the imperial capital vied for the honor of providing his last resting-place, and the capital won. Four years later a plaque was affixed to a dingy dwelling in the Vilna ghetto to mark the spot where the great artist was born.

Antokolski was not by any means the only sculptor, though the most brilliant, who emerged from that quarter. There were at least two others,

Ilja (Elias) Ginsburg and Abraham Eisenberg. Ginsburg, born in 1860, was one of eight children of a widowed mother. He also began making wooden carvings in his boyhood; but his pious mother, who wished him to become a rabbi, was so angry that she threw both carvings and instruments into the street. The engraver, Avner Griliches, however, encouraged the lad and introduced him to Antokolski, who offered to train him as a sculptor. The mother was strongly opposed to her son's going to the capital to "make idols," but his more tolerant grandfather carried the day. Young Ginsburg accompanied Antokolski first to Rome and then to St. Petersburg, where with the generous support of Baron de Guenzburg he studied at the Art Academy for eight years. In 1886 he was awarded a gold medal for his *Lamentation of Jeremiah*. In the course of his successful career he modelled the busts of several of Russia's celebrities in different spheres, such as Tolstoi and Tschaikovski, besides some charming studies of children. Eisenberg, born in 1879, studied in Warsaw and showed a preference for Jewish themes, his most popular works being *The Jewish Funeral*, *Musicians*, and *Studying the Talmud*. He was an honored member of the Warsaw Art Academy, but because of the anti-Jewish boycott, he withdrew his works and arranged an exhibition of them and the works of other Jewish artists in the Luxemburg Gallery in Warsaw. Subsequently he became a director of the Vilna theatrical company and in 1924 settled in America. Another plastic art was represented by Abraham Griliches, born

in 1852, the son of Avner Griliches, the engraver.
He was a medal designer and gem cutter. He
designed various coins and numerous medals to
commemorate historic events, was awarded a gold
medal at the International Paris Exhibition of 1889,
was appointed designer to the Russian Imperial
Mint and devised the State seals of Alexander III
and Nicholas II.

The love of the drama gave birth to the company
which became famous on both sides of the Atlantic
as the "Vilner Truppe." It was founded in February 1916, during the German occupation, thanks
to the enterprise of Alexander Azro and a band of
players, some at first only amateurs, who felt the
need of providing some artistic entertainment to
counteract the sufferings of the time. Azro, born
in 1892, made his first amateur appearance at the
age of thirteen. Subsequently, he studied at Kiev,
and returned to the stage in Vilna. The first performances of the "Vilner Truppe" were given in the
local circus, and they met with such astounding
success that the company was soon able to appear
at the Municipal Theater before an audience that
also included non-Jews, as well as to visit Warsaw
and other cities. Not only plays by Jewish writers
but works by European dramatists were produced.
Azro took as his model the style and technique
created by Stanislavsky in the Moscow Theater.
One of the distinguishing features of his company
was the brilliance of the collective acting, the like of
which had never before been seen on the Yiddish
stage. Although individual performances were not

allowed to stand out, and all members of the company displayed a high standard, at least three actors deserve mention. The first is Sonja Alomis (Lubaka), the wife of Azro, who played leading parts in many cities of Europe and America; the second is Abraham Morevski, who was a well-known actor on the Russian stage for several years before he joined the "Vilner Truppe," his best part being the Miropoler *Zaddik* in *Der Dibbuk*; and the third is Joseph Buloff (Bulkin), who left the company to become the manager of the "Volkstheater" in New York.

A wide gulf separated those who acted imaginary characters on the stage from those who played the most perilous parts in real life — the revolutionaries and fighters for freedom, of whom so many were born in or near Vilna. Drawn both from the working class and student circles, these crusaders agitated under assumed names and changed their abodes in kaleidoscopic fashion. Their pockets stuffed with fiery leaflets, a concealed revolver for their self-defense, they risked their own limited freedom in the hope of achieving the greater freedom of their country; but only too often they were doomed either to be shot, to die in the wastes of Siberia, or to be disillusioned by the Bolshevist Revolution. Of the hundreds of socialists of conflicting parties whose homes or political centers were in Vilna,[1] at least three may be

---

[1] Lists of these fighters for freedom and accounts of the careers of many of them are given in E. N. Jeshurin's *Vilna: A Zammelbuch.*

added to those already mentioned as typical of their varied vicissitudes.

Ossip Solomonovitch Minor, born in 1861, joined the revolutionary party *Narodnaja Volja* when a student of the Moscow University. In 1883, the police arrested him and scores of other students, including Michael Raffalovitch Gotz, who afterwards became a leader of the new party of Social Revolutionaries. Minor was imprisoned for some months, deported in 1884 to Tula, then to Jaroslav where he was in jail for eighteen months, and next to the notorious Butirki prison in Moscow. From there he was deported with many others to Yakutsk, in Eastern Siberia, partly on foot and partly in a rickety cart. Sentenced to penal servitude for life, he was transported to Vilivisk. After languishing for ten years in Siberia, he returned in 1898 to European Russia. He settled in Vilna, under police supervision, where his father had been ordered to live owing to his energetic intervention on behalf of the Jews in Moscow, where he was the rabbi. In 1902 Ossip Minor went to Berlin where he was in contact with Gotz and other revolutionaries, including Gershuni, the organizer of the Terrorists, and Azeff, who was later unmasked as an *agent provocateur*. From there, in 1903, he went to Geneva, where he became a member of the Foreign Committee of the Social Revolutionaries and editor of their fighting organ. Returned to Russia after the revolution of 1905, he was sentenced in 1908 to a long term of imprisonment from which he was released only by the revolution of 1917. He was appointed chairman of the

Moscow Duma, but, disillusioned by the policy and practices of the Bolsheviks, he left Russia for France, where, broken in body and spirit, he died in 1918.

Isaiah Eisenstadt, also known as J. Judin, born in 1867, was the theoretician of Marxism in the socialist circle that gave birth to the Bund. He joined the Social Revolutionary movement as a student and served a first sentence of eighteen months in prison. After living in Berlin for a short time, he returned to Russia, was arrested for organizing a strike and in 1897 was banished to Siberia for five years. He returned to Vilna in 1902, continued his revolutionary agitation, was arrested and deported abroad, and then went back to Vilna. He continued his revolutionary activity in Warsaw and Odessa and was exiled to the Astrakhan Province for four years. After the establishment of the Kerensky government he was given a post at the "Institute of Marx and Engels." When the Bolsheviks came into power, however, Eisenstadt was again arrested a few times, and finally left the country for Paris in 1922, broken and disillusioned. Charles Rappoport, born at Duksty in the Vilna district in 1865, likewise joined the socialist movement as a student. Because of his share in the abortive plot against Alexander III in 1887, he fled to Paris, where he remained and became naturalized in 1899. Although at first opposed to Marxism, he was the founder with Dr. Zhitlowsky and others of the Union of Russian Social Revolutionaries. Afterwards he became one of the most active leaders of the United Socialist Party in France, and later head of the French Communists and editor of their paper, *L'Humanité*. He wrote the best biography of Jaurès and also, among other works, *La Philosophie Sociale de Lavroff* and *La Philosophie de l'Histoire*. He died under tragic circumstances shortly after the Germans entered Paris.

Long before any of these passionate crusaders was conscious of the tyranny which they tried to overthrow, there flourished a Jew who had made such good use of his abilities and opportunities, even within the restricted liberty available, that he rose from obscurity and poverty to a position of great wealth and authority. His name was Yehuda Opatov (1797–1868), who was said to have started life as a bootblack in the Synagogue Courtyard and afterwards acquired such riches that he bought and built a great deal of property, lived in a fine mansion in grand style, and drove through the streets of Vilna in a carriage and pair. He was so dominating a character that he was feared by the elders of the community and even respected by government officials. He belonged to the type of *Gebir* or *Takkif* (magnate) to be found in most communities of the time; but he was charitable and religious withal. In 1848, during the plague, he gave 6,000 roubles for the relief of widows and orphans; on a later occasion, when food was scarce and very dear, he had large quantities of bread baked, which he sold at half-price to all the poor, Jews and Gentiles alike. He built a synagogue and assigned some property for its maintenance as well as for the support of several pious scholars. Opatov befriended the *Balhabessel* in his days of distress by taking him into his house. Nobody less than Mapu[1] was worthy to be the Hebrew teacher of his children, and his daughter Helena became the wife of the celebrated Antokolski.

A notable personality of our own time was Dr. Zemah Shabad[2] (1864–1935), a popular physician and one of the foremost public workers in Vilna from the time of the first German invasion until his death. He was a valiant defender of Jewish interests throughout the turbulent period of 1915–22 as well as later when a member of the *Seym*, and an indefatigable promoter of the social and cultural welfare of the community. He was a member of the "Volkist" (Democratic) party, an enthusiastic advocate of Jewish cultural autonomy, an ardent champion of the Yiddish language and secular schooling, and a founder, together with his son-in-law, Dr. M. Weinreich, the philologian, of the Yiddish Scientific Institute. His death was the occasion of the most imposing demonstration of sorrow and solidarity ever seen in Vilna, for his funeral was followed by 30,000 persons, among whom were also representatives of the municipality, the university, and the government.

Among the multitude of personages who played their parts in the history and development of the community, two were altogether different from all

[1] Opatov is believed to have been the original of one of the characters satirized in Mapu's novel, *Ayit Zabu'a* ("The Hypocrite").

[2] His name was derived from an ancestor who was a *Sheliah Bet Din* (messenger of the Court of Judgment).

those who have already been depicted. They, too, must be included as illustrative of its many-sided and motley character. They were Motke Habad and Sheike Feifer, famous wits produced by Russian Jewry in the first half of the nineteenth century. In a somber and dismal world, in which their people suffered so much oppression, they had the faculty of preserving a constant sense of humor and of amusing and entertaining their generation with their quips and jests, their stories and anecdotes. Motke Habad was the elder and more inventive of the two. He often based his humorous or satirical conceits upon a scriptural text. Sheike Feifer, who owed his cognomen to his expert whistling[1] and sang bass in the *Balhabessel*'s choir, was primarily an impersonator and practical joker. Only a few of their authentic witticisms have been handed down, perhaps because so many of their contemporaries also had a gift of humor, but they live in the grateful memory of the community as men who knew how to make others laugh at times when there was so much cause for tears.

[1] From *pfeifen*, "to whistle."

CHAPTER XX

THE KARAITES

1. TROKI IN THE PAST

FOUR miles from Vilna, on the main road to Kovno, lies the sleepy little town of Troki, whose early history was closely and prominently associated both with the city of Vilna and with its Jewish community. It was the capital of the Grand Duchy of Lithuania before Grand Duke Gedymin transferred his metropolis to the banks of the Vilia, and from a bend in the road one can still see the crumbling ruin of his ancient castle. There were Jews in Troki some two hundred years before the arrival of any in Vilna. They were Karaites, who spoke a Tatar dialect. They owed their settlement in Lithuania to the Grand Duke Witold, who, after his successful war against the Tatars in the Crimea in the latter part of the fourteenth century, took a few hundred Karaites back with him to Troki and treated them as favored colonists rather than as captives. They were given plots of land to till, which their descendants continued to cultivate down to the present day, and were granted not only religious liberty but also the privileges of communal autonomy. Their rights were set forth in a charter granted them by the Grand Duke on June 24, 1388, and subsequently confirmed on various occasions. Grand Duke Casimir

Jagiello, in 1441, not only renewed their charters but also conferred upon them the Magdeburg Law, which thus placed them on the same legal level as the Gentile communities of Vilna, Kovno and Troki itself. While reaffirming their religious freedom and communal autonomy, this Grand Duke sympathetically stressed their poverty and promised that they would not be subjected to heavy taxation. Half a century later, however, the Karaites had to share the fate of all the Jews in Lithuania, who were expelled from the country in 1495 by Grand Duke Alexander. They, as well as many Rabbanites, congregated at Ratno, on the frontier of Lithuania and Poland, where they stayed until 1503, when Alexander, upon succeeding to the Polish Crown, rescinded his own decree. They then returned to Troki, and their charters were re-confirmed in 1507 by King Sigismund I.

Even before their temporary exile from Troki, the leaders of the sectarians had entered into correspondence with Elijah Bashiatzi, one of the heads of the Karaite community in Constantinople, for the purpose of obtaining a spiritual leader. In response to his friendly invitation, some promising young men were sent to that city in order to be trained by local scholars. This arrangement proved satisfactory, and from the beginning of the sixteenth century, for a period of a hundred and fifty years, Troki formed the religious and intellectual center of Karaism in Lithuania and Poland. Economic conditions, however, were rather difficult, causing a number of Karaites to abandon their properties

The Karaite Synagogue

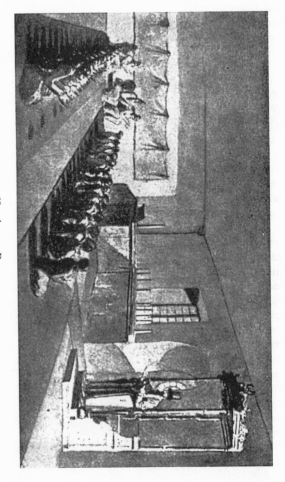

Karaites at Prayer

and to migrate to other towns and villages. Thereupon a warning was sent after them that unless they returned they would forfeit their possessions.

The Karaites held a general assembly from time to time for the purpose of appointing their secular and religious leaders and regulating their internal affairs. The principal dignitary was the *Shofet* (*Wojt* or Mayor), whose office was first mentioned in the charter of 1441. His main duties were to watch over the guaranteed rights of the community, to make any necessary representations to the authorities, and to act as judge in civil disputes. He was elected for a period of two or three years and had to receive the approval of the *Voivode* (Governor), who expected a monetary gift for granting it. The procedure occasionally led to an ambitious person first securing the official sanction and then leaving the community no alternative but to elect him. The *Shofet* could not act as a judge alone, but had to be assisted by two or three *Dayyanim*, who were elected for a year, and in the event of any disagreement the case had to be referred to another committee of three. This triumvirate, which was first appointed in 1533, was charged with the administration of communal affairs, and for a certain period even had authority over the *Shofet*. The emoluments of this dignitary were apparently adequate, if not handsome. He received a fee of 10 per cent of the amount involved in the lawsuit submitted to his decision (paid in equal shares by the two parties); he was exempt from all taxation; and he had at his disposal during his term of office a plot of land from the estates belonging to the community.

The first *Shofet* of whom there is mention was named Abraham, who held office in 1508. From that date, until 1766, when the last of the line was elected,[1] there was a succession of twenty-three (with occasional gaps). No outstanding figure occupied the position in the sixteenth century, but in the first half of the seventeenth the most important incumbent was Ezra ben Nisan, who was appointed in 1640. He came into contact with Joseph Solomon Delmedigo, when that romantic personality was staying in Vilna as physician to the Duke of Radziwill, and he may have studied medicine under him. Delmedigo, who showed a partiality for Karaite friendships, is also believed to have studied with him Rashi's commentaty on the Pentateuch, with Elijah Mizrahi's super-commentary and Ibn Ezra's exegesis. Ezra, who died in 1666 at the age of seventy-one, was on friendly terms with the Rabbanites, and composed some liturgical poems. The ablest representatives of the office were four generations of the Labanos (Labanowski) family, who watched over the welfare of the community from 1671 until the last decade of the eighteenth century. The first member of the family to attain the honor was Abraham ben Samuel. King John III Sobieski invited him to choose a number of families and settle

---

[1] The complete list, with dates, and accounts of the careers of the most important holders of the office, will be found in Jacob Mann's *Texts and Studies*, Vol. II, *Karaitica*.

with them at Kukizov, near Lwow, which belonged
to the king's son, Constantine. This action was a
tribute to the ability of the pioneers chosen, but it
affected adversely the progress of the community
which lost them.

In the first decade of the eighteenth century the
Karaites at Troki suffered a number of disasters:
the occupation of the town in 1706 by Swedish
troops, who levied contributions upon them, famine
in 1709, and plague in the following year. Owing
to the intolerable conditions, Samuel ben Abraham
Labanos, the *Shofet* elected in 1713, as well as Solomon ben Aaron, the religious leader, lived in Vilna
for a few years and did not take up residence at
Troki until 1719. By the middle of the century the
community was so heavily indebted that the *Shofet*,
Abraham ben Samuel, furnished with letters of
introduction from the Rabbanite leaders of Vilna
and Brest-Litovsk, went to the Crimea for help in
1755, and also to Sluzk in 1761. Abraham's son,
Samuel, was the last of the line. He was elected in
1776, the year in which the charters of the Troki
sectarians were confirmed for the last time. The
Second Partition of Poland, in 1793, brought the
entire province, including Vilna and Troki, under
the rule of the Russian government, which probably
never recognized the Karaite charters. The political change resulted in reducing the dignity of *Shofet*
to a merely nominal title, and at the assembly which
met in 1806 to elect a small council to look after
communal affairs, that office was not even mentioned. Another effect of the change was that the

Troki congregation no longer exercised any jurisdiction, as it had previously done, over the Karaites in other towns in northern Lithuania, the chief of which were Nowomiasto, Poswol, Poniewiez, Birze and Salaty.

The office of rabbi, or *Hakam*, was not filled as regularly as among the Rabbanites, partly, presumably, because of the lack of qualified candidates, and partly because the *Hazzan* (cantor) was often learned enough in Karaite law and lore to act as teacher of the young and even to compose prayers. The rabbi, who pronounced decisions on dietary and ritual laws, marital matters and questions of the calendar, was usually a member of the triumvirate who directed the affairs of the community. His tenure of office was not limited like that of the secular head. The earliest incumbent was Solomon of Adrianople, who flourished early in the fifteenth century. In the following century a notable *Hakam* was Joseph ben Mordecai (1553). A more distinguished successor was Joseph Malinowski (ben Mordecai), a disciple of the famous scholar, Isaac ben Abraham Troki. Joseph was spiritual leader at the end of the sixteenth and the beginning of the seventeenth century. Apparently after a dispute with his congregation, he went to minister to the sectarians at Luzk. In the first half of the eighteenth century the ecclesiastical head was Solomon ben Aaron, of Poswol, who presided over the Karaite *Bet Din* in Vilna before settling in 1719 in Troki, where he continued in office until his death at an advanced age in 1745. A functionary at the other end of the scale was the *Shoter* (constable), whose duties, like those of a beadle, were to enforce the decisions of the leaders, to announce the *Herem* (ban) in the synagogue against lawbreakers, and to inflict punishment in the courtyard upon anyone who was sentenced to flogging.

The most important scholar produced by the Troki sectarians was Isaac ben Abraham, who engaged in disputations both with Christian theologians and with Rabbanites. He was born in 1533 and in the latter half of the sixteenth century was regarded as the leading Karaite scholar in Lithuania and Poland.[1] Nothing is known of any official status he may have occupied, apart from his acting, when a young man of twenty, as secretary of a communal assembly; but he achieved greater fame than any of the community's long roll of dignitaries through his work, *Hizzuk Emunah* ("Strengthening of Faith"). This book, a defense of Judaism against Christianity, was completed by his disciple, Joseph Malinowski, but was not published for over a century. A disciple of Malinowski, Zerah ben Nathan, wrote to Menasseh ben Israel, some time after 1629, proposing that he should publish it in Amsterdam. The suggestion, however, did not bear fruit, although the book was eventually printed in that city in 1705. Isaac ben Abraham, who died in 1594, also composed some poems, which were embodied in the Karaite

[1] Dubnow, *Weltgeschichte*, vol. VI, p. 381, rather strangely, doubts whether Isaac b. Abraham was a Karaite, a doubt upon which Jacob Mann tartly comments, *Texts and Studies*, vol. II, p. 553.

458

The Jews of Vilna

liturgy. His *Hizzuk Emunah*, before being printed, was widely circulated in manuscript and handed down in various distorted versions as well as in German and Spanish translations.[1] It was a defective version that was included, with a Latin translation, by Johann Wagenseil in his collection of anti-Christian writings, published in 1681 under the title of *Tela Ignea Satanae* ("Satan's Fiery Darts") for the purpose of giving Christians the opportunity of refuting it. It aroused considerable attention in the Christian world, was used by eighteenth century freethinkers in their attacks upon Christianity, and was even quoted with admiring approval by Voltaire.

Apart from his completion of *Hizzuk Emunah*, little else is known of Joseph Malinowski's literary work, except that he wrote some liturgical poems. For a time he was the teacher of Zerah ben Nathan, who was born at Troki in 1580 and acquired a reputation for scholarship. Zerah visited Constantinople in 1618 to extend his studies. He, too, enjoyed the friendship of Joseph Delmedigo, to whom, in 1620, he addressed a letter containing twelve questions relating to mathematics, astronomy and the Cabala.[2] He contributed some prayers to the Karaite liturgy and kept up a learned correspondence with scholars in distant lands. He died in 1657.

The only other scholars worthy of note were Joshua ben Judah, in the first half of the seventeenth century, who was first a *Shofet* and then a rabbi, and

[1] There is an English translation by Moses Mocatta (1851).

[2] The answers were published under the title *Iggeret Ahuz* by Abraham Geiger in his *Melo Hofnayyim* (Berlin, 1849).

composed some prayers; Abraham ben Joshua (born in 1636), who was both a liturgical poet and a physician and wrote medical works both in Hebrew and Latin; and Solomon ben Aaron, at the end of the seventeenth and the beginning of the eighteenth century, who was the author of polemical works, a grammar in dialogue form, and a religious codex in two volumes, entitled *Apirjon* (which is preserved as a manuscript in the Leningrad Library).

The relations between the Jews of Vilna and the sectarians at Troki began very early and followed a fluctuating course. At times they rendered a friendly service to one another, and at other times there were serious recriminations. Before the Jews of Vilna had a cemetery of their own, they took their dead to Troki for burial. Yet, when some of them wished to live in the town, the Karaites angrily objected to the arrival of competitors and even complained to the authorities that their livelihood was imperilled thereby. Nevertheless, after the destruction of the Troki community in 1655 by the invasion of the Muscovites and Cossacks, the Vilna Kahal appealed in 1664 to the Lithuanian *Va'ad* to assist the Karaites in their work of restoration, especially because of the valuable charters they possessed. The Rabbanites also gave help to the sectarians when they fled to Vilna from the plague that afflicted Troki in 1710, although the Karaite leaders murmured at some of the younger members of their community of both sexes for accepting employment as domestics in the homes of the Rabbanites.

It was chiefly in connection with the payment of their taxes to the state that the Karaites were brought into regular relations with the Rabbanites. At first they paid these taxes directly to the government officers. Towards the end of the sixteenth century they were required to remit them through the organization of Lithuanian Jewry; and from the year 1623, when the separate Lithuanian *Va'ad* was constituted, there were official relations between this body and the Karaites for such fiscal purposes.[1] The sectarians originally contributed only their quota of the poll-tax (which the Troki assembly apportioned among the various Karaite settlements in the country), but after the middle of the seventeenth century they were also called upon to bear their share of the general financial burdens of Lithuanian Jewry, which had increased because of the necessity of ransoming Jews from Tatar captivity and maintaining poor refugees, as well as on account of the upkeep of the *Va'ad*. They repeatedly complained, on the ground of poverty, both of the amount of the poll-tax as well as of the additional imposts demanded. Although their quota was considerably reduced in the course of time, representatives of the *Va'ad*, first from Brest-Litovsk and then from Vilna, now and again had to pay visits to Troki to collect the money. These fiscal disputes did not cease until 1765, when, in consequence of the government's abolition of payment by the Jewish community of a general assessment and the imposition

---

[1] J. Mann, *Texts and Studies*, vol. II, pp. 626 ff.

of a poll-tax payable by each member of the population, the Karaites could no longer blame the Rabbanites for the amount that they had to contribute.

Not only in the fiscal sphere, however, did the Karaites come under the control of the Rabbanite *Va'ad*. In consequence of this subordination they also lost a certain measure of independence in communal affairs. Each Karaite settlement was placed under the authority of the nearest important Kahal with its *Bet Din*, so that from 1643 the Vilna Kahal regularly asserted its authority over the sectarians of Troki in matters of litigation. In that year the Kahal had a conflict with the *Shofet* Nisan ben Joseph, because he had pronounced a ban against a sectary who invoked their intervention. The Vilna Kahal thereupon annulled the ban, and threatened to proclaim one against the *Shofet* himself. They pointed out that his predecessor, Ezra ben Nisan, had accepted their ruling. The sequel to this dispute has not been handed down. On the other hand, the Troki community often lent its charters to the Vilna Kahal, and almost as often complained of the delay in their return. The Kahal needed these documents in their dealings with official bodies, either for the purpose of asserting their civil rights, or for combating a "ritual murder" accusation, or for vindicating the right of Jews to employ Christian servants.

The control of the Vilna Kahal over the sectaries of Troki inevitably lapsed from the time when the system of taxation was changed and the major community was no longer responsible for its neighbor. The cultural prominence of the Karaites had

long faded away, and their charters failed to protect
them from a violent attack upon their quarter in
1772 by a number of Polish noblemen, who broke
open the synagogue and damaged its interior. Some
twenty years later the synagogue was destroyed by
fire, and the sectaries of Luzk and the Crimea were
called upon to help in rebuilding it.

Under Russian rule the Karaites secured exemption from all the manifold hardships and disabilities
to which Jews were subjected. In 1853 the sectaries
of Troki even sought permission from the government not to call themselves Jews any more, but
"Russian Karaites of the Old Testament Faith,"
because "they rejected the Talmud, and were distinguished from the Jews by their mode of life,
industry, calm, exemplary honesty, and loyalty to
the tsar." The government, after deliberating for
ten years, granted them this permission, which they
retained until the end of the tsarist regime. Their
attitude to the Rabbanites had become increasingly
hostile. About the middle of the nineteenth century
they insisted upon their expulsion; but after the
lapse of a couple of years the Rabbanites were
allowed to return and live in peace.

2.   TROKI IN THE PRESENT

A visitor to Troki at the present day will find that
mechanical progress, even in this part of Eastern
Europe, appears to have overlooked the little town.
It has not yet been linked up with any city by a
railway, and a journey from Vilna, which has to be

made in a small motorbus along a rough and dusty road, is apt to be more adventurous than enjoyable. But the discomfort of the trip is well repaid when, after being driven across a wooden bridge into the main street, one can gaze upon the idyllic charms of an island retreat. For Troki is surrounded by a circular lake, on which there are pleasure boats and fishing keels; and, though the prevailing peace seems incapable of disturbance, it is ensured by the water-police, athletic young fellows clad in white and blue uniforms, with round white hats. The entire population scarcely exceeds five hundred families, of which a hundred are Jewish and a hundred are Karaite, while the rest consist of Russians, Poles and Tatars.[1] The Karaites do not show any friendship towards the Jews. They are mainly vegetable gardeners, who convey their produce every morning to the market in Vilna, and may be met on the country road in the afternoon returning in their long rumbling carts. The Jews are artisans and shopkeepers. They also provide the fishermen, who have a cooperative society, which pays the local authority an annual rent for the right to exploit the beautiful lake.

Most of the Karaites live in small, one-story houses of timber, on the principal street, Kowenski Ulica, so called because it leads to Kovno. In appearance they differ strikingly from the Jews. Though they are mainly dark, they have the Tatar physiognomy; while some of them, especially the

[1] The author visited Troki in the summer of 1932.

girls, present a fair type. Their synagogue, which is also situated on this street, is a small structure of simple design, which has replaced an earlier building. It is approached by a path leading from an iron gate, flanked on either side by brick columns, on which is inscribed in Hebrew lettering and Arabic numerals the date of construction — 1894. Its cupola was originally surmounted by a Shield of David, but the removal of this emblem was ordered some ten years ago by the local *Hakam* as smacking too much of traditional Judaism.[1] The offending symbol, however, still remains on the iron gate, from which it could hardly be removed without causing a conspicuous blemish.

The interior of the synagogue is somewhat similar in plan to that of an orthodox house of prayer, with a gallery for women, except that there is no raised platform for the cantor, who has only a small reading-desk on the floor. A Turkish carpet covers the gangway leading to the Ark of the Torah at the upper end; but no one may advance more than a few feet without taking off his shoes, for the ground is considered sacred.

The Ark is draped with a red plush curtain Above it, on one side, are the initial words of the Ten Commandments in gilt lettering; and on the other side are twin tablets with the complete text of the Com-

---

[1] It is interesting to note that one of the earliest references to the *Magen David* is in a work *Eshkol Hakofer* by the famous Karaite scholar, Judah b. Elia Hadassi, who lived in Constantinople in the middle of the 12th century.

mandments in Hebrew. The Ark contains only one
scroll of the Torah, for at the outbreak of the World
War of 1914–18 all the other Hebrew scrolls, together
with many parchment manuscripts, were sent to
Moscow for safekeeping. The solitary scroll is
taken out of its receptacle every Sabbath and opened
on the cantor's desk, but the worshippers who are
called to its presence are unable to decipher the
unpunctuated script and read their portion from
a printed Pentateuch. The Karaite prayer-book,
printed in Vilna in 1863, differs radically from the
orthodox Hebrew liturgy, and the *tallit* is likewise
different from that worn in the Rabbanite synagogue, as it is more like a scarf and has, instead of
fringes, a blue thread emerging from a cluster of
white ones.

In one important principle the Karaites have
departed from the teaching of their founder, for
they have light — even electric light — on the
Sabbath. They defend this innovation on the ground
that the biblical prohibition — "ye shall kindle no
light in your dwelling places" — does not apply to
their house of prayer, for this is not a dwelling place.
They have a large cemetery, situated about a mile
away, which is reputed to be five hundred years
old, though it contains no tombstones that can boast
of such antiquity. Most of those I saw were of the
nineteenth century: many were of black marble,
with Hebrew or Russian epitaphs in gilt lettering,
and there were also several family vaults with black
marble columns. A peculiar sanctity seemed to

cling to the place, for pious Karaites in Vilna always express a particular wish to be buried in its soil rather than in that of the great city.

The Jewish synagogue, which is in another part of the town, presented a striking contrast to the Karaite place of worship both in its lack of neatness and also in the obvious hard wear to which it was subjected by the devout members of the local community. There is a schoolroom adjoining it, where a teacher of the *Agudat Israel* shade of orthodoxy gave instruction to a mixed class of boys and girls.

3. THE SECTARIES IN VILNA

The settlement of the Karaites in Vilna is comparatively modern and does not number more than forty families. Their synagogue, situated in a fine residential quarter, is a handsome building of white stone, erected as recently as 1923. It is semi-Moorish in design and is crowned with a cupola, which is surmounted by an iron circle containing the initial words of the Decalogue in two columns. The interior is in general like that of the synagogue at Troki, but rather more ornate. There are rich carpets of Oriental design in front of the Ark; while on either side of it, in an alcove, lies a bright red silk covering, beneath which, so the cantor told me, is simply a Hebrew Pentateuch. Facing the Ark stands the cantor's reading-desk, and on either side of this is a comfortable armchair, one for the cantor himself and the other, somewhat more ornate, for the *Hakam*. Aloft there is a gallery for women, where they can easily hear but not easily be seen.

The cantor, a middle-aged man, with slight black beard and mustache, and high cheek-bones, wore a black tight-fitting robe bound by a dark blue sash, and topped by a round black hat. He told me that the synagogue was supported partly by the members of the Karaite community and partly by the government. Besides the local congregation there were also small groups of the sect at Halicz and Luzk. They maintained that they were not Jews by race, but Tatars. Their Hebrew prayer-book, which I examined, contained many prayers in the Tatar dialect, but they spoke Polish among themselves. Their religious head was invited to all important official functions held by the government and the local authorities, and I was told (though not by the cantor) that he was not at all particular about the food that he ate. This indifference even to biblical prohibitions seemed to have resulted from declining contact with the traditional form of the Law of Moses, for the scroll was for the most part kept safe in its repository and was not brought to light except on special occasions, the readings for the Sabbath taking place, as in Troki, from the more convenient text of the printed book.

I remarked to the cantor that the number of Karaites had now dwindled to such an extent that it appeared to be only a matter of time before they would become as few as the Samaritans and perhaps have a similar struggle for existence. He thereupon replied that there were 300,000 Cossacks on the

Volga who were also faithful to the Karaite doctrine. But inquiries made afterwards in other circles convinced me that this figure was a fantastic exaggeration, and that whatever Karaite Cossacks there might have been before the first World War had, in consequence of the changed conditions, most probably shed their Karaism.

CHAPTER XXI

EPILOGUE

How doth the city sit solitary,
That was full of people!
How is she become as a widow!

She weepeth sore in the night,
And her tears are on her cheeks.

Lamentations, 1.1–2.

THE second devastating war launched upon Europe within a quarter of a century by the unscrupulous aggression and overweening ambition of Germany, bringing enslavement, desolation, and distress to so many countries, and entailing unspeakable suffering for millions of Jews, affected the fate of Vilna radically and ruinously. From September 19, 1939, when the city was seized by the Russians without resistance, its inhabitants anxiously wondered whether the change of regime would become permanent. They had not long to wait. Three weeks later, on October 10, the Russians announced that they would cede the Vilna district to the Lithuanians, although it was not until October 27 that the Russians actually withdrew and the cession was effected. Under the rule of the Lithuanians the people breathed more freely and the Jews enjoyed a feeling of comparative relief such as they had not known before. But this condition was destined to

prove only transitory; for after eight months it
came to a sudden end. The Russians, watching the
irresistible advance of the Germans into Norway
and Denmark, Holland and Belgium, and the
northern half of France, resolved upon counter-
action. In the summer of 1940 they recovered
possession not only of Bessarabia (together with
Northern Bukowina), but also of the Baltic States —
Lithuania, Latvia, and Estonia. On June 15, 1940,
the Lithuanian Republic was occupied by the Russian troops, and one month later formally incorporated within the Soviet Union. Thus, after the
lapse of twenty-five years, the city of Vilna, which
had been lost to tsarist Russia by the first World
War and had then undergone so many changes of
government, was brought back under the rule of
Russia by the second World War. But only for
twelve months, for on June 24, 1941, the Germans
were again in control of the city and of all the
surrounding country.

Within the brief period from the capture of the
city by the Russians in September 1939, until they
retook it in the following June, the Jews underwent
a medley of emotions and experiences, in which
anxiety alternated with hope, and relief with despair. Before the city was ceded to the Lithuanians,
the Russian soldiers bought freely whatever they
needed, especially clothing, tea, sugar and other
comestibles, thus depleting the local stocks. Besides,
the Russian authorities themselves requisitioned
considerable material. The result was seriously to
affect the economic position both of large numbers

of Jews and of the community as a whole, and to aggravate severely the main problems with which both the municipal and the Jewish authorities had to deal — the relief of a great host of refugees. The city of Vilna, which had been a place of refuge so often in its checkered history, was now called upon once again to serve as an asylum to those who had fled from the new dangers. At least 25,000 people swarmed or smuggled themselves into the city from districts which had fallen into the hands of either the Germans or the Russians, and of that number some 15,000 were Jews. These fugitives included about one thousand *Halutzim* (young Zionists of both sexes who had been training with a view to settlement in Palestine), and a large number of students and teachers from a dozen talmudical academies in Poland. They also included many Jews who had been expelled at the point of the bayonet from Nazi-occupied Poland to the no-man's land dividing it from Lithuania, and who were admitted across the guarded frontier only upon the assurance of the Jewish relief committee that they would be supported. A number of prominent men, both Zionists and socialists, had been taken away by the Red Army before it made its first withdrawal from Vilna. On the other hand, some thousands of Jews, free from any ideological prepossession, and anxious to secure a livelihood, accepted the invitation of the Soviet authorities to follow them into Russia.

Once the Lithuanian government was in undisturbed control of the Vilna district, systematic measures were taken for the relief of the refugees. Under its auspices a co-ordinating committee was formed, consisting of representatives of the American Jewish Joint Distribution Committee, the American Red Cross, the Commission for Polish Relief, and the Lithuanian Red Cross, while the government itself gave a subsidy equal to fifty per cent of all the funds received from abroad. The British government, too, provided assistance in the form of medical supplies which were not available in the country and which were brought by airplane. Nor was any discrimination shown on the ground of race or religion; for a number of Polish refugee journalists, including some notorious anti-Semites, were housed and fed by the Joint Distribution Committee. So far as the Jews were concerned, the task of providing relief was seriously aggravated by the fact that not only the 15,000 refugees but also the great majority of the local community of 60,000 souls were in urgent need of support. The relief committee therefore devoted its efforts to reducing the swarm of refugees, partly by dispersing a certain proportion among the provincial districts, and partly by expediting emigration in whatever direction was practicable. The Zionist leaders who had escaped from Warsaw, with the cooperation of the local Zionists, organized training centers for the refugee *Halutzim*, so that these might be sent to Palestine with a minimum of delay. The Soviet authorities, after first refusing, granted visas for the transit through Russia of those with certificates for Palestine; but the efforts of Jews to migrate to other countries were frustrated by the refusal of travel agencies to sell tickets to persons between the ages of eighteen and fifty.

The plight of those remaining in Vilna, although mitigated by the relief agency, was anything but enviable, for, on January 21, 1940, a decree was issued prohibiting the refugees to obtain work, to start their own enterprises, or to engage in any form of political or organizational activity. Moreover, they were exposed to anti-Semitic attacks. The "Endeks," who had not yet learned what evil had been wrought to their own country by Nazi practices, organized anti-Jewish riots, under the pretext of protesting against the increased price of bread, both in Vilna and other cities. The first of these riots, on October 31, 1939, was checked only by the arrival of troops and tanks, but not before fifty Jews had been injured, shops plundered, and a Lithuanian policeman killed. A Jewish deputation from Vilna hurried to Kovno and was assured by the Premier, Jonas Cernius, and the Minister of the Interior, Kazys Stucas, that any further disorders would be firmly suppressed by the police. Although one Polish nationalist was, indeed, sentenced to death and another to fifteen years' imprisonment for participation in the riots, further anti-Jewish assaults took place some weeks later. Disorders continued for some time: a synagogue was wrecked in a suburb of Vilna on March 26, 1940, and two culprits were arrested.

The attitude of the Lithuanian government itself, however, was one of gratifying tolerance. It issued a manifesto in Yiddish to the Jews of Vilna, guaranteeing them equality of rights. It formally recognized the legal status of the *Kehillah*. It approved the appointment of a Jew as vice-mayor. It allowed the *Vilner Tageblatt* and two other Jewish papers to resume publication. Four streets in the city were renamed in honor of the popular Jewish writers, Mendele Mocher Seforim, Perez, Dick, and the distinguished Jewish communal worker, Dr. Shabad. The Lithuanian minister in Moscow was instructed to secure the assent of the Soviet authorities to the repatriation of a number of prominent Jews of Vilna who had been deported to Russia. And for the first time in Lithuanian history a government official was tried on charges of anti-Semitism made by fourteen non-Jewish colleagues. No wonder that the Jews in Vilna, both the regular inhabitants and the refugees, despite their material distress and the occasional hooliganism of the "Endeks," regarded themselves as particularly fortunate when they heard of the slavery, torture and starvation of their fellow-Jews under the Nazis. No wonder that hundreds of Jews who had been caught in the German trap risked life and limb in their attempts to escape to the city of refuge, for there, at least until the Nazi invasion of the western countries, it was still possible to keep in touch with the outside world and even to reach it. No wonder, too, that as month followed month, they began to indulge in the hope that they would be spared any further political upheaval.

This seemingly idyllic state of affairs came to an

early end. The Germans' victorious march into Western Europe stimulated a counter-move on the part of the Russians in Eastern Europe, with the result that the Lithuanian Republic, after having been allowed to enjoy the possession of Vilna for eight months, was absorbed (together with Latvia and Estonia) in the Soviet Union. This change of regime had a very profound and unsettling effect upon the Jewish community of Vilna, both economically and spiritually. True, the rights of citizenship, in accordance with Soviet policy, were granted to all persons who had been resident in the country since September 1, 1939, thus including a goodly proportion of the population of the city who had hitherto been without civic rights. True, the offices of the Jewish community were allowed to continue functioning in the interests of social welfare, and a Jewish labor leader, Solomon Gavenda, was elected a vice-mayor. But the characteristic and distinguishing features of Jewish life in the famed city were abolished; the pillars of its sacred traditions were shattered. Its elaborate religious organization, which had flourished for centuries, was disrupted. All forms of expression of Jewish nationalism were banned and suppressed. All Zionist societies and kindred bodies were dissolved. The Palestine Immigration Office was closed. Even the Yiddish papers had to cease, though a successor was soon provided in the shape of a Communist daily.

Nevertheless, however harassing the Jews may have found their new mode of life under the Soviet dispensation, it seemed to them almost heavenly

by comparison with the torments of hell which they
had to endure as soon as they came into the grip
of the Nazis. On June 22, 1941, without warning,
Hitler hurled his massed and armored battalions
in full fury against the whole length of the new
Russian frontier. Two days later the German army
was in control of Vilna and of a large area surrounding it, and from that date began the martyrdom of
the Jewish community, which reached dimensions
unparalleled in its history. All the sufferings which
had been inflicted upon the Jews in Western Poland
were now visited upon those in Vilna, as in the rest
of Poland, as well as in Lithuania, Latvia and
Estonia. They were treated not merely with a lack
of humanity and justice, which they did not expect
from the paladins of Nordic *Kultur*, but with deliberate and persistent cruelty and methodical and
unbridled barbarism. Hitler's myrmidons were
unscrupulous and thorough in the fulfilment of his
will to exterminate the Jews.

The Jews in Vilna had to endure the whole
ghastly program of Nazi savagery, which had
already been applied in so many places in Eastern
Europe, and which was far more malignant than
that meted out to the Poles. Assault and pillage,
vandalism and sacrilege, imprisonment and murder,
were the order of the day. Many were seized and
shot or hanged on the charge that they had given
help to the Soviet army or that they were Bolsheviks.
All who survived the first outburst of ferocity were
robbed of whatever property they still had and
left with only some trifling belongings. Rabbis were

subjected to special indignities and ill-treatment.
Their beards were shorn off, and they were brutally
beaten. The entire Jewish population, which had
increased with refugees to over 80,000 souls, were
confined in two ghettos, the old one in the neighborhood of the *Schulhof*, and a new one in the Bakshta
quarter. There they were treated like slaves, condemned to starvation rations and denied fuel and
medical drugs, so that, with the additional evils of
overcrowding and defective sanitation, they were
a prey to epidemics. They had all — even children — to demonstrate their Jewish identity by
wearing a white band marked with the "Shield of
David," a practice based upon the mediaeval yellow
badge, which was imposed with severe penalties upon
the Jews in all Nazi-dominated countries. Any
attempt to escape from the ghettos, which were
strictly guarded, was followed by execution. Thousands were seized and drafted to forced labor, with
no regard to their physical fitness. They were
marched in serried ranks to the scene of their toil
by soldiers who used whips or rifles to egg them on
to finish their task in the shortest time. They were
employed on day and night shifts to complete the
rapid conversion of the Russian to the German
railroad gauge from Vilna to Minsk, as well as on the
construction of roads and fortifications; and in consequence of brutal maltreatment, hunger, and ex-
haustion, scores died daily.

By the end of January 1942, it was reported in
Polish circles in London that, since the German
occupation, over 30,000 Jews had disappeared from

Vilna — half of them transported to the labor camps on the East European front and the remainder either interned or executed. Appalling as this report was, it was entirely overshadowed by another far more horrible a few months later. A fugitive from Vilna, who had escaped on May 25 and made his way to Gdynia, from where a Swedish ship brought him to Stockholm three weeks later, related that he had been the witness of a wholesale slaughter of Jews. After the declaration of the so-called autonomous status of the Baltic States at the end of April, he said that special Lithuanian police began persecuting the Jews and the Poles. All the Jews in the city were herded into the Bakshta Ghetto, then arrested in batches and sent with their belongings to the local prison. From May 7 began the transportation to their death of these innocent and helpless victims of Nazi sadism. They were driven at sunset in trucks — men, women, and children alike — to the suburbs of Ponary, where they were machine-gunned. Night after night, for fourteen days, these mass butcheries continued until a total estimated at about 60,000 had been exterminated. Some 20,000 Jews, who were still regarded as useful, including doctors, scientists, and technical workers, were spared.[1] Terrible as was the fate that thus befell the

---

[1] *Evening Standard*, London, June 16, 1942. It is naturally impossible to check the accuracy of these figures. According to Dr. I. Schwarzbart, member of the Polish National Council, out of a Jewish population of 65,000 in Vilna, 50,000 were slaugh-

majority of the Jews in Vilna, and exaggerated
though the number of victims may appear, the
outrage was unfortunately paralleled by the calamities that overtook many scores of other Jewish
communities in Eastern Europe in the course of the
invasion of the German vandals. The silence that
the German government has consistently preserved
concerning the many reports published in the
western world of mass murders of Jews by the Nazi
soldiery can be regarded only as a tacit confirmation
of their substantial truth.

So the story of the Jews in Vilna, which began
with the dream of Gedymin, closes with a horrible
nightmare — with a scene of bloodshed and barbarity, beside which the massacres of Chmielnicki
and the pogroms of the tsarist "Black Hundreds"
pale into insignificance. The sylvan outskirts of the
city, so often compared to the picturesque land-
scape of Switzerland, were converted into a vast
reeking shambles, from which the moans of dying
Jews rose to Heaven, while those still left alive
walked in daily expectation of being doomed to share
their fate.

Will the glorious traditions of the "Jerusalem of
Lithuania" ever be renewed? Will the Jews ever
rise again from the desolation and devastation
around them, rebuild their ruined lives, and restore
their shattered community? It would be hazardous,

tered by the Germans and Lithuanians, in the Ponar mountains,
over a period from November 1941.

and perhaps idle, though natural, to indulge in the
consolation of pleasant prophecy, and yet the
accumulated experiences of a long and eventful
past counsel hope.

> *Knowest thou not this of old time,*
> *Since man was placed upon earth,*
> *That the triumphing of the wicked is short,*
> *And the joy of the godless but for a moment?*
>
> Job, 20.4–5.

However dense the gloom that has fallen upon
Jewish Vilna, however sad and sick its remnant of
thinkers and scholars, of writers and teachers, who
may perhaps still pace the cloistral seclusion of the
Synagogue Courtyard, the spirit that has reigned
in its midst during four hundred years and more of
creative and idealist activity will not soon be
quenched. The memories of its long roll of illustrious
sons, who have enriched the annals of Israel with the
wealth of their works and the pattern of their lives,
and inscribed their names on the scroll of Time in
imperishable letters, will remain a source of comfort,
of pride and of inspiration to their people for countless generations.

SUPPLEMENTARY NOTES

1. THE FOUNDATION OF THE COMMUNITY

CHAPTER I, PAGE 3

The date of the actual foundation of the Jewish community of Vilna is wrapped in some obscurity, which even Israel Klausner, the latest local historian, has not attempted to clear up. Although the Russian historians, Narbutt and Bialinsky, maintained that there was a considerable settlement by the middle of the 14th century, the evidence upon which their view was based is unknown. Their claim, supported by some Jewish writers, was carefully examined by Sergei Berschadski, another Russian historian, who made a thorough scrutiny of all the Vilna archives and stated that he could not find any evidence of a congregation having existed before the middle of the 16th century. The results of his investigations were published in *Litowskije Jewrei* ("The Jews of Lithuania"), St. Petersburg, 1883, and (the period 1595–1649) in *Voskhod* 1886, 10–11, and 1887, 5–8. Berschadski's conclusion (which is accepted by another local historian, Baer Ratner, see *Jewish Encyclopaedia*, X) is supported by some scattered references in various Hebrew writings, of which the most important is the following passage in Responsum no. 4 of R. Solomon Luria of Lublin (commonly called *Maharshal*, 1510–1573):

> We, the undersigned, hereby certify and witness with our signatures that, whereas we have been chosen to decide the controversy which has taken

place at Vilna, between R. Isaac ben Jacob and R. Jonah ben Isaac, in the matter of the taxation of Polotzk, and whereas the disputant parties appeared before us, and the aforesaid R. Jonah has given to the aforesaid R. Isaac security in behalf of R. Abraham ben Jacob and his brother, R. Menahem . . .

Signed in the city of Vilna, on the last day of the week, 7th Shebat, in the year 5316 (1556):

Menahem b. Eliakim Trivush
Meshullam b. Yehiel
Meshullam b. Judah

Although there is no mention of these three rabbis in any other rabbinical writing, the names of the litigants, R. Jonah b. Isaac, R. Abraham b. Jacob, and his brother Menahem, are mentioned in the official records, and are cited by Berschadski (*Russko-Yevreiski*, No. 69) as tax-farmers for certain localities, appointed by King Sigismund II in 1556.

In the Responsa of R. Joel ha-Levi Sirkes, 2nd collection (Koretz, 1785), the closing paragraph 75 has the following:

The above is the testimony given before us by Jacob b. R. Menahem Kaz. Signed in the city of Vilna, on the 4th day of the week, 23rd Tammuz, in the year 5323 [1563].
Jonathan ben R. Samuel, Eliezer ben R. Joel, Menahem ben R. Samuel Margolis.

According to Finn and Noah Maggid Steinschneider, the first rabbi of Vilna was Abraham Segal, who lived in the latter part of the 16th and at the beginning of the 17th century.

2. THE BLOOD LIBEL BALLAD

CHAPTER III, PAGE 54

The Yiddish ballad on the martyrs of the "ritual murder" accusation in 1690 has been preserved in a single copy in the Bodleian Library, Oxford. It consists of eight pages, the first of which, containing a descriptive title of the ballad, gives Amsterdam as the place of publication, but without a date. The ballad is bound together with several other little works, mainly Hebrew prayers and pamphlets, which were printed in places as diverse as Prague, Frankfort, and Venice, all dating from the 16th century. The entire volume, bound in leather, is only 6x4 inches, about half-an-inch thick, and is secured by a metal clasp (the Press Number is Opp. 8°.556.7). Dubnow refers to the copy of the ballad in the Bodleian as a "booklet," which is, strictly speaking, not correct.

The description on the title page, which is quaintly phrased and partly rhymed, states that the ballad was composed in the form of an acrostic upon the Hebrew alphabet, used twice over, and that the names of the three martyrs, R. Yehezkiel, R. Moses, and R. Abraham ("may the Almighty avenge their blood!") are introduced therein. The ballad is in rhymed strophes of four verses, each strophe beginning with a letter of the alphabet. The reason why the alphabet was used twice, runs the explanation, is that it contains 22 letters, and twice 22 makes 44. Now this number is indicated in Hebrew by the letters *Mem Dalet*, which, when reversed, form the word *Dam*, which means "blood." "Thus," says the anonymous poet, "the Torah that comes out of the alphabet shall intercede before the Divine Presence for the pure blood of the mar-

tyrs that was shed. And all slanders shall cease from
Israel. Amen."

The complete text of the ballad has been reprinted by
Dr. M. Weinreich in his book *Shturmvint*, pp. 201–220
(Vilna, 1927).

3. THE RIGHTEOUS PROSELYTE

CHAPTER IV, PAGE 74

The adoption of Judaism by the Polish nobleman, Count
Valentin Potocki, in the earlier half of the 18th century,
was all the more remarkable in view of the intolerance and
hostility towards Jews generally displayed at the time by
members of the Polish aristocracy, and in view, particularly, of the dreadful penalty it entailed. According to one
version of the story, Potocki and his friend Zaremba set
out from Poland for Paris together; according to another,
they first met and became attached to one another in
Paris. After Potocki went to Rome, to make sure that
he would be acting rightly in adopting the Jewish religion,
Zaremba returned to Poland, where he married the daughter of a rich nobleman. A few years later his conscience
pricked him regarding the vow he had taken with
Potocki to become a Jew. He therefore went with his wife
and young son to Koenigsberg, from where they sailed to
Amsterdam, and there all three were accepted into the
Jewish faith. But nothing is known of a subsequent meeting between Potocki and Zaremba.

The discovery of the "righteous proselyte" by the
Polish authorities was due to a comparatively trivial incident. While Potocki was studying a sacred book in the
Bet ha-Midrash at Ilye, a townlet some miles from Vilna,
he was disturbed by a little boy who was playing about
and making a noise, and as the youngster refused to be

quiet or to leave and even became impudent, Potocki took him by the ear and put him outside. He is said to have remarked at the time that a boy who misbehaved like that could not be a real Jewish child and would probably be baptized later. The boy immediately hurried to his father, a tailor, who was so indignant at the implied reflection upon his child's paternity and religious fidelity that he went posthaste to the local squire and betrayed the identity of the "righteous proselyte." When the latter heard of the tailor's act he fled some miles to a village inn. Afraid that he would be punished if he concealed him, the innkeeper gave him up to the squire's servants, who took him in shackles to Vilna. The judicial authorities ordered the staunch proselyte to be tortured in the hope that he would return to Christianity; but as neither torments nor the pleadings of his family and friends had any effect, he was burned at the stake. Legend relates that his mother succeeded in obtaining a pardon either from the Pope or from the king, but when it was brought to the jail it was already too late. The Jew, Leiser (Eliezer) Zhiskes, who managed to bribe the executioner and so obtain the martyr's ashes, was said to have been beardless and to have worn Christian clothing for the occasion, so that he was not detected (the entire community having thought it wise on that day to remain indoors).

Legend also relates that when Potocki was arrested he uttered a curse that neither the informer nor any of his descendants for ten generations should be spared some affliction. According to A. Litvin (E. Jeshurin's *Zammelbuch*, pp. 841–7), who visited Ilye about 1930, all the descendants of the tailor had some physical defect: they were either deaf, dumb, or lame, although the duration of the curse had about expired.

Several historians have investigated the Vilna archives as well as the *Pinkas* of the Ilye community. Although they have found no trace of the event, there appears to be no doubt that it occurred. The text of the legend was first printed, under the title *Ma'ase Ger Zedek* ("Story of the Righteous Proselyte") in 1862, at Johannisburg (Prussia), although a Polish translation by Ignatz Kraszewski of the same text was published twenty years earlier. A drama on the theme, *Der Dukus*, written by Alter Kacizne, was performed in Warsaw in 1925 and afterwards in America.

4. THE GHETTO

Chapter VI, page 91

The three streets which formed the outer limits of the officially designated ghetto — namely, Zydowska (Jews'), Jatkowa (Slaughterers'), and St. Michael — were all closely situated to the transport route in mediaeval Vilna, which ran through the Wielka street and its continuation, the Zamkowa, extending from the Ostrobrama Church up to the King's Castle beside the river Vilia. Nearly every house in the Wielka has a yard leading to the Jatkowa, which is parallel to it, and the houses on the opposite side of the Jatkowa have yards and alleys leading to the Zydowska. Thus the entire locality is intersected by numerous yards and passages in a maze-like fashion. Its peculiar design was partly determined by the commercial character of the area. A peasant arriving in the city by the road leading through the Ostrobrama Church would hurry down to the town after having stopped, with bared head, to kneel before the sacred image of the Madonna. He then went in search of the goods that he needed and found a short cut through the various alleys to the ironmongers' shop in the Jatkowa and the leather dealers in the Zydowska.

Although the ghetto was never enclosed within walls, its general conformation and its dwellings have remained practically unchanged. Every house is still called to this day by the name derived from some ancient owner, and the present inhabitants of the quarter can seldom state the number of a house. Of the cellars existing beneath several of the houses, the most notorious is in "Reb Leizer's Hof," which consists of three subterranean floors: the first, or upper-most, having been occupied by a baker's family; the second by an orphans' nursery; and the third by a solitary lunatic. Another cellar, with latticed windows, in the "Kalches Hof," is believed, according to a local tradition, to have once been the prison of the Kahal in mediaeval times.

A revolutionary change in the condition of the ghetto was brought about in 1861, when it was officially declared to be abolished and the Jews were legally permitted to live in any part of the city. There was then a general urban development resulting from the economic progress in Russia and from the building, in that year, of the first railway connecting the city with the outside world. The various business firms moved to the vicinity of the railway station, while their owners sought more comfortable and hygienic dwellings in other quarters, their places being taken by the poorest element in the community. Among those born within the ghetto area were the sculptor Antokolski, the communal leader Dr. Zemah Shabad, and the journalist Abe Cahan. The period of relative prosperity that had previously characterized the ghetto was locally termed that of "the golden brick." A further stage in its decline was due to the World War of 1914–18, when the evacuation of the city by the Russians drained the locality of the remaining well-to-do people, their abandoned homes being occupied by the war's victims of other towns and by many who escaped from the pogroms in the Ukraine. The area has for the most part degenerated into a slum which harbors the beggars and the underworld.

5. THE KLAUSEN

CHAPTER VI, PAGE 108

The Klaus, which is (or, after the devastating effects of the second World War, shall one say "was"?) a characteristic institution of most Jewish communities in Eastern Europe, probably reached its highest efflorescence in Vilna. It was a combination of house of prayer and house of study, in which all the time not needed for prayer was devoted to the study of the Talmud or other rabbinical literature. Only in a minority of cases were the students men training for the vocation of rabbi; for the most part they were students for love of the sacred lore, to which they applied themselves with remarkable zeal and concentration. Many of them were engaged in business or manual trades during the day and were thus able to "learn," as the expression went, only in the evening; others, who were supported by some charitable society, pored over the talmudical tomes day and night. Some studied under the guidance of a teacher or *Rosh Yeshibah* (principal of the academy); others studied in couples, in the interest of mutual help in the unravelling of knotty passages; and others again ploughed their lonely furrow. Most of them, at night, used candles to illumine the island of text surrounded by a sea of commentaries; and some even slept in the Klaus on a hard bench, from which they rose at dawn, eager to resume, with renewed zest, where they had left off the previous midnight.

In Vilna, at the time of the annexation by Soviet Russia, there were over a hundred Klausen, many of which belonged to the members of a particular trade. Thus, there were separate Klausen for the bakers of white bread and for the bakers of brown bread, for glaziers and woodchoppers, for drapery sellers and skin-dealers, for shopkeepers and shop assistants, for tailors and cap-makers, butchers and fishmongers, furriers and skin-dressers, carters and candlestick-makers, window-cleaners and water-drawers, painters and sign-writers, musicians and bookbinders, saddlers and embroiderers. Each Klaus had its wardens and various societies for the study of particular subjects, and there was a separate teacher (*Rebbe*) for each subject, e.g., the Scriptures, the Talmud, the Mishna, the Midrash, the *Shulhan Aruk*, and so forth. Each Klaus also had its preachers, who discoursed on the Sabbath evening in the winter or the Sabbath morning in the summer; and some supported three or four teachers, each of whom was a specialist in his subject. In many of them there was a collection box, by means of which large sums were obtained.

Some Klausen were named after famous rabbis who had prayed and studied in them, like that of the *GeRA* (Gaon Rabbi Elijah) or of R. Israel Ginzberg, the teacher of Professor Chwolson and Kalman Schulman; some were named after their personal founders, like *YeSoD* or Strashun; others were called after the societies responsible for them, like that of the gravediggers or of "hospitality to wayfarers;" others again after the suburb in which they were located, like that of Zaretzie, where R. Israel Salanter lectured to forty picked students (called the

Fertziglach—("forty-lets"), who, in their desire to escape being seized for military service, married but continued their studies in pious seclusion. A few Klausen were known by a double name, like that of the beadles', which was also called by the name "Devorah-Esther," a woman of exemplary piety and charity, who plied the humble trade of a hawker in cakes and saved enough to pay for the rebuilding of the house of study.

6. THE COMMUNAL DISPUTE

CHAPTER VIII, PAGE 138

The latest and fullest account of the dispute about Rabbi Samuel ben Avigdor, which developed into a communal battle-royal, is by Dr. Israel Klausner. In his *Vilna bi-Tekufat ha-Gaon* (Jerusalem, 1942) he has devoted to this inglorious episode nearly 250 out of 300 pages, and lavished upon it an abundance of industrious and circumstantial research. The controversy, which began as a struggle for power between the rabbi and the Kahal, gradually developed in bitterness and extent, not only splitting the Vilna community into two warring parties but also disturbing the peace of neighboring communities, and ultimately engaging the attention of the civil authorities and various law courts, with painful results for many of the Jews involved and injurious consequences for the life of the community. The dispute raged for nearly thirty years, from 1762 to 1791, and it underwent such numerous shifts and changes and was crammed with such a multitude of incidents — decisions, judgments, appeals, revised judgments, counter-appeals, arrests, sentences, and imprisonments — that only a summary can be attempted here.

The initial cause of all the trouble was the wish of Rabbi Samuel ben Avigdor to increase his power and prestige, and the determination of the Kahal to thwart him. Ben Avigdor was an unusually wealthy rabbi, who also engaged in commerce (he was styled "the Vilna rabbi and merchant" in a Royal Law Court judgment of 1779), and he became richer still after inheriting considerable property from his father-in-law, *YeSoD*, who died in 1762. It was in that year that the struggle began, as the rabbi was bent upon securing communal positions for his sons and sons-in-law (including the succession to the rabbinate for his son Israel) and to exercise control over the Kahal and the *Bet Din*. After the death of the Vilna *Voivode*, Michael Casimir Radziwill, Ben Avigdor obtained from his son, Carl, on January 24, 1763, a document confirming him in his office and forbidding the Kahal to interfere in matters belonging to his ecclesiastical province. When Carl was deposed and Oginski was appointed *Voivode*, the rabbi got a further confirmation from the latter for 500 gulden; but when Carl returned to the Governorate in 1767, he was no longer partial to the rabbi, but extended favor to him and the Kahal alternately, according to the monetary inducement that he received. The elders of the Kahal decided to try to depose the rabbi by securing statements from various persons accusing him of improper conduct as president of the *Bet Din*, and they were actively supported by most of the *Dayyanim*, who were opposed to his sharing in the legal fees they received. On the strength of the accusations brought against him (such as bribery, wrongfully annulling judgments, and excluding *Dayyanim* from certain hearings), the Kahal deprived him of the right to take part in sittings of the *Bet Din* dealing with disputes between the Kahal and individuals, or with cases between individuals; forbade him to attempt to confer any kind of privilege upon his relatives; declared that he must address any complaint or claim to the local *Bet Din*; and prohibited him from appealing to the civil authorities against the modification of the original terms of his contract of 1750. At a formal session of the Kahal, Samuel ben Avigdor, under duress, promised to comply with the changed conditions of his office.

Despite this promise, the rabbi went to Troki on November 9, 1767, lodged at the Fortress Court a protest against having had to renounce some of the terms of his original contract, and claimed damages. The Kahal thereupon demanded that he must renew his promise to them, failing which they would have the right to depose him. The *Bet Din* approved this decision, and the rabbi was obliged to comply. But, in accordance with the provisions of the constitution of the Lithuanian *Va'ad*, the rabbi invoked the intervention of the Grodno Kahal, which absolved him from the pledge made to his Kahal under compulsion. After a futile attempt to get the matter dealt with by an arbitration board consisting of rabbis of neighboring communities, the Grodno Kahal further decided that the restrictions imposed upon Samuel ben Avigdor were null and void and that the Vilna Kahal must pay him 600 gulden a year for every year that he had been excluded from the sittings of the *Bet Din*. The Vilna Kahal would not accept this judgment and requested the Brisk Kahal to summon Ben Avigdor to a fresh hearing. The Brisk and Slutzk Kahals supported the decisions of Grodno, but Pinsk was against them. Since the Vilna Kahal elected in 1771 contained a majority of the rabbi's friends, they decided to abide by his original contract of 1750, but the following year found a majority of his opponents in the Kahal, who began to agitate against him anew. Thereupon he invoked the intervention of the Slutzk Kahal, who requested the Vilna elders to respect the original contract.

During the next few years Samuel ben Avigdor increased his range of business and his wealth, particularly by visits to Prussia and Russia. In order to strengthen his influence and enhance his prestige in Vilna, he acquired the office of rabbi (by purchase) in Koenigsberg, Orany, and Danzig, without any obligation to minister to those communities; and as Vilna merchants regularly visited those cities he was able to exercise authority over them. In 1777 there was an arbitration in Vilna, which decided that all the terms of the 1750 contract remained in force and the restrictions were annulled. Samuel ben Avigdor was given by the Kahal an I. O. U. for 700 gulden (although more was due to him), on which he was to receive interest until the total amount was paid off; he was to receive his original weekly salary; and if he left the community he was to receive 50 gulden a year for 7 years. His son Israel was appointed a regular *Dayyan* for 15 years, and various privileges were conferred upon his sons-in-law (such as membership of the electoral assembly, *ReHaSh*, without payment, and exemption from communal taxes for a few years). The Vilna Kahal and its rabbi exchanged formal documents confirming the settlement, and the Lithuanian Kahals ratified it. The Vilna elders promised henceforth to support their rabbi in accordance with the original terms of his appointment, and thus, after the struggle had lasted 15 years, Samuel ben Avigdor triumphed.

But four years later the conflict broke out afresh and was conducted with much greater animosity and fury than before, and with the participation of a much larger number of people. Samuel ben Avigdor precipitated the second campaign against him by pressing his financial claims against the Kahal, his business having suffered a decline, and he thus aroused several new opponents, of whom the most active and energetic was R. Abba ben

Zeev-Wolf. A new factor in the controversy was the fact that the populace, especially the artisan class, were on the side of the rabbi, because they wanted his support in fighting against the heavy taxes imposed by the Kahal. The Hasidim were also on the side of the rabbi, who was probably in sympathy with them, despite his official position, as his son-in-law, R. Baruch Mordecai Ittinga, the rabbi in Bobruisk, was a leading Hasid. His partisans included a number of rich men and *Maskilim*, who were opposed to the autocracy exercised by the elders: their leader was R. Simon ben Zeev-Wolf. The Gaon Rabbi Elijah sided with his opponents, as twelve men swore to charges of improper professional conduct against the rabbi (bribery, miscarriage of justice, etc.). In this second phase of the dispute the neighboring Kahals played a minor role, but the Christian authorities, civil and ecclesiastical, played a major part, as the rabbi invoked the help of the bishop, and the Kahal was supported by the *Voivode* and his officials.

The dispute was reopened through the Kahal having to meet the claim of the Piarist Friars to some property, which partly belonged to Rabbi Samuel ben Avigdor. The latter ceded his share on condition that the Kahal would compensate him; but the Kahal did not fulfill the promise to do so. The rabbi, in 1782, insisted upon his claim and got the Slutzk Kahal to summon the Vilna elders to judgment. Thereupon the elders, with the co-operation of the Vilna *Dayyanim*, began collecting statements from various persons, accusing the rabbi of professional misconduct, with a view to deposing him. They were apparently not particular about the truth of the charges, for which in some instances they offered payment. The rabbi therefore sought the protection of Bishop Masalski, a wealthy ecclesiastic, who also engaged in commerce, and who had previously lent him a considerable sum to satisfy a creditor in Koenigsberg. In 1783 the rabbi gave the bishop a promise that he would repay the money in a month out of his professional income; and, as he failed to do so, the bishop summoned both him and the Vilna Kahal to the Fortress Court at Novogrodek, which pronounced judgment against them for 75,000 gulden. The Kahal was obliged to come to a settlement with Samuel ben Avigdor, compensated him for his share of the aforementioned property, but at the same time deprived him of some of his prerogatives.

As the elections of Passover, 1784, resulted in a majority in the Kahal for the opponents of the rabbi, they determined to depose him and collected further accusations against him (including partiality, negligence of study, and indulgence in drink). On Shebat 19, 1875, the Kahal discussed means of getting *ReHaSh* to vote on the question of the rabbi's fitness for office and appointed three of their members to collect the votes. The triumvirate, on Shebat 23, summoned the members of *ReHaSh* individually, without previously informing them of the purpose, submitted the charges against the rabbi, and exercised pressure upon them to vote for his dismissal. A protocol was then drawn up, stating that by a decision of the majority the rabbi had been found unworthy of his office. The Kahal sent two beadles to the rabbi, requesting him to appear before them to receive judgment; but he declined. The Kahal thereupon invited three *Dayyanim* to join them in a formal session, at which they solemnly pronounced the deposition of the rabbi, and afterwards despatched three beadles to the rabbi to inform him of their decision. The Kahal also sent a delegation to the *Voivode* to secure his approval of their act as well as permission to appoint a successor. The principal member of the delegation was R. Abba b. Zeev-Wolf, who himself aspired to the office of rabbi.

Rabbi Samuel ben Avigdor resolved to fight for his position. He also addressed himself to the *Voivode*, who issued a rescript, on March 5, 1785, ordering the Vilna Kahal to appear with the rabbi before the Slutzk *Bet Din*; but as the rabbi did not appear on the date fixed, the *Voivode* appointed a special commission of three Christians, who began to hear the case at the end of March. Besides the Kahal and the rabbi, the populace was also represented (its leading spokesman being R. Simon b. Zeev-Wolf); but, after the proceedings had dragged on for some time, Samuel ben Avigdor declared that he would not appear any more, but would appeal to the *Voivode*. The commission gave judgment for the Kahal; but the *Voivode*, in response to an appeal from the rabbi, quashed the decision of the commission and referred the case to the Slutzk Kahal. As the rabbi's opponents refused to go to Slutzk, the *Voivode* first ordered the litigants to appear before an arbitration tribunal of seven rabbis at Mir, and then appointed a commission of two Christian lawyers to deal with the matter. This legal commission found against the rabbi (who accused them of bribery). The *Voivode*, Carl Radziwill (a rather dissolute character), confirmed the decision of the lawyers on November 28, 1785, removed Samuel ben Avigdor from office, and authorized the appointment of a successor. He issued his written authorization with a blank space in which the name of the new rabbi could be added later, a procedure that was without precedent, and for which he was given the unusually large fee of 2,000 gulden. The recipient of this document was Abba b. Zeev-Wolf, who, until he could be elected rabbi, was appointed "Administrator of Rabbinical Affairs," a position entitling him only to receive the income due to the rabbi and to pay the interest on the loan borrowed by the Kahal to obtain the *Voivode's consens*.

Although his deposition was confirmed by the *Voivode*,

Samuel ben Avigdor was determined to continue the struggle, and therefore went to live in a suburb of Antokol, under the jurisdiction of Bishop Masalski, who recognized him as rabbi of the Jews in that district. The harassed rabbi then lodged a protest against his sentence with the District Court at Troki on December 12, 1785, and the Bishop transferred his debt to Hilary Wichert, who applied to the Royal Court in Warsaw to quash the *Voivode's* judgment, as this would prevent him from recovering the debt. A new development in the feud resulted from the accusation circulated by some members of the Vilna populace that Abba b. Zeev-Wolf had become a Christian some fifty years before and then returned to the Jewish fold, a charge that was entirely without foundation. The Bishop's Court began investigating this charge and summoned both Christian and Jewish witnesses, whereupon Abba b. Zeev-Wolf appealed to the Lithuanian Supreme Tribunal. In revenge for the action against their leading colleague, the Vilna Kahal instigated officers of the *Voivode* to take punitive measures against the principal representatives of the populace. R. Simon b. Zeev-Wolf was arrested, at night on June 6, 1786, and thrown into prison; many partisans of Samuel ben Avigdor hid themselves, and others fled. As a reprisal, officials of the bishop arrested Abba b. Zeev-Wolf four days later. A delegation of the populace, headed by R. Isaac b. Leib, then went to Warsaw and appealed both to the Vice-Chancellor and to the king for protection from the Kahal, and the king issued a rescript on July 7, forbidding the Kahal to prosecute representatives of the populace or to impose any taxes beyond those approved in 1766 by the Liquidation Court. R. Simon b. Zeev-Wolf was released on July 19 and began a more energetic agitation against the Kahal for its abuse of authority and imposing heavy taxation. He cited the Kahal before the Treasury Commission, while the *Voivode*

sued both Kahal and populace before the Royal Court in
Warsaw for ignoring his authority. On November 24,
1787, the Royal Court, which had also had to deal with
the case of Samuel ben Avigdor, confirmed his deposition
and rejected his claims for compensation, but it decided
that he should receive 78 guldens a year for the rest of his
life, besides arrears of salary from February 26, 1785.

The charge of conversion against R. Abba b. Zeev-Wolf
was quashed in the summer of 1787, when Bishop Masalski
sent him a letter, stating that he had given instructions
that no further action be taken against him as there was
no valid evidence in support of the charge. But a few
months later R. Abba had to undergo a further trial. His
son Hirsch, a youth of seventeen, fled from his parents'
home on December 2, 1787, to the Dominican monks in
Vilna and asked to be received into the Christian faith.
He had married at the age of fifteen, and his wife and child
were at Tikotzin. It was a terrible blow to R. Abba, who
still hoped to become Rabbi of Vilna, and he accused
Samuel ben Avigdor's partisans of having been responsible for his son's step; but Hirsch maintained that he had
acted of his own free will and without any material
incentive. Despite efforts made to prevent it, the baptism
of Hirsch took place in the Church of the Dominicans on
January 13, 1788, and he was given the name of Wicenty
Neumann. But ten days later he was kidnapped by
friends of his family, with the help of a young Jewish convert, Kwiatkowski, from Grodno, and taken to Dünaburg
(Dwinsk). The Vilna authorities thereupon arrested R.
Abba b. Zeev-Wolf on the charge of kidnapping, and also
22 other leading Jews, including the Gaon Rabbi Elijah,
to take statements from them regarding the attitude of
the Jewish religion to cases of conversion. The Gaon persistently refused to answer all questions, and after being
in prison during the whole of February 1788, he was re-

leased together with all the others. R. Abba b. Zeev-Wolf, the Gaon, and the others thereupon took action for having been wrongfully arrested; but it was not until after Kwiatkowski was caught in Warsaw, in the following October, that it was proved that they had not taken any part in organizing the kidnapping. Kwiatkowski stated in evidence that he had been taken three times to the Gaon Rabbi. Elijah, who had tried to induce him to return to the Jewish faith and to persuade Hirsch to do likewise. Subsequently, in September 1782, the Lithuanian Supreme Tribunal found a number of persons guilty of some technical offense in connection with the incident, including R. Abba b. Zeev-Wolf, his wife and his son Simon, the Gaon Rabbi Elijah, and several others, and sentenced them to 12 weeks' imprisonment in addition to a fine of 500 gulden. The conditions of their incarceration were rather mild, as they were merely detained in a large house called "the wayfarers' hostel," in which they were allowed to rent a separate room for religious worship. It is doubtful, however, whether the Gaon, owing to his advanced age, was compelled to serve the entire sentence. His name is not included in the list of those who were released on December 12, 1789.

The Lithuanian Supreme Tribunal also dealt later with the slander against R. Abba b. Zeev-Wolf regarding his alleged conversion. On November 24, 1790, it declared the charge entirely unfounded and awarded him 8,000 gulden damages (the costs of litigation), and in August 1791, he acknowledged having received this sum from the priest Krushevsky. His son Hirsch absolutely refused to return to the Jewish fold, and R. Abba's chances of succeeding to the rabbinate were thus irretrievably ruined.

R. Simon b. Zeev-Wolf, together with some other partisans, was again arrested on July 3, 1788, at the instigation of the Kahal, as a reprisal for their taking action

against it before the Treasury Commission; and they were
removed in fetters to the fortress-prison at Nieswicz,
where they were subjected to ill-treatment. While in
prison R. Simon had ample time to reflect upon the Kahal's
abuse of its authority, and when he learned that the Great
Seym of 1789 (which was somewhat influenced by the ideas
of the French Revolution) was considering questions of
constitutional reform and also proposals for revising the
status of the Jewish community, he wrote a pamphlet in
Polish, entitled *The Prisoner at Nieswicz to the Seym with
regard to the need of Jewish Reforms*. In this pamphlet,
which he composed at the end of 1789, when he despaired
of ever being released, he levelled a bitter indictment
against the Kahal, which had continued to abuse its powers
by afflicting the community with burdensome imposts and
failing to hold legal elections; and he urged that the Kahal
should be abolished, that the Jews should merely be permitted to administer their religious affairs themselves, and
that in other respects they should be subject to the general civil laws. Early in January 1790, he was liberated,
together with his fellow-sufferers, and as soon as he was
free he resumed the fight against the abuses of the Kahal
especially in regard to financial matters, in which he had
the effective support of the Treasury Commission.

The final act in the long protracted feud began in the
latter part of 1790, when the Kahal, morally weakened
and financially exhausted, came to a settlement with
Samuel ben Avigdor on the basis of an agreed amount of
damages, and on condition that he should not present any
further claim or demand. The Kahal also promised that
on his death he would be shown the same honor as all
previous rabbis, and that a fitting tombstone would be
placed on his grave. Samuel ben Avigdor also wanted a
promise that R. Abba b. Zeev-Wolf (who had retained the
Voivode's authorization for the appointment of a rabbi)

should not succeed him. Without making such a specific promise, the Kahal decided that no new rabbi should be elected except in accordance with the customary and statutory procedure, no matter whether he already possessed the official *consens* or not. On Tebet 2, 5551 (January 1791), a meeting of *ReHaSh* formally ratified the settlement, and nineteen days later Samuel ben Avigdor was gathered unto his people and called to his final account. After his death a stone was fixed in the place of his seat on the left side of the Ark in the Great Synagogue, which is regarded as confirmation of the tradition that the Kahal enacted an ordinance never again to appoint a president of the *Bet Din*. Nevertheless, in 1836, the Vilna Kahal invited Rabbi Akiba Eger to fill the vacancy, but he declined; and the titular position was not revived until after the first World War.

7. NAPOLEON'S RUSSIAN CAMPAIGN

Chapter XIV, page 263

A remarkable sidelight upon the relations of the Jews of Vilna to Napoleon's ill-fated campaign in Russia is provided by an article by S. Posener, which appeared in *L'Univers Israélite* of August 1934. The writer claims to have discovered in the *Archives Nationales* in Paris reports written by a certain Alexander Facquz de Belem, who had been employed to organize an espionage service among the Jews in Vilna and other districts in support of the Grand Army. Facquz, who is described as a Belgian nobleman by origin and an adventurer by profession, was wanted in 1824 for a number of common frauds, and when the police arrested him, they also seized the copies of the reports written by him in Warsaw twelve years earlier. He had then been engaged by Fouché, the head of the imperial police, although the latter knew that he had formerly been a spy in the Russian service. He was assigned to the Ministry of Foreign Affairs, and accompanied the Grand Army on its eastward adventure. Napoleon stayed in Vilna from June 28 to July 16, 1812, to reorganize his forces and create a local government; but the French army did not leave the city until the following December 10, at the time of the general retreat. It is not known exactly when Facquz arrived in Vilna; he was there at the beginning of November, and held the rank and title of "Lieutenant-Colonel, Secretary of Marshal Berthier, Chief of Staff."

According to the documents found by S. Posener, Facquz undertook to establish in Vilna "a correspondence and observation center," with mobile agents throughout the country. He advised that Jews should, by preference, be engaged for this purpose, as they could more easily travel to all the principal points still occupied by the Russians without arousing any suspicion. Such a center was formed on November 8, 1812, under the name of "L'Agence Juive," a strange namesake of the body provided for, over a century later, in the Palestine Mandate. Facquz writes:

> The Jewish Agency was definitely organized yesterday at 10 in the evening. The three following members of the Kahal are its chiefs: Samuel Klaczki, Seelmanon Urias, and Gerson Jochel. The operations of this Agency remain unknown to the rest of the Jews and even to the other members of the Kahal ... This Agency vows an inviolable attachment to the French cause and promises the greatest secrecy concerning its activities. It recommends the Jewish nation to the benevolence of the Government.

The afore-mentioned trio recommended agents to Facquz, who, according to his own account, dictated instructions to one of the three, which were translated by the latter into Hebrew and handed over, in the presence of Facquz, to an agent, together with a letter of introduction to different Kahals, whose help might be necessary. The travelling agents were to establish "points of information and communication where materials will be found for all travelling agents who would afterwards present themselves." The Agency was to continue to function even after the departure of the Grand Army, and to send communications to Facquz to certain addresses agreed upon. The organizer of this espionage service left Vilna about December 9 for Warsaw, and there, in his last report dated December 22, he wrote that he had not received any letters from his agents. The precipitate retreat of the French army had put an end to this Agency.

The author of the article in *L'Univers Israélite* advances as a reason why the Jews of Vilna refused to render any information service to the French that they were subjected to exactions and extensive requisitions for the benefit of the Grand Army. In the surrounding country districts, including Troki, the Jews were pillaged by the wandering and hungry soldiers, while in Vilna itself, the Kahal, apart from having to allow the synagogues to be used as barracks and to see the cemetery turned into a place of grazing for the soldiers' horses, had to provide foodstuffs, beer and brandy, to the amount of 500,000 Polish florins, another 200,000 florins towards the equipment of hospitals, and a loan of 75,000 florins for the municipality. The Kahal was also called upon by Kosielski, the Commandant of the National Guard in Vilna, to have all members of the community registered for military service, a demand to which it strongly objected on the ground that "no formal order of the Emperor has ever appeared requiring that the

Israelites must be employed in military service, for which they have no aptitude." The Kahal further protested against the entire burden of the upkeep of the army being imposed upon the Jews, who were altogether excluded from the municipal service, whereas in all states under the protection of Napoleon all nations were treated equally. Facquz adds in his report that the Kahal presented itself in a body to him on the night of December 9–10, on the eve of his departure, to reiterate "inviolable attachment" to the French government. Nevertheless, he never heard a word from the Jewish Agency, which apparently evaporated in the night.

S. Posener appears to accept Facquz's story as absolutely trustworthy; but in view of the Belgian's record it is permissible to doubt his veracity. Facqus fails to explain how he made himself understood by the three members of the Kahal, since it is doubtful whether any of them understood French and equally doubtful that he spoke Hebrew or Yiddish. In one place he states that the operations of the Jewish Agency were to be kept secret by the three members of the Kahal, while in his last report he says that the Kahal visited him as a body. He doubtless had to furnish a plausible report to justify his expenditure.

In *L'Univers Israélite* of January 1935, there is another article by S. Posener, in which he discusses at great length the following remarkable passage in the *Histoire du Consulat et de l'Empire* by Thiers:

> Horrible thing to relate: the miserable Polish Jews, who had been obliged to receive our wounded, as soon as they saw the army in retreat, began to throw these wounded through the windows and sometimes to throttle them, thus getting rid of them after having despoiled them. A miserable tribute to offer to the Russians, whose partisans they were.

This history was first published in 1856; and when Thiers was asked, in 1863, by the society of Polish emigrés in Paris, *L'Alliance Polonaise*, to modify the charge contained in this passage in future editions, he declined to do so. S. Posener subjects the charge to a thorough critical examination in the light of numerous French works on Napoleon's Russian campaign written very soon after its débâcle and for the most part based upon records kept by French officers who were in Vilna at the time of the retreat. He shows that the accusation made against the Jews was unfounded, and that the latter were blamed for acts committed by the Cossacks.

Despite the confiscations to which they were subjected, the Jews, who, unlike the Poles, remained for the most part in Vilna as the army approached, behaved very hospitably to large numbers of French soldiers, many of them sick or wounded, whom they lodged and fed in their own homes. But when the Cossacks, in pursuit of the Grand Army, approached Vilna, all who befriended the French soldiers were warned that, if that fact became known, they would be cruelly dealt with by the Russian troops, and that they risked being sent to Siberia. They were therefore urged to put the French guests out of their houses immediately. The Jews, for the most part, acted upon this advice, as also did any Poles who had shown similar kindnesses. When the Cossacks, under Platov, entered the city on December 10, they cut down all French soldiers whom they came across and forced their way into private houses, where they also slaughtered any Frenchmen whom they found. Since many outrages were committed in Jewish houses, rumor, in the prevailing confusion, attributed them to the Jews instead of the Cossacks. The rumor was spread among the ranks of the defeated army, who, suffering from cold, hunger, despair and disease, readily believed any story that reached them in

their bedraggled flight. Hence arose the legend of "Jewish
atrocities." When Emperor Alexander came to Vilna on
December 23 and was informed of what had happened,
he issued orders that those guilty of the atrocities should
be punished. As one might have expected, no Cossacks,
but only some Jews were arrested and executed for a crime
they had not committed. This injustice, added to the
slander, had the effect in many circles of confirming belief
in the legend (*Mémoires du Sergent Bourgogne*, p. 238).

8. THE BEGINNINGS OF ZIONISM

Chapter XVI, page 346

The first Society *Ohabe Zion* was founded in the house
of Elijah Eliezer Friedman, editor of *Ha-Zofeh*, who invited for the purpose his friends, Isaac L. Goldberg,
Michal Uriassohn, Solomon and Albert Vilkuriski, Bezalel
Lipshitz, Issachar Sluzki, Zevi Hirsch Vilkuriski, and S.
Feigenson. The meeting was held in the house of Friedman, because he had written an elegy on the death of
Empress Marie, wife of Tsar Alexander II, and received
two letters of thanks from the government, which were
framed and hung up on a wall, so that if the police made
a sudden entry they would immediately see convincing
evidence of officially acknowledged loyalty. In order
further to avert suspicion, the little group sat round a
table on which were displayed not only glasses of tea,
but also a chess board and some packs of cards. Of the
two directing spirits in the early years of the movement,
Finn represented the religious and Lewanda the political
element. The name of the society was soon changed to
Tikvat 'Aniyim ("Hope of the Poor"), so as to make it
appear a purely philanthropic body. The official positions
held by these two men, Finn as head of the *Zedakah*

Gedolah and Lewanda as head of the Jewish department in the Chancery of the Governor-General, made it impossible for them to participate in a movement resembling anything political. For the same reason neither of them could attend the Kattowitz Conference, the official invitations to which began with the words "With the approval of our dear brethren and lovers of Zion in Vilna." Rabbi Yankele Harif (the *Moreh Zedek*), the appointed delegate, had to turn back from the frontier, as he could not, in his conspicuous rabbinical garb, pose as a commercial traveller for a timber business, the capacity in which it was intended to get him past the frontier officials. The historian, S. P. Rabbinowitz, who travelled to the Conference from Warsaw, met Rabbi Yankele at the frontier to help him across, but had to advise his return. (The memory of Lewanda is perpetuated by the Lewanda Library and Lewanda Street in Tel Aviv.)

The Vilna Zionists showed their practical interest in the resettlement of Palestine by purchasing land there at an early date in the settlements of Gederah, Hederah, and Rishon le-Zion, and by sending K. Z. Wissotzky to investigate the conditions in the settlements. In 1890, as the result of the visit to Vilna of Barzilai Eisenstadt from Palestine, there was formed a secret society, *B'nei Moshe* ("Sons of Moses") for the purpose of speaking Hebrew and studying Jewish history. Its active members included David Notik, Zalman Gurland, Aryeh Naishul, Isaac L. Goldberg, and Benzion Alitar. This society decided to found a girls' school where Hebrew would be taught as a living language, and David Notik was appointed inspector. The school was closed by the authorities, but was reopened in 1893 by the *B'not Zion* under the name of *Yehudiah*. The girls always spoke Hebrew with one another and in the streets, and several of them qualified as teachers. Mrs. Rachel Goldberg was the in-

defatigable manageress and benefactress of the·institution
from 1897 to 1915.

The manner in which invitations to the First Zionist
Congress reached Vilna illustrates the difficulties with
which Theodor Herzl had to cope in establishing his movement. Dr. M. Ehrenpreis (now chief rabbi in Stockholm),
who was one of the secretaries in the Zionist Bureau in
Vienna, had previously written to Ephraim Moshowitzki
in Vilna for data about the life of a certain rabbi who had
flourished there in former times. As Moshowitzki, in
his reply, signed himself "a lover of the people of Zion
and Jerusalem," he was honored by a personal invitation
from Herzl to attend the Congress. Communication having thus been established, further invitations were sent
from Vienna to the address of Moshowitzki, but they were
all suppressed by the Russian postal censor. The Jews
of Vilna subscribed for 6,600 shares in the Jewish Colonial
Trust, when its prospectus was first published in 1898;
and as the bank needed £250,000 with which to begin
operations, Isaac L. Goldberg (who, years later, presented
the site of the Hebrew University in Jerusalem) gave it
a loan of 30,000 roubles (£3,000).

Among the host of workers in Vilna for the Zionist
cause the most militant and adventurous was Michael
Halperin (1860–1920), the son of a rich man. He went to
Palestine in 1885 with a great deal of money, took part
in the establishment of Yesod Hamaaleh and also bought
the land of the settlement Ness Zionah on which to found
a workers' colony. On the day when Ness Zionah was
dedicated, Halperin appeared at the head of his band of
workers, all on horses, with a blue-white flag in his hand,
which he afterwards buried in the soil. He also made a
demonstration at the head of his horsemen in the streets
of Jaffa, singing a Hebrew song: "Raise a flag and banner
for Zion, the banner of the camp of Judah!" He returned

to Vilna penniless in 1894; but four years later went to Palestine again, and returned to Vilna once morè in 1901 and helped to found the Po'ale Zion. He trained thirty young Jews in athletic exercises with a view to fitting them for life in Palestine, and in 1903 organized a Jewish self-defense corps against pogromists. He attended the Sixth Zionist Congress in that year as a delegate for the Po'ale Zion, opposed the East Africa project, and publicly sang for the first time the Zionist workers' anthem, the *Shevu'oh*. He returned to Palestine for the last time in 1906, organized the system of watchmen (*Ha-Shomer*) for the Jewish settlements, and acted as watchman himself. After he had saved one pound, he sent it to an English newspaper to insert the following advertisement: "I, Michael Halperin, shall stretch out my head publicly to be removed by the man who will lend me 50 million dollars if I do not build and establish the Jewish State in the land of Israel with this money in 25 years." Halperin had a restless and tempestuous temperament. He believed that he was descended from King David and longed to see the restoration of the Davidic Kingdom. He spent his last years in the Galilee district, a lonely visionary.

9. THE BANS OF EXCOMMUNICATION

CHAPTER XVII, PAGE 371

The following is the text of the ban proclaimed in the Vilna Great Synagogue on August 26, 1918:

> Order of the *Herem* which was proclaimed in the Great Synagogue of the Holy Community of Vilna, on Monday, Ellul 18, 5678, in the presence of the rabbis of the city and a great congregation.
> Six o'clock, after the *Minhah* prayer. The candles were kindled. Three venerable rabbis ascended to

the Holy Ark. The oldest rabbi put on a *Kittel* (white robe) and praying-shawl. In a few words he explained to them the reason that had made imposition of such a solemn ban necessary, and impressed upon them the enormity of the sin of anyone who transgressed the ban and the punishment that awaited him and his family. The doors of the Holy Ark were opened. The rabbi began in a trembling voice to read this text of the ban:

"With the consent of the Omnipresent and the consent of the *Bet Din* of the rabbis of Vilna, we solemnly declare that we place under the same ban that Joshua invoked against the city of Jericho, and under the same curse wherewith Elisha cursed his servant Gehazi, and under all the bans and curses that have been uttered since the days of Moses our Master until this day, all those Jews, men and women, who will export, for the sake of business, from Vilna and all its suburbs (a) corn and (b) barley, whether as kernels, flour, or groats, and (c) potatoes. The prohibition against export refers to the aforesaid kinds that are now in Vilna, and also to the aforesaid kinds that will be imported into the city, or that will be brought either on carts or by train. Even if the goods are not brought into the city but only sent from a place to Vilna station, then they may not be sent farther either by train or by cart. The ban falls upon the merchants and also upon their agents, upon the buyers, the sellers who sell themselves or their agents, if they know that it is being bought for the purpose of export, also upon the carters who carry such goods and any persons who help them, whether they do the work alone or even if they employ messengers who are not Jews. The ban applies to all Jews, whether they live in our city or come here from another city, whether they are now here or whether they are not now here. And whoever shall transgress this our aforementioned decree 'breaks the fence and a serpent shall bite him.' Cursed be he by the Almighty and cursed in all his ways! His path shall be dark and slippery, and the angel of the Lord shall pursue him. The Lord will not pardon him but will be wroth against that man, and all the curse that is written in the book of the Torah shall lie upon him."

And afterwards the rabbi who pronounced the ban concluded as follows:

"And ye that cleave unto the Lord your God are alive every one of you this day. And He who blessed our fathers, Abraham, Isaac and Jacob, shall bless all this holy congregation together with all holy congregations, excepting him who transgresses this ban. And the Almighty in His mercy shall preserve them and deliver them from all trouble and distress, from all plague and disease, and shall send a blessing and deliverance unto all the works of their hands, and they shall be inscribed and sealed for a good life on the Day of Judgment that is coming unto us for good. And so may it be His will; and let us say Amen."

All the people answered "Amen" in a loud voice, and after that they sounded on the *Shofar* — *Teki'ah*, *Shebarim*, *Teru'ah*, *Teki'ah*. The lights were extinguished.

The order of procedure in the case of the second ban, which was pronounced on November 26, 1918, was the same, except that the ceremony took place at three o'clock in the afternoon and two of the rabbis, each holding a scroll of the Torah, stood on either side of their venerable colleague, who uttered the declaration. It was launched against all who were engaged in the distilling of whisky, or who were in any way connected with its manufacture, either by providing raw materials, utensils, or premises, or by acting as vendors, agents, or carriers; but it allowed a respite of two weeks for the disposal of any liquor already made.

10. THE MORGENTHAU MISSION

CHAPTER XVII, PAGE 381

The mission consisted of Mr. Henry Morgenthau, Brigadier General Edgar Jadwin, and Mr. Homer Johnson. It had been appointed by the "American Commission to Negotiate Peace," which sat in Paris, in 1919. The letter of Secretary Lansing, dated June 30, 1919, stated that the Mission was to make "careful inquiry into all matters affecting the relations between the Jewish and non-Jewish elements in Poland," which would not only involve "the investigation of the various massacres, pogroms, and other excesses alleged to have taken place, the economic boycott, and other methods of discrimination against the Jewish race," but also the discovery of "the reason lying behind such excesses and discrimination with a view to finding a possible remedy," and that it should "evolve some constructive measures to improve the situation which gives concern to all the friends of Poland."

The Mission was in Poland for two months, from July 13 to September 13, 1919. Its report, which was published in full in the *New York Times* of January 19, 1920, provoked a controversy which raged on both sides of the Atlantic for several months. Of the four closely-printed columns of small type, only a paragraph occupying a quarter of a column was devoted to Vilna, confined solely to the incidents of April 19–21. The report was strongly criticized on the ground that it was inadequate, superficial, and in parts even inaccurate; that it betrayed a lack of sympathy with the sufferings of Polish Jewry, a lack of knowledge of the full extent of those sufferings, a lack of courage to apportion the blame for the various outrages, and failure to make suitable recommendations for improving the Jewish position.

I preceded the Morgenthau Mission on a similar investigation on behalf of the World Zionist Organization, and was in Poland from January 1 to February 1, 1919. The Zionist Organization published my *Report on the Pogroms in Poland* in April, 1919; I contributed articles on the results of my inquiry to the London *Times* of February 8 and May 22, 1919, and also delivered a verbal report at a public meeting in the Queen's Hall, London, on April 9, 1919, under the chairmanship of Lord Parmoor. My criticism of the report of the Morgenthau Mission is therefore based upon the results of my own investigations on the spot. The Morgenthau Mission listed and described only "eight principal excesses" between November 11, 1918 and August 8, 1919, whereas my report gave a list of 132 towns and villages in which there had been outrages up to April 5, 1919. The Morgenthau report stated that the responsibility for the excesses was "borne for the most part by the undisciplined and ill-equipped Polish recruits," and failed to criticize either the commanding officers or the Polish government themselves who, for months, though fully acquainted with the facts, refused to issue a condemnation of the pogroms. Its concluding recommendation was to send a commission of experts to Poland, who should "devise a plan by which the Jews can secure the same economic and social opportunities as are enjoyed by their co-religionists in other free countries." That was the very object of the Allies' Treaty with Poland, which had been signed on June 28, 1919, over six months before the report was published.

11. COMMUNAL ORGANIZATIONS AND INSTITUTIONS
CHAPTER XVIII, PAGE 399

The elaborate and highly developed character of the Jewish community may be gathered from the following list of its principal organizations and institutions, apart from its numerous synagogues and talmudical "houses of study," before its annexation by Soviet Russia:

Social and Philanthropic:

"Jekopo," founded in 1919, devoted mainly to reconstruction and relief work, particularly in aid of war-victims, as well as to emigration, cultural work, and housing for the poor.

"Ort," founded in 1918, for the furtherance of training in industry and agriculture; maintained a technical institute and workshops.

"Help through Work," society founded in 1903 (temporarily interrupted in 1915), maintained training workshops and evening courses in many trades.

"Oze," for the promotion of health, founded 1918, maintained clinics, nurses' institute, foundlings' home, sanatorium for consumptives, Froebel courses, playgrounds for children, and medical inspection of schools.

Home for the Aged and Needy; Soup-kitchen for the Intellectual Class; Committee for Orphans; Societies for providing dowries for poor brides, and for comforting mourners.

Religious Organizations:

Tiferet Bahurim Society, founded 1902, for the propagation of religious observance and knowledge among the the working-class.

Talmud Torah institutions; *Torat Emet*, for the religious education and maintenance of children and finding them employment.

    i (a)   Central Education Committee, administering a network of Yiddish secular schools (elementary and upper grade) and evening classes, and schools in the provinces.

- (b) *Tarbut*, in control of Hebrew secular schools in Vilna and provinces.
- (c) *Va'ad ha-Meuhad*, in control of religious schools (Hebrew and Yiddish) in Vilna.
  ii (a) Teachers' Association (Hebrew and Yiddish).
- (b) Jewish Students' Union (mainly students of the Vilna University).

Culture:

Historical and Ethnographical Society.
Writers' Association (Authors and Journalists).
Art Society (arranged art exhibitions, musical evenings, lectures, etc.).
Strashun Library.

Medical Institutions:

The Jewish Hospital; Zwierzyniecka Street Hospital, *Mishmeret Holim* Society, maintaining a hospital, dispensary, laboratory, etc.
Medical Association (gave lectures, demonstrations, etc.).
Dentists' Association.

Economic Organizations:

Merchants' Association (with Board of Arbitrators); Timber Merchants' Association; Manufacturers' Association.
Artisans' Society; Retailers' Cooperative Society.
Central Jewish People's Bank; Jewish Bank; Retailers' Bank; Commercial Club.

Sport and Recreation:

"Maccabi" Athletic and Sport Association (including rowing, swimming, boxing, cycling, and the training of instructors).
"Z.A.K.S." Sporting Club (*Zydowski Akademiczny Klub Sportowy*, Jewish Academic Sporting Club, recognized by the Vilna University).

BIBLIOGRAPHY

The following works, apart from the periodicals and newspapers mentioned in the notes, have been consulted in the preparation of this book:

AGNON, S. J., and ELIASBERG, AHRON, Das Buch von den polnischen Juden, Berlin, 1916.

APEL, JUDAH, Betok Reshit ha-Tehiyah (Memoirs), Tel Aviv, 1936.

BALABAN, MEIR, "Ha-Keraim be-Polin," in Ha-Tekufah, vol. 25.

BRAFMANN, J., Das Buch vom Kahal, 2 vols., Leipzig, 1928.

BROIDES, IZHAK, Vilna ha-Zionit ve-Askaneho ("Vilna Zionism and its Workers"), Tel Aviv, 1939.

BUNIMOWITZ, ISRAEL, Memoirs (Yiddish), Vilna, 1928.

COHEN, ISRAEL, Jewish Life in Modern Times, revised edition, London, 1929.

——, A Report on the Pogroms in Poland, London, 1919.

DUBNOW, SIMON, Pinkas ha-Medinah (Records of the Jewish Council of Lithuania), Berlin, 1925.

——, Geschichte des Chassidismus, 2 vols., Berlin, 1931.

——, Weltgeschichte des jüdischen Volkes, vols. V–X, Berlin, 1925–29.

——, History of the Jews in Russia and Poland, translated by I. Friedlaender, 3 vols., Philadelphia, 1916–20.

FINN, SAMUEL JOSEPH, Kiryah Ne'emanah ("Faithful City"), revised edition, Vilna, 1915.

FRENK, E. N., Yehudei Polin bi-Yemei Milhamot Napoleon ("The Jews of Poland in the Days of the Napoleonic Wars"), Warsaw, 1912.

——, Ha-'Ironim ve-ha-Yehudim be-Polin ("The Burghers and the Jews in Poland"), Warsaw, 1921.

FRIEDLAENDER, ISRAEL, The Jews of Russia and Poland, New York, 1915.

FRIEDMAN, ELIEZER ELIJAH, Sefer ha-Zikronot, Tel Aviv, 1926.

GINZBERG, LOUIS, Students, Scholars and Saints, Philadelphia, 1928.

GRONEMANN, SAMMY, Hawdolah und Zapfenstreich: Erinnerungen an die ostjüdische Etappe, 1916–18, Berlin, 1925.

GROSSMANN, LEONID, Die Beichte eines Juden, Munich, 1927.

GROSSMANN, MORITZ, Iddische Vilna in Vort un Bild ("Jewish Vilna in Words and Pictures"), Vilna, 1925.

HURWITZ, SAMUEL, Dreisik Yor, 1903–1933, fun entwicklung und Organizirung fun Yiddisher Meloche in Vilne, Vilna, 1933.

JAZKAN, SOLOMON J., Rabbenu Eliyahu mi-Vilna ("Rabbi Elijah of Vilna"), Warsaw, 1900.

JESHURIN, EPHIM H., ed., Vilna: A Zammelbuch ("Vilna: A Miscellany"), New York, 1935.

KLAUSNER, ISRAEL, Toledot ha-Kehillah ha-'Ivrit b'Vilna ("History of the Jewish Community in Vilna"), vol. I, Vilna, 1938.

———, Vilna bi-Tekufat ha-Gaon, Jerusalem, 1942.

LESTSCHINSKY, JACOB, Hurban Vilna ("Ruin of Vilna") in *Wirtschaft un Leben*, fortnightly review issued by Verband "Ort," Berlin, Nos. 2–4, September 1928–February 1929.

LEVIN, JOSHUA HESCHEL, and GRODNO, NAHMAN VON, 'Aliyot Eliyahu ("Ascents of Elijah"), Stettin, 1856.

LEVIN, SHMARYA, The Arena, London, 1932.

LEWIN, LOUIS, Die Landessynode der grosspolnischen Judenschaft, Frankfort, 1926.

LIBNI (WEISSBORD), DAVID, Yerushalayim d'Lita, vol. I, Tel Aviv, 1920.

LOEWE, LOUIS, Diaries of Sir Moses and Lady Montefiore, London, 1890.

LUNSKI, HEIKEL, Me-ha-Gitto ha-Vilnai: Tippusim u-Zelalim ("From the Vilna Ghetto — Types and Figures"), Vilna, 1921.

MANN, JACOB, Texts and Studies in Jewish History and Literature, vol. II, *Karaitica*, Philadelphia, 1935.

MARKON, ISAAC DOV, "Golei Vilna bi-Shenat 5415" ("The Exiles of Vilna in the year 1655"), in *Yehudith*, organ of the Judith Lady Montefiore College, Ramsgate, April, 1940.

MEISL, JOSEF, Geschichte der Juden in Polen und Russland, 3 vols., Berlin, 1921–25.

———, Haskalah: Geschichte der Aufklärungsbewegung unter den Juden Russlands, Berlin, 1919.

MERESCHIN, S., Bund und Zionismus, Warsaw, 1908.

MICHELSON, M., Tadeusz Kosciuszko, London, 1904.

MINKIN, JACOB S., The Romance of Hassidism, New York, 1935.

MORFILL, W. R., Poland, London, 1893.

RABINOWITSCH, WOLF, Der Karliner Chassidismus, Tel Aviv, 1935.

RAISIN, J. S., The Haskalah Movement in Russia, Philadelphia, 1913.

REISEN, ZALMAN, ed., Pinkos far der Geschichte fun Vilna in die Yohren fun Milchomo un Okkupazie ("Records for the History of Vilna in the years of War and Occupation"), Vilna, 1922.

————, Lexicon fun der Iddischer Literatur, Presse, un Filologie ("Lexicon of Yiddish Literature, Press, and Philology"), 4 vols., Vilna, 1926–29.

RHINE, A. B., Leon Gordon, Philadelphia, 1910.

ROSENBERG, L., Die Juden in Litauen, Berlin and Munich, 1916.

SHABAD, Dr. ZEMAH, ed., Vilner Zammelbuch ("Vilna Miscellany"), Vilna, vol. I, 1916; vol. II, 1918.

SCHALIT, MOSES, Pinkos: Auf die Churvos fun Milchomos un Mehumos, 1919–31 ("Records of the Ruins of Wars and Upheavals"), published by the Vilna Committee of the "Jekopo," Vilna, 1932.

SCHECHTER, SOLOMON, Studies in Judaism, 1st series, (London, 1896). Philadelphia, 1916.

SCHUL-PINKOS, "Finf Yor Arbet fun Zentralen-Bildungs-Komitet," Vilna, 1924.

SLOUSCHZ, NAHUM, La Renaissance de la Littérature Hebraïque, Paris, 1903.

————, La Poésie lyrique Hebraïque contemporaine, Paris, 1911.

STEINSCHNEIDER, HILLEL NOAH MAGGID, 'Ir Vilna, ("The City of Vilna"), Vilna, 1900.

STRUCK, HERMANN and ZWEIG, ARNOLD, Das ostjüdische Antlitz, Berlin, 1920.

TEIMANAS, DAVID B., L'Autonomie des Communautés juives en Pologne aux XVIme et XVIIme siècles, Paris, 1933.

VILNA, R. ABRAHAM, Sa'arat Eliyahu ("Storm of Elijah"), Vilna, 1894.

VOROBEICHIC, M., Rehob ha-Yehudim b'Vilna ("The Ghetto in Vilna"), with Preface by S. Schneur, Zurich, 1931.

WEINREICH, MAX, Shturmvint ("Stormwind"), Vilna, 1927.

WIENER, LEO, History of Yiddish Literature, London, 1899.

WOLF, LUCIEN, The Legal Sufferings of the Jews in Russia, London, 1912.

WYGODZKI, JACOB, In Shturm ("In the Tempest"), Vilna, 1926.

Various articles in the *Jewish Encyclopaedia*, *Jüdisches Lexicon*, and *Encyclopaedia Britannica*.

INDEX

Index

523